To the Glory of Her Sex

Women of Letters
Sandra M. Gilbert and Susan Gubar
General Editors

To the Glory of Her Sex

WOMEN'S ROLES IN
THE COMPOSITION OF
MEDIEVAL TEXTS

Joan M. Ferrante

INDIANA UNIVERSITY PRESS
Bloomington & Indianapolis

The paper used in this publication meets the
minimum requirements of American
National Standard for Information Sciences—Permanence of Paper for Printed
Library Materials, ANSI Z39.48-1984.

Manufactured in the United States of America

Library of Congress Cataloging-in-Publication Data

Ferrante, Joan M., date
To the glory of her sex : women's roles in the com-
position of Medieval texts / by Joan M. Ferrante.
    p.   cm. — (Women of letters)
Includes bibliographical references and index.
ISBN 0-253-33254-0 (cloth : alk. paper). —
ISBN 0-253-21108-5 (pbk. : alk. paper)
1. Literature, Medieval—History and criticism. 2.
Literature, Medieval—Women authors—History
and criticism. 3. Women and literature—Europe. 4.
Authors and patrons—Europe. I. Title. II. Series:
Women of letters (Bloomington, Ind.)
PN682.W6F39   1997
809'.89287'0902—dc20

96-43546

2   3   4   5   02   01   00   99

For Carey

omnis homo . . . querit sibi amicum fidelem in cuius
consiliis confidat . . . quid dulcius est, quam habeas illum,
cum quo omnia possis loqui ut tecum?
—Eangyth to Boniface

CONTENTS

PREFACE

So many people have helped me in this work, directly and indirectly over the ten years I have been thinking about it, that I could not hope to acknowledge them all. But I would like to thank in particular those who read the manuscript at its longest and most unwieldy: Constance Jordan, whose own work on feminism in the Renaissance is such a strong model; Robert Hanning, whose interest and collaboration in medieval women's studies has cheered and encouraged me over the years; and Carey McIntosh, whose understanding and support have made this work and my life so much richer. I am very grateful to Caroline Bynum, who read this version; her comments were scholarly, generous, meticulous, and practical. And I would like to offer special thanks to the many graduate students who helped me with research and copyediting and enthusiasm at different stages: Suzanne Akbari, Julie Crosby, Mary Agnes Edsall, Thomas Hill, Bruce Holsinger, Claudia Papka, Margaret Pappano, Karen Sorensen, and Karen Green.

Two parts of this study have been published, in shorter versions, in "Whose Voice? The Influence of Women Patrons on Courtly Romances," in *Literary Aspects of Courtly Culture,* ed. Donald Maddox and Sara Sturm-Maddox (Cambridge: D. S. Brewer, 1994) and "Women's Role in Latin Letters from the Fourth to the Early Twelfth Century," in *The Cultural Patronage of Medieval Women,* ed. June Hall McCash (Athens: University of Georgia Press, 1996). I regret that Simon Gaunt's *Gender and Genre in Medieval French Literature* (Cambridge: Cambridge University Press, 1995) came to my attention after the book went to press so I have not been able to include it in my discussion.

ABBREVIATIONS

ANTS	Anglo-Norman Text Society
BFR	Bibliothèque française et romane
CC	Hildegard of Bingen, *Causae et Curae*
CCCM	*Corpus Christianorum Continuatio Medievalis*
CCM	*Cahiers de civilisation médiévales*
CCSL	*Corpus Christianorum Series Latina*
CFMA	Classiques français du moyen âge
CSEL	*Corpus Scriptorum Ecclesiasticorum Latinorum*
DB	Dronke, *Women Writers* (Berlin ms.)
Gb	*Guiberti Gemblacensis Epistolae*
GRA	*Gesta Regum Anglorum*
HGF	*Historiens des Gaules et de la France*
JMRS	*Journal of Medieval and Renaissance Studies*
LDO	Hildegard of Bingen, *Liber Divinorum Operum*
LVD	Elisabeth of Schönau, *Liber Viarum Dei*
LVM	Hildegard of Bingen, *Liber Vitae Meritorum*
MFN	*Medieval Feminist Newsletter*
MGH	*Monumenta Germaniae Historica*
MGH AA	Auctores Antiquissimi
MGH AWB	Die Ältere Wormser Briefsammlung
MGH BDKz	Briefe der Deutschen Kaiserzeit
MGH Ep Kar	Epistolae Karolini Aevi
MGH Greg I Reg	Gregorii I Pape Registrum Epistolarum
MGH LL	Libelli de lite
MGH MK BL	Epistolae Merovingici et Karolini Aevi, Sancti Bonifatii et Lulli Epistolae
MGH MK Ep Austr	Epistolae Merovingici et Karolini Aevi, Epistolae Austrasicae
MGH SRM	Scriptores rerum merovingicarum
MGH SS	Scriptores

MGH ZHIV	Briefsammlungen der Zeit Heinrichs IV
MLR	*Modern Language Review*
MS	*Medieval Studies*
Pi	*Analecta Sancte Hildegardis Opera*, ed. J. B. Pitra
PL	*Patriologia Latina*
RBMAS	Rerum Brittanicarum Medii Aevi Scriptores (Rolls Series)
RHCHO	*Recueil des Historiens des Croisades, Historiens Orientaux*
SATF	Société des anciens textes français
VA	*Hildegardis Bingensis Epistolarium*, ed. L. Van Acker
VMRA	*Vita Mathildis reginae antiquior*, MGH, SS 10
VMRP	*Vita Mathildis reginae posterior*, MGH, SS 4
ZrP	*Zeitschrft für romanische Philologie*

Part One
Background

Introduction

"AN OCCASION OF PRAISE IS PREPARED FOR YOUR SEX"

When I was asked to write on medieval women of letters for this series, I hesitated. Peter Dronke's *Women Writers of the Middle Ages* had recently appeared, covering most of the women I was interested in with scholarly care and human sensitivity, and I was not sure I had much to add. Asked to consider different perspectives, however, I began to think about letters in the broadest sense, including not only religious and secular literature but epistolary literature as well. I decided to look into the letters of early medieval women, before the period of vernacular correspondence which had had some attention.[1] I expected, perhaps because I am not a historian, to find only a small number of formal documents which would not reveal much about the correspondents. Instead I found over twelve hundred letters in printed sources alone, most of them from men to women but many from women to men and even some from women to women. To my greater surprise, I also found that they revealed more than a little about the women involved: their public roles in secular and religious life as rulers, regents, consorts, or abbesses and their private roles as colleagues, friends, and family.

As I read through the letters, I became slowly aware of two things which struck me as particularly significant: they show women at the center of public life, and the women so involved, even when they are playing male roles, are aware of themselves as women. Women had a role in political, religious, and cultural developments from the earliest centuries of the Christian era, not continuously or ubiquitously but frequently and consistently enough to make it clear that medieval history in any form from the Middle Ages to the present which does not include the role of women is not true history. As Carolyn Heilbrun has pointed out in *Writing a Woman's Life*, history looks different with a woman at the center. It even looks different just with women sharing the stage. I became more and more interested in the letters until they dominated my research, and I finally had to readjust my project, so that instead of presenting them in an introductory section to this study, I have made them the subject of a separate work, a guide to women's correspondence from the fourth to the thirteenth century. Nonetheless, the letters remain a presence in this work even though I discuss them only briefly here, because they profoundly influenced the way I read the other texts, the works written for women and the works written by women.

What I came to see was that despite the theoretical and even legal obstacles to women's holding power, they did inherit land and sometimes position, and they frequently served as regents, exercising significant authority. Despite the period's intense misogyny, which has been carefully documented, women could be respected colleagues, friends, and relatives, whose affection, support, even advice were sought and cherished—or whose antagonism had to be confronted carefully. The letters, official or personal, showed men and women working together in all spheres of public and private life, with occasional friction but often with successful collaboration. At the same time, I have had enough experience as a woman in what was when I began very much a man's world and remains with all the changes of recent decades dominated by men and by male prejudices— the university—to know that holding a position of authority does not protect a woman from misogyny or her male friends from hostility. Women can be accepted and used as capable allies in a cause, but their opponents are likely to see and attack them not as worthy opponents but as women who have no place in the conflict. I was therefore alert to suggestions in the letters that medieval women rulers, regents, and abbesses were aware of the problems of being a woman in a position of authority not accepted by all men. I was not surprised that they seemed to look for models of women whose authority or accomplishment could not be questioned—the Virgin Mary as the queen of heaven, the highest-ranking human being there, or Judith, whose militant action saved her people from a tyrant. I noticed that historic and even fictional works written for women gave much more attention to the role and actions of women than other works in the same genres. And I began to suspect that works by women might well say something to women in the audience that they did not say to men, because both the writer and her female reader or listener were aware of the problems women faced and at the same time of what certain women had been able to do.

The study of medieval women has progressed considerably in the last two decades. One of the most exhilarating moments for me during my research was to participate in the conference on "The Roles of *Women* in the Middle Ages: A Reassessment," October 15–17, 1992, at the State University of New York in Binghamton. Twenty years after the first conference on "The Role of *Woman*," at which five men and one woman spoke, four of them about representations of women in literature and art, the 1992 conference had forty-seven regular sessions and four plenary sessions on women in science and religion, in politics and the arts, in marriage and heresy, with over 170 speakers. I too had progressed from a work in which I looked at the image of *woman* in men's writings (*Woman as Image in Medieval Literature,* 1975) to this study, in which I am concerned with real women, what they did, what they said, and what they hired men to say. An even more important event for me personally was the two weeks I spent at the University of Northern Illinois in the spring of 1993 giving a series of lectures on women's letters, patronage, and writing. There I found myself in a group of women colleagues working on medieval women in different disciplines, something I had not experienced before, and their critical responses and enthusiasm for what I was doing gave me the courage and the impetus to complete the work.

What I hope this work will do is contribute to a sense of what medieval women could and did do, despite the patriarchal systems in which they lived. I do not deny that religious and secular patriarchy, not to say misogyny, inhibited women in many ways, but I think it is far more important to recognize that it could not exclude them from all power or influence. To concentrate too much on the negative is to play into the hands of the patriarchal view that women were able to do little, therefore they did nothing valuable, therefore we do not need to include them in our studies. That many women were victims I certainly do not deny, but that not a few were able to control their lives is an equally important fact. If aristocratic society disadvantages women in some ways, by treating them as marriage pawns, valuing and guarding their chastity to preserve the purity of lineage, it also advantages them for similar reasons. If family is key, a female heir is better than letting property or position go outside; women often carry the prestige and legitimacy of their lineage to their husband or son; women are more often than not the safest choice for a regency because of their connections, their prestige, even their skill and experience, but most of all because they are likely to preserve the power for the husband or son, not to steal it for themselves or their line as men might.

Theory and doctrine are one thing, practice and experience another. Though I am not impervious to the hostility active women face, nor to the legal, social, religious, and psychological limitations placed in their way, in medieval or in modern life, I am concerned in this study with examples of positive practice, rather than of negative theory. In this approach, I associate myself with scholars like Marjorie Chibnall, Edith Ennen, Mary McLaughlin, Caroline Bynum, Barbara Newman, Peter Dronke, Charity Cannon Willard, Jo Ann McNamara, and Katharina Wilson, to name only a few of those who have focused on the achievements of medieval women in life and literature. To do so is not to deny for a moment the misogyny in medieval culture.[2] I have fought the misogyny in modern life enough to be, I think, alert to it in medieval texts. I know what Jerome and Peter Damian and others said about the women they did not approve of, but I am more interested in what they said to the ones they respected and admired and worked with. It is not that enough has been said about medieval misogyny—it is something we must always be aware of in any study of medieval culture because it is a fact of medieval life—it is rather that there is much more to be said about women who were active and effective despite the prejudices against them.

Of course there is an underlying misogyny to the fact that when women act competently in a male role, they are called "virile," just as when men act viciously, they can be called "womanly." It may be that the men who speak to women of the glory and praise to their sex in their accomplishments speak out of astonishment that a woman could achieve so much; but their praise is strong nonetheless, and it is given not only for religious but also for political and intellectual achievement: pope Hormisda told empress Euphemia that "great occasion of praise is prepared for your sex, if at your urging Christ joins the members that were divided of his church" (PL63, c.437–48). Hildebert of Lavardin said to the empress Matilda, her father's chosen heir to the English throne, that her mother had given birth to her and been completely reborn in her, "lest the glory of the female sex decline" (*Carmina minora*, 35) and told her aunt, the formidable countess Adela, chosen administrator of the lands of her husband's family, that "the grace of God heaped up titles to be praised in you by which you might be to the glory of [your] sex" (PL171, ep.1.3); through her, Hildebert says, "her sex aspires to glory, and her family retains its slipping dignity" (ep.3.8, a reference to her husband's retreat from the crusade). Hildebert seems to have sought out "glorious" women; he spoke to the poet-nun Muriel of the great glory to her sex in the ten sibyls, implying even greater in her single and singular existence (poem 26). Hildegard of Bingen addressed the Virgin in words that others might have used of her: "O female form, sister of Wisdom, how glorious you are." And Abelard spoke, in a sermon on the annunciation, of a woman conceiving the lord "that a creature might bring forth the creator. This is the common salvation of mankind, but the special glory of women."

The range of women who are called the glory of their sex is striking. It is not just the ultimate paradox, the virgin mother, the unrealizable model. Virginity, of course, gave women a particular standing—it lifted them above their sex and gender, perhaps above either sex. It would be easy to say that since general condemnations of the sex did not normally apply to virgins, men who wrote or thought misogynistically could be friends with virgins without contradicting themselves; but in fact it is more often married women, widows, and mothers who are singled out for special praise, who are numbered among the men's closest and most respected friends, sometimes while they are still active in the secular world. I suggest that when medieval men write theoretically about the female sex, they may condemn it or relegate it to subordinate roles, but when they—even the same men—deal with individual women, they treat them as colleagues or even as superiors. Whatever they may think of the idea of women in such a position, they accept the fact. If many medieval men continue to mouth traditional misogyny despite the examples of women all around them, many women in positions of authority or endowed with undeniable talent belie those conventions with their achievements. Some women no doubt resented successful women, but others cherished their example. Some of the men around them recognized and encouraged them, and it is because they recognized and encouraged that we have, in many cases, any record of that achievement at all.

The correspondence of women, as I suggest in chapter 1, shows that they were involved in all aspects of their society to a greater or lesser degree, in secular and ecclesiastical politics, in religious and intellectual life, as well as in the affairs of their families, and that their influence in those spheres should not be overlooked.[3] It is against this background of women's presence in medieval life, and their influence over the writings of men, which I shall discuss in the next three chapters, that I think their own writings should be read, as I shall do in the last two chapters. What is particularly striking in the letters and in texts commissioned by women is how much women, even those playing male roles in secular government or rising above sex in their religious lives, are aware of themselves as women and identify with powerful or effective, not oppressed, women in history—with Mary as queen of heaven or mother of God; with Judith and Esther, who saved their people; with the queen of Sheba, who traveled far to hear Solomon's wisdom; with the Christian empresses Helena, who found the true cross, Galla Placidia and Pulcheria, who fought heresy, and queen Clothild, who converted her husband and thereby his people. These are women to be reckoned with, women for a woman in power to identify with. Such models are evoked by friends and counselors not only from biblical and ancient history but also from contemporary history, sometimes from the women's own families.

Though some women may suppress the fact of their womanhood at times and act despite it, it is rarely irrelevant, either to them or to the men in contact with them. They act as their position demands, as a ruler rather than a woman if they are ruling, as a religious virgin rather than a physical woman if they are dedicated to God, but that does not mean they are unaware of their sex, of the problems it creates for them, of the prejudices against them. How could they be? Some women, like Hildegard of Bingen, use the disadvantage of their sex to their advantage, turning the perceived weakness to strength. None is able, like the men around them, to speak for the whole of mankind as if there were no other sex, though Hildegard comes close, since she speaks for God. And most of them look to other women in the past to support and justify them in the present.

In the histories and romances which women commissioned or which were dedicated to them, there is a strong emphasis on women active in public life, women with wealth and power and wisdom and education, who run countries and defeat enemies and further culture and religion. Their positive qualities and achievements are emphasized, the negative are downplayed or suppressed. Semiramis is mentioned often in histories written for women as a woman who extended her empire by conquest, who founded cities, who governed effectively. The Amazons are admired for their successful civilization without men as well as for their fighting. Adam, rather than Eve, is held responsible for the fall; women seem not only to resent the emphasis on Eve's role but also to be alert to the logical inconsistency of saying women are weaker and need guidance and then blaming the woman rather than the man for what happened.[4] Women seem to take pride in the achievements of other women, in the present as well as in the past: queens look to the achievements of their mothers and grandmothers, abbesses to their illustrious fellows. The histories written for women give more attention to women in history, naming queens as well as kings, mothers as well as fathers, since a mother's illustrious genealogy can be a major claim to her son's legitimacy in a disputed succession; they record allegiances by marriage as well as wars, and they tell the stories of women of note, biblical, ancient, and modern. The romances written for women differ in similar ways from the romances written for male patrons: instead of presenting women in need of rescue by dashing knights, who then marry them and raise them in social status, the heroines of women-sponsored romances are often heirs to their own lands, educated and effective rulers, who raise the lower-born heroes to their rank by marriage.

Women writers also focus more often than men writers on women, their deeds, their emotions, their strengths, and their needs. Hrotsvit tells the stories of women saints and martyrs and features royal women in her historic epics; Elisabeth of Schönau writes the history of Ursula and the eleven thousand virgins and looks to other women saints and the Virgin for information and support; Clemence of Barking expands the life of St. Catherine, who conquered learned men in debate; Marie de France gives a sympathetic reading of women trapped in oppressive marriages. Hildegard of Bingen writes about women's medical and psychological problems and gives encouragement and support to other women in the church; she herself looks to the feminine aspects of God, Sapientia, Caritas, the "lux vivens," as her sources, as Christine de Pizan relies on a series of female personifications to deliver her messages.

Some may question whether people dealing with abstractions in a gendered language identify those abstractions sexually. Certainly when they present them as personifications, they are forced to. But I would suggest that even if some men can speak of God's feminine qualities without consciously positing a female side to God, it is less likely that women can.[5] If you live in a linguistic world in which the masculine is universal, the feminine limited, in which you as a female can be subsumed under masculine nouns and adjectives while feminine words mark women off as different from men—*essi* can stand for men or for men and women, *essae* can only be women—you must be alert to feminine words, including abstractions as marked in a particular way with which you identify.[6] When God spoke to Hildegard as the "lux vivens" or Sapientia, she responded at some level to a female voice. None of the women I discuss here went so far as the Guglielmites, for instance, who believed in a female holy spirit and proposed a female pope and cardinals, but many of them played male roles in life or in their imaginations and all of them knew what it was to be female in a male world.[7]

Christine de Pizan speaks of herself becoming masculine in body as well as in spirit in order to cope with the exigencies of her life, then writes not only on male subjects for male audiences (war and chivalry) and female subjects for female audiences (a manual of appropriate behavior for every rank) but also striking defenses of women for general audiences. Marie de France and women who wrote lyric poetry in Provençal, the trobairitz, respond to the female situation by speaking out for themselves (or their characters), asserting their need to take action or to express themselves. All of them, religious or secular, are aware of themselves as women and speak to women in their audience, though none of them writes exclusively for women.

Though my main interests are in the high Middle Ages, from the late eleventh to the early thirteenth century, I have included material in the first three chapters from the earliest centuries of medieval culture—some of which might be considered late classical—because it is indispensable background and very relevant to the later works. At the end of the book I have included a section on Christine de Pizan, although she wrote in the late fourteenth and early fifteenth centuries, because she is too major a figure both as a writer and as a woman concerned with the problems of women in the secular world to be omitted. I do not pretend that all the women included in this study had similar experiences or similar feelings about their experiences. They live in different times, in different cultures; they have different opportunities, different limitations. While I am aware of the dangers of assuming that women in different periods and different environments react similarly as women, I am also struck by how much women who take an active part in public life (i.e., the male world) do share, however different their circumstances. All the women discussed here might be seen as feminists by virtue of the life they led or the works they produced, though they are not necessarily feminist in all their opinions. That should not be held against them. A woman who does not fight sexual stereotypes in her words but who does in her actions makes a significant and positive contribution to the history of women.

1 Women in Correspondence

"WHAT WE HAVE LOST IN MEN LET US RECOVER IN WOMEN"

Because letters taught me to see women's roles in a new way which influenced my understanding of women's patronage of or collaboration in literary works by men and encouraged me to read a more feminist message in works by women, I want to give some idea of the letters, though I must refer the reader to the guide, now in preparation, for more detailed information.[1]

I would also caution the reader not to dismiss the few examples I give here as unusual but to remember that there are many, many more such extant, and what we have is probably a very small proportion of what there once was. The letters offer a counter to the misogynist texts and help recreate to some extent medieval women's complicated sense of woman's place in the world—on the one hand, frequently hearing how weak and dangerous women were, how unfit, indeed forbidden, to rule or to teach; on the other, seeing women in positions of authority in government and even in the church.

The correspondence of women through the Middle Ages, whether official letters involving women in power or more personal exchanges between colleagues, friends, or family members, is remarkably consistent in what it reveals about women's roles. The letters show that women's authority, political and intellectual, is recognized by the men who work with them, that women collaborate and cooperate with men in politics, religion, and scholarship as colleagues, that their friendship and support is valued and trusted. In some cases, the men might have preferred to work with a man but accept the woman God assigned; in other cases, whatever their theoretical views, they are clearly happier working with a woman who shares their concerns, who is willing to mediate and negotiate with no need to save face, or who is a trusted friend, not a rival, to whom they can confess anxiety with no shame.

The letters which have been preserved are mainly letters to and from women who live in a male world of secular or religious government (even if they are in convents), of scholarly investigation or documentation. These women are of necessity aware of themselves as women, even as they perform the functions of men "virilely." They seem to identify with other important women, to be alert to women's history and problems. Even though history plays down or suppresses the role of particular women, correspondence of women shows that they and the men who wrote to and for them were aware of striking figures from the distant and near past. Even though the actions of particular women may be dropped from official memory within a few generations, their names are often preserved in texts written for women. Even when the knowledge of individual women and their work is lost to later generations in the same country—Hildegard does not seem to have known of Hrotsvit, or Christine de Pizan of Marie de France, but Hildegard knew about Elisabeth of Schönau and the women ruling in Western Europe, and Christine knew the queens of France and Joan of Arc—the same women's problems come up again and again. Medieval women writers write with the knowledge that we so frequently lack of the presence of women in the political, religious, and cultural life of their society and, I think, expect contemporary women in their audience to draw on that knowledge as they respond to their works.

The correspondents, male and female, are in all cases bound by common interests or responsibilities, in some cases also by affection, so the tenor is respectful, friendly, cooperative; even in cases of conflict it is usually conciliatory rather than polemic. These are people who must work together and want to be successful at it. This is not to deny that there were men who resented the presence of such women or their actions and complained about them, conspired against them, or openly opposed them. But as long as the women were there, men had to deal with them. If most of the histories written after the events by monastics and men dedicated to a particular cause slight the role of women unless to criticize or blame, the letters written during the events focus on that role. They show women involved in the day-to-day business of government, in the normal administration of life, even on occasion in war. Women participated either as head of state, as regent for the head of state, or as his consort.[2] The letters show that both the men they governed for and the men they governed expected women to make and enforce decisions or to persuade husbands or sons to do so; to provide justice and protection as well as to mediate among hostile parties; to take an active role in fighting heresy, extending Christianity, and controlling simony; and to give generously to the church. They recognized women's right to be involved in ecclesiastical appointments and negotiations for imperial succession, their right to rule the lands they inherited (or at the very least to claim them), and their right to act as regents for male relatives and to be much more than figureheads when they did. And these are not sporadic or unusual situations.

If the number of women who wielded power in their own name, as their father's or husband's heir, was relatively small, the number who held it for husband or son was rather large. And those who did inherit directly were not without supporters in their claims. It is unusual to have a woman like Countess Matilda of Tuscany, who was her father's only heir, who succeeded to her mother's lands from a second marriage as well as to her own husband's lands, and who was herself the major imperial feudatory in Italy and a formidable figure in imperial and papal politics. But in the twelfth century, empress Matilda was her father's designated heir for the throne of England, Eleanor of Aquitaine was heir to Aquitaine and Poitou and brought them with her to both her marriages, Urraca was the heir to León and Castile through her father, Alfonso VI, and Melisende to Jerusalem through her father, Baldwin II. Ermengard, who inherited and ruled the county of Narbonne, elicited, in a struggle over jurisdiction with one of her men, a strong recognition of her rights from king Louis VII: "if the better sex is lacking, it is conceded to women to succeed and administer their heredity. Remember that you are of our kingdom and we want you to hold to the usage of our rule. . . . Sit therefore in judgment, diligently examining matters with the zeal of him who created you woman when he might have a man, and gave the rule of the province of Narbonne in his benignity to the hand of a woman; by our authority, no person is permitted to turn away from your jurisdiction because you are a woman" (ep.280, HGF 16).

It is not surprising that there are many more examples of women regents than of women rulers. In a regency, the man nominally has the power and the woman is technically only filling in for him while he is away or too young to exercise it, though in fact if the woman was successful and (or) ambitious, she might continue to exercise power well into her son's majority.[3] Women often seem to combine birth, wealth, connections, and experience with skill and a willingness to negotiate or compromise in ways that might be awkward for a man who has to protect his honor. Thus there are numerous instances of women regents in the East and the West from the fifth to the thirteenth century, sometimes several at the same moment, who corresponded with and were often praised by popes and other rulers, from Pulcheria, who ruled the Byzantine empire for her brother in the fifth century,[4] to Blanche, who was chosen by her husband to rule France for their son Louis IX, and her sister Berenguela, who inherited Castile and ruled it for her son in the thirteenth century. And the regencies were not necessarily temporary: Brunhild ruled her husband's lands, Austrasia and Burgundy, for thirty-eight years as regent for their son until his death in 596, then for their grandsons and briefly for a great-grandson.[5] An unusual record of the husband's recognition of his wife's authority is found in a letter from Stephen of Blois, written while on crusade to his wife Adela, who because of her royal blood, personal wealth, and political acumen had considerable power and prestige in her husband's family: "I send [the wish] that you do well and dispose of *your* things superbly, and treat *your* sons and *your* men honorably, as befits you" (italics added; RHCHO, 3.2).[6]

A striking example of women—regents and consorts—directly participating in political affairs is the "colloquy of ladies" (*colloquium dominarum*, MGH BDKz 2.62), as Adalbero of Rheims calls it, that occurred in the tenth century. He was referring to a female "summit" that probably included the Ottonian empresses Adelaide and Theophanu, regents for Otto III (their grandson and son respectively); perhaps Adelaide's daughters by different husbands, queen Emma of France (who would briefly serve as regent for her son, Louis V, the following year), and Matilda, abbess of Quedlinburg (who would later be named by her nephew Otto III as his regent); Adelaide, wife of then duke Hugh Capet (who often sent her to negotiate for him with Theophanu); and certainly the addressee of the letter, countess Beatrice of Upper Lorraine (a sister of Hugh Capet and related through their mother to the Ottonians).[7]

I will come back to many of these women in the chapter on women and the writing of history. For now I will mention only one other well-known woman who was deeply involved in the political scene throughout her long life, often in opposition to her husband: Eleanor of Aquitaine. After her divorce from Louis VII of France, she chose the future king of England, Henry II, as her second husband, bringing her inherited lands of Aquitaine and Poitou into the marriage in 1152.[8] It was not a peaceful union, but in the course of it Eleanor served as regent for her husband, gave birth to eight children, took active control of Aquitaine in 1168, and encouraged her sons to revolt against their father, which led to her imprisonment in 1174 (a kind of house arrest). After Henry's death in 1189, she resumed an active public role in the political lives of her remaining sons, Richard (she was his regent during his captivity and raised the money for his ransom) and John (she led an army to Anjou to support him), and in negotiations for family marriages virtually until her death. Her letters show her willing to take on opponents in verbal as well as political battle. Early on, in 1161, she wrote to pope Alexander III that she confidently took his side and was not afraid to do battle for him and subdue his enemies with her arguments (HGF 15.767, PL200, Alex. ep.2); three decades later, she wrote to pope Celestine III pleading with him, preaching to him, and rebuking him in very strong language for not doing more to free her captive son: "what excuse could modify your sloth and lack of care, when it is clear to all that you have the power of freeing my son and lack the will?" "Give my son back to me, man of God, if you are a man of God and not a man of blood" (PL206, c.1265–72).[9]

I have focused on women regents or rulers because the highest authority is concentrated in them at such times, but women could also be involved in the governments of their husbands as royal or noble consorts, having jurisdiction over their own holdings or carrying out various administrative or diplomatic duties at their husband's behest. Throughout the Middle Ages, wives are exhorted by popes to persuade their husbands to do the right thing or to stop doing wrong (to convert to orthodoxy, restore church property, or combat corruption in the land or the family).[10] Wives are charged by their husbands with delicate negotiations the husband would find awkward; they are approached by secular and religious leaders for advice and information, for help by mediation. And, of course, at any moment a consort might become a regent. What all this means is that men, religious and lay, recognized the authority of women in positions of power and worked with them accordingly. Not many, perhaps, encouraged women to retain power in the world rather than retiring to save their souls, as Gregory VII did countess Matilda, but most accepted them while they were there (even if grudgingly in some cases).[11]

"VIRILE STRENGTH RULES IN HER FEMININE BREAST"

There were, of course, conflicts. Churchmen complain that the women or the men serving under them have committed injustices against churchmen or others, interfered with ecclesiastical matters, supported evildoers; but the very existence of the complaints testifies to the women's authority. And many women had to fight to exercise authority, to claim their inheritance, or to oppose an unwanted divorce; like men, they often had to fight to retain power or defend their rights, and they often did. In their official functions, they were treated like men, that is, as the ruling authority irrespective of sex. The highest praise that could be paid women in authority through the centuries was that they indeed acted like men. The ninth-century Byzantine empress Theodora, regent for her son, Michael III, was praised by pope Nicholas I for defending the church, even against her husband while he was alive, and for fighting heretics as regent, "when you were ruling *alone*" (italics added), so that they "sensed in you a virile breast and, wondering at your unconquerable strength, doubted you were a woman" (MGH, EpKar 4, NicI, ep.95).[12] Peter Damian wrote to Adelaide of Savoy, who ruled Savoy until her death in 1091, that "you rule your land without the virile aid of a king, and they come to you for judgment" (ep.114).[13] Ivo of Chartres praised queen Matilda for her religious devotion and God for putting "virile strength in a feminine breast" (ep.174); Matilda herself wrote to pope Paschal II in support of Anselm, promising to strive with all her ability as much as womanly powers allow — "muliebribus viribus," perhaps a pun, "womanly manliness" (Anselm, ep.323). Melisende, who inherited the kingdom of Jerusalem from her father (Baldwin intended her to share it with her husband, but she asserted her right to govern it herself), was encouraged by Bernard of Clairvaux, when her husband died, to "show a man in a woman" so that "all who see you think you to be a king rather than a queen from your works" (ep.354).

Chroniclers writing about women, not to them, used the same form of praise. Hugh of Flavigny said that countess Matilda, the only one who scorned the power of the king, was "deservedly called 'virago,' who surpassed even men by the virtue of her spirit" (*Chronicon*, MGH SS 8.462). The *Gesta Stephani*, written in support of empress Matilda's rival, commented on her flight from Winchester, riding astride like a man: "the countess of Anjou, always above feminine softness, had a mind steeled and unbroken in adversity."[14] Sometimes virile implies human perfection rather than masculine action; an anonymous love letter (which its editor thinks may have been by Abelard) praises a woman's mental skills by calling her "virile in strength beyond her age and sex."[15] When Hildebert of Lavardin writes to nuns that they should struggle so "the enemies who attack a woman will find a man" (ep.1.4), he is implying that it can be a mistake to assume "womanly weakness," but when he writes of an abbess that she gave up all female acts, did "nothing womanly, but was altogether virile" (PL171, c.1305–6), he means that in her virtue she rose above her sex and acted like a man.

It may seem demeaning to compliment women by calling them "manly," but in a culture which assumes the male as the norm, to recognize maleness in a woman, particularly when encouraging her in a male role in the male world, can be a positive affirmation. Women strengthened themselves and each other with the same injunction. An early abbess Caesaria (not Caesarius's sister) urged Radegund and a fellow nun to fight against the devil "strongly and virilely, as if you were men" (MGH MK 3, part 7, 450–53); in her intense repetition of the injunction, four times in four lines, she seems to be telling them to look out for themselves in a hostile world. Elisabeth of Schönau told the abbess of Dietkirchen to be strong against the devil's plots, to act virilely and bear the temptations of the world (6.13).[16] Christina of Markyate told herself to act like a man when she was fleeing home to escape marriage and pursue her religious purpose ("virilem animum induce et more viri in equum ascende," s.34, p.92).[17]

Women were aware of being women in a male world, even or perhaps particularly when they were praised for rising above it; they were aware of performing roles others and perhaps they themselves considered male roles. Though the office might put them above gender, they nonetheless represented their sex in those roles, setting a model for others, showing it could be done just as professional women have done through the centuries, and if they were not aware of doing so, others pointed it out, either by praising them as the glory of their sex or by identifying them with models of effective and heroic women from history. The prime model was the Virgin Mary, not as the humble handmaid of the Lord, nor as the devoted, sorrowing mother, but in her glory as mother of God (Theotokos), Mary was a model for an Eastern empress (Pulcheria), and as queen of heaven for Ottonian empresses.[18]

It is not surprising that someone writing to or about a queen or empress would cite a biblical queen as a model. The queen of Sheba and Esther are the most frequent models, Esther primarily as an example of a woman who courageously, even forcefully, exerted influence on her husband and thereby saved her people. Nicholas I to Eudocia, to enflame her husband toward recovery of the church of Constantinople, says she too was placed in the king's house to free her people (ep.96). Peter Damian, attempting to persuade Adelaide of Savoy to take action with a bishop against priests living with women, cites Esther, "who virilely exposed herself to death to save her people" (ep.114), and lists her with women who took forceful, even violent, action against men: Deborah, Jahel, Judith, the woman who fatally wounded Abimelech (2 Kgs. 11:21), and "the wise woman who threw the severed head of Sheba, son of Bichri, to Joab, and so averted the danger of siege from the city" (2 Kgs. 20:16–22). The queen of Sheba is a model of learning, and generosity, though often as a foil. Amalasuntha is favorably compared to her as "one whom princes here learn from with wonder" while the other "came to learn the wisdom of Solomon" (Theodahad, 10.4.7). Pope Nicholas I prefers the industry of queen Ermentrude, who offers her gifts to an immortal king and his princes, while the queen of Sheba bestowed hers on a mortal king (ep.28). Peter Damian compliments retired empress Agnes for her humility by comparing her to the queen of Sheba, who came to Jerusalem with a retinue and mysteries to be solved by the wisdom of Solomon, while "our queen" Agnes came to Rome to hear the foolishness of a fisherman alone with her sister-in-law to loose the bonds of sins (ep.104). Bernard of Clairvaux reminds Melisende that the queen of Sheba came to hear the wisdom of Solomon, to learn to be ruled and thus *know how to rule* (ep.289).

More interesting is the invocation of nonbiblical queens and empresses as models for later women, which not only provides a lesson but also preserves a historical memory of them. Helena, revered as the woman who found the cross, is an expected model: Euphemia is told she will surpass the glory of Helena, as "the unity of the church found its sign through her, through you it will have its remedy" (pope Hormisda, ep.33). But Pulcheria, who wielded power directly in the empire and was called a "new Helena" for protecting the faith against heresy, is also cited: Gregory I prays that empress Leantia will have "the clemency of Pulcheria Augusta, who for zeal of the Catholic faith is called a new Helena" (13.42).[19] Even more striking is the reference Nicholas I makes to a letter from empress Galla Placidia to her nephew Theodosius to reinforce his own words to empress Eudocia—a pope citing the written authority of a woman teaching a man (ep.96).[20]

It is not only queens who offer women models of atypical action in God's service; biblical figures like Sara and Judith are cited, Sara for correcting her husband. When Peter Damian tries to persuade a countess to change the corrupt ways of her husband's family, he offers a list of biblical women who corrected men—Judith, Abigail, Manoe's wife (Judges 13.23), and Sara—saying "if man were never to submit to woman, the Lord would not have said to Abraham 'In all that Sara tells you, hear her voice'" (ep.143). Judith's heroism is often used allegorically. Peter Damian mentions her to Adelaide of Savoy as a courageous woman who tackled a difficult problem, and bishop Azecho, in a letter to a nun, perhaps an abbess, justifies the friendship of men and women, answering those who cite Delilah against women with Judith, "when desire lay murdered in Holofernes's neck" (MGH AWB, 45).[21] Judith is God's tool, taking up where priests fail: Hildebert of Lavardin encouraged a widow in her devotion with the example of Judith, who liberated Bethulia when even the priests were afraid (ep.1.10), and when Thomas of Canterbury asked a nun, Idonea, to undertake a delicate diplomatic mission for him, he reminded her that the virtue of a woman extinguishes the swelling arrogance of Holofernes, when men are deficient, leaders dispirited, and priests deserting the law (PL190, ep.196).

Thomas reinforces his suggestion that women must make up with their strength for male defects by pointing out that with apostles staggering and fleeing or fallen into perfidy, it was holy women who followed Christ.[22] Much earlier, Jerome made a similar point; defending himself for writing to women, he gives a catalogue of glorious biblical women who achieved what men did or could not. He mentions Deborah, Ruth, Esther, and Judith and also Mary Magdalene, who announced the resurrection to the apostles and believed when they doubted; Sara, to whom Abraham was subject; the virgin who devoured sex; the woman of Thecua, who taught king David; the queen of Sheba, who showed up all the men of Israel; Priscilla, who taught the apostle Apollo; and many others. He addresses this list to Marcella "so that you do not regret your sex and its name, nor raise men up in whose condemnation the life of women is praised in scripture" (ep.65).

On at least one occasion a man encourages a woman to fight in the name of other women. When Lothar II tried to divorce Theutberg, with whom he had had no children, in order to marry his concubine and legitimize their son, Theutberg appealed to pope Nicholas I, who took her side. When, after much suffering, she was coerced into confessing to adultery and asked for a separation, Nicholas tried to dissuade her with a series of arguments, including the good of other women. He said that if Lothar succeeded, all men could compel wives they hated to confess to crimes by intolerable pains, "for who can do more harm . . . than a husband to his wife?" (ep.45).

The evidence in the letters that some women did identify with other women and their needs in such a way is slight but suggestive. Radegund, for example, who had suffered as the spoils of war and been forced to marry the man who murdered her family, founded a convent to help other women, "with the zeal of a mind inclined towards the progress of other women."[23] And abbess Caesaria sent Radegund a copy of Caesarius's rule with a letter of strong encouragement and practical advice for what would clearly be a difficult endeavor in a hostile world. There are instances of women defending other women—empress Ermengard taking the part of her daughter Bertha, an abbess, against bishop Hincmar (Ep Kar 6, ep.11, 12); countess Adela taking the part of her adulterous cousin Adelaide, to the distress of bishop Ivo of Chartres (PL162, ep.5)—though how much the women were motivated by family loyalty or female solidarity is not clear. When Agnes was regent, she supported the claims of an abbess over the angry complaints of the Bamberg canons, who had accused the abbess of various misdeeds and fiercely resented Agnes's action: "there may not be much glory in defeating a woman, but there is certainly great shame in being defeated by one" (MGH ZHIV, Meinhard ep.61).

"EVERYONE SEEKS A FAITHFUL FRIEND TO CONFIDE IN"

There are letters between abbesses which imply a vast correspondence linking women and women's houses across Europe and personal contact through travel: Elfled of Whitby asked Adolana of Pfalzel to receive a third abbess en route to Rome (MGH MK6 BL, ep.8), and abbesses who met Hildegard of Bingen on her preaching tours wrote to her for advice and comfort and to keep the relationship alive. Letters from abbess to abbess appear in the Boniface letter collection, as well as in the correspondences of Hildegard and of Elisabeth of Schönau. The letters express or request affection and support, advice and sympathy, or recommend other women to their care. Women took comfort not only in the advice and moral support of Hildegard of Bingen but also in her success, a pride expressed by the abbess of Bamberg: "Christ made us particularly happy in this, that he not only foresaw and predestined you for this from the female sex, but illumined many through doctrine by his grace" (VA61).

Hildegard, abbess of Bingen (1098-1179), and her younger contemporary, Elisabeth, magistra (presiding nun) of Schönau (1128-64/65), were visionaries whose books were widely read and sought after across Europe by influential people, and both reveal a concern with women in their works, which I discuss in chapter 5, but both were also correspondents whose advice was widely sought by letter. It is extraordinary to have any letters by a woman author and even more to have the large correspondence connected with Hildegard (the new edition lists 390 letters). For Elisabeth, whose life was much shorter, we have twenty-two letters collected among her works. The letters show these women—women especially chosen by God, but women nonetheless—in the role of transmitter of the highest authority, the divine will. Through the voices that speak to them in their visions, Hildegard and Elisabeth have access to the final word on a variety of subjects, a word that takes precedence over the knowledge of any living male. They are consulted on religious questions and personal matters; even pope Eugene consulted Hildegard's writings, as John of Salisbury noted when he asked a friend to check his copy for him (ep.186).

Of Elisabeth's twenty-two known letters, thirteen are addressed to men, nine to women. Most of them, as befits a visionary, answer questions or report messages from the heavenly voices that speak through her (an angel, a saint, the Virgin), and these are confident statements of moral guidance or injunctions to bishops to read and publicize the message of her book. At the command of an angel, she sends her *Liber viarum dei* to the bishops of Cologne, Trier, and Mainz, because God wants them to preach it widely (4.20); to archbishop Hillin of Trier she writes a second time, reminding him of the message, reproving him for defrauding God of the jewels and pearls in his care, and advising him to look in the book and see what was said about pride and avarice in the apostolic see.[24] But usually she answers religious questions asking for information about particular saints, or personal ones, such as whether a brother should go on a pilgrimage.[25] One of the most interesting problems put to Elisabeth came from Gerlach, abbot of Deutz, who was worried about the host which had been sneezed up by a boy during communion in their church (6.6). Elisabeth answers him in a lively dialogue with her angel: "My lord, what happened to the venerable sacrament that was thrown up from the throat of the sneezing boy in the church of Deutz-Köln? Was it trampled by the feet of bystanders and perished?" He reassured her: "'The sanctity of that sacrament restored the spirit of the one taking it, and when it fell from his mouth, it was caught by an angel of God who was present and hid it in a secret place.' And I said: 'Lord, do I dare ask in what place it is stored?' And he said 'Don't ask' ('Noli interrogare'). I said again: 'What service should the brothers offer to God for this negligence?'" And the angel gives the penance with detailed instructions in case blood was spilled or the host placed among relics (6.7).

In her letters to other nuns, Elisabeth speaks mainly about leading lives to be worthy of the eternal spouse, being wise *and intelligent* virgins (6.10), keeping their lamps lit, loving each other, bearing each others' burdens (something her sisters frequently do in the vision books), and caring for the infirm, because God has called them to this vocation and chosen them his heirs. When there are problems, she promises penance and healing: "the wise doctor wants to cure the languors of your souls, first with bitterness, then with gentle stroking and smooth unguents to heal the wounds" (6.10, to sisters of Dietkirchen). She can be forceful in her criticism, as to the sisters of the holy virgins in Cologne, whose "feet trample the blood of God's saints that was poured out on earth, they have soiled the bed in which he should lie with his saints" (6.11). But she can also share her own sufferings; after she describes and explains a vision to an unnamed woman, perhaps the abbess of Dietkirchen (see Clark 164, n.60), she tells her how she had wept because her fevers made her miss the Easter celebration, and the angel consoled her by bringing her in spirit to a lovely place and letting her drink from a fountain with a gold vessel. "All these things," she says, "I took care to tell you, dearest, so that you might have some consolation from them and be comforted in the lord" (6.14).

To Hildegard, Elisabeth goes much further, sharing her anxiety about her visions in her first and very long letter (3.19), hoping for consolation and advice and perhaps encouragement from the older woman who had had such experiences herself. She wrote because she had heard of Hilde-gard's sympathy for her, indeed that Hildegard had had a revelation about Elisabeth's anxiety.[26] She does not say that being a woman was part of her problem, but it is implicit in her story and in her choice of Hildegard as a confidante and supporter. Elisabeth explains that she is distressed by what people, particularly religious people, have been saying, ridiculing the grace of God in her, even writing letters in her name, with prophecies which she would never presume to make. She tells Hildegard the whole story, so she can judge whether Elisabeth has acted presumptuously or not. The story reveals a lot about Elisabeth's fears and the hesitation of some members of her society to accept the word she brings them. Elisabeth had hidden God's revelations in order "to avoid arrogance and not to seem the author of novelties"—perhaps a tactless remark to make to a famous visionary—until her angel whipped her for keeping back the word of God that was given to her to be revealed. But even then she did not reveal them publicly; first she showed the book she kept of her visions to the abbot, who apparently accepted them as genuine and brought her message to men of the church. Some received it with reverence, others raised questions about her angel, presumably questioning her sanity or veracity and shaking the abbot's confidence. He was clearly torn between established (male) authority and a young woman's unsupported claims, but each time he was swayed by her reports. The angel speaks to her, never to him, but it is he, not she, who preaches the message publicly. When someone else began to relate terrible prophecies as though they came from her, however, Elisabeth was afraid she would be ridiculed. She tells all this to Hildegard so that Hildegard will know her innocence and the abbot's and can reveal it to others, and she asks her for prayers and words of consolation.

Hildegard, having no woman model to turn to, had sought support and received it from a male mystic—her first extant letter was to Bernard of Clairvaux, who recognized the grace of God and inner erudition teaching through her (VA1r).[27] But she is sympathetic to Elisabeth's needs and becomes a model for Elisabeth as visionary, author, and public source of authority. Hildegard's one certain letter to Elisabeth encourages her with the understanding of one who has suffered in the same way: "I too lie in the cowardice of my mind (in pusillanimitate mentis mee), making a little sound, at times, like the small sound of a trumpet from the living light" (VA201r). But she has accepted the responsibility. Speaking not for herself, "a poor little earthen vessel (paupercula et fictile vas)," but from the serene light, she tells Elisabeth that God fashioned the human being as a vessel through which he might accomplish his works, that the world is weary in its virtues and God must strengthen some lest his instruments be idle. That is, she and Elisabeth must carry on Christ's work, since others do not. Those who wish to accomplish the works of God must remember they are earthen vessels, simply reciting the mysteries of God, like a trumpet which sounds only when one blows in it, and leave heavenly things to God. In other words, they should deliver the messages God entrusts to them and not be tempted to act on their own, a temptation Hildegard has presumably known and not always, some might add, overcome.[28]

Elisabeth's second letter to Hildegard is less personal and much more assured in its praise of Hildegard—a praise which must at least in part reflect back on her—in its recognition that she is filling a void left by the church hierarchy, and in its declaration of revelations and concerns they both share (6.20-21): "Rejoice with me, my lady and venerable daughter of the eternal king, that the finger of God writes in you, that you may pronounce the word of life . . . you are the organ of the Holy Spirit, your words enflamed me as if fire touched my heart . . . the stimulus of God works in you with wondrous fortitude in the edification of his church. . . . Who chose you, will crown you with the crown of happiness . . . the lord placed you in his vineyard to work it. For the lord sought workers in his vineyard and found them all lazy, because no one led them. The lord's vineyard has no cultivator, the lord's vineyard perishes, the head of the church languishes and its members are dead. . . ."

Other women seem to have been emotionally dependent on Hildegard, abbesses who sought her comfort, advice, and support, who must have seen her as a role model and taken pride in her prestige. As the abbess of Bamberg said, "Christ gave us special joy in this that not only did he foresee and predestine you for this from the female sex but also illumined many through doctrine by his grace. . . . We ask eagerly that you deign to receive us in the consort of your fraternity and commend us to your sacred convent and strengthen us with commonitory letters" (VA61). Other women revealed their needs more directly. The abbess of Altena implied that Hildegard might give a little less time to her heavenly husband and a little more to her friends on earth. Complaining that Hildegard has not written in a long time, she suggests, "I believe that if you could redirect the sharp sight of your mind from the intuition of your beloved and move your foot outside your dwelling of quiet, you would not fail to console me more often through your messenger . . . for if it is not given to me to see your beloved face again in this life, which I cannot say without tears, yet

I will always be happy about you, whom I have loved as my own soul" (VA49).

Gertrude, nun of Bamberg, laments: "The wine of sorrow, by which your divine absence made me drunk, has so afflicted me that it generated an aversion in me not only of dictating but even of living. It would have been better for me, I believe, never to have seen you, never to have felt you having such benign and maternal deep feelings for me, than that separated by such distance, I grieve for you without pause, as if I had lost you." Hoping, if she cannot see her in this life because of her sins, she will see her "there where we shall never be separated from his vision," she asks Hildegard, "most chosen mother, as you rest in his embraces continually and beneath his shadow lie quiet from the fervor of temptations and vices like a young mule, deign to pray for me . . ." (VA62). This letter elicited a long and encouraging response from Hildegard, drawing from the Song of Songs, rejoicing in what she has heard about Gertrude, and telling her to rejoice in God since she will live eternally (VA62r).

If Hildegard's concern for Gertrude was maternal, she seems to have felt some of the intensity of Gertrude's affection for another young nun, Richardis of Stade, whom she struggled to keep with her. Richardis had helped Hildegard in her work on the *Scivias*. From an important family, she and her niece Adelheid were both trained at Rupertsberg, destined to become abbesses themselves, but when they received the offers in 1152, Hildegard was not ready, and did everything she could to stop them, including virtually accusing their brother Hartwig, archbishop of Bremen, of simony (VA12).[29] Hildegard insisted it was not God's will for the young nuns to take those posts, perhaps hearing her own emotional needs as God's words. Her letter to Richardis reveals her pain and disappointment: "Hear, daughter, your mother saying . . . pain grows in me, pain kills the confidence and comfort I had in a human being. . . . I was wrong to love a noble [human] so. . . . Woe to me, mother, woe to me, daughter, why did you forsake me like an orphan? I loved the nobility of your customs, your wisdom, your chastity, your soul and the whole of your life, so that many asked me 'what are you doing?'" (VA64). Richardis seems to have returned the affection, at least her brother later said she desired Hildegard's cloister in tears and with her whole heart, and would have returned if death had not intervened (VA13). Hildegard does not betray the same intensity of feeling for Adelheid in the one letter extant (VA99), but Adelheid, now abbess of Gandersheim, sends a conciliatory letter asking her former abbess to pray for her and her flock and to exchange visits among their nuns, promising to visit herself, implicating Hildegard in her own success or failure, and acknowledging her past and future influence: "a good tree is known from its good fruit . . . do not let the flower of ancient nourishment dry up in the heart which flourished when you sweetly brought me up" (VA100).

Hildegard did her best to help other abbesses, as well as to give them advice. If she encouraged an abbess to stay with her duties, she also wrote to her nuns to do their part. She told the abbess of Bamberg not to run away from working her field lest weeds grow, not to hide the light of her rationality, allowing her daughters to be covered by the black cloud of the devil's deception (VA61r); to the nuns she says, "let that summer be in you that makes roses and lilies grow," not weeds (VA63). To Hazzecha, abbess of Krauftal, who wanted to retire to solitary life in a cell, Hildegard wrote of the dangers of such an intense life, where "recent things become much worse and weigh like the throwing of a stone" (VA159r) and warned that "if you begin a greater task than you can bear, through the devil's deception, you will fall" (VA161).[30] And she exhorted Hazzecha's nuns to amend their ways with a parable of a fig tree planted by God which used to give fruit but dried up because of winter and a stream fouled by animals, horrid beasts blowing fire of malignant vice against the whiteness of innocence; the nuns had been holy in the first planting but have abandoned the Rule, so their fruit—the works of love, obedience, perseverance in good—has dried up; yet God has not abandoned them but wants to keep them as they were in the first planting (VA162). When the sisters of the Holy Cross in Woffensheim were unable to elect a new abbess because of their disagreements, Hildegard told them to "flee the evil of contradiction . . . so the true sun might emit its rays to you to choose a mother to have the place of Christ (vicem Christi) with good intention toward you" (VA239), an interesting comment on her view of the abbess's role. She also wrote to their prioress, encouraging her to take on the position: "no man should flee, if he has the capacity, from sustaining a congregation of holy people with God's staff" (VA238).

Hildegard believes deeply in the abbess's responsibility to God, in her acting "in the place of Christ" according to God's will, which she describes forcefully in a letter to Sophia of Kitzingen, whose nuns were giving her much trouble: "In the true light, I see a fire-ring like a wheel circling you. And you change the narrow path on which you look to the sun. Then storm clouds come over you, because your spirit wanders, and you cry, 'When will God free me?' He answers, 'I will not let you go. This is my will: seize the net so it does not tear, for when you let it go, it pulls in another direction'" (VA151). At the same time, Hildegard saw the nun's role as the highest aspiration of woman, a return to her prelapsarian state, when she related directly to God without the interference of Adam. She tells the nuns who had asked her help in correcting their negligence a parable about a nobleman and his beautiful spouse, who did not persevere in her nobility, which was like Eve "before God presented her to Adam, when she looked then not to Adam but to God." So should woman "look to God, and not to another husband (*virum*) *whom at first she did not want to have*" (VA250r).[31]

The letters suggest that women looked to Hildegard particularly as a mentor in the modern sense: she was a respected abbess, who founded and ran a successful monastery for decades and was not afraid to oppose the ecclesiastical hierarchy for the things she believed in; she was a woman chosen by God to carry his word to the church and all its members, who was listened to with respect rather than ridicule by powerful men in the secular and church hierarchies. Though she declared her preference for the single life in terms that seem to put down the male sex, Hildegard actually worked effectively with men in the religious hierarchy and with her male secretaries, who were devoted to her. She preached to bishops and opposed them in the name of God, and she strongly admonished popes and kings, but she had a number of male friends who sought her advice for their lives, and she applied the same standards of responsibility and justice to them. Her predictions of divine wrath are clothed in complicated images, which allow for various interpretations.[32] They were, however, believed, and pope Eugene and emperor Frederick Barbarossa testified to their truth. It is no wonder, then, that men and women, religious and lay, people of importance and minor figures, emperors and kings, popes and archbishops, as well as queens and abbesses, nuns and priests, turned to her—if they could not come, they wrote—for forecasts and for practical advice about their careers, their medical problems, their marriages; about the state of the world or the church; and about theological questions.

The theological questions are perhaps the most striking; because Hildegard has a direct line to the Word, she can respond to very delicate questions with answers that are more reliable than those of the most respected teachers of the church. So she is asked about major issues by a bishop, even by a master of Paris: Eberhard, bishop of Bamberg, asked about eternity, equality, and connection in the trinity (VA31), a ticklish subject in the twelfth century because of the controversies around the ideas of Abelard and Gilbert of Poitiers; Odo, a Paris master, asked about paternity and divinity and whether they are God, issues directly related to Gilbert's discussions (VA40); Rudeger, a monk of Ebrach, asked about Christ in the Eucharist (VA89). Guibert and the monks of Villers sent sixty-nine questions about contradictions in the Bible, scientific matters, unexplained details, interpretations of text, and theological problems: whether the waters above the firmament were natural, how God spoke to Adam, in what species God appeared to him, by what reason the souls of infants in their mothers' wombs are believed to contract original sin, and with what justice they are punished.[33]

Hildegard was considered a source of universal knowledge but her answers combine revelation from the "living light" with common sense. The requests range from a bishop's desire for advice toward his salvation, having no confidence in his own actions to attain it (Henry of Beauvais, VA32), to a wife's concern with her husband's illness (Pi124) or extramarital affair

(Pi95). Lay women write about legal (Pi161) or medical problems (Pi36). Priests ask how to cure their own nightmares (DB8), parishioners' sterility (VA70), or demonic possession (PL60).[34] For nightmares, she suggested that the priest read himself to sleep (with the gospel of John), relax (his hand over his heart), and pray for quiet. For the demon, she first recommended a ritual of exorcism but later treated the woman directly by letting the demon talk itself out. In her letters Hildegard attacks willful obstinacy, pride, corruption, failures in leadership at all levels, and Cathar beliefs, but she also preaches the need for justice and mercy in any leader, king, or abbess. She preaches love as a more effective teacher than fear, though inspiring fear may sometimes be necessary (VA61r), and healing and comfort over angry punishment (VA213). When abbots and abbesses ask whether they can leave their posts and accept new ones or retire to solitude, Hildegard speaks firmly about their God-given responsibilities, but she recognizes the need for occasional rest. She believes in discipline to keep the monastic flock from straying but opposes excessive austerity.

People also wrote to Hildegard asking for the sermons they had heard her preach in a series of preaching tours which God forced her to make and clergy and bishops came to hear. This unusual circumstance is justified by an admirer who says she is exempt from the condition imposed by Paul that does not permit women to teach in church because she is instructed by the spirit (Gb18.240ff). Though Hildegard presents herself as "indocta," unlearned, so that whatever learned words come from her are God's, not hers, she does not claim ignorance. What she seems to mean is that she has had no formal training in philosophy and theology, whereas she is, of course, literate if not polished in Latin and seems to be well read.[35] She is not modest about the significance of her visionary experiences, which she compares with those of Paul and John; nor did she shrink from battle with those who opposed her, because she saw their stands as opposition to God. She implicitly compares herself to Mary and those who oppose her, like the monks of her old house at Disibodenberg, to Lucifer, who did not praise God, while God foresaw that a work would be done in female nature that not angels or men or other creatures could carry through (VA77r). When the bishops of Mainz laid an interdict on her convent after she buried a nobleman who had once been excommunicated, she implied that they were repeating Adam's fall in their disobedience to God's will (VA23). These two battles seem to be matters of principle, but they also suggest a perhaps unconscious desire to assert her independence from ecclesiastical authority.

But among those closest to her, her nuns and her secretaries, Hildegard seems to have inspired affection and awe. Her secretaries were among her most devoted admirers, aware of her importance for the world, taking pride in her gifts. The first, Volmar, worried what would happen when she died: "Where then will be the answers to those asking about all events?

Where the new interpretation of Scriptures? . . . the voice of unheard melody and of unheard language . . . the new and unheard sermons on feast days . . . the revelation about souls of the dead . . . about past, present, future . . . the exposition . . . with divine grace, with sweetest and humblest customs, and maternal affection to all . . . ?" (VA195). He thanks God for infusing his gift in her to the edification of the whole church. Abbot Ludwig of St. Eucharius, who helped her edit her texts after Volmar died, wrote what is to me the most appealing variation of the humility topos: "It seems ridiculous enough if butterflies saluted eagles with their letters, or fleas stags, or stomach-worms lions, so even more than wondrous, or if I might truly say, laughable, that a sinner worth little or nothing in divine or human arts should presume to write to one whom God with the marvelous prerogative of chastity magnifies so high and with such great excellence of wit that not only you exceed the heights of philosophers and dialecticians, but also of the ancient prophets" (VA215). Guibert wrote to her in Marian language—"Hail, full of grace after Mary, the Lord is with you, blessed are you among women, and blessed the speech of your mouth"—and connects her with Paul, calling her a "chosen vessel" (Gb22).[36]

Guibert was aware that some men in the church did not approve of his sojourn among women in Hildegard's convent, but he justified himself, as so many men did throughout the Middle Ages, by comparison with Jerome (Gb32). Jerome's letters, like his commentaries, so many of them addressed to women, were known and read, and they provided an unimpeachable model for male-female friendship among religious. However misogynist men like Jerome might have sounded in their moral writings, in their personal relations, as reflected in their letters, they were capable of great affection and respect for their women colleagues. As Christians they were equal before God, and as religious they were "equal by vocation," as a later abbess reminds an abbot devoted to the same patron saint.[37] As missionaries or scholars, male and female religious shared the same interests and goals; as women they could not be rivals within the ecclesiastical hierarchy and as religious, they were not likely to threaten the man's chastity.[38] They were siblings in the family of Christ.[39]

Sometimes they were siblings in the family of man as well. Both Jerome and Augustine had sisters who were nuns, and Augustine probably wrote a rule for his sister's house (as Caesarius of Arles did). We have no letters from Jerome or Augustine to their sisters, though both wrote to other women, nor from Augustine to his mother, who was such a presence in his life. But Ambrose sent sermons with letters describing his adventures to his sister Marcellina, his "spokesman" in Rome.[40] The Boniface collection includes moving letters of affection and loneliness from nuns to their brothers (epp.143, 147, 148) and from a monk (who might be Boniface's colleague Lull) to his sister (ep.140), as well as letters of intense friendship between Boniface and Bugga, Eadburg, and Lioba. Peter Damian wrote religious advice to his sisters (ep.94) and a theological tract to one, encouraging her interest in such matters (ep.93), and letters of deep affection to empress Agnes when she lived as a nun.[41] One wonders if the natural sibling relation made it easier for some men to form such relations with strangers.

But the most interesting letters are those between friends and colleagues —Jerome to Marcella and Paula, Abelard and Heloise—particularly when they shared the intellectual excitement of scholarly discovery. Jerome worked with women in his biblical studies in Rome and Jerusalem, corresponded with them about textual problems and heresies, and wrote many of his works at their request (see chapter 2) and over a third of his extant letters to them. He defended his work with women by biblical examples of women who taught, asking "if to be taught by a woman was not shameful to an apostle, why should it be to me to teach women?" (ep.65) and insisting that he judged not by sex but by spirit (ep.127.5). Their questions push him to investigate, to study, to work out the answers, and he encourages them to continue to study biblical texts and commentaries, to oppose heresy even publicly. He writes as one scholar to another, expecting a "friendly mind" to understand his excitement when he is comparing Aquila to the Hebrew: "I have found much . . . you see that nothing can be put ahead of this work" (ep.32 to Marcella). He unburdens himself about enemies, knowing he will have a sympathetic ear, and writes secretly by his own hand about dangerous doctrine (ep.33 to Paula). He recognizes the intelligence and the learning of the women he worked with and applauds one, at least, for imparting her knowledge to men: Marcella "answered any arguments that were put to her about scripture, including obscure and ambiguous inquiries from priests, saying that the answers came from me or another man even when they were her own, claiming always to be a pupil even when she was teaching, so that she did not seem to injure the male sex because the apostle did not permit women to teach" (ep.127.7), a resounding justification of a woman teaching theology even to priests.

The women who worked with Jerome were wealthy, highly educated, and deeply devoted to religion and religious study. Marcella turned her home into a community of religious women; Paula spent her fortune building a monastery for men and three communities for women, and giving to the poor. There were many such women who supported the early church and the work of men like Jerome (and Augustine and John Chrysostom), but Jerome's letters record more of them than do the letters of his colleagues.[42] The women who worked with Jerome were also devoted to each other, as his letters to women about other women and the one extant letter from Paula and Eustochium to Marcella (ep.46) testify. The existence of these women and their friendship with Jerome is not simply an interesting historical fact, it is an important precedent for the Middle Ages, because Jerome's letters were known and cited by later writers, male and female, in defense of similar relations. Gisla and Rotrud, a sister and a daughter of Charlemagne, who asked their friend Alcuin for a commentary on John, reminded him that Jerome "dedicated many works on prophetic obscurities" to women, that "epistolary pages flew often from Bethlehem . . . to Roman citadels" (ep.196). Azecho, who sees no reason to avoid conversation with all women because some may be dangerous, justifies his writing to a nun in the eleventh century with the claim that Jerome wrote many things to Paula and Eustochium that he did not want to write to men. Guibert of Gembloux, admirer and last secretary of Hildegard of Bingen, wrote defending his friendship with the nuns of her convent that Jerome had many religious women friends and wrote to them often (Gb32). Goscelin, writing a book of advice for the recluse Eve, cites Paula, Eustochium, and Blesilla, scholars and saints of the simple life (citing Jerome's "sancta rusticitas et docta sanctitas," 3.6), as models for her to follow; the justification of his relation with Eve is implicit. Heloise and Abelard look to Marcella and Jerome as models, both citing the passage in which Jerome says Marcella "did not simply accept everything I said, but examined it and with a perceptive mind thought it all out so I felt myself to have not so much a disciple as a judge" (Abelard in ep.9, Heloise in the *Problemata*).

When the relation between Heloise and Abelard began, it was of course very different from the friendship of Marcella and Jerome. Abelard admits that his intentions in tutoring Heloise were to use her literary interests to seduce her; knowing her knowledge and love of literature, he thought she would be all the more ready to consent and that they could enjoy each other's presence even when apart by an exchange of letters in which they could speak more openly than in person (*Historia calamitatum*). But she would later use those same interests to seduce him intellectually into writing a series of works, most of his extant output, for her and the nuns of the Paraclete. She presented him with textual problems, problems of translation and of understanding, and elicited in response answers, commentaries, hymns, sermons, and a rule. She often directed his thoughts specifically to the problems of women, sometimes provoking strong feminist arguments from him by using antifeminist statements. Both Abelard and Heloise have been accused of antifeminism, but it seems to me that Heloise's remarks are meant to move Abelard to counter them with greater authority than a woman's word would have, not to express her own convictions. It is always possible that a strong and intelligent woman might feel some scorn for those women who do not act on their own behalf, but it is also likely that as a woman who has achieved success in the world (and an abbess was a worldly as well as a religious figure), she had had enough experience of female effectiveness and male hostility to have serious doubts about the clichés of womanly weakness. Certainly in the actions of her life and in the effects of her letters, her sense of her own dignity and the enhanced sense she provides for other women seem to me to predominate. Abelard's occasional misogynist outbursts may be more deeply ambivalent.[43] Medieval correspondence gives many examples of men who can attack women in one context and praise them in another, who can speak of women as an inferior sex but treat them as political or intellectual equals and even superiors, who seem to have one view of the sex in general or in theory and another of the individuals they knew. In this, despite his great intellect, Abelard is like the men of his and other times. But he does finally cast his lot with Heloise and the Paraclete; and therefore to exalt them and their role is to justify his own, and in exalting them, he goes very far indeed (see chapter 2).

It is a testament to the respect and confidence Abelard felt for Heloise, not unlike what Jerome clearly felt for Marcella, that it was in a letter to Heloise that Abelard made his "confession of faith," his response to those who hated him because of his logic, who accused him of understanding philosophy better than religion. He declares the tenets of his faith in direct terms, reminiscent of the credo, though he carefully dissociates himself from the heresies of Arius and Sabellius. But he ends with a classical reference, "safely located here [on this faith], I do not fear the barking of Scylla, I laugh at the whirlpool of Charybdis, and have no horror of the fatal songs of the sirens." The text of the letter appears only in a letter addressed by one of Abelard's students, Berengar of Poitiers, to Bernard and Abelard's other accusers at the Council of Sens, but it is clearly addressed to Heloise, "my sister, once dear to me in the world, now most dear in Christ."[44]

Abelard was not the only man who was attracted to Heloise for her learning and responded to her unusual gifts. Peter the Venerable wrote expressing his affection and admiration, saying he had been aware of her reputation for learning from their youth, when she was known for her secular studies and had gone further in the pursuit of wisdom than almost all men; then she turned to philosophy in the true sense, left logic for the Gospel, Plato for Christ, the academy for the cloister. Moreover, she conquered the old enemy of women, the devil, to her eternal glory; he says she is one of the animals Ezekiel saw, associating her with the evangelists, a disciple of truth, who leads others to salvation, and compares her to the Amazon Penthesilea and the biblical judge Deborah, women who fought against men for their people (ep.115, also R277–84). Hugh Metel, a canon who had not met Heloise but admired her from afar, also wrote letters of praise for her writing of prose and poetry in which she "rises above the female sex and surpasses or equals the pens of doctors," as well as for her life devoted to heavenly delights; he begs for letters, saying his soul "covets at least to see and be seen, to hear and be heard in an exchange of letters."[45]

The relations Heloise had with Abelard despite the complications of the physical affair, like those Jerome had with Marcella and probably even more with Paula, were based on deep affection and trust and mutual respect. But they certainly were nourished in large part by the shared intellectual excitement of working out philosophical, theological, and textual problems together, the mutual stimulation of exceptional minds. I know of no other couples quite like them, but I have no doubt that other men and women in the Middle Ages felt that kind of excitement from time to time. There are traces of such in a letter from Adam of Perseigne to a countess of Chartres, describing how he had felt "compelled with a certain pious violence to remain with you two days" while they shared thoughts: "the sweet words of new friendship come into my mind, the conversations in which we conferred equally about hatred of sin, contempt of the world, studies of virtues, words of scripture, examples of the saints, and the joys of heavenly life" (PL211, ep.27).

"LET MUTUAL SONGS COMMEND US TO EACH OTHER"

A different kind of intellectual stimulation is evident in the last body of letters I will mention, the exchange of epistolary poems between men and women religious.[46] Although such poems openly display a higher level of self-conscious artistry, of literary artifice, than the prose letter, however carefully constructed that may be, they are nonetheless a means of communication between friends. Even in those exchanges in which only the man's side is preserved, the woman's technical knowledge is referred or deferred to. From the sixth century to the twelfth, there are exchanges of occasional poems between men and women, poems which express affection and respect, sometimes emotional dependence, sometimes appreciation of the other's skill. Many of the late-Roman bishops were not only literate but also accomplished practitioners of Latin letters, prose and poetry, and engaged in exchanges of occasional verse with their friends, male and female. At the request of Euprepia, Ennodius composed epitaphs of women they both admired and sent them to her, expecting her to detect the flaws, since, as he says, she had often pointed out the poverty of his wit (ep.5.7).[47] Venantius Fortunatus exchanged poems and gifts with his close friends, queen Radegund and her abbess, Agnes. In this case, too, we have only Fortunatus's part of the exchange, but since he complains when they do not send poems or delights when they do, we know it was reciprocal. And we know that Radegund was an accomplished poet from her three extant poems, all epistolary. Two are to relatives. One is an elegy on the destruction of her land and her people, which she wrote to her cousin Hamalafred, to whom she had been particularly close as a child and whose absence she feels most strongly. The other, to her nephew Artachis, also begins with a lament for her fallen land and dead father and uncles.[48]

The exchange with Fortunatus seems to have been in a lighter vein, celebrating the small events of their daily lives—gifts of food, festive occasions, their "Daedalan art" in decorations, visits and separations. Radegund and Agnes were devout, loving, and learned women who provided Fortunatus with much that he seemed to need, and probably he did the same for them. Like Radegund, Fortunatus was an exile, and he valued the love and intimacy they offered, as well as the mutual respect and delight of poetic exchange.[49] He and Agnes worry in verse about Radegund's health, begging her to drink wine, as Paul ordered Timothy to do (11.4). He laments when they are separated: "although the sky is serene with clouds fleeing, when you are hidden, the day is without sun to me" (11.2), and "absent from you, feasting, I cultivated fasts, food without you could not satisfy me" (11.16). He rejoices when they meet: "you bring back my joys with you and you make Easter twice celebrated . . . though seeds just now begin to rise . . . I seeing you here today reap the harvest" (8.10). He complains when they do not send poems: "did passing time so distract you that you did not distribute the usual wealth to me? nor give sweet modulations of the lady tongue to one who, while you speak words, is fed by your mouth?" (11.5). He delights when they do: "The flattering master [*magistra*] recreated him with words and foods and sates with various delighting play" (11.23a); "in brief tablets you gave me great songs, you were able to give honey to empty wax [the writing tablets] . . . to me, avid, your words are more than food" (app.31).

When Fortunatus speaks of Radegund as a "master" he is probably complimenting her skill. But in British double monasteries in the eighth century, poetry was taught and composed by men and women, and Boniface's missions carried their style of administration and education to Germany. Among the letters of Boniface and his colleagues, there are many references to the exchange of poems and the texts of a few poems. One, probably from his colleague and successor, Lull, thanking an abbess and nun who cared for him when he was very sick, is sent with apologies for its errors, which he is confident they will not judge too harshly, and a request that they correct anything in it contrary to the rule of grammatical art (ep.98). Other letters in the collection bear witness to the exchange of poems between siblings: a brother writing to his sister about the approaching end of the world includes his poems and a request for hers (ep.140); a lonely sister, writing of her desire to see her brother, thanks him for his gifts and sends religious poems in return (epp.147, 148).[50]

In the late eleventh and early twelfth centuries, there seems to have been a whole circle of poets, men and women, who played an elaborate literary game, exchanging rhetorical elegance and literary flirtation, such desire as may have been felt sublimated through the poetry. The poets included bishops Hildebert of Lavardin and Baudri of Bourgueil.[51] The women were nuns—Cecilia, perhaps the daughter of William the Conqueror, who became abbess of Caen in 1113; a Muriel who lived in a convent and inspired poems by Serlo of Wilton as well; and many others.[52]

Hildebert's attitudes toward women are complex, depending on the mode. In his role as bishop, Hildebert encouraged the regent Adela of Blois to be like a man (ep.1.4) and inspired a widow with examples of David, small but terrible in the name of God, and Judith, who liberated Bethulia when even the priests were afraid (ep.1.10). As a traditional moralist, he could tell a nun that "flesh and woman are a double infirmity" (ep.1.6) and write in verse that "woman is a fragile thing, never constant except in crime" (PL171, c.1428). In his role as secular subordinate, he could write worldly flattery to countess Adela—"he is foolish and sins who equates you to mortals / it is small praise, but you will be to me first among goddesses" (10)—and courtly sentiments to the abbess Cecilia: "Who is accustomed to be more skillful at speaking before men than Cicero, / is less eloquent when he comes before Gods. / So I, while in the midst of the people I speak with a skillful mouth, / to your face can say little" (46).[53] But he expresses his most exuberant enthusiasm in the literary exchange, responding to a poem from Muriel: "Former times boasted ten sibyls / and there was great glory to your sex. / Present times rejoice in the wit of one / . . . Whatever you breathe out is immortal and the world / adores your work as divine. / You put down by your wit celebrated poets and bards, / and both sexes are stunned by your eloquence. / Looking ten times over at the songs sent to me, / I am amazed. . . . It is not human to do such sacred labors, / . . . The weight of the words, grave sense, beautiful order / have the face of divine condition. /. . . The cares of exile and the harsh weight of labors / you, virgin, can alleviate with your song. /. . . Do not deny your words to me" (26).

One might assume that the extravagance of the praise indicates the rarity of a woman poet, but the number of women, including Muriel, with whom Baudri of Bourgueil (1046-1130) exchanged or hoped to exchange poems belies that assumption. Baudri is reminiscent of Fortunatus, writing with a playful and affectionate tone. To the experienced poets, like Muriel, he writes in praise of their abilities; to those I take to be younger women, he sends encouragement to study and write; to all he expresses a desire to receive their poems. Muriel had long attracted Baudri by her fame, and when he first heard her recite, he wrote enthusiastically: "with what honeyed charm are your words anointed / how sweet sounds your voice . . . the words sound a man, the voice a woman."[54] He longs for a time when they can speak together, asking and answering each other's questions; meanwhile, "let mutual songs commend us to us," let us be the first to know each other's secrets (72-73). Emma, too, must have been a recognized poet, since when he praises her poems ("flavored with nectar, her wisdom sustained with honey"), he speaks of the swarms of (female) disciples who rush to be revived by the honey of the parent bee—if her order allowed male disciples, he would be one (75-76). In a longer poem accompanying a book of his poetry, he wonders how she has received his poems in the past, with love or laughter, and describing himself as a raucous cricket in comparison to her, asks her for critical editing and appraisal of his collection, to read it carefully, to censure rather than flatter, to extol, correct, or add (80-82).

Baudri's tone with Agnes and Beatrice is less diffident, more playful. He plays on Agnes's name ("little lamb because gentler than a lamb"), encourages her in her studies and her poetry, promising to return the tablets—evidence of an exchange—and asking her to return his greetings in verses (74-75). He complains to Beatrice that she never responds in song despite his requests, and he attempts to coax her with mockery: she puts her finger over her mouth and pretends to hide behind her veil; he begins to see an ass before the lyre; men are often at a loss for words before a virgin, no woman is before a man—a courtly, not a religious view; "let her praise or damn our songs in song, / but not be a mute and mutilated sheep / . . . she wrote, she dictated, she said almost nothing" (77-78).

With Constance, the one woman from whom we have an answering poem, there is a different tone again, an intensity beneath the flirtatious surface that suggests a stronger attachment. His shorter poem to her does not reveal much: he says he greets everyone in verse, using his poems to cover his rusticity and jesting in writing, though in fact he speaks quite seriously about her vow of virginity and her sacrifice to God; at the end, he asks her to renew the covenant of friendship, to commit anything she wants to convey to tablets, and to greet Emma for him (78-79).[55] But the longer poem—written, he says, by his own hand—declares his love for Constance, protesting its innocence, perhaps too frequently, in the language of romantic love, and aware that others might interpret it differently, telling her to embrace the physical poem as though it were a substitute for him, but assuring her that it is harmless: "read through and cautiously embrace the sheet you've read, / lest a malign tongue harm my fame . . . no poison is hidden in it . . . you can place it in your bosom" (83-87). Though he protests that "Foul love never drove me, / with you I wish to live a fellow-citizen in virginity . . . I swear by all that is, I don't wish to be a man to you / nor that you be a woman to me," still he says she is more to him than Helen to Paris or Venus to Mars, evoking relations which were far from chaste, and describes her features as a worldly lover might, lips that heat and swell with a fiery color, a body to suit the face so that she might bring down the highest Jove from heaven, if Greek fable were true. He insists, "I love you vehemently, / I love you vehemently, I wholly shall love you whole, / you alone I enfold in my gut," but "it is a special love which flesh does not accompany, / nor desire make illicit." It is her virginity he says he loves, the purity of her flesh. If his love is as pure as he proclaims, it is because it is consummated only in song and is finally a game, but it also seems a stronger emotion than what he feels for the other women he writes to.[56]

Constance answered with a poem of the same length (179 lines) and the same intensity of emotion and language: "I read your sheet with studious investigation, / I touched your songs with my naked hand. / Rejoicing, I unfolded the volume, two, three, four times / . . . I consumed the day, reading [it] often, / night was hateful . . . compelling me to cease my study. / I refolded in my lap and placed the sheet under my left breast, which they say is closer to the heart." She praises him with learned comparisons; he is a Cato in deeds, Cicero in words, another Homer, "he alone is worth many Aristotles." And writing gives her the means not only to speak but also to say what she could not otherwise: "I shall attack wax, since wax does not know modesty / . . . Many things indeed I may write which I do not wish to say to him present." But she longs for his presence: "A year has passed since I have not been able to see him whom I wish for, / and yet I often read his songs. / . . . He will not come to me, nor will I, thirsting, see him." And she asks him to come to her, since the obstacles are fewer for him: "I would come if I could / . . . but my fierce stepmother [her abbess?] hinders my journey . . . awaited one, come, don't delay long, / I have often called you, come."

All the poems Hildebert and particularly Baudri exchanged with their women friends and fellow poets suggest feelings of affection and shared delight in intellectual games, whatever other emotions may lie beneath the surface. Of their more formal poems to patrons, there is one pair by Baudri which is pertinent to this study. Baudri couched a request to countess Adela for a more tangible exchange, the gift of a cope, or cloak, in rather elaborate praise. The first, a long poem (1,354 lines), flatters her with flights of fancy that might be at home in a romance.[57] After comparing her with her illustrious father—no less in virtue though greater in her knowledge of poetry and her interest in books—Baudri describes her room. He imagines it as decorated with themes to suggest her great learning: tapestries of the Old Testament and ancient history; a mosaic map of the world on the floor, with the heavens on the ceiling; a bed draped in hangings showing her father's conquest of England, surrounded by life-size figures of the seven liberal arts and medicine, which could recite the material of their disciplines. This poem graphically sets Adela at the center of the world, its history, its culture, and implicitly its power. It ends with a modest request for a cope, which the extravagance of the poem might seem to merit.

But apparently the cope was not forthcoming, since Baudri also wrote a shorter poem which focuses on the request. In it, he asks for a cope that will suit both the giver and the receiver, that will turn her from a countess to a queen for him, as his song will spread her fame through the wide world. She has already furnished the matter for the song: "you yourself furnish the song to me, you the pen, / you will give the breath, the mouth, you will fill the void; / you pay the deserved rewards to the poet. / You compel taciturn bards to be loquacious; / therefore come back to your speaking bard, countess, / and restore, O lady, to the writer, his rewards, the cope." He describes the cope he expects, with gold and gems, implying that her honor rests on its value, that she should adorn it as she does churches. Leaving out no detail, he reminds her at the very end not to forget the fringe, "cave ne desit etiam sua fimbria cappae."

Chrétien may be echoing this poem in his prologue to *Lancelot*, which he wrote at the command of Marie de Champagne, who also furnished the poet with the matter of his work. Whereas Baudri says to Adela, "you would be a queen to me from a countess (nam regina mihi tu fies ex comitissa)" if she gave him the garment adorned with gold and gems, Chrétien declares he will not say that the countess is worth as much in queens as a precious gem in brocades and sardonyx, although she is: "dirai je: Tant com une jame / vaut de pailes et de sardines, / vaut la contesse de reines? / Naie voir; je n'en dirai rien, / s'est il voirs maleoit gré mien" (lines 16–20). In both cases, it is the countess who wills the poet to speak, who compels the taciturn (or unwilling) bard to be loquacious. Where Baudri openly offered flattery in return for the rich gift, Chrétien pretends not to flatter but only to do what she asks. But perhaps the echo of Baudri implies that he too writes this work, which made him so uncomfortable, only for a rich reward.[58]

I will return to Chrétien's complicated relationship with his patron and her requests in the chapter on romances; the ambivalence he shows toward her is not characteristic of Latin writers or of other vernacular romance poets who write for women. Whether the mode is a religious treatise, a history, or a romance, I have found that men writing at the request or commission of women seem more than ready to work with them to compose something that is agreeable to both. I have ended this discussion of correspondence between women and men with epistolary poems because they are both an elegant means of communication between literate friends and the most obvious and equal form of collaboration, in which both partners produce texts expressing their own thoughts, and responding to each other's. In the next three chapters, I will look at other kinds of collaboration in which the text is an expression of the interests of both parties but one person sets the structure or content while the other composes the words.

Part Two
Women in Collaboration

2 *Religious Texts*

The presence and probable influence of women in the beginnings of vernacular literatures, particularly Provençal and French, has been much discussed, but the fact that women also influenced literature in Latin, religious and secular, throughout the Middle Ages, probably more than we can trace, has had less attention. As I read through the letters, I was struck by how frequently men mentioned that the work they were sending was written at the request of the woman they were sending it to.[1] I began to see that the women friends and colleagues who asked for commentaries on specific texts or who asked questions that could be properly answered only in treatises were as instrumental in the production of those works as the women who commissioned panegyrics or histories or later romances. Without the man's letter, we might have no idea of the source; with it, we can see something of a collaborative effort. The woman might set the man a program of activity, forcing him to work out his ideas or do more research, or she might frame the structure of his work by the questions she asked; and he responded because the subject interested him and he trusted her to be a sympathetic audience to ideas as he developed them or to be a purveyor of his ideas to a wider public. This led me to a much broader view of women's role in literature written by men, of collaboration as well as patronage.

The two are not necessarily exclusive. Friends and colleagues, even family members, solicited texts and offered various kinds of support (such as gifts or copying manuscripts); formal sponsors sometimes worked closely with the writer, suggesting material, offering information. The woman's role varies from actively soliciting religious works by asking specific questions, requesting commentaries on particular texts, or commissioning a work of history, biography, or romance with a particular slant or plot, to simply receiving works which were dedicated to them in the hopes of or in gratitude for favors. No matter what her role, the woman addressed could and often did exercise some influence over the work produced. The work is usually the product of the writer's and the sponsor's mutual interests, whether intellectual and religious or political, to further knowledge and understanding or support a cause. Even when the writer's interests are very personal—his own advancement—his choice of sponsor involves a political judgment that her favor will be valuable to him. The letters of dedication which describe the relations between writer, patron, and the text, are, of course, written according to conventions which have been thoroughly studied.[2] But since writers do not normally use irrelevant topoi, it is possible to determine from those they choose to employ what their situation is.

The relation between writer and patron differs somewhat from one category to another. The religious works for women are usually exchanges between intellectual equals, or at least colleagues and friends who are engaged in the same enterprise and who respect each other's minds. When a woman requests a rule for women, she asks to be identified as different from a man, but when she asks for an exchange of ideas, she asks and is answered as an equal. In the secular works, histories or romances, the patron is clearly in a socially superior position; her taste, her views, sometimes her political agenda, are privileged.

I will discuss collaboration between women and writers in three areas. In this chapter, I consider religious (Latin) texts whose authors address them to the women who had set the subject matter of the discourse by the questions they posed or had determined the form of the material by particular requests, whether guides or rules for the spiritual life, sermons, or treatises on theology or scripture. In chapter 3, I look at historical narrative, Latin histories and biographies, commissioned by or dedicated to a particular woman, who is addressed by name in an accompanying letter or preface. In chapter 4, my focus is on courtly literature in French, translations of histories from Latin and newly composed romances, from the twelfth and thirteenth centuries, in which the woman patron is directly addressed in the text. One assumes there were many more texts written for women which have lost all trace of the addressee, but I will discuss only works which are clearly identified.[3] Like the histories, the romances for women patrons implicitly argue for women's claims to inheritance and power. Indeed, in all three areas, religion, history, romance, the works I discuss here assume the mental and moral capacity of women to act responsibly in their public world.

Women and men worked together for Christianity from the time of Christ, though as early as the gospels and Paul the women's role was played down or denied. But even after the prohibitions of Paul or pseudo-Paul, men of the church looked to women for help in actively fighting heresy and spreading the faith. They encouraged them in their spiritual devotion, in their scriptural and theological studies, and in their choice of a religious life, writing at their request guides for a religious life, commentaries on difficult biblical texts, and treatises on deep theological questions. The most obvious form such encouragement took was the guide or rule for the virginal life, for the dedicated widow, even for the married woman who chose (with her husband's consent) to live chastely. The women who embraced a life without sex were the equal, spiritually, of religious men; men who could attack worldly women with merciless virulence could be compassionately supportive of religious women.[4]

One might expect that rules and guides, being formal, would offer the least interesting material on women, but they too can show something about the author's attitude toward religious women. In the early church, highly educated, well-connected, and wealthy women, who supported the work of distinguished men like Jerome and Augustine and wanted to devote themselves to a religious life, asked those distinguished men to compose guides for monastic life or for the holy life of widowhood. The men's responses show respect for the women and recognition of their role in guiding others. Indeed, sometimes the response became part of a battle over heresy. Jerome wrote directions for a virginal life for Demetrias, a consecrated virgin (ep.130), because he could not refuse her illustrious mother and grandmother, Juliana and Proba, with whom Augustine and Chrysostom also corresponded. Jerome suggested Demetrias spend her time reading, spinning, fasting, and preparing to teach others holy conversation; he warned her against excessive austerity, to which he said women were particularly vulnerable, and against heresy. The latter warning was not by chance. Pelagius, too, wrote a letter to Demetrias when she became a nun, also at the request of her mother; it was a statement of his teachings, a letter Peter Brown calls "a calculated and widely-publicized declaration of his message."[5] Distressed when he heard about Pelagius's letter, Augustine wrote to warn her mother, Juliana (ep.188), confident from their previous exchange that he does not have to mince words with her; he asks her to examine both her daughter's state of mind and the book, to look for ambiguities in the text not only to protect her daughter and her servants from its teachings but also to note any indication that Pelagius might accept the teaching of grace and to let Augustine know if she found it.[6] Augustine also wrote a work at Juliana's insistent urging on the good of widowhood (*De bono viduitatis liber seu epistola ad Julianam viduam*). In this work, he included some things that might be superfluous to her because they might be useful to others, encouraging her to pass on what she considered worthwhile, taking time from other "most urgent occupations" because her request led him to compose a work that would benefit others as well.

Jerome, who wrote most of his works for women[7] and took their religious vocations seriously, did not hesitate to write on different aspects of the religious life for them: on widowhood for Furia (ep.54) and for Salina (ep.79), on monogamy for Geruchia (ep.123). He wrote rules culled from scripture for a holy married life for Celantia (ep.148) and forty-one chapters on virginity for Eustochium (ep.22), who was one of his most devoted followers and for whom he later wrote many of his most important commentaries. He also wrote a rather progressive letter on the education of a very young woman (ep.107) for Laeta's daughter Paula (who would eventually join her aunt Eustochium and become the recipient of many of Jerome's commentaries). Augustine wrote what is considered a source of the Augustinian Rule for a group of virgins, which his sister headed (ep.211).[8] Ambrose composed three books on virginity for his sister Marcellina, a consecrated virgin who lived at home with their mother (*De virginibus ad Marcellinam sororem suam, libri tres,* PL16, c.219ff); in them he reminded her of things they frequently discussed ("ea quae mecum conferre soles," 3.1) and praised her for equaling and surpassing all instruction with her virtue. Caesarius composed a rule for virgins for his sister Caesaria, which another abbess Caesaria passed on to Radegunde when she founded her house.

Writing to a later Proba about virginity and humility at her vehement request, bishop Fulgentius of Ruspe in the early sixth century sent twenty-three chapters (PL65, ep.3, c.324-39), in which he made every effort to encourage her as a woman to think of herself as equal to men in the eyes of God. He connects *virgo* with *virago*, since woman was formed from man (*vir*), and the *vir*gin (Eve) prefigured the church which came from a man (Christ) who had true *vir*tue (c.326-7), and he notes that God's injunction to those who hope in the Lord to act *vir*ilely (Ps.30:25) is meant for men and women ("tam viris quam mulieribus," c.327), that God inspires the fervor of holy desire in his sons and daughters ("filiis filiabusque," c.325), while the devil fights all God's spiritual servants, male and female ("spiritales Dei famulos et famulas," c.334).[9] In a piece on prayer which Fulgentius sent her later (ep.4, c.339-44), he asks how the first man could heal his infirmity when he could not keep himself healthy (c.340), with no mention of Eve. Fulgentius wrote to Proba's sister, Galla, about widowhood when her husband died, to encourage her in her religious resolution (ep.2, c.311-23); he cited Proba as an example of virginity and humility to be imitated. He also speaks at some length about the holy widows Judith and Anna: Judith, girded with spiritual arms, cut off the head of the wanton plunderer, and Anna knew the head of the church; to Judith was given the destruction of Holofernes, to Anna was revealed the advent of the savior (c.320).

Empress Agnes, when she became a nun, inspired works on the religious life, one from Peter Damian on contempt of the world (*De fluxa mundi gloria et saeculi despectione,* PL145, c.807-20), which compares her favorably to the queen of Sheba—Agnes, who came in humility for the wisdom of Christ, is "truly the queen of Sheba."[10] She is herself an example of proper contempt for the world, having exchanged her crown for a veil, her purple for sackcloth, a scepter for a psalter in contrast to worldly rulers who came to bad ends; the list of men and women includes the suicides of mighty queens, of Cleopatra and of Semiramis, who had subjected many kingdoms to herself. John of Fécamp compiled a collection of scriptural passages on the religious life at Agnes's request, which he sent with some comments, adding something on the life and customs of virgins for the instruction of the nuns in her monastery.[11] He too sees her as "a shining example of holy widowhood" to other noble matrons. Recognizing the hostility she had faced, he answers the barking dogs who are her enemies with a description of her pious works as she travels through Italy and France. He asks her to control the publication of the work, making sure that if others want to have it, they transcribe it diligently, neither adding nor omitting. And he wishes her God's comfort in her dual life, active as a Martha and contemplative as a Mary.

In the same period, Goscelin wrote a *Liber confortatorius* in four books for a little-known recluse of Angers, Eve, whom he had known from her earliest years at Wilton.[12] He worried about her moving to the austerity of the recluse life, then came to see it as the right decision and wrote this book to support and praise her. His tone is friendly rather than formal or polemic, growing naturally out of trust and direct contact. The work reveals his strong attachment to her, his grief over their separation—he is so overwhelmed by grief as he writes that he has to stop and sit in the church, weeping—and his desire to make up for the distance by writing, that is, he seems to be consoling himself more than her. This is particularly obvious in the first of four parts, in which he reminisces tenderly about their life together, his teaching, her lending him books, his sending her a fish, their correspondence, and her departure, leaving her parents and especially him desolate. He compares theirs to the separations of other intensely loving pairs, a list that includes David and Jonathan, John and the Virgin, Peter and Paul, Orestes and his friend, abbess Modesta and her sister Gertrude.

Goscelin uses classical as well as Christian allusions and examples throughout the work, testifying to Eve's education and their shared interests, "our" Boethius, Horace, Seneca, and Virgil, who teach the joys of the austere life and the liberty to be attained in it. Her window can provide a library, which should include the lives of the fathers, the confessions of Augustine, the histories of Cassiodorus and Eusebius, the *City of God*, Orosius, Boethius. Like Aeneas, she has found a place where she can rest despite her struggles (3.8), but where she also has her own living model, a woman recluse who, Goscelin says, prepared the place for her and watches over her, "Benedicta domina" (4.1).[13] Benedicta is one of many positive women models Goscelin offers to Eve. In the struggle against temptation that is the subject of the second part, Goscelin mentions Perpetua and Sara, St. Blandina and the captive woman who converted the

Iberians, while he warns her against the sins of Adam (gluttony, vainglory, and greed). As encouragement for combat with the old seducer of (the first) Eve, there are more examples in the third part, including Jerome's friends Paula, Eustochium, and Blesilla, scholars and saints of the simple life, what Jerome called "sancta rusticitas et docta sanctitas" (3.6). In the last part, on triumph, Goscelin contrasts his own experience, when he was assigned to a place he could not bear but came to love, with that of Eve, who, disdaining the easy life of a nun, should be content with that of a poor recluse. He ends with the eternal joys that await her after the Last Judgment, when all the saints will come together, among them queen Edith (see chapter 3) and the souls from Wilton, and Goscelin will see his dear daughter again, though in his unworthiness he will be far from her.

When, half a century later, Heloise asked Abelard for a rule suitable for women and a history of monastic women, characteristically wanting not just a rule to live by but a justification for their very existence, she supported her request with classical touches like Goscelin's with quotes from Ovid's *Ars amatoria* and Macrobius's *Saturnalia* as well as from religious authorities such as Jerome, Gregory, Chrysostom, and Augustine, and a lengthy, learned, and sensible discussion of the problems the Benedictine Rule posed for women.[14] Heloise's letter, it has been persuasively argued, sketches the outlines of Abelard's response.[15] Heloise uses, as she has throughout the letters, the formula of "the weaker sex" to provoke Abelard to a strong affirmation of women's strengths; but in this letter, which Linda Georgianna has called her "longest and most learned by far" (224), she makes the formula work to show up the problems in the basic assumptions of monasticism. She points out that the same yoke is "laid on the weaker sex as on the stronger" (MS 17.242, R 160), though women have different needs, e.g., of clothing during menstruation; though Gregory I said heavy burdens may be laid on men but women should be gently converted, monastic rules were completely silent about women (17.243, R 162).[16] If Benedict modified his rule for the young, the old, and the weak, would he not have done the same "for the weaker sex whose frailty and infirmity is generally known?" (17.244, R 163). That is, one cannot have it both ways: either women are weaker and therefore should be treated differently or they are at least equally capable of following the precepts of the gospel. Heloise herself notes that women, by the virtues of continence and abstinence, can be the equals of rulers of the church and the clergy, which should be "sufficient for our infirmity" (ibid. and R 164), and warns against imposing a burden on women "under which we see nearly all men stagger and even fall" (17.246 R 167).[17] Heloise returns briefly and almost casually to the question of weakness at the end of the letter, in connection with reciting the psalms: "here at least, if you think fit, you may allow some concession to our weakness, and when we recite the psalter in full within a week it shall not be necessary to repeat the same psalms" (17.252,

R 178); but this too is a loaded concession, since she had noted earlier that monks, by Benedict's rule, are only required to recite the psalter weekly, like the clergy, a watered-down imitation of the fathers, who used to complete it in one day (168). In fact, as Georgianna argues so effectively, what Heloise is primarily concerned with, as in her other letters and the *Problemata,* is not the details of a rule of external behavior, but the problems of regulating the inner life: "her call for help is a reasoned, learned critique of contemporary monastic life in the light of her own history as well as her theology" (253).

Abelard responded with a treatise on the authority or dignity of the order of nuns (ep.6), emphasizing the role women played in the Old Testament and in early Christianity, particularly the women around Christ and those who were associated with the apostles and the early church. Abelard argues Christ's authority for the monastic vocation of women, with some striking points which seem to suggest much more: that women alone were allowed to perform the sacraments, the anointing of head and feet, by which Christ was made priest and king ("Christ was anointed by a woman, Christians by men; his head by a woman, his members by men," ep.6, MS 17.255). Though men are stronger in mind and body, it was the women who showed devotion and courage through the passion and death, who were rewarded with the first sight of the risen Christ, and who announced it to the apostles who then told the world (17.258). Women, in other words, had a clerical role in the gospels, one which Abelard seems to preserve through his identification of contemporary abbesses with the deaconesses of earlier times (264ff). Fathers of the church, Origen, Ambrose, Jerome, gave particular care to the instruction of women.

Abelard's rule (ep.7) emphasizes learning, though it covers other aspects of life. He sets up a number of functions for particular nuns and outlines the duties and responsibilities of each position, suggesting that all but the chantress, who is in charge of reading, singing, writing, and keeping the book cupboard, should be chosen from nuns who do not study letters, leaving the others more freedom for their studies ("litteris vacare liberius queant," 263).[18] Reading is an essential part of the nun's life; indeed, Abelard warns against excessive attention to music at the cost of understanding the words; and the references to Cicero, Lucan, Macrobius, and Ovid suggest that the reading was not necessarily all religious.[19]

In a separate, long letter to the virgins of Heloise's convent, the Paraclete, Abelard strongly encouraged them in their studies, particularly emphasizing the study of biblical languages (PL178, ep.9, Cousin 1.225–36). Noting Jerome's involvement in women's studies of scripture, Abelard cites Jerome frequently and at length on the details and programs of such study from childhood on; on the importance of the three biblical languages, Hebrew, Greek, and Latin; on the part his women disciples played in fighting heresy; on their examining and questioning what he taught them;

and on the approval of women's study even in the Old Testament (the exhortation to parents in Daniel to teach daughters as well as sons and Solomon's rewards to the queen of Sheba for her ardor for learning). Noting the problems translations raise about the meaning of a text, Abelard encourages Heloise's nuns to remember the zeal of the great doctor and of those holy women for the scriptures and, while they can and while they have a mother expert in the three languages ("matrem harum peritam trium linguarum habetis," c.332), to carry their studies to the point of being able to resolve any doubts they might have about different translations. They do not have to travel to have access to these languages, as Jerome did, having in Heloise a mother sufficient for their study. In this study of foreign tongues, they can make up for the deficiencies of contemporary men; "what we have lost in men," Abelard urges, "let us recover in women . . . let the queen of the South again search out the wisdom of the true Solomon in you to the condemnation of men and a judgment of the stronger sex" (c.335-6).[20]

In the course of their religious observances, nuns listened to sermons, and many of the men concerned with the religious life of women composed sermons for them or sent sermons to them, though with rather different purposes. Abelard says he composed his keeping in mind the capacity of the younger members of his audience (*intelligentia parvularum*) and favoring simplicity over eloquence, but in the content a good part of his purpose seems to be to encourage the nuns in their religious vocation by enhancing their sense of themselves as women, as in his history of nuns.[21] Ambrose's sermons, which he sent to his virgin sister, served a different purpose. He was looking beyond her to a larger audience in Rome, for, as Peter Brown comments, "it was through Marcellina that Ambrose chose to speak to Rome" (*Body and Society,* 343); "we know about some of Ambrose's most heroic confrontations with the Emperors in Milan only because he wrote about them in great detail to Marcellina" (342). She was his publisher, so to speak; he sent her accounts of historic events and the texts of sermons he had preached for her to pass on to others (ep.20, 22, 41).[22] Writing in response to her letters of concern for the church and for him, he described the attempt by Arian forces to take over a church in Milan, the people's defense, his own refusal to submit to force, his appropriate readings and comments to the congregation during the siege, the emperor's threat and his own heroic response (ep.20), the discovery of the bodies of two martyrs (ep.22), the burning of a synagogue by a Christian bishop and monks, their punishment and the ordered rebuilding of the synagogue, and his conversation with the emperor after preaching a sermon before him (ep.41). She may not have requested the texts in so many words, but her concern and interest enabled him to preserve both the texts and his account of the events.

The sister for whom Caesarius of Arles wrote a rule did request sermons as well, which he sent with great diffidence, excusing not only his style, which may simply be a humility topos, but deferring to her higher mode of devotion: "not that I can confer anything on your learning or perfection . . . fearing to incur a note of boasting or imprudence, especially that I know you spend time in assiduous meditation on divine volumes and ignore nothing that pertains to your perfection" (PL67, ep.1, c.1125). In another letter-sermon warning against various vices, advising constant vigilance against the enemy and frequent reading, he apologizes not only for his rustic and inexperienced speech but also for his presumption that he, being tepid, admonish the fervent, that being slow and negligent, he incite the running (c.1128–35). Adam of Perseigne, who spent two exciting days in the late twelfth century talking about sin and contempt of the world with the countess of Chartres, sent sermons or the equivalent to various women who had heard him speak or spoken with him and asked for his written words. Though the relationships are not as close as the others mentioned here, the personal contact is important: to Agnes, a virgin, who requested the sermon she had heard him give to a convent of virgins, he sent the text (or a close approximation—the tenor of that sermon has slid away, he explains, but the sense is the same).[23] Adam also sent the sermons she requested to Blanche (of Navarre), countess of Champagne and its regent from 1202–22. He sent them in Latin because they were given in Latin and would lose by translation ("barely will the savor or composition remain in a pilgrim idiom, for liquor when poured from a vessel is altered somewhat in color or savor or odor," ep.30). Like the countess of Chartres, to whom he wrote in Latin, knowing she had some understanding of it, telling her if she had difficulty with anything in the letter to have her chaplain explain it (ep.27), the countess of Champagne must have known enough Latin to understand the general meaning. I assume that when Adam suggests they can have someone expound the text to them, he is referring to underlying subtleties, since it would have been tactless, not to say didactically ineffective to send a requested text in a language they did not know.[24] Adam was writing to the countesses shortly after the death of Hildegard of Bingen, the text of whose sermons had been requested by many men after they heard her preach.

Sermons, like the guides for spiritual life, are essentially public documents, meant for a somewhat varied audience. Far more interesting to me are the detailed works on scriptural and theological questions written at the specific request of particular women. There is evidence of such scholarly exchange from the fourth century to the twelfth. There may be nothing to equal the exchanges between Jerome, Marcella, Paula, and Eustochium or between Abelard and Heloise for scope and quantity, but there is material from Augustine, Alcuin, and Peter Damian which shows that they too could engage in intellectual investigation with women and encourage them in their own scholarly pursuits. I begin with Jerome, whose work with women was cited to justify so many later writers, and end with Abelard, whose work for the Paraclete can be seen as the culmination of religious collaboration between men and women.

Jerome defended himself frequently for writing to women, obviously because he was frequently attacked for doing so. He counters one attack by saying he would not be writing to women if men asked him questions about scripture (in a letter to Principia, a companion of Marcella, accompanying the commentary she had requested on the forty-fourth psalm, ep.65); women take up where men fail, he notes, just as Deborah would not have triumphed over the enemy if men had gone to battle.[25] Jerome gives a more radical example from the New Testament of a woman, Priscilla, who with her husband, Aquila, taught the apostle Apollo, and concludes, "if to be taught by a woman was not shameful to an apostle, why should it be afterwards to me to teach women as well as men?" In the prologue to Sophonia, he responds at length to those who mock him for writing to Paula and Eustochium rather than to men, a justification that is worth citing in full: "If they knew that Holda prophesied when men were silent, and Deborah as judge and prophet overcame the enemies of Israel when Barac was afraid, and Judith and Esther, as types of the church, killed adversaries and freed Israel from danger as it was about to perish, never would they ridicule me behind my back. I say nothing of Anna and Elizabeth, and other holy women, whose starlike sparks the bright light of Mary hides. I shall come to gentile women so that they [his mockers] might see that philosophers of the world sought differences in souls not bodies. Plato brought Aspasia into disputes; Sappho was cited with Pindar and Alcaeus; Themista philosophized among the wisest of Greece; the whole Roman city admired Cornelia of the Gracchi, that is your Cornelia [alluding to the illustrious heritage of their family]; that most eloquent of philosophers and most acute of rhetors, Carneades, who elicited applause among consuls in the Academy, did not blush to dispute on philosophy at home before his wife. What shall I say of the daughter of Cato, the wife of Brutus, whose virtue was such that we do not admire the constancy of her father or husband as much? Greek and Latin history is filled with the virtues of women which demand whole books. Let it suffice to me, since other work presses, only to say at the end of the prologue, that the Lord at his resurrection appeared first to women and that they were the apostles of the apostles ("apostolorum illas fuisse apostolas"), so that men blushed that they did not seek him whom the weaker sex had already found" (CCSL 76A, p.655).

It is not unlikely that Jerome identified with Christ in this, that he too in his teachings appeared first to women. Certainly women like Marcella, Paula, and Eustochium urged him to much of his writing. Paula and Blesilla caused him to write even when they were no longer alive to receive the works, and after Paula's death a third generation, the younger Paula, joined her aunt Eustochium as eager audience for his writings. Still other women were responsible for individual works. He was as willing to take time to answer the specific questions that came up in the course of their studies as to compose larger works. Fabiola, who visited Jerome in Jerusalem and studied scripture with zeal, put questions which he could not always answer, shaming him, as he said, into writing by refusing to accept his ignorance. At her request, he discussed the vestments of Aaron at some length, noting that he had not been able to find Tertullian's work on the subject and asking her, if she should find it, which she is more likely to do in Rome, not to judge his drop by comparison with that river, that is, expecting her to do her own research and weigh his words against other authorities (ep.64). She too inspired him to write for her after her death on a question she had asked about the mansions of the sons of Israel; he dedicated the writing to her memory (ep.78). For Hedybia, who came from such a distinguished family of writers and teachers that Jerome found it necessary to defend his right to answer her by reason of faith and illumination, he wrote twelve chapters answering detailed questions about the gospels and Paul, involving different versions of events in different gospels, contradictory and enigmatic statements (ep.120). Algasia posed eleven questions about the New Testament, "large questions on a small paper" (ep.121), based on close readings, which he answered in eleven chapters, citing Greek passages.

But it was his close friend Marcella who put the most difficult questions to him, as Jerome notes: "you provoke us with great questions and make our wit numb with inactivity; while you ask, you teach" (ep.59); "you write nothing except what tortures me and compels me to read scriptures" (ep.29). He responded to her questions about the ten names for God in Hebrew with Greek and Latin equivalents (ep.25), the reason why words such as *alleluia* and *amen* were not translated from Hebrew (ep.26), metrics in the Hebrew psalms (ep.28), the Hebrew *ephod* (ep.29), interpretations of passages from the psalms (ep.34), five problems from the New Testament (ep.59), blasphemy against the Holy Spirit (ep.42), New Testament discrepancies pointed out by Montanists (ep.41), and criticism of the work of other teachers (ep.37, 40). He answers all her questions, though he notes that having the scriptures in hand, she, before all others, does not need his answers but only wants to get his thoughts on the subject (ep.41).

Marcella had remained in Rome—where, according to Peter Brown (*Body and Society* 369), she had an unusually large library of Greek texts—when Jerome established himself in the Holy Land, but she continued to influence him and his work. When Marcella and two of Jerome's male friends, Pammachius and Oceanus, were distressed by Rufinus's misleading statements about Jerome in his translation of Origen, they sent the text to Jerome with a request for information; he responded with a more accurate translation of his own, now an important source for Origen.[26]

When Marcella's mother, Albina, died, Jerome sent her as "medication for the wound" a commentary on Paul's letter to the Galatians (PL26, c331), a work he had done for Paula and Eustochium. He took the occasion to praise Marcella's scholarly zeal in a passage which Abelard would cite to (and of) Heloise and which must also be read as encouragement to Paula and Eustochium: "I know her ardor, her faith, which she has as a flame in her chest, surpasses her sex, forgets that she is human ("superare sexum, oblivisci hominis"), and hastens over the Red Sea of this world sounding the drum of divine volumes [that is, not just studying but teaching them]. Certainly when I was at Rome, she never saw me but that she asked something about scripture. Nor did she think whatever I answered correct, in the Pythagorean way: she did not value prejudged authority without reason but examined all things and thought about everything with a wise mind, so that I felt myself to have not so much a disciple as a judge" (c.331–2). Independent judgment is a quality Jerome and Augustine respect and encourage in women.

Jerome again includes Marcella as the audience and inspiration for his commentary on Ephesians, although he had also undertaken it for Paula and Eustochium, who worked closely with him in Bethlehem and for whom he did so many others.[27] The elder Paula was also interested in the writings of Origen, whose ideas were then under attack: at her request Jerome compiled a detailed bibliography of Origen's works (ep.33), writing "swiftly, by the fire of a small lantern," what he "would not have dictated with cautious speech" because of the "rabid dogs" who attack Origen, trusting Paula more than his own secretary. He also allowed her needs to interfere with his work. When Paula and her daughter Eustochium complained about other commentaries on Origen's Homilies on Luke that they were "dull in sense and words, . . . played in words and slept in judgments," he did one for them, despite his aversion to writing what is not his own: "hearing a croaking raven altogether dark and laughing at the colors of other birds . . . behold how much your authority and will counts with me. I have put aside somewhat the books of Hebrew questions in order to dictate these which in your opinion are profitable."[28] Speaking of these homilies as works of Origen's youth, Jerome acknowledges the actual and potential role of Paula and Eustochium in bringing Origen's work to the Romans: he says if he had the time to translate the works of Origen's maturity, "you would see, or rather *through you the Roman tongue would know,* how much good he knew before and now began to know." He also notes that Paula's deceased daughter, Blesilla, had asked him to translate Origen's twenty-six volumes on Matthew, five on Luke, and thirty-two on John, but he had not had the strength, the leisure, or the labor.[29]

Jerome did most of his biblical commentaries for Paula and Eustochium, and after Paula's death for Eustochium and the young Paula, inscribing them into the text from time to time so no one could doubt who the first audience was. In the one on Galatians, he begins the third book with an address to them, apologizing at some length for the roughness of his rhetoric, blaming it on his absorption in Hebrew texts for the past fifteen years to the exclusion of Cicero or Virgil or other such gentiles. Since the weakness of his eyes and body require him to use a secretary, who becomes impatient if Jerome hesitates over his words, he cannot take the time to polish them. But he justifies himself to them, and to others who might read it, that he is not writing panegyric or polemic but commentary, that he is not seeking to have his own words praised but to make sure another's words are understood, presenting himself as the servant of the text (and perhaps of those who asked about it). He reminds them that their church was formed on the words of rustics and fishermen and asserts that he does not want others to have to interpret his words of interpretation (perhaps as they do Origen's).

Jerome begins his commentary on Paul's letter to the Ephesians (in which he acknowledges that he follows Origen in part) with an address to Paula and Eustochium about scriptures as the source of wisdom for life, as the most valuable treasure to amass. Again excusing his lack of eloquence, he begs them and "holy Marcella, that unique exemplar of widowhood," who had also requested this work, not to hand it over to the envious who pretend to erudition by attacking others, leaving its publication, so to speak, to their discretion. Tell them, he suggests, to sweat to put three words together so they can learn what the labor is—"you know, who compelled me to this work of explanation." He reminds them that he is commenting on Ephesians, as he did on Galatians, at their request and at the urging of Marcella's letters. At the beginning of the second book on Ephesians, he compares himself unfavorably to Marcella: he, alone in the solitude of a monastery in view of the stable where the shepherds came to adore the child, is unable to accomplish because of inertia what Marcella, a noble woman with a noisy family and the care of a household, can. It is perhaps because he is writing with such women in mind that he distinguishes between the literal or carnal and the allegorical meaning of Paul's injunction that women should fear their husbands ("Mulier autem ut timeat virum"): "frequently women are found to be much better than their husbands and to command them and rule over the house, and teach the children and keep discipline in the household, while they [husbands] give themselves to excesses and run after prostitutes. Whether they should rule or fear their husbands, I leave to the reader's judgment" (PL26, c.570).

Jerome sent his translation of the book of Esther, a woman who had successfully guided her husband, to Paula and Eustochium, who had studied Hebrew, not to enable them to read it but for their approval, expecting them to check his translations: "since you have zealously entered the Hebrew libraries and confirm the struggles of interpreters, holding the Hebrew book of Esther, look at the individual words of our translation so that you may know that I added nothing, but simply transmitted the history from Hebrew to Latin as a faithful witness."[30] One cannot help wondering if it was the example of women like Marcella and Paula that moved Jerome to translate the book of Judith, another impressive woman who saved her people, though he knew it was not in the Jewish canon. He sent it to two men with a preface telling them to "accept the widow Judith, an example of chastity, with triumphal praise, and proclaim her with perpetual publicity. For the rewarder of chastity gave her to be imitated, *not only by women but by men,* and endowed her with such virtue that she might conquer one who was unconquered by all men" (PL29, c.41–42).

Jerome wrote commentaries on several of the minor prophets for Paula and Eustochium, as well as Isaiah, Jeremiah, Daniel, and Joshua, which he finished after Paula's death and dedicated to Eustochium with the rest of the Octateuch.[31] In the preface to Daniel, he asks Paula (the younger) and Eustochium to pray for him that "as long as I am in this little body, I may write something pleasing to you, useful to the church, worthy to the future" (PL28, c.1360), making it clear that the works they asked for were intended for posterity. He dedicated four of his commentaries on the twelve minor prophets to Paula (the younger) and Eustochium and five of them to Pammachius, his old friend and Paula's son-in-law.[32] But Paula (the elder) is present even in the dedications to Pammachius. In Hosea, Jerome mentions her role in the Hosea commentary tradition: twenty-two years before, "at the request of your holy and venerable mother-in-law or rather mother, Paula, for that name is of the flesh, this of the spirit," Jerome asked Didymus to complete Origen's work on Hosea and Didymus dictated three books on it to him, which Jerome now lists among his sources or precursors (CCSL, 76). In the preface to Joel, Jerome asks that Pammachius accept what he had promised to Paula, his holy and venerable relative, as her pious heir; and in the third book of Amos, he mentions the four he had already done for Paula and her daughter Eustochium, that is, Nahum, Micah, Sophonia/Zephania, and Haggai.[33]

Augustine did not work closely with women, as Jerome did, despite—or perhaps because of—his intense relations with his mother and the mother of his son. But he did rely on certain women for support—women like Albina, who was very generous to the church, and Italica, who gave him a house—and he did encourage them both in theological studies and in battles against heresy. He respected their ability to make their own judgments about religious questions. Indeed, his ideal of education was precisely that one learned to think for oneself, as he wrote to a young woman, Florentina (ep.266). He told her to ask whatever she liked, promising to tell her what he knew and try to work out what he did not, wanting her to become learned rather than be dependent on his or anyone else's learning—she might learn something from him, but she will really learn from "the inner master of the inner man." When he wrote to Proba about prayer, answering a question she asked about a passage in Paul, he noted that "many philosophical minds have been occupied and much time spent" on such questions, and suggested at the end that she think it all through, in case "the Lord gives you any other idea on this matter, which either has not occurred to me or would be too long for me to explain" (ep.130). When he corresponded with women about heresy, as with Juliana about Pelagius, he enlisted their help: he confirmed Maxima's faith about the human nature of Christ against the errors she had written of in her province and asked her to send him any writings to the contrary (ep.264); he asked Seleuciana, who had written about a Novatian belief on baptism and penance that he did not know of, to investigate further, to examine carefully if the person she is trying to persuade is really a Novatian or involved in some other error, noting textual problems which have to be checked in Greek (ep.265).[34]

As with Jerome, women asked him questions which helped him develop his own ideas. At least two works which are preliminary studies toward the last book of the *City of God* were written at the request of women. In answer to a question from Italica, Augustine discussed whether God can be seen with the physical eye now or after the resurrection (ep.92), asking her to read it to those who think differently and be sure to write back to him what answer they make.[35] At the end he says, "I leave to your understanding to recognize what a great misfortune it would be [to think the sight of God can be achieved by bodily eyes, with the mind acting wholly in the flesh], and I will not labor to explain it at greater length."[36] To Paulina, also at her request, he did write at greater length (ep.147, fifty-four chapters) about whether the invisible God can be seen. The question gave him a good deal of difficulty, as he makes clear in a reference in chapter 42 to the earlier work and the anguish he experienced in that brief letter ("dolens in illa brevi epistola") of attempting to control the corporeal images of the outer man, relying entirely on divine authority, restraining his own mind from that sort of vanity rather than anyone else's. Emphasizing the difficulty of the question, he tells Paulina not to believe something on his authority, but to find truth in scripture and in her interior sense of truth ("Nolo auctoritatem meam sequaris . . . sed aut scripturis canonicis credas . . . aut interius demonstranti veritati," chapter 2). Distinguishing between scripture, which must be believed, and other witnesses or evidence, which she can choose to believe or not as she weighs their value (4), he repeatedly warns her against taking anyone's writings, including his, on faith without the evidence of her own senses and mind or the authority of scripture (5). He cites other authorities which she may already know, particularly Ambrose and even Jerome, but he insists that he did not cite such great men because they should be followed like scriptural authority (54). He presents his arguments as to a student of philosophy:

"note and recall to see whether . . . if you ask, I answer . . . (37); examine what you have seen, what you have believed, what you still do not know, either because I have not spoken of it, or you have not understood, or you have not judged it credible. Among the points which you have seen to be true, distinguish further . . . (38); after you have carefully examined and distinguished . . . assess the actual weight of evidence" (39). If she has doubts, he tells her to look carefully within herself and find the light (40ff.). At the end, he promises to get to the spiritual body in another work, presumably the *City of God*. In his retractions, he mentions the longer work on the vision of God, "in which I undertook a careful examination of the future nature of the spiritual body at the resurrection of the saints, and whether and how God, who is a spirit, can be seen by a body, but that very difficult question at the end I explained as best I could in Book 22 of *The City of God*" (2.41).

Several centuries later, in a very different culture, the Carolingian court, Alcuin wrote on theological questions and biblical commentary for women in Charlemagne's family who shared his scholarly interests and helped occasionally in his research. At the request of Charlemagne's granddaughter Gundrada, he wrote a treatise on the reason of the soul (*De ratione animae*), which urged her to further research: he mentions a piece of Augustine's on the subject which she should read, if she has it, and a brief but sharp response of Jerome's, which Alcuin read in Britain but cannot find here, along with four other related books which Alcuin does not have, but which she may be able to find in the imperial book cupboard; if she does, he asks her to read them and send them on to him (ep.309).[37] Alcuin sent a work on the Adoptionist heresy to an unnamed virgin, perhaps Gundrada, with questions and answers she might use to conquer her opponents, expecting her to debate on it because she is trained in dialectical subtleties (ep.204).

A work that was close to Alcuin's heart was inspired by Charlemagne's sister Gisla and his daughter Rotrud. Gisla was abbess of the distinguished double monastery of Chelles, and Rotrud, who joined her there, had been tutored in Greek in preparation for a Byzantine marriage, which never occurred.[38] They asked Alcuin for a commentary on the gospel of John, which he answered first in brief (ep.195) and eventually at length. He appended their letter of request to the full commentary as a prologue, so future readers would recognize the zeal of their devotion and the occasion of his obedience, providing us with one of the few such requests from women extant (ep.196). Their letter declares their burning desire to study scripture inspired by his expositions, "after we drank some of the mellifluous knowledge with your wisdom expounding it," knowledge that is to be preferred to all the wealth of the world and is the only true wisdom. They beg him to share his wisdom with them, telling him exactly what they want: "reveal to us the venerable sense of the holy fathers, collect the pearls of many . . . and feed the poor of Christ." But not just the fathers; they want a comprehensive survey of scholarship on the subject: "enter the treasury of the holy doctors and bring forth for us, as a most learned scribe . . . the new and the old." They have Augustine's explanations, which they say are "in certain places much more obscure and embellished with greater circumlocution than can enter the weak intellect of our smallness" ("quam nostrae parvitatis ingeniolo intrare valeat").[39] But despite the humility topos, they do not hesitate to imply a comparison with the women Jerome wrote for ("that most brilliant doctor of divine scripture in the holy church, most blessed Jerome, in no way scorned the prayers of noble women, but dedicated many works on prophetic obscurities to their names"), or even with Christ's disciples ("his grace will be yours on the road of this labor who, to the two disciples going on the road [to Emaus] added himself as the third companion and opened meanings to them that they might understand holy scripture").

In his letter of dedication, Alcuin says he had wanted to do this commentary for thirty years but did not get to it until their good intention excited his pen and called it back to the zeal of writing (ep.214). He laments his own smallness before the task (equally formulaically, using the same *parvitas* they had used). He speaks at some length about the doctrinal importance of John's gospel and its difference from the other three gospels and cites Augustine, Ambrose, Gregory, Bede, and others (ep.213). He offers what he has found for them to taste and see "if it has a catholic savor," and sends his only copy to them asking if they deem it worthy to have it transcribed, that is, to publish it for him, with instructions for the copying and editing.

Rabanus Maurus dedicated two biblical commentaries to empress Judith, the second wife of Charlemagne's son, but they seem to have a political significance as much as a religious one. They are both on books about forceful women, one on Judith, the biblical heroine and the empress's namesake, the other on Esther, a biblical queen, "one your equal in name, the other in dignity," whose extraordinary virtues he says make them models for men as well as women, but whose actions make them particularly apt models for the empress. Though he does not say so, Rabanus strongly suggests that he intends Judith to identify with the historical experiences of both women, one who went out aggressively to destroy the enemy of her people, the other who persuaded her husband to change his policy toward them.[40] Rabanus tells the empress in the dedication to the book of Judith that "your prudence has conquered enemies already and if you persevere in good, you will happily overcome them all in your conflict (*agone*), provided you implore divine help." Judith (like Esther) is presented consistently as a type of the church, and Rabanus may well have been encouraging the empress to identify herself directly with church interests like her namesake, though he may also have supported her political maneuvers. He brings a number of other women into his commentary who are extraneous to the story but in whom Judith might have seen models: Semiramis was the queen of all Asia after her husband's death and founded the city of Babylon, making it the capital of the Assyrian kingdom—she is the first person mentioned who founded a city; Rhea Silvia, the mother of Romulus (who founded Rome) is also mentioned (ch.1); Themaris and Priscilla are mentioned as believers in connection with Paul in Acts (ch.10).[41] The Old Testament Judith is called "Judith nostra" frequently, as though she belonged particularly to Rabanus and the empress. The passages on her beauty and wisdom, admired by all (ch.11), and her counseling the people as the church teaches its children with maternal affection and magisterial authority (ch.14) must be heard as echoes of the praises Rabanus and others lavished on Judith for her wisdom, her beauty, and the care she took over the education of her son. In the dedicatory letters, Rabanus praises her wit, her imitation of holy women, and her learning. He alludes to what Jerome found in the Hebrew but omits Greek references, which an eager reader might supply for herself after examining the preceding: "you, most noble queen, since you well understand the divine mysteries in expositions, will rightly assess what is to be perceived in the rest" (MGH, Ep Kar 3, ep. 17a, 17b).[42] In the last chapter of the Judith commentary (16), we are told the Lord gave the enemy into the hand of woman, who was destined in Genesis to trample his head.

In the eleventh century, Peter Damian wrote a considerable amount of biblical commentary for royal and noble women, some of whom became nuns. Indeed, he included so much material on the Bible in his letters to women that excerpts from them are cited among his biblical commentaries (PL 145, c.1021ff). Letters to countess/duchess Hermesinde, countess Blanche, countess Adelaide, and the empress Agnes are cited throughout the Old Testament commentaries that were culled by a disciple from Peter's letters and sermons. But the most intellectual of Peter's letters to women is one he wrote to one of his sisters in response to her weighty questions about what existed before creation and what would exist after the end of the world (ep.93). Though, like Jerome, he says she draws him to unknown things and compels him to teach what he has not yet learned, he does not discourage her curiosity; he says it is fruitful to inquire, that the mind cannot be free from thoughts, and wickedness cannot hold a mind that is engaged in sober cogitation on useful things. He talks about infinity and the finite, referring her to Augustine's *City of God,* Jerome on Daniel and the Apocalypse, and his own letter to Blanche about the day of judgment (ep.66).[43]

There were probably many other collaborations that have not left records, but the only collaboration between a man and a woman on religious texts that comes close to Jerome's with his friends is the work Heloise persuaded Abelard to write for the Paraclete. She asked him for a history of nuns, a rule suitable to women, sermons, hymns, an exposition of Genesis, and answers to theological and scriptural questions that came up during their studies. She is thus directly responsible for much of Abelard's extant writing. Two of her letters of request are extant: the one that asked for a history of women's monasticism (how it began and what authority there was for it) and for a rule suitable to women (ep.5, discussed earlier), and the one that accompanied the questions (the *Problemata*). But in Heloise's case, we have some of the "personal" letters, and they reveal how she brought Abelard out of a psychological crisis and focused his attention on his work by persuading him of her own psychological as well as intellectual needs. Since this is such an unusual opportunity to trace the stages of the collaboration, I will go briefly through the earlier correspondence.

After she read the *Historia* and was worried about the danger Abelard seemed to be in, she began to manipulate him by emphasizing her own moral anguish and danger, in order to draw him away from the life that threatened his body and soul. Physical danger is what she mentions, but his psychological state must have distressed her even more: the despair (the word occurs in different forms through the *Historia*), the self-pity, the paranoia, the possibility of suicide.[44] Abelard mentions the story of Malchus, a captive monk who lived chastely in the same house as his wife; what he does not say, but Heloise no doubt remembered, is that when the marriage was forced on them, it was the woman who suggested they live together chastely in order to save the man from suicide. So Heloise reminded Abelard of his responsibility for herself and the nuns of the Paraclete, his "creation," of their vulnerability as women in a new house, and offered their obedience and need in the place of his rebellious monks, "stubborn pigs."

More subtle and probably more effective was her presentation of her own desperate need. By describing her grief and shame, by admitting to the anguish of her illicit desires and the guilt of her hypocrisy, she invited him to worry more about her spiritual state than his own situation. Heloise's open expression of strong feelings, her confession of truths that others do not suspect under her pious exterior, have disturbed readers who find it inconsistent with her position and reputation, but it is not inconsistent with her acute sense of self-awareness and ethical responsibility, nor with the concern she and Abelard share for intention in sin (see his *Ethics*). It is not her actions, which by all accounts have been exemplary, that matter to her; it is her innermost thoughts. To Abelard she can confess a guilt others would not understand. At the same time, of course, she can make him feel guilty for the suffering which others would not suspect.[45] It could be argued that her struggle with her feelings might also be edifying for the nuns, who certainly knew something of the facts of her story, but perhaps not of her inner torment.

But Heloise is speaking primarily to manipulate Abelard in order to save him under the pretext of his saving her.[46] There is a dual purpose in the strong declarations of the lover—"you know, beloved, . . . how much I have lost in you . . . you are the sole cause of my sorrow and you alone can grant me the grace of consolation. . . . God is my witness that if Augustus, Emperor of the whole world, thought fit to honour me with marriage and conferred all the earth on me to possess for ever, it would be dearer and more honourable to me to be called not his Empress but your whore" (ep.1, R 113–14). Heloise wants to convey the total devotion of her love untainted by wealth or status; at the same time, she wants to shock him into concern for her soul so he will stop feeling sorry for himself and begin to act positively to save her and her nuns. At least he can give her words, of which he seems to have an abundance; reminding him of the many letters and poems he wrote to her when his desires were foul ("turpes voluptates"), she asks if it would not be far better now to call her to God.

Abelard rises to the bait. Answering (ep.2) that he had believed that any teaching of his would be superfluous, that she did not need him, he promises to send anything she asks pertaining to God. He reminds her how women's prayers for their loved ones and wives' for their husbands are particularly effective, affirming their past relation in a positive way, with a brief passage on the effect of women's prayers in the Bible and the way women in the Old and New Testaments were singled out for special miracles of resurrection—Heloise's self-deprecation often has the effect of eliciting feminist arguments from Abelard, as in his history of the order of nuns. Heloise continues her attack in her next letter (ep.3), railing against fortune, the injustice of the penalty he suffered (his castration). Her anguish at being the instrument of such a crime leads her to attack women, beginning with Eve, as the ruin of great men; though she is careful to note that she, unlike Eve and Delilah, never participated willingly in his fall, she accepts some responsibility in her yielding to the pleasures of carnal desire, indeed in her continuing longings and fantasies, despite her confessions and mortification of the flesh: "men call me chaste; they do not know the hypocrite I am" (R 133). It is Abelard, she insists, not God she has always tried to please, and she has deceived even him to the extent that he asks for her prayers and praises her, but she begs him to recognize her need: "Do not suppose me healthy and so withdraw the grace of your healing. Do not believe I want for nothing and delay helping me in my hour of need. Do not think me strong lest I fall before you can sustain me" (R 134).

Abelard responds very carefully and logically to her arguments (ep.4), even admitting to a particular guilt of his own he had not acknowledged in the *Historia,* his uncontrolled lust, which he sometimes forced on her against her will. If he paid the greater physical penalty, she deserved it less,

as weaker in sex and stronger in continence. He asks her, now his "insep-
arable companion in grace and in guilt" (R 149), to join him in giving
thanks: God bound them in marriage because he had something bigger in
mind, more worthy of the talents he had bestowed, their knowledge of
letters. Heloise now pays God great usury on her talent in the spiritual
daughters she bears him, turning the curse of Eve into the blessing of
Mary: "how unseemly [it would have been] for those holy hands which
now turn the pages of sacred books to have to perform degrading services
in women's concerns" (R 150). This sense that her intellectual gifts destined her for a higher life is the crucial shift which will enable Heloise to
focus Abelard's energies on something positive, on the series of works
which she will request from him for the Paraclete.

Now Heloise can accept Abelard's injunction to control the expression
of her grief and ask him to help distract her thought (and his). The
remaining correspondence, in which Heloise continues to direct Abelard's
thought, but intellectually rather than emotionally, is more technical or
professional: she requests and gets a series of works for the instruction of
her nuns, assuming or resuming the role of abbess, the person in authority
over her own house and the abbey and five priories that grew from it, who
commissions or requests works to suit her needs. As such, she is directly
responsible for what Mary McLaughlin calls "a remarkable—indeed
unique—body of works."[47] Heloise can use the female monastic's humility
topos of the "weaker sex" to provoke Abelard to strong affirmations of
women's strengths, but now she can also note that women, by the virtues
of continence and abstinence, can be the equals of rulers of the church and
the clergy, which should be "sufficient for our infirmity" (R 164), and
warn against imposing a burden on women "under which we see nearly
all men stagger and even fall" (R 167).[48]

It is implicit in the other requests Heloise makes of Abelard that women
can also hold their own intellectually. That she shared his concern for
textual authenticity is evident in her series of questions as well as in her
request for the hymns. The letter that accompanied the questions shows
the intellectual sophistication that she and perhaps some of her nuns
brought to their studies (Cousin, 1.237-38). Like so many of her prede-
cessors in theological study, she cites Jerome on Marcella, commending her
for her study of holy letters, her questions about her studies, her unwill-
ingness to accept authority without examining, thinking everything
through, so that he felt himself to have not so much a pupil as a judge.
This is a passage Abelard cites in ep.9, and it reveals a lot about Heloise's
intellectual independence—there is no humility topos here. Apparently
identifying with Marcella, as Abelard clearly did with Jerome, she notes
that Jerome proposed that Marcella teach others (in the letter to Principia),
but she reminds Abelard that the responsibility for her nuns is his, since
he brought them, handmaids of Christ and his own spiritual daughters,

together in his oratory and exhorted them to the study of scripture. Scripture is a mirror of the soul in which a bride of Christ must look for her beauty and defects, but scripture not understood is like a mirror placed before unseeing eyes. Now that they have given themselves to this work, now that they are caught up in the love of letters, they are perturbed by many questions and cannot get on with their reading; they are less able to love what they do not understand, and their labor seems fruitless. So they ask and beg him as teacher and father to answer their questions, which they put down as they occur in their daily reading. The request is put in the plural, but the questions arise from Heloise's philosophical interests particularly in sin and judgment, intention versus action, law and punishment, damnation and repentance (1, 2, 8-16, 19, 20, 24-26, 42), as well as her scholarly interests in meaning, to clear up apparent contradictions or discrepancies, to explain odd references or implications (3-7, 17, 18, 21-23, 27-41). Some questions arise from episodes involving women in the Bible (e.g., 5, on differing accounts of the risen Christ's appearances to women; 8, on the implications of Christ's stopping the stoning of the woman taken in adultery; 31-34, on various small points in the story of Hanna in 1 Kings, which focus attention on her importance as both a prophet and the mother of Samuel).[49]

Heloise's request for a commentary on the beginning of Genesis (*Expositio in Hexameron*, Cousin 1.626-79) was far more demanding.[50] Abelard's preface emphasizes the difficulty of the task; citing Origen and Jerome, he defines Genesis as one of the three hardest parts of the Old Testament to understand (the others are the Song of Songs and Ezekiel). Only Augustine, he says, attempted to expound Genesis, and that without certainty and with many more questions than answers. Since Abelard cannot refuse "sister Heloise, once dear in the world, now dearest in Christ," who asks begging and begs asking, he asks her and her spiritual daughters who compel him to do it to pray God to make it possible and he covers himself with a Pauline variation of the humility topos: "I am become a fool; you have compelled me" (2 Cor. 12:11). Though the commentary is evoked by Heloise's request and addressed to her, it is written with a larger audience in mind. In it, Abelard intends to make mankind (*homo*) understand "what obedience he owes God, who created him in his image and put him in paradise over other creatures" (628).

Abelard goes through creation day by day, giving physical explanations for each stage; but almost half the commentary is devoted to the sixth day. Man, *homo*, standing for the rational mortal animal, both male and female (656), was created in the image of God. Then man was differentiated into male and female, the male (*vir*) in the image, the female (*femina*) in the similitude of God; God made the male wiser, so he loved God more and was not seduced by the devil, not susceptible to his lies about God. Abelard's remarks are based on the biblical text and are in many ways traditional, but they include some interesting comments and some suggestive omissions. The male is more worthy, more similar in his members—presumably more like Christ in the physical body—but both male and female imitate God in the possession of reason and the immortal soul, in the exercise of divine virtues of power, wisdom, and love. Man was made by God, woman was created from man, so that man is one step closer to God; but in being made by God alone, not from another creature, man is like Christ, the Son from the Father, whereas the holy spirit is said to be from the Father and the Son (659). This suggests an unstated analogy between woman and the holy spirit, which nuns devoted to the holy spirit (the Paraclete) were not likely to miss.[51] In the general "Allegoria" at the end of the commentary, Abelard first says that Adam stands for mankind (*homo* from *humo,* earth, 671), then notes that God put man (the text Abelard cites gives *hominem,* but he specifies *virum*) into paradise, that is, he was made outside from earth, while woman was made inside paradise from man (672). She would, of course, eject herself and him from it, whence Abelard deduces that habits pertain more to salvation than places, since woman was made in a better place and was worse in seduction. But does this not also set up a greater potential for woman when her habits are appropriate to paradise?

In the hymns and sermons Abelard wrote for the Paraclete, where he was not bound in the same way by a particular biblical text and was writing for the particular use of women, he went much further in his suggestions about the female sex.[52] We do not have the letter requesting the hymns, but Abelard discusses it in some detail in his response. He was hesitant at first, he says, to compose new ones when there were ancient hymns by saints, but after consulting various people, he was finally persuaded by *her* arguments about textual authenticity which he cites at some length: that the Latin church, and the French church in particular, follow customary usage rather than authority, that they do not know who did the (Latin) translation of the psalter they use in the French church, that it is of doubtful authority and they have no way of deciding among the various translations. Even when they know the authors of certain hymns, like Hilary, Ambrose, Prudentius, the words are so irregular in scansion that they cannot fit them to the music. Some feast days have hymns which are clearly not for that occasion or which strain our knowledge of the truth, of which she gave many examples, or they have no hymns of their own at all, like those for holy women who were not virgins or martyrs (preface to book 1).[53] For all these reasons, Abelard acceded to her request, sending three large collections of Latin poems.

The first group of hymns are praise of God in the trinity and in his creation, daily hymns for the days of the week, Abelard explains in the letter that introduces the second group.[54] The hymns of the second group are for feast days, the first four celebrating the virgin in an active role.

They begin with "Verbo verbum virgo concipiens (virgin conceiving the word by the word)," the sound suggesting a very close identity between Mary and Christ (30); the second (31) begins "Dei patris et matris unicus (only child of God the father and the mother)." In the third (32.1), the birth of Christ is described in a way that reverses the birth of Eve from Adam: "how blessed the bed of straw that the side (*latus*) of the virgin pressed, from whom the little one was drawn out"; other queens give birth in pain, that bed was without pain. In the fourth, Mary is praised as "glory of virgins," "adornment of mothers," whom God promised to the patriarchs, whom the enigmas of the law prefigure and songs of prophets sing, our only hope after God (33). At the presentation of Christ, she is called "royal virgin" ("virgo regia," 39.3). Every sex and age, man and woman, are to rejoice that she, ignorant of man, brought forth the man whom God put on ("virum, quem Deus induit, / ignara viri peperit," 41.2), a construction in which Mary is the active subject not passive object. Virgins are to rejoice for the virgin, the mother of the almighty, married women for the married woman who now publishes her conception (41.3); the old man and the widow (Simeon and Anna) confess the lord's presence (41.5). Mary is the means by which we know God and he us: "through you God made his descent to us, through you [is the] ascent to him for us" (78.2).

Other women are also given active roles in the hymns. An Easter hymn begins, "give the drum to Mary, the lord is risen" (59), referring both to the Mary (Miriam) in Exodus 15, the prophet who led the women in celebration of the lord's triumph, and to Mary Magdalene, who "merited first to see him rising . . . with the other faithful including women, narrating this to the disciples" (59.3-4).[55] The women keeping vigil "do not want to yield to men yielding, / fearless, they see the guards, / secure, they discern threatening swords. / The beating which the shepherd bore, / dispersed the rams of the flock in fright; / love kept the sheep intrepid, / and charity dispelled fear" (51.1-2). In the third set of hymns, which Abelard says are in praise of the court of the supernal palace, the saints, women are not lacking in the army of Christ's soldiers who participate in his victory and glory ("nec huic militiae, / vel tantae victoriae, / praemiique gloriae / desunt quoque feminae," 99.1); the weak sex fights and triumphs like the strong, amazons with men, those weaker by nature are more wondrous in their victory; men and women, brothers and sisters, sons and mothers, fight together; the wife animates her husband, the mother strengthens her sons, sister provokes brother, admonishing him with words and examples. How can the young not fight when they see virgins at war? They share the struggle as they share the guilt: "from both sexes we have the wound, from both we take the cure, God put on man in the virgin ("*vir*um Deus induit in *virg*ine," 124.1) that men and women ("tam viri quam feminae") might be saved." The sex that became lower in nature after the guilt, divine mercy raised higher in grace (124.2). Mary sets the example but others follow: "who could number the choirs of virgins imitating her, the widows embracing sacred vows?—even in matrimony some burn with that desire" (124.3).

The virgin is, or course, the ultimate source of her sex's glory—"the singular honor of the virgin, so strong that she could be the mother of God" (125.1)—whose steps Abelard traces through sacred history: Adam formed outside of paradise, woman inside, an indication of the excellence of their (*harum,* women's) creation, formed from the rib of man to be strong as bones (125.2). When the virtue/power of men dried up, this strength invaded many women like the judge Deborah and the widow (Judith) who killed Holofernes, the mother of seven brothers (2 Mach. 7) meriting a solemn mass (125.3); and the daughter of Jephthah who chose to die rather than let her father betray his vow (125.4). Jephthah's daughter is the first example of constancy in another hymn: if men contend with men in constancy, who among men can compare for fortitude of mind with Jephthah's daughter (126)?[56] She is followed by the virgin martyrs and those who freed the faithful from their enemies, like Esther (126.3); "the more fragile the sex, the more wondrous its virtue/power" (126.4).

The Virgin conquered flesh, the martyr conquers the enemy; the double palm (virgin and martyr) is rarer among men, richer among women (120.2); as their sex is weaker, so their virtue is more wondrous, and their sacrifice the more pleasing as it is the purer (ibid.); whole in spirit and body, the true sacrifice is from the virgin (120.3). When God gives victory to women, who does not set this grace above others (121.1)? As the sex is more fragile, so the virtue is more wondrous (ibid.); the constancy of women conquers exquisite kinds of torments (121.2); waters cannot extinguish the flame of their unconquered love, for it is never weak, however frail the sex (121.3); let the stronger sex blush when the weaker sustains so much (121.4). The virtues of the sex culminate in the most startling claim Abelard makes for women—that a woman anointed Christ's feet, a woman made him Christ physically, the mysteries of priest and king were taken from a woman (127). The sex which gave him birth also transmitted the sacraments: "Christi pedes capit unguens mulier, / Christum eum fecit corporaliter. / Sacerdotis et regis mysteria / suscepisse constat hunc a femina, / et qui eum sexus peperit / sacramenta quoque tradidit," 127.2). This is said in a hymn which celebrates the divine grace of Mary, Anna, Elizabeth—who will not say that women excel in grace after seeing them (127.1)?—but it makes a claim which comes perilously close to priestly powers, a claim Abelard repeated in a sermon about the passion (11).

What is so strongly implied in the hymns, the active role of women in religious history, is more explicit in the sermons, as it was in the history of nuns, whose purpose seems to be to encourage the nuns in their religious vocation by enhancing their sense of themselves as women.[57] Abelard's letter to Heloise introducing the sermons ends with a frank

acknowledgment of the range of their relations and their common responsibility and purpose: "Be well in the Lord, his handmaid, dear to me once
in the world, now dearest in Christ: wife then in the flesh, sister now in
spirit, and consort in the profession of holy purpose" (Cousin 1.350, R
34). Abelard accepts the traditional definition of women as the weaker sex
but turns it into strength (as Hildegard does, see chapter 5), a strength that
originates in Mary, who reverses the order of creation. The first sermon,
on the annunciation of the Virgin (1.351–8), opens: "The beginning of our
redemption today is the conception of the lady mother. A woman conceived the lord that a creature might bring forth the creator. This is the
common salvation of mankind, but *the special glory of women.* The first
Adam was fashioned from earth, not born from woman: but woman was
formed from his rib. The second Adam, maker and redeemer of all, determined to assume the form of our sex from a woman, that grace might be
in both sexes, as guilt had been in both, and the medication came through
who inflicted the wound." Abelard tells the young virgins to choose God
not man as their spouse, to assume the form of sacred profession from
Mary. He asks why she was called "blessed among women," not among
men and women, and answers it was because of the special grace of
virginity. Few men imitate Christ, but the grace of Mary has many followers among you, whose virtue is more pleasing as the sex is weaker; virtue
indeed is perfected in weakness (354). The sermon ends with praise of the
humility which women like Mary ("queen of the heavens") and Elizabeth
show despite their exaltation; "great are such praises of feminine nature
and glory excelling human infirmity." The repetition of the weakness of
their sex in conjunction with the extraordinary accomplishments of Mary
and the saints has the same effect as in Hildegard's writings of suggesting
unexpected, even heroic, accomplishment.[58]

In the second sermon, on the birth of Christ (1.359–69), Abelard says
that "a woman alone, out of her own substance, without the mixing of
virile seed, furnished the body with which divinity clothed itself, taking the
form of a man in her" (360). He describes the virgin's uterus as a perfect
circle, whose integrity was not disturbed by conception or birth. Like
Hildegard, Abelard makes the connection with Eve: as Eve was formed
from the father alone, so Christ was born of the mother alone. The apostle
said God sent his son made from woman (Gal. 4:4); Abelard says she was
a woman by sex, but unacquainted (*ignara*) with womanly weakness
(364)—since she is usually said to be "ignara" of men, it is very tempting
to equate womanly weakness with the knowledge of men.[59]

Abelard makes a point of the apostle's saying "made from woman
(factum ex muliere)" rather than "born from (*natum*), as some say" (in
the [fifth] sermon on the purification of Mary, 390–98). Christ assumed
flesh in the virgin womb not from nothing, not from elsewhere, but from
the maternal flesh: "In utero virginali carnem non de nihilo, non aliunde,

sed materna traxit ex carne" (392). The exaltation of Mary as the mother of God reaches its climax in sermon 26, on the assumption of Mary (520-27). Abelard begins the sermon with the doubt or admiration expressed by the angels at Christ's ascension, "Who is this king of glory?" and imagines the wonder at "such exaltation of the weak sex" when the virgin is assumed: "who is this who ascends like the rising dawn, beautiful as the moon, elect as the sun, terrible like an ordered line of battle?"[60] Only angels came to meet Christ—there was no one else in heaven—but when Mary arrived, she was met by the whole supernal court; angels and saints came with Christ to receive her in whom he had received soul and flesh (522). Even on earth, the apostles who fled in fear at Christ's death came together to honor his mother when she died (523). Christ was so solicitous for his mother's honor and material needs that he provided a spouse for her before he was born.[61] Abelard tells women to weigh carefully how the lord raised their lower sex in glory so that the heavenly and earthly paradise seems natural to them: Adam was created outside paradise, Eve within, Christ was resuscitated on earth, his mother's body in heaven; the female sex was created body and soul in the earthly paradise, raised soul and body into the heavenly (523). The lord showed the glory of the resurrection to men in himself, to women in his mother, to incite in both sexes desire and hope of future beatitude (524).

Though certainly the most awesome, the virgin is not the only exemplary woman in the sermons. The women who ministered to Christ are singled out in the sermons for the passion and for Easter. In the supper at Bethany, Martha ministered food, Mary unguents, Abelard says; women received the lord whom men persecuted, restoring him and not fearing the mighty persecutors (11, on the events of the passion, 428-54). Christ ministered to his disciples, an example of humility to men, but only women are commemorated in scripture ministering to Christ, an example to women of their dignity, "who merited ministering to him in all things" (430-31). A woman not only washed his feet with her tears but also anointed his head: "she made him Christ corporally, she accomplished the sacraments of king and of priest." Indeed, the greater devotion of women is shown in their repeated ministerings, a second anointing of Christ's head at a second meal (Abelard treats the meal mentioned in Matthew 26 and Mark 14 as different from the one in John 12, 438-39).

The sermon on Easter (13, 460-65) begins, "How much the paschal exaltation of solemnity pertains to the devotion or honor of women, both Old and New Testament testify." Again Abelard pairs Mary (Miriam), who led the women in celebration of the lord's triumph (Exodus 15), with the Mary to whom Christ revealed his resurrection, the "apostle of the apostles, legate of legates," who told the news to other women before she told the apostles. One Mary foretold first, the other saw first. In the Old Testament celebration, men preceded the women, in the New, women

preceded men, the inverted order more blessed and honorable ("prae-
posterus quidem ordo beatior et honorabilior pensandus est," 461).
Christ's resurrection is compared to the phoenix, not unusual in itself, but
when he notes that the bird is unique, of neither male nor female sex (464),
Abelard adds an unusual observation: "just as in the body of Christ which
is the church, diversity of sex carries no dignity" (465). Christ attends not
to the quality of sex but of merits.

A sermon on Susanna (29, 537-46) makes another unusual point, offering a married woman as an example of virtue to virgins, because of her
courageous willingness to die rather than sacrifice her chastity. It also
includes a comment on the importance of education for women, citing
Jerome's commentary on Daniel in support of parents' educating daughters
in divine words and the law of God (539), and criticizing modern parents
who, from avarice, do not educate their daughters as Susanna's parents
did (540). In the sermon on St. Stephen's birthday (31), citing Paul, Cassiodorus, and Jerome, Abelard speaks of women participating in the early
church as deaconesses, of virgins and widows who chose Christ as their
spouse, and of the holy men who worked with them, like Stephen, and
Origen, who castrated himself so he could instruct women without infamy
(555-56). In a sermon in praise of Stephen's martyrdom (32), Abelard says
he received the power to do wonders and signs after he began serving
women, as if the more he humbled himself in service to the weaker sex,
the more the lord exalted him, so that he appeared to excel over other
saints (558). The reflections of Origen and Stephen in Abelard's life would
be hard to overlook. At the end of the sermon, Abelard reminds his
"dearest sisters" that "these things which are preached about the first
ministry especially pertain to your glory" (566), so they will remember
him who was a faithful minister to them among men (Stephen) and pray
to him as their advocate. Implicit in this ending is the hope that they will
think of the man who ministers to them, whose glory is enhanced by his
service to them (Abelard), and pray for him.

Abelard, like Jerome, was motivated to do a large part of his writing
by women. The two are unusual in the quantity and particular focus of
their attention, but not in the fact that they composed religious, scholarly,
or theological works at the request of women. While many men wrote on
virginity and the spiritual life or commented on biblical texts of particular
interest for women, distinguished figures like Jerome, Augustine, Alcuin,
Peter Damian, and Abelard wrote serious works on complicated questions
with respect for the minds and learning of the women who had asked for
them, often with great enthusiasm because they were being pushed to
develop ideas that interested them. They show no sexual discrimination in
their answers, writing them as they would to men, and expecting most of
the texts to reach a larger audience than the women they are addressed to.
Jerome and Abelard, however, the men most intimately involved with

women in their studies, do make a point of the sex of their first audience, partly to justify their writing for women to a hostile world, partly to defend and encourage those women as active disciples and students of Christ. It is true that religious women rise above sex by their profession of chastity, but Jerome and Abelard also recognize and respect the selfless devotion of those women as women, their intellectual and moral strength making them more than the equal of men, including themselves.

3 Women and the Writing of History

Women who exercised secular power could also rise above their sex by virtue of their official roles. And men who supported them often collaborated with them in the writing of historical texts that championed their families or furthered their political destinies. Medieval women play various roles in the preservation of history quite apart from the texts. Secular women were frequently in themselves important links to past as well as to present prestige within a family; their ancestry is often what gives legitimacy to their husbands' claims.[1] Their regency for husbands and young or even grown sons enables a line to continue in power and preserve its place in history; they provide continuity within the line. Religious women were expected to pray for the souls of the dead of their families or the families of their convents' founders, for which purpose they were given lists of the dead; thus they became keepers of the written record, however simple, of the family history.

But women were also actively involved in the writing of history texts. Secular women commissioned men to write histories of themselves, their husbands, their families, or the world, usually to further a political agenda, directly or indirectly. Men accepted the commissions because they shared the political interests, because their fate was tied to the woman's, or because they wanted to win or show gratitude for favor, in any case recognizing the actual or potential power of the woman they served. Other men dedicated histories to women to support the women's positions or to enhance their own. The men who wrote the histories for women were clerics, who may have accepted the woman's position as the will of God or welcomed it because they respected her abilities and trusted her motives. If women were not usually able to lead troops, they were often better at negotiating peace.[2] If women upheld the authority of secular power when they represented it, they were also more likely to work with rather than against the church. Women were also more likely to support culture, and because they so often outlived their husbands and were regents for their sons, some historians may have directed their works to women rather than to men in the hopes of having a more lasting influence through them. There is no small irony in the fact that the same institution that produced such virulent misogyny, the church, also produced very strong propaganda for women's claims, in the commissioned histories, another instance of theory giving way to political reality.

I know of no evidence of secular women in the West writing history themselves, though it is not inconceivable, and we do have the Byzantine example of Anna Comnena's history of her father.[3] But certainly religious women wrote lives and annals and histories, sometimes for their abbesses, sometimes at the request of men who wanted lives of famous members of the family or histories of the family. The abbess of Quedlinburg, Matilda, daughter, sister, and aunt of Ottonian emperors, had her nuns compile the *Annales Quedlinburgenses;* Gerberga, abbess of Gandersheim and a member of the Saxon imperial family, asked Hrotsvit to write a history of the Ottonians and one of her monastery, works which were clearly intended also for the imperial court; Charlemagne's sister, abbess Gisla of Chelles, may have had her nuns compose the *Annales Mettenses Priores.*[4] Otto II requested the life of his ancestor, *Vita Mathildis reginae antiquior,* probably from a nun of Nordhausen, and there is a possibility that the later life of the same queen, written at the request of emperor Henry II, was done by a nun of the same convent.

I am less concerned here with female authorship of histories or lives than I am with the question of cooperation between men and women in the composing of history. The purposes of medieval histories, chronicles, and lives were not to give objective reports or analyses of events but to establish claims (legal claims to property or rights, dynastic claims to power), to offer models of behavior to be followed and avoided, even to entertain.[5] Since it was propaganda, whether spiritual or political, history could be slanted to favor one side or another, historic figures and events chosen selectively to make particular points, awkward details equally selectively left out. The histories that are written for or by women are invariably slanted to a greater or lesser extent toward women and the active roles they can, do, and perhaps should play in history. When women write, they usually give more space to the actions and relations of women. But both women and the men who write for them seem to focus on human relations, to see the family more as the center of historic events, probably because it was through their family connections that women were able to hold public positions, while male-oriented histories are more concerned with the often hostile relations between nations (wars) and between institutions. Great women are presented as models of the effective exercise of power, usually though not always for justice, peace, or dedication to a good cause, and as such they can also be models of behavior not only to other women in power but also to men. Bad women are presented like bad men as models to be avoided, a traditional component of medieval history, though the proportion of good to bad women is considerably lower in texts not concerned with women.

Writers thinking primarily of a male audience either pay little attention to women or see them mainly as a problem. Bede, for example, a monk writing in the eighth century, is not misogynist in his *Historia ecclesiastica,* but he relegates women's action to the religious sphere, alluding only briefly to mothers or wives of rulers. He gives most attention to abbess Hilda, who trained five bishops and the poet Caedmon (4.23, 24) and presided over a synod (3.25). Bede also cites a letter from pope Boniface to queen Ethelberga encouraging her to convert the king of the Northumbrians by teaching him the laws of God (2.11), though he attributes the major influence in the king's conversion to a vision (2.12). Their infant daughter is the first Northumbrian to be baptized (2.9).[6] Gregory of Tours, a sixth-century bishop, has much more to say about secular women in his *History of the Franks,* particularly in the contemporary material, because he dealt with them directly. A few are holy, but most are problematic, best exemplified by Fredegund, queen of the Franks, who plots scores of assassinations, tortures her real or imagined enemies, attacks anyone who crosses her, even her own daughter and certainly bishops—in short, she is one of the major villains of the story.

In the early centuries, much medieval history was written by bishops and by monks, some of them attached to secular courts, most of them dependent in some way on the good will of local secular authority, having a personal or institutional stake in the political situation. When a woman had power or influence in that situation, it did not hurt to court her favor, and when she was a trusted friend, it could be (or seem) beneficial to the larger community to serve her interests. All the histories and lives written by male clerics for women that I consider in this chapter have at least an implicit, many an explicit, political agenda. From Paul the Deacon's *Historia Romana* for countess Adelperga to William of Malmesbury's *Historia novella* for empress Matilda, the histories are written with a clear sense of the woman's present and potential power.

I have chosen to look at the texts in chronological rather than generic order since I have not been able to discern a clear difference in attitude or motivation between the histories and the lives, and there does seem to be a development in the use of the histories across time. The earliest histories written for women that I have seen, by Paul the Deacon and Freculf of Lisieux in the eighth and ninth centuries, seem to be intended to support the women in potentially difficult political situations, and at the same time to ensure their good will toward the writer. The next group of texts, all connected with the Ottonian dynasty in the tenth century, were written by or at the request of nuns of major imperial monasteries vying for the support and protection of the imperial family. Finally, in the eleventh and early twelfth, a series of lives and histories were commissioned by or for women of the English royal line, some to justify the actions or claims of a particular woman or her family to her contemporaries, some to record their glory for posterity and presumably thereby to strengthen the position of their contemporary descendants, which would do no harm to the author or his institution.[7]

When Paul the Deacon, a Lombard and monk of Monte Cassino then residing at the court of Charlemagne, wrote the *Historia Romana* (c. 770) for Adelperga, countess of Benevento, daughter of the last Lombard king, wife and mother of the last surviving Lombard rulers, the position of the Lombards was tenuous. Both pope and emperor were uncomfortable with their Byzantine connection. Charlemagne would defeat her father in 774; a year later her refugee brother would be involved in an unsuccessful conspiracy against Charlemagne which included Paul's own brother; and when her husband and older son died in 787, her remaining son would be a hostage at Charlemagne's court. Adelperga was left to run Benevento until Charlemagne could be persuaded to send her son Grimoald back in 788.[8] Paul could not have known that these events would occur when he responded to Adelperga's request for the Roman history, but as a Lombard living at Charlemagne's court he could not have been unaware of the dangers and may well have intended his history to strengthen her resolve when the trouble came.

Whether or not Paul was Adelperga's tutor (he was tutor of Charlemagne's daughter, Rotrud), he says he has always been a promoter of her elegance (in studies), and he did advise her in her reading.[9] In his letter dedicating the *Historia Romana,* which she had urged him to write, he praises her devotion to learning: "you search the secrets of the prudent with subtle wit and very wise zeal so that the golden eloquence of philosophers and jewels of poets speak readily to you, you engage also in divine as well as worldly histories."[10] When he gave her Eutropius's history to read, she examined it avidly, as was her custom, but was displeased by its brevity and failure to mention divine history; she wanted him to extend the history in suitable places, to add to it from scripture, and to clarify the chronology. He says he has expanded Eutropius from other sources and added six books, coming up to the time of Justinian, and promises, if she wills and he lives, eventually to bring it up to their time.[11] At the end of book 10, Paul says Eutropius composed the history and Paul added to it, with the help or support of the most Christian lady Adelperga, duchess of Benevento: "iuvente domna Adelperga" is a topos, perhaps, but one which implies collaboration.

In the history, one is struck by the presence of women, some named only as the relatives of men and important as the links between nations, but important enough to be named in that role, others actively taking part in government, choosing their husbands' successors, plotting, advising, being the object of plots. Bad, good, strong, weak, clever, foolish, ineffective or neutral, they are, like the men, a part of Paul's history. Either Paul knows that Adelperga is alert to the role of women in history and expects him to acknowledge it or he thinks she should be aware of the part they have played and have models to follow and avoid—perhaps both.[12] In any case, he certainly gives women more play than Eutropius had. He also gives most attention to women in the last books of his history, where he is no longer following Eutropius, though he interpolates passages about women in other books, from different sources.

What matters, of course, is what he chooses to include. Even in Roman history, he shows women actively participating. In his brief history of Aeneas, based on Virgil's *Aeneid* and Jerome's *Chronicon,* he mentions that Aeneas built and named Lavinium for his second wife, Lavinia, and Paul implies that she later controlled the kingdom: when Ascanius went to found Alba Longa, he "left the kingdom of his stepmother" ("derelicto novercae suae Laviniae regno," HR 1.1). The rape of the Sabines leads to war and then to peace, because of the relationship through the women; Paul adds the phrase "whose daughters they had taken" to his sources (1.2). Women free their people from tyrants: the rape of Lucretia leads to the end of Tarquinius's rule, an event Paul connects in time (as well as in theme) with Judith's killing of Holofernes (1.8). Women resist conquest sometimes more fiercely than men: in book 5, Paul adds from Orosius a battle between the Romans and the Cymbrian women in which the women disposed their wagons like a camp and fought from above, resisting for a long time until the Romans began to scalp them, leaving a shameful wound; then the women killed themselves and each other. The uncivilized nature of the Roman attack foreshadows descriptions in later works of Greek attacks on the Amazons, as though fighting men go crazy when women resist them, even if Paul speaks of some of the women killing themselves and their children "in female fury" ("femineo furore," 5.2).[13]

But it is in the last books of the history, which Paul added at Adelperga's request, that women are most in evidence, saving their husbands or their people, guiding their husbands to proper action, peace or conversion. The daughter of one emperor saves her husband from her father's murderous plots (10.3); the widow of another keeps the Goths from destroying Constantinople by distributing much money to the people and so preserving the kingdom "faithfully and virilely" for her kin (11.11). The younger empress Galla Placidia was seized by the Goths and joined to their king in marriage, which Paul says turned out well for the state (*reipublicae*), since she moved her husband by her very sharp wit ("acerrimo ingenio") and subtle flattery to seek peace from the Romans (12.15); later she and her son by another marriage were appointed rulers of the western kingdom (13.9).[14] Cesara, wife of a Persian king, came to Constantinople with a few faithful companions, disguised in the dress of a private person, because of her love for the Christian faith. When her husband sent legates to look for her, her identity was discovered, but she sent back a message saying she would never share his bed unless he believed in Christ as she did. He came without delay, "peacefully" bringing sixty thousand soldiers, was baptized with the emperor as godfather, and departed with many gifts and his wife (17.27). Even in modern history, women protect their people: the emperor cannot for the present conquer the Lombards because a certain queen built a church to John the Baptist in Lombard territory, and so the saint intercedes for them (17.28).

Not all Paul's examples are positive. There are, as is to be expected in a comprehensive history, examples of evil to be avoided, women who offer themselves to the conquerors of their people (14.13, 16) and heretic empresses who persecute true believers but nonetheless retain their authority (17.10, 12–14). And there is the unfortunate Amalasuntha, daughter of Theodoric and his chosen regent for his heir, her son. When her son died, to secure her position Amalasuntha associated Theodatus (her cousin) with her in the government, but he quickly had her murdered (16.12). She, however, had had the foresight to commend herself and her son to emperor Justinian, who eventually sent his armies against Theodatus. Her daughter was seized and married by Theodatus's successor, presumably because she, like her mother, carried the legitimacy of rule (16.15).[15] It seems likely to me that Paul intended a warning to Adelperga with this story of the daughter of a king, widowed and regent for a young son, who turns in her attempt to retain power to a relative who betrays her, something that could easily have happened to her. Amalasuntha might have done better to rely only on her emperor, Justinian, who did avenge her, as Adelperga presumably should rely on Paul's other patron, the emperor Charlemagne.

The next major history written for a woman that I know of was dedicated to Judith, the second wife of Charlemagne's son Louis the Pious. Judith, a Welf/Guelph, worked hard to advance the position of her son, Charles the Bald, against the interests of her three stepsons in plans to divide the empire. She was a notable patron of letters, partly because of her cultured background but no doubt also because friendly pens could help her and her son.[16] Among works written for her which praise her and her royal role (and not coincidentally look to her for help) is Ermold's verse biography, *In honorem Hludovici*, which describes Judith's elegant outdoor meal during a hunt and her conspicuous place in royal processions and banquets; it ends with a plea to Judith, "you who by right hold the heights of empire with him" (2644–45: "Tu quoque, digna sibi conjux, pulcherrima Judith, / quae secum imperii culmina jure tenes") to help the disgraced author.[17] Walafrid Strabo, who tutored her son Charles, compares Judith in his *De imagine Tetrici* to Rachel leading Benjamin (the favored son, which Judith was doing her best to make Charles). Rabanus Maurus dedicated commentaries on the biblical heroines Judith and Esther to Judith, "one your equal in name, the other in dignity/position," women who had saved their people by taking clever or forceful action (see chapter 2).

Judith, young, beautiful, and cultivated, seems to have had considerable influence over her husband, but not surprisingly she was mistrusted by others; the object of accusations and attacks, she was at least twice banished from court. Freculf, bishop of Lyons, who presented her in 829 with the second volume of his world history (before the exiles but not before the plottings), was certainly aware both of her power and of the precariousness of her position. Still, given her youth and influence, it was not unlikely that she would outlive her husband and be able to exercise power through her son.[18] The first volume of the history, which covers the creation to the birth of Christ, is dedicated to Freculf's "teacher," Elisachar; the second treats the more relevant history of the Romans and Goths, who would be succeeded by the Franks and Lombards.[19] He offers it to Judith as a mirror by which she can educate her son to what he should do and what he should avoid, as Bathsheba educated that wisest of earlier kings, Solomon, who according to Freculf remembered his mother's teaching in Proverbs 4:3–6. Freculf praises the wisdom with which God endowed Judith and the learning of her natural wit in divine and liberal studies, endowments which have astonished hearers, including him; and he offers his work to her judgment and perhaps praise, since *Judith* means "judging" or "praising" (PL106, c.1115–16).

It might have been impolitic to suggest that Judith too could learn something from the historic examples Freculf presents, but I have no doubt he hoped she would. Certainly he gives many examples of women whose experiences might be relevant, women involved in religious and secular struggles, imperial and noble women, women who influenced their husbands and sons, women who succeeded and women who failed.[20] Freculf describes women whose devotion to Christ estranges them from their husbands and women who convert their husbands: Domicilla, daughter of Domitian and bride of emperor Aurelian, was exiled because she believed in Christ and took the veil, while Theodora, who also professed chastity when she was converted, converted her powerful husband and through him many others, including nobles and friends of the emperor (Freculf, *Chronicon*, 2.2.10). Freculf tells the story of Helena, mother of emperor Constantine, "a woman incomparable in faith, religion of soul and singular magnificence," as a supreme example of mutual support between mother and son: Helena not only found the cross but also gave her son the nails from which he made armor (presumably to fight in God's cause), and he in turn founded a city in her honor, Helenopolis (2.3.18).

Some women try to influence their men in the wrong direction and are punished for it: Justina, an Aryan empress who could do nothing while her husband was alive, after his death took advantage of her son's youth and persecuted Ambrose and others with some success, but when her plots led to war, putting her son to flight, he finally recognized that his troubles came from his mother's advice ("cognoscens quae mala matris consilio sustineret"), and she ended her life in exile (2.4.24).[21] The cautionary message of this story is clear, but it is not always easy to know how to read the stories of mothers and sons: when a devout woman brings her little son to be martyred in Mesopotamia and deflects the emperor's wrath from Christians (2.4.17), are we to applaud her religious zeal and her courage in facing her enemies or to question her willingness to sacrifice him to the cause she believes in?[22]

In the stories of Mommea and Placella, however, Freculf offers positive examples which can also be read as compliments to Judith. Mommea, mother of emperor Aurelius Alexander, was a Christian and a religious woman who took care to hear learned men like Origen and summoned him to Antioch in highest honor. Freculf also mentions that Origen wrote letters (still extant) to another emperor, Philip, "the first Christian among Roman kings," and his mother (2.3.2). In his praise of Placella's charity and teaching and the comments about the learned men of the time, Freculf probably intends Judith to read allusions to the intellectual splendor of her court (2.4.29). Placella admonished her husband often about divine laws, which she had first learned thoroughly, not exalted by worldly dignity, but enflamed by divine love; as soon as she came to the purple, she cared for the lame and weak, not through servants but directly, offering whatever she had, ministering to the sick with her own hands, advising her husband to distribute gold, reminding him what he had recently been, what he now was, what he owed his benefactor in gratitude (2.4.28). The intellectual distinction of their reign continued under Theodosius's sons, Arcadius and Honorius, during whose rule Ambrose, Jerome, and Augustine were writing. Freculf even lists a number of Jerome's writings, mentioning some to women (to Eustochium about preserving virginity, to Paula about the death of her daughter, a letter to Paula and Eustochium, a book of letters to Marcellum [sic], 2.5.3), perhaps implying a connection with his own work.

After the Carolingians, the next major medieval dynasty was the Ottonian, in which women played significant roles and were involved in a large body of history for, by, and about women. Most of the history was monastic in origin and orientation, which is not to say that it was not concerned with the lives and roles of secular women or of religious women in the secular world. Since the monasteries concerned were all imperial foundations, to some extent rivals for imperial support, and their abbesses were mostly members of the imperial family, there was considerable intercourse between them and the court.[23] Matilda, abbess of Quedlinburg but also daughter of emperor Otto I, sister of Otto II, and aunt of Otto III, would be sufficiently adept in secular matters to serve at times as regent for her nephew and to support the position of her sister-in-law Theophanu against her mother, Adelaide, on the imperial claims to Adelaide's dower lands. It is not surprising, then, that Widukind, a monk of Corvey, should have written a (secular) history of their people, the Saxons, for Matilda when she became abbess at a very early age, nor that the history should glorify her (and perhaps his) ancestors in secular as well as religious life.[24] Widukind may not give as much attention to particular women as Hrotsvit does in the same period, but he is very aware of the importance of maternal relations and possessions; wars and rebellions are fought by Wichmann the younger and Thangmar over claims through their mothers. What is different from earlier histories for women is that in Widukind and the other Saxon histories, the models are not just historic women but men and women who are the direct ancestors and relations of the sponsor. What is striking in this history directed to a nun is that all the models are secular women.

Widukind, in his prologues to the three books of the *Res Gestae Saxonicae*, makes it clear that he sees Matilda as a secular as well as a religious figure. He praises her virginity, wisdom, and imperial majesty and offers her the deeds of a most powerful father and most glorious grandfather to read and improve herself by ("unde ex optima et gloriosissima melior gloriosiorque efficiaris," prologue 1). He calls her mistress of all Europe by right ("domina . . . iure totius Europae," prologue 2), the most serene splendor and brightest gem of the world through the imperial dignity (prologue 3). His history includes the famous women of the dynasty, queens Matilda, Edith, and Adelaide. Matilda, mother of Otto I, the namesake of the abbess (and the subject of her own lives), is said to be beyond the power of Widukind's pen to describe or praise (3.12, 74) for her religious devotion, her care for the sick and the poor, her humility without detriment to royal dignity, her instruction of servants in arts and letters, which she had mastered after the death of the king (3.74). Her death is related just before her son's (3.75), as the fitting end of the history (except for the brief notice of the election of the next emperor, 3.76).[25] Edith's death is described at the end of book II, with the grief of all the Saxons; she shone as much for her holy religion as for the power of her royal birth from the Angles (2.46). Adelaide is described as a "queen of singular prudence in many things," who was persecuted by Berengar (3.7) and rescued by Otto, after he had tested her good faith, in a marriage which brought him the royal seat of Pavia (3.9).

The heroic story of Adelaide's escape, which Hrotsvit tells in such lively detail, is not mentioned by Widukind nor by the *Annales Quedlinburgenses*, which abbess Matilda, who was Adelaide's daughter, had her nuns write.[26] Adelaide is, however, featured in the *Annales*, where there is considerable focus on the political as well as religious roles of contemporary Ottonian women; even when they are nuns, they are described as "imperial ladies." The history makes the monastery a center of public functions, meetings of the imperial family and the important people in the land of both sexes (*utriusque sexus*), and it makes religious functions (dedications of churches, installations of abbesses, an imperial princess taking the veil) public affairs. It also emphasizes the family ties, indeed the love that binds siblings in particular. In its function as a record of events of the year, the *Annales* mentions the marriages and deaths of the main women in the line and the birth of the future abbess, Matilda, "a very bright gem in the imperial crown" (AQ955). It records church buildings and dedications: the foundation of Quedlinburg by queen Matilda after the death of her husband and her continuing maternal care for it (936); the monastery abbess Matilda constructed in honor of her only and beloved brother and dedicated to Mary, "mother of God" (986); and the presence of imperial women at other church dedications.

But we are also told much more of Adelaide's story—her marriage to Otto as the widow of the illustrious king Lothar, a queen "beautiful in face, provident in counsel, illustrious by the honorableness of her behavior," born of established royal stock, the chosen heir of her husband to the Lombard kingdom (951)—and her role in preserving the kingdom for her grandson. When the duke of Bavaria seized the young Otto III after the death of his father, messengers were sent to his grandmother, the imperial empress in Lombardy; she hastened to come, met with her daughter-in-law Theophanu, her daughter abbess Matilda, her brother, the king of Burgundy, and leaders of Europe, who were ready to die for the young king.[27] Henry, terrified by a sign in the heavens, was compelled to surrender the king to his grandmother, mother, and aunt, and the "imperial ladies" came back to Saxony, stopping at Quedlinburg (984); Henry humbled himself before the three imperial ladies who had charge of the kingdom and the king, and they received his submission, "since it is the custom of the pious not only not to render evil for good, but rather to render good for evil" (985). In the entry for her death, we are told that the illustrious empress had worked with her consort, she with merits and customs, he with strengths and triumphs (suggesting that her role was a crucial complement to his), and after his death she never stopped in her care for the poor (999); the young emperor Otto III is said to have depended on the pope, his grandmother empress, and his aunt, the imperial abbess, as three pillars (1000).

If the *Annales* is discreet about abbess Matilda's actions during her lifetime, it explodes in a very long chapter about her when she dies, describing not only her virtues from earliest youth (she became abbess at eleven) but also her skills in government as her nephew's regent: she kept peace in the land not with arms but with vigils and prayers, but she also conferred effectively with secular and religious leaders, princes, bishops, judges; she was merciful to the poor, severe to the evil. Her loss was felt by all, but particularly by her nephew and her nuns, who chose her niece to replace her (999). Whatever the qualifications of the niece, Adelaide, it did not hurt the monastery to have as abbess a dearly beloved sister of the emperor; we are told that he came out of love for her and hated to leave the sister he dearly loved ("sororem quam intime diligebat") when he returned to Italy (1000). A second sister, Sophie, became abbess of Gandersheim (and later of Essen as well), and she and Adelaide kept up their relations with the empire after the election of their second cousin, Henry II, going to meet him and his wife when the election was announced (1002).

Sophie's predecessor as abbess of Gandersheim was her father's cousin, Gerberga, daughter of Henry of Bavaria, brother of the first emperor Otto.[28] Gandersheim was another major convent founded and supported by the imperial family. Among Gerberga's nuns was the writer Hrotsvit, whose poems and plays will be discussed in a later chapter. Gerberga commissioned Hrotsvit to write two historical epics, one the life of the emperor, the other the history of the convent.[29] Together they illustrate the divine origin of the imperial dynasty and the monastery of Gandersheim and the intimate connection of the two. We know Hrotsvit intended her verse-epic (a style more suited to panegyric than prose) about Otto to be read at the imperial court, since she sent it both to Otto I and, after his death (973), to his son Otto II, and it is likely that the history of the monastery, which is also in verse and also a history of their ancestors, was meant for the same court audience. Even though both epics were probably intended for men as well as women, Hrotsvit gives much more attention than most writers to the deeds of women and their participation in public affairs.[30]

For the *Gesta Ottonis*, commissioned by Gerberga but presented to the emperor and his son, Hrotsvit has no written model; hers is the first life of the emperor. In it, Hrotsvit emphasizes human relations, the marriages of women in the imperial family which are shared responsibilities like their public functions and harmonious partnerships, and she gives short shrift to military operations. She uses the excuse that it is not for a frail woman in a monastery to talk of war, but she had not hesitated to talk of brothels in her dramas, presumably without direct experience of them, so it seems more likely that she prefers to emphasize Otto's gifts and virtues as a ruler over those of the warrior. She is anxious to show him as a wise and merciful king who forgives his enemies and eventually brings them around.

Hrotsvit begins the history with the first king in the line, Otto's father, Henry, and his illustrious wife and co-ruler, Matilda ("*con*regnante sua Mathilda *con*iuge clara," *Gesta Ottonis*, 22), whom none can now surpass in the highest merits; they had three sons, Otto, Henry, and Bruno, who became bishop of Cologne and the only man in the family in the tenth century to be called a saint.[31] The father sought a bride, a worthy friend or companion ("dignam . . . amicam," 71), for his son Otto among the

Angles, and the king of England (AEthelstan) carefully prepared his sister by instilling sweet love for Otto in her mind.[32] He sent both Edith, "outstanding daughter of an illustrious mother," descended from great kings, beautiful, shining with goodness, considered the best of all women in her land (81–92), and her younger sister, Adiva, lesser in age and merit, along with treasure.[33] Edith's goodness pleased all, and she and Otto married.

Though Otto was a model king of strength tempered by mercy, his early rule was disturbed by a series of rebellions involving his brother Henry, the father of Hrotsvit's abbess and sponsor, Gerberga. Hrotsvit is very careful in her presentation of Henry to play down his treacherous role. She presents him first as victim, then as protagonist, hoping he did not agree in his heart but was compelled by force (11.223–24), though she offers no evidence of force. She describes Otto's mercy to Henry and his grief over the many deaths caused by rebellion, comparing them to David and Saul, but says little about the battles fought. The one positive thing she can say is that Henry married ("joined to himself legally with worthy love," "sibi condigne legali iunxit amore," 156) Judith, shining with beauty and goodness, the noble daughter of a distinguished duke.

The death of Otto's queen, Edith, is described with great sympathy for the distress of the people, whom she had treated more as a loving mother than as a stern ruler (403–4). She leaves her two children equally bereft, though Otto cares for them with affection and benign piety. The son, Liudulf, is said to be good in habit, sweet in mind, kind, merciful, humble, faithful, and filled with sweet love for his father, even when absent (that is, with no instinct for rebellion), though he too would later revolt. The lack of faith in brother and son contrast, though this is never said, with the virtue and loyalty of the women in the royal family. Of the daughter, Liudgard, we are told that she is like her venerable mother in habits and face (422) and "the only hope [her father] had of female sex," "unica feminei quae spes sexus fuit illi," 445, presumably an allusion to the value of women in alliances through marriage, though nothing is said of political imperatives (and indeed the Ottonians seemed as anxious to place their women in important abbacies as to marry them well). Otto arranged the marriage of his daughter, whom he cherished and loved, to Conrad (of Lorraine), a distinguished and powerful duke, and of his son to Ida, the daughter of another illustrious duke, Herman (of Swabia).

Otto himself married again, a queen, Adelaide, whose dramatic story Hrotsvit tells in some detail, giving her active role more play in contrast to other versions. Adelaide's first husband, Lothar, king of Italy, left his kingdom in her hands when he died. Descended from a long line of great kings, she was noble, beautiful, and so shining in wit that she would have ruled the kingdom worthily, if that people had not plotted treachery ("Scilicet ingenio fuerat praelucida tanto, / ut posset regnum digne rexisse relictum, / si gens ipsa dolum mox non dictaret amarum," 478–80). Beren-

gar seized her throne and her treasures, removed her ministers and atten-
dants, and imprisoned her, with no companions but a girl and a priest.
When a bishop, Adelhard, offered help if she could get to him, she and her
companions dug a secret tunnel through which she escaped, hiding in caves
and grainfields, protected by God from searching armies, until the bishop
found her. Meanwhile, Saxons who had known her kindness when they
were in Italy told Otto her story, saying there could be no worthier successor to Edith. Otto was hesitant because of all the conspiracies around her,
but he remembered that she had helped him sympathetically when he was
in exile and he must not be ungrateful, and he was not unaware of the
advantage of joining the Italian lands to his. With the help of his son, Otto
established a position in Italy, sent messages of peace and love to Adelaide,
and invited her to join him. When Otto's first son, Liudulf, died, the way
was left open to the son of Otto and Adelaide, Otto II.

Hrotsvit's second epic, the *Primordia Coenobii Gandeshemensis*, begins
a century before the events of the *Gesta*. It attributes the foundation of
the monastery to the Saxon chiefs Liudulf and his son Otto (grandfather
of the emperor Otto I), but in fact shows the key role played by the women
in the family, who seem to be preferred by God to do his work and are
aided by divine signs. Liudulf's wife, Oda, descended from a distinguished
Frankish family, is the figure who links the story from its beginnings to
the birth of the first emperor at the end. Her mother, Aeda, a noble woman
of good repute and religious devotion, had a revelation from John the
Baptist, who prophesied both the foundation of a cloister for virgins and
the future fame and power of her family, to be fulfilled in her great-great-
grandson the emperor Otto. Though overcome by terror at the vision "in
the way of women" ("obstupuit mentis iuxta morem muliebris, / pro-
cumbens subito magno terrore coacta," *Primordia* 50–51), Aeda instilled
in her daughter the mission to build the convent. Oda, following the
example of her venerable mother, persuaded her husband to construct the
monastery. Her "faithful husband" yielded to the counsels of his "chosen
wife" and they served God together (99–102).

They began with a small church, destining their daughter, Hathumoda,
to be the abbess, to prepare for which they placed her in the care and
instruction of a venerable abbess. Acting always together, they obtained
permission first from their king, Louis, and then from the pope, going to
him for his blessing and the privilege of his immediate authority. A miraculous light, seen first by swineherds, revealed the site for the new buildings,
but stones could not be found until Hathumoda, after fasting and prayer,
was led by a bird to a stash of rocks, enough to build the monastery and
church. Before the work was complete, Liudulf died, leaving his wife and
sons with the responsibility of finishing it. Perhaps, Hrotsvit conjectures,
God took him so that the mind of the illustrious lady Oda might be free
to devote itself to God's affairs. Then Oda turned her persuasive powers

on her son Otto, who "responded with his deeds to his holy mother's vow" (369) and finished the building, though God also helped by making Oda's daughter queen of France, giving her access to wealth which she and her husband bestowed on the monastery.

When the first abbess Hathumoda died, she left her sister Gerberga in charge. But Gerberga, who was a secret nun, had to get free of her betrothal to a man who refused to give her up. Her struggle suggests the pressure women in the family felt from their secular obligations. Torn between her desire for Christ and her fear of civil war, she continued to live in the world richly clothed, that is, giving no outward appearance of her profession, but avoided meeting with her fiance, Bernard, until he persuaded her mother, Oda, to insist on it. Her behavior toward him then showed more royal diplomacy than saintly obstinacy. In the face of his threats to force her to break her vow when he returned from war, she answered that she entrusted herself to Christ—a trust that was not misplaced, since Bernard died in the war and she was able to keep her vow.

Gerberga was a solicitous abbess, but her mother, Oda, continued to exert an influence over the convent, keeping a watchful eye on all the activities to be sure no one tried to live by her own law. She herself set an example with the sweet love of a prudent mother toward her dear foster children ("caras . . . alumnas," 420), persuading them to virtue and frightening them away from vice. When her granddaughters and grandsons came to do her honor as their grandmother and the mother-in-law of the king and to bestow gifts, she urged them to give to the nuns, "our ladies" ("nostras . . . domnas," 436). Even the lands her son-in-law gave her she bestowed with his permission on Gandersheim, and at the urging of her daughter, the king gave his own gifts of land under the jurisdiction of abbess Gerberga, his wife's sister. When Gerberga died, she entrusted her sheep pen to a third sister, Christine, who followed the example of her two sisters in way of life and virtue, with her mother's constant encouragement. Oda continued to be solicitous for the needs of the nuns, her "adoptive children" (505), and to encourage her son Otto to help; he never refused to carry out for them what his mother ordered (514), treating them as a kind father. His death was deeply felt by the nuns, who wept for three days beside his body, as if their tears could restore it. Eight days before his death, his grandson Otto, destined to be the first emperor and to fulfill the prophecy given to Aeda at the beginning of the poem, was born. Six months later, Oda died, aged 107 years, having seen the monastery built and enriched through several generations of her family.[34]

Hrotsvit's poems were valuable arguments for the importance of Gandersheim for the imperial family. She does not mention that Gandersheim had earlier produced the first commemorative list of names of its members, which Van Houts notes.[35] Later, in 968, abbess Matilda of Quedlinburg was given a roll with the names of the dead by her grandmother queen

Matilda, a list Van Houts suggests was an updated version of the one at Gandersheim (58). There were most likely rivalries among the family convents for support; certainly they produced many histories to draw attention to themselves and their most distinguished members or supporters. Nordhausen, founded by queen Matilda and connected with Quedlinburg, which Matilda and her husband had founded, produced two lives of the queen, at least one by a nun of the convent. Though the two lives were written at the request of Matilda's male descendants Otto II and Henry II, it is likely that abbess Richburga, who had been an intimate of queen Matilda's, was involved in their production as a major source if not as author and that she was anxious to keep the needs of Nordhausen in the minds of the two kings to prevent alienation of its lands.[36] Indeed, Althoff argues, the two lives were occasioned by the gift of Nordhausen as part of her dower lands to the new empress, first Theophanu, wife of Otto II, then Cunegund, wife of Henry II. The lives were thus intended to remind the emperors of their ancestors' wishes and their own obligations to the convent. Both are cast as examples of a virtuous public life for her male descendant to strive to imitate.[37]

Matilda is an unusual saint in that she was, according to the lives, happily married, was the mother of five children (and two imperial lines), and does not seem to have rejected her secular life, though she was intensely devout—her sons compelled her to take the veil when they seized her possessions because they thought she was giving too much away in charity, but she was reinstated through the offices of her daughter-in-law, queen Edith (VMRA, 8-9; VMRP, 11-12).[38] In both cases things went badly for the king as divine punishment until he was reconciled with his mother. In the first life, the queen notes and resolves the problem directly; in the second, priests and other princes urge the queen to admonish the king to recall his mother to her position in the kingdom for the good of the land. In both lives, the wife's influence over her husband is recognized as good for the country; she moves him to mercy (VMRA, 5) and he acknowledges her role himself at his death: "you calmed our wrath and gave us useful counsel in all things, you very often called us back from iniquity to justice and zealously admonished us to be merciful to the oppressed" (VMRP, 8).

In her life as queen mother, Matilda is most active in her lavish charity to the sick and the poor and her devout, even fanatic, religious observance, but at the same time she does not neglect her son's secular needs. After the reconciliation, his life becomes more like his father's, implicitly because of her influence (VMRA, 10); together they found church institutions (not an exclusively religious endeavor), and her prayers help him to be victorious in Italy (VMRA, 13). She preserves family history by presenting the list of the names of their dead to her granddaughter abbess Matilda of Quedlinburg to remember their souls (VMRP, 26). In the later life written for

Henry—and this is a major difference from the earlier life—she becomes a prophet of his accession and an advocate for his line, descended from her favorite son, Henry, who was named for his father. In each generation, her preference is for the one who bears that name, and her hope is that eventually the name will return to the royal office. The implication is that the present Henry II owes his succession to his sainted great-grandmother and therefore will attend to her deepest wish, that her posterity care for the younger convent she founded, Nordhausen.

The rivalry among the most important royal institutions for women, Gandersheim, Quedlinburg, Nordhausen, and Essen, seems to underlie all the histories produced by them. Corbet (36) suggests that Hrotsvit mentions the revered mother of her protagonist, queen Matilda, only briefly, because of her role in the foundation of what would be the major rival to Gandersheim, Quedlinburg. Abbess Matilda of Essen, a granddaughter of Otto I through his son by Edith and thus a niece of Matilda of Quedlinburg and the first cousin once removed of abbess Gerberga of Gandersheim, worked hard at building up the artistic and literary reputation of her monastery to "rival the splendour of Gandersheim, Quedlinburg and Nordhausen," in the words of Van Houts (61). As the last surviving member of Liudulf's line, she commissioned or requested a history of her distinguished English forebears from an English cousin, AEthelweard, who seems to have adapted the *Anglo-Saxon Chronicle* into Latin for her.[39] The work was certainly intended to serve the prestige of her monastery and its abbess, but it could not have hurt AEthelweard to call attention to his heritage and prestigious relations, as he implies by his enthusiastic acceptance of the commission. He composed the *Chronicon* celebrating her glorious lineage in response to a letter which he says he "desired, . . . clasped . . . to my soul, I have not merely read it, but have laid it away in the treasury of my heart." His work emphasizes their common descent and the importance of women and marriages in their heritage, but otherwise, like its Anglo-Saxon source, it sees history primarily in terms of notable events like battles and successions.

AEthelweard and presumably Matilda intend the work for a larger audience, not only her nuns, whom he mentions in the prologue to book 4 ("deus . . . conservet te . . . tecumque socias tuas"), but men as well, if they are not unworthy (*indigni*) and read in love ("caritate suademus cunctos preposita legi," *Chronicon*, 4.2). But Matilda is his prime audience. He addresses her directly throughout, imagining her reading the work aloud to others "so that attention may be increased by the gentle voice of the reader and the desire of the listener to hear" (prologue 1); unable to include everything, he leaves it to the wise reader to select other, deeper passages from holy and secular history (prologue 2). He exhorts her, "darling of all my desire" ("omni desiderii mei charissima"), not to find the long reading tedious, "for to you above all I dedicate it. The more my mind travels regions afar, the more the spirit of love is engendered nearer by" (prologue 3). Apologizing for the quantity of material to the "dearest sister of my desire," he asks her not to judge him too severely, but "as these things were written in our love for you, so may they be read in your love for us" (prologue 4).

Though AEthelweard says he has already written to her about their common family and the migration of one part from England to Germany, he proposes to set it in the context of world history, beginning from the beginning. First he sets forth their common genealogy: king AEthelwulf had five sons, including AEthelweard's ancestor, king AEthelred, and king Alfred, from whom Matilda is descended. Alfred sent his daughter AElfthryth to Germany to marry Baldwin (II of Flanders), and they had four children, two sons and two daughters, all named in the text;[40] indeed, Matilda's neighbor count Arnulf descends from AElfthryth. Of Alfred's granddaughters (children of Edward the Elder), two were sent to Gaul, Eadgyfu to marry king Charles, Eadhild to marry duke Hugo; two others were sent by their brother AEthelstan to Otto for him to choose, the episode related by Hrotsvit in the *Gesta Ottonis*. The one he chose was Matilda's ancestor Eadgyth (Edith); the other married a king near the Alps, about whom AEthelweard has no further information. He expects Matilda to find out about that family for him, since it is her family connection and she is not far from them—and, as Van Houts notes (67), it is woman's task to keep track of members of the family, past or present.

The first of the four books runs from the creation to early Christianity in Britain, the second from the arrival of Augustine to Byrhtric, king of the West Saxons. In the course of book 2, AEthelweard mentions two women of some importance, one secular, one religious: Seaxburh, widow of the king of the West Saxons (Cenwalh), who succeeded him in 672 and ruled twelve months (2.7), and Hilda, abbess of Whitby, who died in 680 (2.8); the book ends with the marriage of Offa's daughter Eadburh to Byrhtric (2.20). In book 3, AEthelweard mentions that marriage again (3.1) and notes two other marriages, one of their ancestor AEthelwulf to the daughter of Charles the Bald (great-granddaughter of Charlemagne) (3.4). The fourth and last book, in which AEthelweard is least dependent on his source, deals most directly with their family. AEthelweard breaks into the middle of chapter 2 to speak directly to Matilda when he comes to their common ancestors, the sons of AEthelwulf, embracing the zeal of her sincerity, interrupting the flow of his work not of necessity but in love, rededicating the work to her, and rejecting other readers as unworthy, unless they too receive it in love (4.2). He repeats that AEthelwulf's wife was a daughter of Charles of France, notes the death (in 888) of queen AEthelswith (4.3) and much later (in 917) the death and burial place of AEthelflæd, the king's sister (4.4), and then of queen AElfgifu (wife of king Edmund), who was later sanctified (*sanctificatur*); miracles have occurred at her tomb in the monastery known as Shaftesbury up to the present day (4.6). This royal "saint" is, perhaps fittingly in a work composed for an abbess of royal extraction on both sides, related to the major royal dynasties of western Europe, the last woman to be named.

There is one other secular history connected with the Saxon imperial house, also motivated at least in part by the welfare of a monastery, which should be mentioned here, Donizo's life of countess Matilda of Tuscany (1046-1115). Matilda was, through her maternal grandmother, Matilda of Swabia, sister of empress Gisela, a first cousin once removed of Henry III and second cousin of Henry IV. She was also the heir to her father's vast holdings in Italy and to those she and her mother acquired by marriage with the dukes of Lorraine; she administered them first with her mother, then on her own. Matilda was the major imperial feudatory in Italy, a force in imperial-papal politics, a supporter of the reform papacy and close friend of Gregory VII, and a mediator between him and her cousin the emperor.[41] She was a secular ruler with close ties to the church but not a saint, and so the life portrays her, though Donizo does suppress her two marriages and one pregnancy and treats her as a kind of virgin queen.[42] She offers a striking example of a woman who inherited land and power, who ruled over large territories, put down rebellions, and took part in major events. Since her life has not been translated and little has yet been written of her in English, I will discuss the biography in some detail.

The life was written by Donizo, priest and monk of the monastery of Canossa, founded by her family. He emphasizes the devotion of her family to the monks and presents the fortress of Canossa as the symbol of the family and its strength, clearly appealing to her and her heirs to support it for their own good. Donizo inscribes himself in an acrostic at the end of the two books ("Presbiter hunc librum finxit monachusque Donizo," 2.1358-99).[43] He inscribed Matilda at the beginning as the daughter of Boniface and Beatrice, now handmaid of God and worthy daughter of Peter ("Filia Mathildis Bonefacii Beatricis nunc ancilla Dei filia digna Petri," 1.1-61). Donizo's stated intent was to glorify her life and deeds and the deeds of her ancestors in verse for her, but as he explains sadly in an epilogue added after her death, she died before he could present it to her. Although Donizo mentions as his models earlier prose histories (of the Franks, presumably Gregory of Tours, and the Lombards, presumably Paul the Deacon), he chooses to write in verse, probably thinking of Virgil, whom he cites (1.682, 685), and certainly intending a greater compliment to Matilda with the more exalted style.[44] Noting that Matilda's honor throughout the world is greater than her forebears', Donizo declares that he wants posterity to know such a ruler/ruling lady ("Posteritas nostra tantam dominam volo noscat," 1.57), a woman "to be venerated and loved" ("veneranda Mathildis amanda," 1.60). She combines the secular and religious virtues in a perfect balance: Donizo praises her exercise of the four cardinal virtues in her rule, prudence, temperance, justice with piety, and fortitude, at the beginning of the first book, emphasizing her public role: "sua temperat acta ducatrix" (1.44), "indicis observat caelestis iura timenda: / fortis in adversis" (1.46-7); he praises her theological virtues at the beginning of the second book. She is the heir and culmination of a family tradition of devotion to justice and peace, loyalty to kings and emperors who are not always grateful or deserving, and support of their religion, which never wavers.

The impregnable fortress of Canossa, which her family built and which symbolizes them, speaks in the poem for the family and seems to represent the formidable countess herself—a mighty woman, often besieged but never taken (1.279-429). Canossa begins her role in the family history as the refuge of a wronged queen, the heroic Adelaide of Hrotsvit's *Gesta Ottonis:* when the widow of king Lothar escapes from Berengar, with the help of a girl and a priest, it is to Canossa that she comes for refuge. The story differs from Hrotsvit's in certain details, which make Adelaide's role even more active: after the priest makes a hole in the wall and extracts the two women, supplies them with men's clothes, and brings them to a lake, where he negotiates with a fisherman to take them across, the queen takes over. It is she who decides to ask the bishop of Reggio for help, and he suggests Canossa, the fortress of his knight, Atto (Matilda's ancestor), which will be secure against Berengar. From Canossa, Adelaide sends to the pope, asking advice, but suggesting that she be married to Otto. Pope John agrees and Atto acts as the mediator between Otto and Adelaide, a detail for which there is apparently no historical evidence; after the marriage, Atto is besieged by Berengar, but resists successfully and is rewarded by Otto.

Canossa tells her own story, describing how Atto raised her walls, and protected them with the relics of two saints, a man and a woman (appropriately named Victor and Corona); she debates with the city of Mantua (1.597ff.), accusing her of having stolen the bodies of Canossa's lords who should have been buried within her walls. Donizo seems to envisage Canossa as a kind of monument to the family, a symbol of their impregnability, a shrine to be tended by his fellow monks. The debate is staged to embarrass Mantua, a city which had rebelled against Matilda and resisted her rule for many years. Canossa reminds her that she may be a city, but she has little honor; that she must fear every rebel, while Canossa need fear no king; that her church is subject to the patriarch of Aquileia, while Canossa's is directly under the pope, that even Virgil, Mantua's native poet, spoke against her.

In her history of the family, Canossa carefully names and identifies all the women: Atto's wife, Hildegard, was a learned governor (*gubernatrix,* ruler, director), a prudent, upright counselor, often persuading her husband to better things, like founding a monastery (1.430-4); their son Tedaldus, who succeeded his father, married a woman apparently of higher rank, Guillia, called duchess (*ducatrix*, 1.452), who pleased high and low with her piety.[45] Their son and heir, Boniface, Matilda's father, married twice: first, Richilde (daughter of the count palatine, Giselbert), who gave much charity to the poor (1.521) but died childless; then the "great Beatrice" ("magna Beatrix," 1.782), Matilda's mother, who was of royal descent.[46] Beatrice is described by comparison with biblical women (Leah, Rachel, Sara), as Boniface is compared to biblical heroes. Donizo goes out of his way to present Boniface and Beatrice as equals ("pares"): just as their names begin with the same letter, B, they are equal in goodness, resemble each other in nobility, and both are blessed by Olympus (1.787-94). He enriches her and is enriched by her (1.813); he holds servants, male and female, castles, and towns through her, he is lord of Gaul through her (1.814-15). And Matilda (their only surviving child) is the worthy heir of both. Matilda resembled both parents, with her mother's features and her father's color; the honor of her father, the love of her mother, she is the glory of both (1.839). Promising that Matilda will have her own "felix carmen" in time, Donizo in the voice of Canossa devotes the rest of book 1 to the deeds of her parents: Boniface's military achievements in support of emperor Conrad II and the attempt of the ungrateful Henry II to capture him; Boniface's interest in divine matters, his love for the clergy, but particularly monks, and his acceptance of penance for having followed the German custom of selling churches; after his death, twenty-four years of prudent rule by Beatrice, her careful tutoring of "lofty Matilda, modest in mind" ("excelsam Mathildim mente modestam," 1.1144), with whom she founded monasteries, both of them venerating monks more than other clerics; and the opposition of "learned Beatrice" ("docta Beatrix," 1.1177) to the antipope of the young emperor Henry IV and her mediation between him and the new pope, Gregory VII.

Henry is presented as a villain whose own mother, Agnes, saw him as a dragon in her womb (1.1163-65). Donizo suppresses Agnes's antichurch role during her regency, blaming the young Henry for actions which were probably carried out by his mother, and emphasizes her later help as mediator between the pope and her son. The two women, Beatrice and Agnes, are credited with working for peace in the kingdom (1.1226-1354), though Henry kept going back to his bad ways, despite promises to the pope through his mother. Through all the troubles between emperor and pope, whatever others did, Beatrice and Matilda, the "great countesses" ("Comitissae / Magnae," 1.1348-49, the enjambment emphasizing the adjective) remained firm as rock; they were saddened when the king went the wrong way, but they never deserted the pope. The first book ends with the death of Beatrice, buried in Pisa to the grief of Canossa, whose last words express her hope of receiving Matilda's remains, "austere Matilda, the celebrated lady, whose uprightness is known to all" ("severam / Mathil-dim, claram dominam, probitate notata / omni," 1.1383-85).

The second book is devoted to Matilda. If the first flowers and shines with the renowned dukes, the second will flower and shine even more vigorously with the deeds of "ducatrix" Matilda (2.9-12). The book begins with Matilda's theological virtues, her love for Christ and his modest servants, her hatred for vice—she knows how to soothe the pious and terrify the evil (2.25)—and her learning. She composes letters (that is, she is literate in Latin), she knows the German language and speaks it as well as French. She acts always with discretion; her fame extends to all kingdoms, from Greece and Russia across Europe to Britain (2.28-37).[47] Canossa, who loved her ancestors, loves Matilda even more, for she exalted and cherished the castle, always restoring it and making its name grow in Rome.

Matilda is treated as a major force in the relations between emperor and pope, the emperor seeking the help of his cousin Matilda, asking for a meeting with the pope in Lombardy, and the pope agreeing to what Matilda asked. Both came to Canossa, which glories in having been the site of such a summit meeting, with pope, emperor, secular and religious princes of Italy, Gaul, and Germany seeking terms of peace.[48] After three days of fruitless discussion, the emperor begged Hugh of Cluny to help, but the abbot said no one could help if not Matilda, so the emperor begged her on his knees, reminding her of their close relation: "consobrina [maternal cousin] valens, fac me benedicere vade" (2.97). When Matilda spoke for him, the pope believed her and accepted Henry's penance—standing barefoot in the snow—blessed him, and made peace. The Lombard bishops persuaded Henry to new plots, but Matilda learned of them and foiled them. Donizo describes the conflict as between the emperor, goaded to evil by Guibert of Parma, and the pope, supported in the right action by Matilda, with Guibert and Matilda as the active figures. She resisted Henry and Guibert with military force, money, and writings: "she writes to the Germans and princes dear to her, to shun the errors of the rebel king" (2.296-97), and so generates fruit for God (2.298). Her home became a refuge for religious enemies of the empire. When cities of Lombardy and Italy rebelled against Matilda, she put down their revolt: "illustrious Matilda was a terror to them all" ("Inclita Mathildis terror fuit omnibus illis," 2.365). Matilda made the church her heir, and the pope declared the church of Canossa free from any other authority (2.173-79), an independence the author is presumably anxious to preserve; after Gregory died, the next pope wrote to Matilda, presumably seeking help, even more often (2.330).

As Henry becomes a more serious enemy of the holy church and of lady Matilda, "so worthy of love" (2.439-40), Matilda is more closely identified with the church. When the emperor seized some of her land, attacking her city, Mantua, its citizens betrayed Matilda as Judas did Christ (2.478-80), but the *ducatrix* remained firm as adamant and the bishop fled to the "great catholic countess" ("grandem Comitissam catholicam," 2.553). The king's attempt to take Canossa by surprise failed and he lost his banner; that was taken as a sign of his defeat (2.718), and the countess began to win back what she had lost. Popes held synods under her auspices (2.763ff. and 1089ff.), and pope Urban II preached a crusade which Matilda supported and which drew participants of both sexes (2.814).

In her many services to the church, Matilda played the role of a series of biblical heroines: she was a Martha and a Mary when she kept the pope safe from the emperor for three months (2.169-72); attentive to the teachings of the pope and Christ, the wise countess listened like the queen of Sheba to the blessed words of Solomon (2.188-89); when Henry's second wife, Praxedes, left her husband and took refuge with Matilda, the countess was a Deborah and a Jahel defeating Sisara (2.743-50); when Henry attempted unsuccessfully to take Nogara, Matilda was a Judith defeating Holofernes (2.796-99); and when Henry's son Conrad left his father and put himself under the broad wings of Matilda, she was an Esther to Henry's Haman (2.846-51).[49] Though she continued to support the church under Paschal, Matilda, who had always been prompt, strong, and vigilant in her response to the needs of the church and fervid in war even against the king (2.1069), toward the end of her life sought quiet and happily received the new king's messages of peace (2.1095-96). Donizo reminds us how she alone had often stood against the king, a report confirmed by other contemporary historians, how the German princes had wondered at her, a woman (2.1152-56).[50] When the pope agreed to crown Henry V in Rome, the king came seeking peace and when new trouble broke out, Henry met with Matilda, made her his viceroy for Liguria (2.1255), and helped persuade even the Mantuans to return to her fold (2.1260ff.).

Though Donizo understandably concentrates on the most public, political and military of Matilda's actions, he also alludes to her role as a patron: after the death of Anselm, bishop of Lucca, Matilda had books compiled about him, records of miracles that occurred at his tomb, lives by Bardone and Rangerius; the latter's dedication of a second book (*Liber de anulo et baculo*) to Matilda is quoted at length by Donizo (2.395-434). Donizo does not mention another work that was probably written for Matilda or while the author was taking refuge with her, Bonizo of Sutri's *Liber ad amicum* (c. 1086), perhaps because Bonizo later turned against her. The *Liber* discusses the problems facing the church and contrasts Matilda's mother, Beatrice, a lone woman fighting the enemies of the church, with the empress Agnes, who, deceived like a woman and "with feminine license," assents to the evil of the antipope; the book ends with praise of the warlike Matilda and an exhortation to the soldiers of God to imitate her.[51] Donizo mentions at the end of his poem that Matilda had a large supply of good books in all the arts and sciences, that she made gifts to monasteries and churches of land, books, pallia, and jewels. She helped the poor, conquered priests by love, and gave studious attention night and day to sacred psalms and religious offices in which she was expert. Not even bishops were more zealous (2.1369), and she was particularly close to wise clerics (2.1367). She waged God's wars, conquering because she stood defenseless (2.1373). And finally she left everything to Peter.

When Matilda died before he could present the book to her, Donizo added an epilogue to express his amazement and distress at the news; he envisaged the end of honor for Italy, the ruin of churches, the corruption of mores. Addressing Matilda in his grief, he remembers her religious zeal, her desire to fast, weak with love, until priests forbade it, her generous charity, her orders that numerous servants be freed after her death (2.1487-88), her long illness (seven months), and her death at sixty-nine (in 1115) with the crucifix in hand, offering herself to God. He prays for her to all the saints she had served, but he addresses his last words to her temporal heir, the emperor Henry V and his wife, Matilda, when they came to Canossa in 1116. Donizo points out that the empress is also a Matilda, probably hoping she will identify with her illustrious cousin by marriage and be sympathetic to the monks' cause. This Matilda, the daughter of Henry I of England, would have a history written in support of her claim to the throne by another monk, William of Malmesbury, which I will come back to at the end of this chapter.

Two English queens, Emma and Edith, had already commissioned histories to serve their cause shortly before the Norman conquest, in hopes of retaining power through a son or a brother. Emma (died 1052), queen of AEthelred and of Cnut and queen mother of both Harthacnut and Edward the Confessor, commissioned an unnamed monastic to write a history ostensibly in praise of Cnut but also and primarily to justify her actions and her continuing role in English politics; it is known as the *Encomium Emmae Reginae*.[52] Edith commissioned a life of her husband, Emma's son Edward, to further the chances of one of her brothers. Like countess Matilda, Emma is presented by the monk who writes for her as a virgin when she marries Cnut ("Placuit ergo regi verbum *virginis,* et iusiurando facto, *virgini* placuit voluntas regis," *Encomium,* 2.16.15-16), though she too had been married and had living sons, and she is cast as a central figure in the history, responsible for the order of succession. Historic facts are not just exaggerated, however; they are severely distorted in this life. Without directly lying, the author allows us to believe that Cnut is Emma's first husband, that Harthacnut is her first son, that her (older) sons by AEthelred are really Cnut's, and that Cnut's older son Harold was illegitimate and low-born.[53]

It seems clear that Emma did not wish to be associated with the king who had been put to flight by the Danes and was anxious to justify her support of her son by the Dane over the claims of her sons by the English king. She wants to be seen as a "peace-weaver" (Eleanor Searle), a "bearer of legitimacy" (Eric John), but beyond that, there is much disagreement over the intended audience and message of the work.[54] Was it addressed to the Flemish, as Felice Lifshitz argues, or to the English, as Eric John and Miles Campbell argue? Is it supporting Harthacnut or Edward? Is it an attack on Harold or Godwin or even Edward (who seized his mother's lands shortly after her accession)? All we know of the author is that he was in a Flemish monastery, where he was a witness to the visiting Cnut's generosity and to Emma's while she was in exile. One assumes that the details he gives of English history come from Emma and not from his own knowledge. Of Emma, we know that she was the daughter of a Norman father and a Danish mother, and therefore may have been mistrusted by the English when she was AEthelred's queen (Searle, 284–85), but that she did persuade Harthacnut to name his half-brother Edward as his successor (286).

The author says that his work praises Emma by praising Cnut, as Virgil praised his emperor in the *Aeneid* even though he scarcely mentioned him. Who could deny, he asks, that this work gives praise to the queen, when it is not only written for her glory but she also seems to obtain the greater part of that glory in it? (Argumentum, 7–12). Amidst lavish praise of her ("preeminent over all in her sex by elegance of customs," Prologus, 1–2, "her virtue shining brighter than the sun," Prol.5), and the assurance that he would die to advance her cause (Prol.6–7), he carefully establishes Emma's influence over the text: "as you order, I long to give posterity the remembrance of things done;" "since I see that I cannot avoid writing, I believe I must choose either to be subject to the various judgments of men or remain silent about those things which are ordered to me by you, lady queen."[55] He seems to be worried about the issue of truth and audience reception of his work. He insists that history requires truth, because any error or embellishment of truth makes the audience suspicious, and he would rather be accused of chattering (*loquacitatis*) by the envious than let the truth be hidden (Prol.18–23, 26–27). This could simply be a topos, but his insistence on it suggests that he is aware of the propagandistic nature of his assignment. Consciously or not, and it is hard to believe it is unconscious, he does distort history to present his patron and her sons in the most favorable light.[56]

The author suggests in the summary that precedes the work that divine will favors Emma and her family: England would probably not have been free of war when Cnut succeeded his father if he had not made a marriage favored by God with this "most noble queen" (Arg.22–24); though their son was ruling in Denmark when Cnut died and his kingdom was usurped, divine vengeance restored the kingdom to the one who should have had it

(Arg.28–29). God's will is reenforced by a pattern of family devotion, particularly between brothers and sons to their mother: Harthacnut, "obeying in all things his mother's counsels," obtained the kingdom and shared the dignity and wealth of the kingdom with his brother (Arg.30–32). The pattern is hinted at even in Cnut's early history: he and his brother showed great affection for each other and were able to differ on serious matters without rancor (2.2); together they prepared the army to reconquer England and went to bring their mother back to Denmark (2.2), and before Cnut departed he took leave of his mother and brother (2.4).

Once he was established, Cnut sought an appropriate wife through various kingdoms and cities and found Emma, "very wealthy in family and substance, but with the delight of beauty and prudence, most outstanding among all women of that time as a famous queen" (2.16.5–7). She was also, though the author does not say so explicitly, politically astute. She refused to marry him until he swore that no son of his by anyone else would succeed him, because "it was said that he had sons by another woman" (2.16.11–14), a disingenuous reference to his legitimate heir, whose paternity the author denies. The king accepted Emma's terms and the author praises her prudent providing for her own.[57] After a happy marriage with such joy on both sides that it is hard to believe ("difficile creditu est quanta repente in utrisque alteri de altero exorta sit magnitudo gaudii," 2.17.2–3), Cnut died, and Harold seized the throne. Though some of the English preferred him to "the noble sons of the distinguished queen," the archbishop refused to consecrate Harold while Emma's sons were living, stating, "Cnut committed *them* to my faith, I owe this faith to *them*, and I will keep it to *them* faithfully" (3.1.17–18), thus reinforcing the idea that they were all Cnut's sons. Harold forged a letter purporting to be from Emma inviting her sons to return (33.2–3), and when Alfred came, Harold had him tortured and murdered. This deed is described in detail, with apologies to the mother for adding to her pain, but in fact the author glorifies the death by presenting it as a martyrdom ("martyrium narrando," 3.6.2, "finemque hujus martyrii," 3.6.15, "innocenter enim fuit martyrizatus," 3.6.20), complete with miracles at the tomb. Thus Emma has a patron in heaven in place of the son on earth, not to say strong political ammunition against her enemies.[58]

Emma went into exile in Flanders and worked to regain her position through her two remaining sons.[59] Edward came from Normandy at her summons but refused to help, saying the English had sworn no oath to him (3.8), so she sent for Harthacnut, who prepared to come to avenge his brother and obey his mother (3.8.11–12), an attitude that implies he was more fit to succeed his father than Edward would have been. Meanwhile Harold, "the unjust invader of the kingdom" (3.9.17), conveniently died; Emma and Harthacnut set sail together ("Hardecnuto materque," 3.11.1) and were received by the Angles as king and queen ("regi reginaeque," 3.13.2). The tale ends with Emma's greatest coup: Harthacnut sends for Edward with fraternal love, and together the brothers assume royal power, ruling harmoniously with their mother; the covenant of maternal and fraternal love flourishes inviolable, "mater amboque filii regni paratis commodis nulla lite intercedente utuntur. . . . hic inviolabile viget faedus materni fraternique amoris" (3.14.1–3).[60]

An anonymous life of Emma's son, Edward the Confessor, was written for his queen, Edith, around the time of his death.[61] Like her mother-in-law before her, Edith has the author slant history to favor her and her family, her father Godwin and her brothers, particularly Harold and Tostig, the king's protectors, putting the best light on their actions and on the royal marriage. It was probably begun before the childless Edward's death, in support of one of Edith's brothers—Harold did succeed Edward briefly— despite the fact that the king had named the Norman William as his successor, but its stated aim is to praise Edith, the poet's patron, who, he says, restored him to life, and who presumably wished to preserve a position of influence in the kingdom after Edward's death. If it was finished after the Norman Conquest, Edith, as the only survivor of the Godwin family left in England, may have wanted to be seen and called on as a potential source of peace between the Normans and the English, at the very least, to change her reputation from a partisan of herself and her own family to a devoted wife and dedicated queen.[62]

The work, written in prose and verse, begins with a conversation between the poet and his muse, which suggests a literary rather than political motivation, but only thinly disguises the main purpose. The muse may well represent the queen; she certainly encourages the author to bestir himself in the midst of poverty and envy and write what will be the first life of Edward. Whatever she orders, the poet declares himself willing to serve in praise of the lady "to whom you especially vowed me" (*Vita AEduuardi*, 30–31). He recalls how she commiserated with him, fixed his "feet" (metric as well as physical?), brought him back from death, and restored his abandoned pens. The muse tells the poet to celebrate the queen while he lives as the king's more-than-equal: "another part of the man, the same kind of probity, deeper in wit and swift in counsel; she has no equal anywhere; with twin body, they are considered one person" ("altera pars hominis, species eadem probitatis; / altius ingenium, consiliumque citum; / convenit nusquam terrarum par sibi quicquam; / corpore nam gemino unus habentur homo," 67–70). The poet replies that nothing is more pleasing to him than to speak the praises of those who, and primarily the lady, protect him (91–92).

The story begins with Edith's father, Godwin, his service to Cnut, his prudence, loyalty, and general affability, and his relation by marriage.[63] In this version, Godwin persuaded the English to accept Edward as their king when their servitude to barbarians ended and then Edward married his daughter.[64] The poet describes the queen, by whose counsel peace bound the kingdom on all sides, as worthy of her husband (296-97), who was devoted to God's cause and to justice, but her story cannot be dissociated from her family's. Unfortunately, we are told, the king surrounded himself with French friends who did not get on with his native advisors and Godwin was the victim of their malice. When Edward appointed a Norman (Robert of Jumièges) to the archbishopric of Canterbury though the monks had elected someone else, they sought Godwin's support for their candidate, so when Robert got the see he sought revenge on Godwin by accusing him of the murder of Edward's brother Alfred, though the poet claims that Harold, illegitimate son of Cnut, was responsible. Godwin was forced to leave the country and, not satisfied with the exile, Robert persuaded the king to separate from his wife. Edward, we are told, balked at the idea of divorce, but to keep the peace he let Edith retire for a year of prayers and tears to the abbey of Wilton, where she had been educated. This did more harm to the court, the author comments, than the departure of the duke, because Edith was a moderator in all royal counsels and the principle of all honesty, preferring what was appropriate to the king to any praise or wealth (493-98). This is the only hint in the life of her political role, though her interventions on behalf of her family were probably substantial.[65] Instead, Edith is presented as an innocent victim; the king's treatment of her is compared to the stoning of Susanna (509-11). Eventually, Godwin and his sons returned to popular acclaim, restoring Edith to the royal bedchamber and, we are assured, continuing to support the king; after Godwin's death, his sons kept the kingdom going, despite the (considerable) problems between them, which the author describes as obliquely (but honestly) as possible, with allusions to Thebes, Cain and Abel, and the banquet of Thyestes.

Edward, meanwhile, led a quiet life of hunting and religious devotion, a gentle "Christicola," taking no delight in the pomp of royalty which the offices of his royal wife supplied, but grateful to her for her service (905ff.). Edith is presented both as a model, demure Christian wife and as a great patron of the church. She not only did not hold her husband back from dispensations to the kingdom's poor and weak but urged him on and seemed to precede him in many things—while he gave, she lavished ("cum ipse interdum daret, illa largiebatur," 920), to his honor. Though her royal seat was by custom at the king's side, she preferred to sit at his feet, except in church and at the royal table, unless he invited or compelled her to sit beside him (922ff.). In sum, a woman to be set before all noble matrons or persons of royal and imperial dignity as an example of virtue and honesty, both in Christian worship and in worldly dignity (927ff.). Edward built a noble edifice at the abbey of Westminster, where he wanted to be buried (974ff.), and Edith, in emulation of his action and out of her own devotion, built a stone monastery for the nuns at Wilton, where his ancestor, her namesake Edith, was venerated (1014ff.). This is the one episode in which the poet shows a forceful intensity in the queen. Edith had a special purpose in endowing this building, believing as she did that it was much harder for women to raise money to build: "nowhere were alms more soundly given than where the weak sex, less effective in building, feels the anguish of penury more."[66] Church building provided a happy rivalry between king and queen, pleasing to God, in which she finished sooner, having begun more modestly. The blessed heroine ("benedicta virago," 1044, the choice of the noun suggesting a stronger personality than the poet has otherwise portrayed) pushed ahead for the dedication. Even when the devil's envy caused a fire which destroyed almost everything but the church, the mind of the faithful woman was not terrified. Instead of drawing back, she accelerated her plans, and the dedication was properly celebrated with a huge multitude of dignitaries and the faithful. Here the author inserts an epithalamium to the Virgin (1066ff.), a tacit compliment to the queen, who is presumably also a virgin.

Edward's final illness is attributed to the loss of his mainstay, Edith's brother Tostig, as a result of new rebellions; without him he is unable to control the pride of the wicked, falls sick, and never recovers. The queen too is unable to act; confounded by the dissension of her brothers, Tostig's exile, and her husband's impotence, Edith was not able to carry out her counsel "in which the grace of God would have been evident." She who was accustomed to support the king in adversities, to dispel them with effective counsel and keep him serene, now gave the signs of future ills with her tears, by which the whole palace fell inconsolably into mourning (1203ff.). The author is loath to describe the war—such a page full of death would not please the queen (and would remind the audience of the destructive actions of her family)—and the muse, speaking one senses for the queen, urges him on to better matters, the beauty of Edward in his life and death, reminding him that the queen supports him and that whatever he writes is to her praise and honor; no page will be more pleasing to her than the descriptions of Edward. She reminds the author how the queen spoke to him of Edward as a father and of herself as a daughter (1341–42); he was, in fact, at least twenty years older. If he rejects the muse (and the queen) now, who will raise him, who reward him? That is, his fortunes are tied to hers. She reminds him that his will be the first life, that the book is dedicated to the queen, that the description of the man God favored alive and declares to live in heaven will please the queen. So the poet carries on, with a sad heart, orphaned from such a lord, perhaps identifying himself with the queen in his filial relation to Edward, and finally moves into a hagiographic mode.

Clearly the highest compliment he can pay the queen is to paint her husband as a saint, making their nonmarriage a virtue rather than an embarrassment and putting the responsibility for it on God's will. He claims that Edward was selected and divinely consecrated by God, that he conserved the dignity of that consecration with his chastity and led his whole life in true innocence, for which God glorified him with miracles in this life and the next.[67] After his death, God reveals that Edward is a saint living in heaven and still living in the world through the miracles performed at his tomb. Just before he dies, with the queen sitting on the ground holding his feet in her lap, Edward has a prophetic vision of the future, of the evils his land will suffer for its sins; and the queen and those who fear God know that the Christian religion has been violated in their land. The king thanks the queen for her devotion as a daughter, which will bring her eternal felicity, and commends her with the kingdom to her brother Harold, calling her his "lady and sister" ("domina et sorore," 1563–64), suggesting that she is to retain a public position after his death.[68] The author leaves us with a picture of Edith as a woman who accepted her husband's religious preference (that it might have been sexual is not suggested) and accommodated her public life to it. He suggests that she played an important role as counselor and mediator within the court, a likely role for one who was both wife of the king and daughter and sister of some of his most powerful native nobles, but gives no details about it, as if more attention to Edith's political role would have thrown her husband's ineffectiveness into sharper relief and undercut the author's purpose of glorifying her by emphasizing Edward's saintliness.

Edith's brother Harold was in position to seize the throne when Edward died, but he lost it to William of Normandy within the year. The dynasty that William established in England would include a series of women active in public life and in commissioning the writing of histories. Queen Matilda, wife of Henry I and descendant of English kings, countess Adela, sister of Henry I and mother of king Stephen, and empress Matilda, daughter of Matilda and Henry I, chosen heir of her father and mother of Henry II, all had significant roles to play in the public sphere, and all had (Latin) histories written for them.[69]

The stories of Adela and the two Matildas are closely connected by their family ties, and even their patronage of histories overlaps to some extent. William of Malmesbury wrote the *Gesta regum Anglorum* at the request of queen Matilda—it was the history of her family—and it was later presented by his fellow monks to the chosen heir to that line, her daughter empress Matilda; when Hugh of Fleury dedicated his history of modern French kings to empress Matilda, he mentioned that he had collected material on Roman emperors and French kings (presumably the *Historia ecclesiastica*) for her aunt Adela and that this work was a "supplement of that history." All three women were powerful figures in their public spheres who would have appreciated the accomplishments and struggles of the women in those histories and would probably have found a history that did not include such women lacking if not inaccurate; at the same time the presence of those historic models in the histories reinforced their own positions.

Adela, countess of Blois, was born after her father ascended the English throne. Her heritage through her mother, Matilda of Flanders, was even more distinguished, descent from French and English kings going back to Robert the Pious and Alfred. On both counts, Adela had particular prestige in the family of her husband, Stephen. She was co-ruler with him until he went on crusade in 1096, a venture she underwrote with her personal wealth, and then ruled as his regent until he died in 1102;[70] she continued to rule for their sons and even for her childless brother-in-law, Hugh, count of Troyes, while he was on crusade. Adela has been called "one of the most prestigious, influential, and effective power brokers in the turbulent secular and ecclesiastical politics of the late-eleventh and early-twelfth centuries."[71] Letters to her about her administration are extant from bishops Hildebert of Lavardin ("you administer as a woman who does not need the help of a man," PL171, ep.1.3); Ivo of Chartres, with whom there was some friction over secular interference with the clergy; and Anselm, who was grateful for her hospitality, protection, and negotiations during his exile. She retired to the convent of Marcigny in 1120 and died in 1137.

Many works of poetry and prose were written for Adela of Blois.[72] Hugh of Fleury wrote the *Historia ecclesiastica* for her, explicitly slanting it toward her interests. He sent it to her in 1110 with the assertion that "members of the female sex should not be deprived of knowledge of deep things, for [as we shall show clearly in the following text,] great industry of mind and the elegance of most upright morals have always existed among women."[73] In his prologue, Hugh praises Adela as "one of the foremost among princes of our time ("nostri aevi multis preponenda proceribus") for her generosity, probity, and erudition in letters, which is the great statesmanship (*civilitas*) of our people." He compiles the history to delight her and exhort her to do good—not that she is not already adorned with great virtues, but one can always be even better—and particularly as a monument/memorial to her name, to leave to posterity a record of her unceasing array of good works. Hugh justifies his writing such a work for a woman to those who might object with examples from religious history: Jerome's many writings honoring Paula and Eustochium, pope Gregory's sending four books of dialogues to Theudelinda, Christ teaching the woman who sat at his feet, better and more devoted even than Christ's own ministers.[74] Hugh's letter ends with a brief poem: "Live, be well, rejoice with most worthy praise / progeny of kings, column of clergy and people, / whom probity of customs and nobility of ancestors / adorn equally; may all prosperity yield to you." In the epilogue, Hugh repeats much of his praise, but adds that he has dedicated this compendious and honorable volume not to illiterate princes, for whom the literary art is an object of scorn, but deservedly to her. He notes that if her brothers are the heirs to her father's lands, she is the heir to his elegance of custom and affluence; Gaul, which is supported by her liberality, can bear witness to that.

In the history, as Kimberly LoPrete shows in her study of the *Historia ecclesiastica*, Hugh emphasizes the role of ruling and otherwise notable women, good and bad, selecting, using, or omitting appropriate details from his sources. He begins with Semiramis, who has to dress as a man in order to govern an unruly populace, who surpasses men as well as women in *virtus*, extends the borders of her realm, and rules long after the majority of her son, until he kills her. The Amazons, Scythian women who fought and governed their own lands under the rule of two queens, also expanded their territory, through Europe and Asia, where they founded cities as well. Despite the occasional defeat, by Hercules in battle, by Alexander in bed, they had a long and glorious history, including Penthe-silea's exploits in the Trojan war and Thamyris's revenge on Cyrus for her son's death.[75]

Women play less active roles among the Romans in Hugh's work, as they did in his sources, but they do play an important part in the dynastic succession of the imperial family by marriage, many of them formally recognized as Augustae, acting with their husbands or for minor sons. Justina, the Arian, was ultimately unsuccessful in her fight against ortho-doxy and Ambrose, but she had been in authority as recognized regent for some years. Irene ruled jointly with her son Constantine VI, making peace with the Arabs, defeating the Slavs, and negotiating with Charlemagne. Then she fell out with her son, imprisoned him, and ruled on her own for five years; though he came back with foreign help, he was so inept she was able to return once again as empress in her own name for five more years. When she is finally deposed, Hugh lets her make a rather heroic speech, accepting God's will and defying the faithless usurper. As LoPrete points out, it is thus a woman who voices "Hugh's oft-depicted moral of the divine source of all legitimate earthly rulership," in contrast to most West-ern historians, who saw her as an illegitimate ruler, allowing the Roman imperial dignity to be transferred to the Franks.[76]

Queen Matilda, married to Adela's brother Henry I, never had the power Adela exercised after her husband's death, but she too brought prestige to the marriage, acted as regent when he was away, and partici-pated in public affairs, particularly in relation to the church. Educated at Wilton, like Edith, Matilda was involved with the church, though always aware of the needs of the kingdom. She mediated for her husband with churchmen and secular rulers, like her son-in-law, Henry V. She was in correspondence with popes and bishops about the exile of her friend and advisor, Anselm of Canterbury, and other matters, including lay investi-ture. Ivo of Chartres commended her "virile strength in a feminine breast" (PL162, ep.174); Hildebert commended her intelligence and understanding in his letters and praised her virtues in his poetry, as Marbod of Rennes did. Anselm exchanged many letters with her, about his situation and the stand he was taking, but also about her treatment of the churches in her hands; and six of her letters to him are included among his, on the state of negotiations for his return and on her own feelings for and worries about him.[77]

Matilda commissioned at least two histories, a life of her mother, "saint" Margaret, from a monk of Durham who had known the family well, and a history of the kings of England, a more extended history of her family, from another monk, William of Malmesbury.[78] The life presents Margaret as a model queen who was consort and mother and considered a saint, like the Saxon Matilda. The monk of Durham acknowledges the commission from the queen because of that intimacy and congratulates her on wanting to have a permanent record of the life of her mother, whom she did not know well, which she could read rather than being satisfied with what she was told about her; he accepts despite the magnitude of the subject, out of obedience to her authority and love for her mother. Precious in her deeds as well as her name and family, Margaret ("pearl") is a descendant of native English kings. The monk notes the prowess of her grandfather Edmund Ironside and the religious devotion of her great-uncle Edward the Confessor, and mentions Edward's mother, Emma, and her father, count Richard of the Normans; though they were not related by blood to Margaret, they are a link with the family her daughter married into.

Margaret is presented as an active and effective queen in her public and private roles. She participated in religious and secular affairs; she was particularly concerned with justice and her orders were carried out, laws were disposed on her counsel, religion was advanced by her industry, and the people prospered (3). She was devout but intellectually alert; she is compared to Mary sitting at the Lord's feet, praised for her study of divine readings, but also her "acute subtlety of wit to understand anything, great tenacity of memory to retain it, and facility of gracious speech to express it" ("Inerat ei ad intelligendum quamlibet rem acuta ingenii subtilitas, ad retinendum multa memoriae tenacitas, ad proferendum gratiosa verborum facilitas," 3). The cares and tumults of the kingdom never kept her from her religious readings, and she regularly discussed or debated (*conserebat*) subtle questions with very learned men, none of whom was deeper in wit or clearer in expression. Indeed, the monk comments, it often happened that many who came to her learned went away more learned ("Evenit itaque saepius, ut ab ea ipsi doctores, multo quam advenerant, abcederent doctiores," 6). She worked to eradicate whatever was wrong in the Scottish church, arguing effectively at councils for proper (Roman) observances, citing the gospels and Paul (8). The debates are quoted at length, with Margaret having the last word because the others are unable to answer her, giving a vivid picture of Margaret as a public debater in the style of Saint Catharine.[79]

But her concerns were human as well as intellectual. When she walked or rode in public, widows and orphans flocked to Margaret for help (9), and with her husband she served the poor in the royal hall (10). Her husband (Matilda's father) was so devoted to her, according to the life, that though he could not read, he fondled the books he knew she loved (6). She combined sternness with playfulness, so she was loved and feared by all who served her, men and women (4);[80] and she made sure her children were brought up with suitable discipline (5). Though she was another Esther, trampling ornaments in her mind, nonetheless she made sure the royal halls were suitably ornamented and decorated for royal dignity (7). That is, for all her religious devotion, she was conscious of and attentive to her secular role and could therefore serve as an excellent model for her daughter as queen of England.

The *History of the Kings of England (Gesta Regum Anglorum)* which her daughter, queen Matilda, commissioned from William of Malmesbury is filled with active women who could serve as models for queens or saints, most to be imitated, some to be avoided, and much is made of the birth and family connections of women.[81] What is striking about the work is the large number of women whose actions are chronicled and the even larger number who are identified by name. The families of kings and other princes are usually listed beginning with the wife's parentage; then the daughters are named as well as sons, and their dispositions given, whom they married or what monasteries they went into (see 2.121, 126; 2.214; 3.276).[82] The importance of the woman's family is made particularly clear in a reference to king Godfrey of Jerusalem, son of Eustace of Boulogne but "more ennobled maternally by his mother, Ida [as Matilda's children were], who was descended from Charlemagne" (4.373). Some women are remarkable for their wealth, often bestowed generously in the building of churches and monasteries, but sometimes employed in secular causes: the mother of Henry I, another queen Matilda, is said to have supplied her son Robert with military forces out of her revenues (3.273); later Henry is said to be supported by the "blessing of his father, together with his maternal inheritance and immense treasures" (5.391).[83] Some women are active in other ways in support of their sons: Elfrida, wanting her son to be king, plotted and abetted the assassination of his half-brother Edward (the Elder), an infamous act, William comments, though he is careful to mention that she was faithful to her husband (2.162). In contrast, the French queen, mother of Odo and Henry, preferred her younger son for the throne as more able, though their father, Robert, favored the elder; since women persevere, she did not stop until she won over all the chief nobility with presents and promises, and Henry was crowned before his father died (2.187).[84]

William mentions a number of women who participated directly in their husband's or even brother's governments, some who ruled on their own: AEthelwulf held his foreign wife, Judith, in highest esteem, and placed her beside him on the throne against the custom of the West Saxons (who had reacted to the crimes of Offa's daughter, Edburga, with injunctions against the king's consort, 2.113); Cnut tried to conciliate the Angles by marrying the wife of their former king, assuming that in giving service to their accustomed lady (Emma), they would mind Danish rule less (2.181); Constance, a sister of Henry I who married Alan Fergant of Brittany, was so severe in her justice, we are told, that she incited the people to poison her (3.276).[85] AEthelfleda, sister of Edward (the Elder) and widow of AEthelred, who refused to marry again, perhaps because of a difficult birth, is described as a great help to her brother in counsels and no less in constructing cities, a most powerful heroine ("virago potentissima"), who protected men at home and terrified them abroad, whether by fortune or by her powers one could not easily tell (2.125). When Kenwalk, the seventh-century king of Wessex, died, he left the government of the kingdom to his wife, Seaxburh, "who did not lack the spirit for discharging such duties, to raise new armies, keep the old in service, rule her subjects with mercy, rage threateningly at her enemies, in short to do all things so that one could discern no [difference] but her sex; but life deserted her, breathing more than female spirits, after scarcely a year in power" (1.32).[86] But women are not necessarily done in by assuming male roles. The countess/marchioness Matilda (of Tuscany) actively retained the duchy in opposition to the empire, especially in Italy (4.373): a woman "forgetful of her sex," not unlike the ancient Amazons, a woman in armor who led her troops to battle, Matilda espoused the just cause of pope Urban against the empire and kept his throne secure for eleven years.[87]

If few women have the opportunity to rule alone, many have an influence on their ruling husbands or an active role as consorts.[88] When Edwin, exiled from Northumbria by his brother-in-law, took refuge with Redwald of East Anglia, it was Redwald's wife whose counsel gave him the strength ("uxori pectoris consiliis roboratus," 1.47) to withstand the brother-in-law's threats and keep faith with his friend. Ine, king of Wessex, went to Rome at the end of his life and gave himself to God, incited by his wife, who went with him to soothe his suffering and keep up his resolve by her example (1.37).[89]

It is not surprising, since William is a monk, that he makes much of the religious devotion of the women he describes. Many of them prefer God to marriage and either leave their husbands to retire to a monastery or refuse to marry in the first place. William frequently praises holy women: he speaks of a chorus of devoted women at Shaftesbury who "irradiate the lands with the brightness of their religion," who "through their prayers sustain the progress of the world which before vacillated in sins" (2.163);

if all virtues have not left the earth, they are to be found only in the hearts of nuns, women who, despite the weakness of their sex, vie in the preservation of continence and ascend triumphant to heaven (2.217-19). The history is filled with royal women virgins and saints, even a female genealogy of saints, which mentions the royal fathers but focuses on the women: the three daughters of Anna, king of the East Angles; Etheldrida, who married twice but was "a model of saintly continence" and was proclaimed a saint; Sexberga, who became a nun after her husband died; and Ethelberga, who was a nun and then an abbess. This Sexberga had two daughters, Earcongota, of whom Bede speaks (*Historia ecclesiastica* 3.8), and Ermenhilda, who married the king of the Mercians and then became a nun, following her mother as abbess at Ely, while her daughter Werburga was a holy virgin (2.214).

But William does not simply glorify holy women or model queens, triumphs to pursue and wisdom to imitate, he also gives examples of misfortunes to be avoided and folly to be scorned, as a medieval writer of history was supposed to.[90] He tells of a woman who participates in the death of her stepson (2.162), a sister who murders her brother (1.95), a woman who causes her husband to give up his faith (1.97), and the daughter of Offa, who persuaded her husband to destroy innocent people and poisoned those she could not falsely accuse (2.113), a woman of such uncontrolled lust that she left one husband to go to another several times (4.388). Though William does not whitewash the worst kinds of action or influence, he does give a balanced view, blaming men for their own actions where others have been quick to attribute them to the seductive powers of women.[91] When a king marries his stepmother, he has to overcome her sense of propriety (1.10). When an envoy of a king decides to keep for himself the woman he is inspecting for the king and lies about her, she is an unwitting victim of his treachery; but when the king announces he is coming to visit and the man tells his wife to make herself unattractive, she understands what has happened and makes herself as attractive as possible, taking an active part in the man's punishment (2.157). William does not condemn a nun for having an affair with a cleric but implies that it is the fault of her brother, the emperor Henry III, who insisted on keeping her at court.[92] William also tells many stories of women as victims of men's abuses: rape (punished, 2.158, outwitted, 2.159), murder (2.177), and a false accusation of adultery (successfully answered, 2.188).

When he speaks of the women whose histories have been mentioned earlier in this chapter, William is generally but not entirely favorable. Edith, the wife of Edward the Confessor, is praised for erudition—she has a "gymnasium of all the liberal arts in her breast"—and for purity of mind and beauty (2.197). But Emma is more complicated, presumably because of her preference for her Danish husband over her English sons. Though William seems to applaud her indignation at her first husband's sexual promiscuity (2.165), he deplores her second marriage to the enemy and invader, Cnut, "entering the bed of the man who killed her husband and put her sons to flight" (2.180).[93] She did, however, encourage him to give and gave herself with "prodigal sanctity" to religious institutions, while he was concentrating on wars (2.181). But, William says, she hated her (English) son, Edward, transferring her feelings for his father to him, preferring Cnut, living or dead, to Edward and refusing to give any of her treasure which she hoarded to help him or the poor (2.196), though she continued to give to Winchester.[94] Little is said about Adela, countess of Blois, whose son Stephen would succeed her brother Henry, though what is said is positive: she is named as one of the five daughters of William I and the first Matilda, who was celebrated for secular activity but recently took the veil at Marcigny (3.276); we are told only that her husband went on crusade and was martyred (4.34) and that there was enmity between the French king, Louis, and Henry because of her son Thibaut (5.405). More, naturally, is said about queen Matilda, William's patron, and her mother, Margaret: Margaret's marriage and children are listed (2.228), and she is praised for her piety, her alms and vigils (4.311), and the virtues of three of her sons, who shared her piety (5.400).

Of the queen who commissioned his history, William reports that she descended from an illustrious line of kings, that she was educated at Wilton and Romsey and devoted to letters, that she wore a veil, not because she was a nun but to discourage suitors (questions had been raised about her religious status at the time of her marriage). Henry, we are told, had long been attached to Matilda before he married her, despite her small marriage portion, the result of her being an orphan although she is a (great-)grandniece of Edward (5.393). She possessed the most admirable public and private virtues: she was satisfied with one child of either sex and stopped at that ("et parere et parturire destitit"), an indication of continence; she was kind, generous, and hospitable, holy and pious like her mother, beautiful and chaste. She wore haircloth under her royal garments during Lent, washed the feet of the sick and kissed their hands. If she had a fault, it was in her support of scholars and artists: she was prodigal to clerks, generous to scholars, poets, and singers, particularly foreigners who could spread her fame abroad, sometimes ignoring natives; indeed, her liberality led her to exploit her tenants, for which William partly blames her servants, who seized or wasted what they could (5.418). Of her official life, we know little, except that she is mentioned as a signatory, with the king, bishops, and abbots, of a document asserting the primacy of the see in Canterbury (3.298).

About her daughter, the empress Matilda, to whom the history was finally presented, William reports that she married the emperor of Germany, Henry V (5.420), who struggled with the pope over investiture but eventually gave up his claims. The younger Matilda is said to be like her father in fortitude and her mother in religion; piety and action vie in her character, so it is hard to tell which of her good qualities is most commendable (5.438). William would tell the story of her struggle for the crown in some detail later in the *Historia novella*, after her husband and father had died. The relevant details of her life which fill out William's accounts can be briefly summarized: Matilda was betrothed to Henry V and sent to his court when she was eight years old, in 1110.[95] They married in 1114, and she participated in his reign; she traveled with him, was included in official acts, and served as his regent in Italy. Since they had no child for whom she could be regent, after he died she returned home to her father in 1125 and was married, probably against her wishes, to Geoffrey of Anjou, ten years her junior, with whom she had the future king Henry II. Among her most loyal supporters after her father died were her uncle, David, king of Scotland, and her half-brother, Robert of Gloucester, who commissioned the *Historia novella* in her cause. Gilbert of Foliot, abbot of Gloucester, wrote a summary of arguments in favor of her claims, and the monks of Malmesbury acknowledged her claim with enthusiasm when they presented William's earlier history to her while her father was still alive. Though she was recognized as "domina," and exercised some administrative powers in England, she never became queen. She did not, however, retire from public life. She achieved the succession of her son, and once he was king, she acted for him in Normandy and mediated between him and his major opponents, Thomas, the archbishop of Canterbury, and the king of France, Louis VII.

While Matilda was a young empress, the monk Hugh of Fleury presented his history of the kings of the Franks to her. He offered her the work as a record of the loftiness of her family, running through her "splendid genealogy," including William, who did what only two Roman emperors had dared do before, conquer England, and was glorious in his magnanimity and magnificence beyond all kings and princes of our time.[96] Hugh may not have had a political purpose in dedicating his work to Matilda beyond hoping to win her favor for himself and his monastery, but the monks of Malmesbury who presented William's history of the kings of the Angles to her, were concerned with her succession to the throne. They recognize her as the heir to the king with some eagerness ("we seize your rule in our spirit," "dominationem vestram . . . animo rapimus") and offer her the examples in the book so she can follow in the footsteps of her illustrious ancestors: in it "you can document that none of those whom the present book remembers, no king or queen awaited the legal powers of the hereditary kingdom of the Angles more royally or splendidly than you."[97] And when Robert of Gloucester, Matilda's half-brother and loyal supporter, commissioned William to write the *Historia novella*, it was in direct and undisguised support of her cause.

The *Historia novella* was written after Henry's death and deals with the struggle between the empress and her cousin Stephen for the crown. As William describes the events up to the queen's escape from Oxford, where he left the story presumably because the hoped-for ending never occurred, legitimacy and decency are all on the empress's side, bad action on Stephen's. Before he comes to her English claims, William establishes Matilda's credentials as empress, saying she was reluctant to leave her new country and large possessions, and in succeeding years, princes came from Lorraine and Lombardy to ask her to return as their lady (*dominam*, 1.450). But she did as her father wished and married the count of Anjou to keep peace between them, and her father had his nobles and bishops and abbots swear an oath to accept his daughter as their sovereign, should he die without male heirs. William gives her descent from (Norman) kings back to her grandfather on her father's side, and from West Saxon kings back to the year 800 on her mother's (1.451). The first laymen to take the oath were both related to her through women, her mother's brother, David, king of Scotland, and her cousin by her paternal aunt Adela, Stephen (1.452).

When Henry died, Stephen was first on the scene, but he would have had no success if it had not been for his brother, the bishop of Winchester and papal legate, who expected him to follow the example of his grandfather William in his governing and his relations with the church (1.460). He did not, however, keep his promises; he spent the king's treasure on soldiers who sought only plunder, and his mismanagement led his brother and men like Robert, who had given only conditional support, to return to Matilda (1.465-67). As people deserted Stephen, his malice erupted in revenge; he seized castles of bishops, which his brother insisted he return (2.468, 471). The empress, more inclined to justice and open to a church decision, accepted terms for peace, but the king, listening to people who wanted only war, delayed and then rejected them (2.486). Matilda and Robert pledged to honor the rights of the church (3.491), and the papal legate, Stephen's brother, addressed an assembly of bishops supporting Matilda's legitimacy, reminding them of the oaths they had sworn, explaining that Stephen had been allowed to rule for the peace of the country but had acted against justice and peace and the church, and electing Matilda as the ruler of England and Normandy (3.493).[98] Stephen's supporters, always anxious for war—many had joined him for plunder, not because they disliked the empress, William comments (3.522)—continued to act badly, burning an abbey of nuns because partisans of the empress were inside (3.499).

Though the lines of good and bad behavior are clearly drawn on the same sides as the supporters of Matilda and Stephen, the behavior of women and men is treated differently, if no less arbitrarily. With one exception—Matilda's half-brother Robert is loyal, courageous, and energetic in her support throughout—men on both sides tend to behave poorly, like the king and his supporters, his brother the legate, who keeps shifting allegiance, and Matilda's husband, the count of Anjou, who instead of sending help, first draws Robert away from her to help him and then refuses to come. Women, on the other hand, again with a single exception, are loyal and courageous:[99] not only the empress but also the countess Mabilia, Robert's wife, who negotiated the exchange of Robert for Stephen when they had both been captured (3.507), having her husband's full confidence in her to act for him, and Stephen's queen, yet another Matilda, who represented the king in negotiations for peace and later, when her husband was captured, kept watch on the roads so no supplies got through to the empress and finally took her husband's place as surety when he was released.[100]

Though their roles in this history are minor, they are characteristic of the roles women are shown to play throughout the histories written for women. Those roles can vary from the more traditional ones—the link to a distinguished or powerful family, the influential wife and mother, mediator, or devoted supporter of the church—to the more strikingly active negotiators, regents, and rulers. When they are writing for women in power, men (and women even more) emphasize other women in power, accepting them as a normal, indeed essential, part of history. They do not eschew women who abuse their positions, because history is meant to give models to avoid as well as to follow, but they decidedly favor women who use their positions for the good of their people and often for the good of the author's church. Like the biblical heroines who take matters into their own hands, fighting to save their people in God's cause (Judith, Deborah, Esther) or seeking wisdom (the queen of Sheba), the Amazons and Byzantine empresses who appear in the universal histories show women effectively engaged in a man's world, governing, negotiating, manipulating, plotting, even fighting. And the more contemporary women, the Ottonian regents, countess Matilda of Tuscany, the English queens, take an active part in diplomacy and in government, as well as in religious and cultural patronage. All these histories not only accept the fact of women in authority but also seem to argue at least implicitly that women in power can be beneficial to society and that these particular women are especially valuable in the situations for which the work was written. Clearly the women patrons, but to some extent perhaps also the men who wrote for them, admire active, forceful women who play a role in the destiny of their people. The patrons are themselves active women, both in the public sphere and in the patronage of letters, commissioning works that implicitly or explicitly support their positions. If not so directly involved in producing the literary work as the women who inspired religious tracts by their questions, the women for whom the histories and lives were written did influence the content of these works by their position or their political needs and did thereby influence our sense of that history—if we do not ignore them.

4 *Courtly Literature*

THE LADY IN COMMAND OR THE DAMSEL IN DISTRESS

The women who commissioned romances, asking the poet to tell a particular story, perhaps to give it a particular slant, may also have had a political agenda. The approach is less direct, more subtle, than in the histories and lives, but the message is frequently similar. Romances composed for women present educated and intelligent women, capable of ruling their lands, of organizing people and events to achieve their ends, women who guide and protect the immature hero, preoccupied with winning glory in combat. They may operate in a fantasy world with the help of magic, but the problems they face and the personalities they deal with are very much of the world the patrons and poets live in, where men pick fights to assert power and claim possessions and women negotiate and administer to keep society working. This is, of course, a simplified description, but my point is that the romances composed for women are, like the histories, asserting the abilities and political rights of women in a fictional disguise. They are less overtly propaganda, therefore perhaps less threatening, but nonetheless an effective way of making the same points, even to audiences less receptive to such messages, and making them in a language accessible to a much larger audience.[1]

Women were deeply involved with the vernacular literature which was written in and for secular courts from the mid-twelfth century on. They commissioned works to be translated or composed, sometimes insisting on particular storylines, and they formed a significant part of the audience for these and other works. If Dante's suggestion that a poet first wrote in the vulgate rather than in Latin so a lady could understand his words (*Vita Nuova*, 25) is oversimplified and even inaccurate,[2] there is no question that women were a major force in the development of vernacular literatures, particularly in the courtly genres of lyric and romance. Whether they were interested in entertainment, flattery, propaganda, or some combination thereof, women actively encouraged vernacular poets. They exerted an influence not only by their presence as interested members of the audience and as sponsors of individual poets—it is perhaps too obvious to say that at the very least the courtly love game would not have developed as it did if women had not been part of the audience as potential patrons or potential lovers, not to say fellow poets—but also as commissioners of verse translations of secular Latin works which helped create the audience and the taste for new vernacular literature.[3]

There are reflections of the political sphere in the relations between men and women in all courtly genres, even the lyric, where poets posturing as lovers depict the woman they love as a powerful figure, using the language of political power—"midons," "my lord," rather than "my lady." I take a brief look in this chapter at women's patronage of the earliest romance lyrics in Provençal, then at their role in commissioning translations and adaptations into French of Latin works which influenced the beginnings of courtly romance, the fictionalized "histories" of the *romans d'antiquité*. Then I concentrate on the romances which were commissioned by or dedicated to particular women. Like the histories written for women, these romances show a distinct preference for powerful and active women, particularly as compared to romances written for male patrons. While we cannot know whether poets slanted the literature they wrote for women because women asked them to, though some poets imply it, we can trace the recurrence of certain motifs in the romances that women are said to have commissioned or encouraged or designed. Taken together, the motifs suggest a strong pattern of complimenting, even supporting, the lady by enhancing the powers and roles of women characters.

Though all the motifs do not occur in all such romances, they do occur frequently enough to indicate that women patrons responded to them. They include women as the only heirs to their father's land or as effective rulers or regents, some so independent they refuse to marry (at least at first); a hero who is lower-born and raised in status by marriage to the heroine, and who often needs the help of women more than he serves them; women who recognize and reward merit where they find it (perhaps a hint at the relation between woman patron and poet). The heroines of such romances are often unusually well educated, which gives them extraordinary, even magic, powers; some are able to manipulate the hero's actions and the events of the story, so they seem to be surrogates for the poet, an identification which at times is virtually explicit. If the poet is writing at the woman's suggestion, so is in some sense her spokesman, then by making his heroine his surrogate, he is extending and emphasizing their collaborative effort. In romances written for male patrons or for a general audience—not for a specific woman—the woman's role is far less striking: the hero usually rescues a damsel in distress and raises her rank by marrying her; heroines are not highly educated and do not control the action; if they are heirs to their lands, the fact is downplayed, or extenuating circumstances negate its significance; male bonding and fighting are featured.

It was particularly in the Anglo-Norman courts of Henry I, under the influence of queens Matilda and Adeliza and then of Henry II and Eleanor of Aquitaine, that secular French literature began and developed. In Eleanor's court, themes from Provençal love poetry, the first romance vernacular literature extant, could combine with narratives from the French adaptations of classical stories and of Welsh legends in the fertile beginnings of courtly romance. Eleanor's grandfather Guilhem, the ninth duke of Aquitaine, is the first poet whose work we have in Provençal, and Eleanor must have been familiar with the traditions of early Provençal poetry; certainly she encouraged poets who wrote in Provençal as well as French. Bernart de Ventadorn alludes directly to her in one poem, "Huguet, mos cortes messatgers / chantatz ma chanso volonters / a la reina dels Normans" (33.43–45: "Hugh, my courtly messenger, sing my song willingly to the queen of the Normans"), and less directly in another, as his lady far off in the Norman land, beyond the wild, deep sea (26.38ff.).[4] Unlike Guilhem and a few other early poets, Jaufré Rudel and Raimbaut d'Aurenga, who were nobles and not in need of patronage from women or men, Bernart was a professional poet, who needed support.[5] He sent another poem to a woman who might be the countess of Narbonne: "Lo vers mi porta, Corona, / lai a midons a Narbona, / que tuih sei faih son enter" (23.57–59: "Carry my poem, Corona, to my lord [=my lady] of Narbonne, for all her deeds are whole/true"). The countess is mentioned by Andreas Capellanus as an arbiter of courtly love matters along with Eleanor and her daughter, Marie of Champagne.[6]

Whether he is addressing a queen or any other lady, a patron or his love, Bernart often takes the posture of a vassal, offering his service for her reward, a reward that can be explicitly sexual. He complains regularly about his lady's treatment of him, seeming to wallow in his suffering, which not coincidentally gives him the subject matter of his songs, but occasionally there is a hint of a happier relation. Indeed, one poem suggests private communication: "ela sap letras et enten, / et agrada'm qu'eu escria / los motz, e s'a leis plazia, / legis los al meu sauvamen" (17.53–56: "she knows and understands letters and it pleases me that I write the words and that she, if it please her, read them to my salvation"). This may even suggest an exchange of letters or perhaps of poems, something that rarely occurs in extant Provençal poetry.[7] The debate poems between men and women indicate that there were lively oral exchanges between real men and women, the kind of repartee that would go on in a sophisticated court. There are reflections of such exchanges in Raimbaut's debate with a lady (25) and in the pastorelas, though the woman there is disguised as a peasant; the relatively large proportion of women's poems in Provençal which are debates shows that women certainly engaged in them.[8]

In courtly lyrics, the poet says that he is writing to gain a lady's favor, even if he often seems to be writing as much for men in the audience; it is true that for the most part the courtly love game is played out by men before and with a public audience. Trobairitz usually address their cansos directly to the men who are the objects of their love, while trobadors mainly write about, rather than to, women who remain at a social or emotional distance. Although their laments about the lady in the third person might also have been meant as messages to her and she is presumably in the audience, male poets address themselves to other men, to love, even to the poem, but only briefly to the woman.[9] Nonetheless, some poets, Arnaut Daniel and Raimbaut, address the lady more frequently;[10] and even Bernart de Ventadorn directs at least one stanza and sometimes two or more to a lady in over half his poems. The game of courtly love as virtually all these poets play it is based on the concept of the poet serving the lady by writing poetry in her honor, which is at the very least a parody of the traditional relation between poet and patron.

The *vidas* and *razos,* written later to accompany performance of the poems, suggest that women were particularly interested in the honor they derived from being the subjects of such poems and that they encouraged poets in order to enhance their reputations to the envy of other women. A *razo* for Bertran de Born claims that the duchess of Saxony, "for the great desire she had of worth and honor and because she knew that Sir Bertran was a man so valued and worthy that he could greatly exalt her, did him such honor that he considered himself well paid and fell in love with her, so that he began to praise and glorify her." A *razo* of Uc de Saint Circ says that a lady Ponsa, "courtly and educated, was so envious of the lady Clara, for whom Sir Uc had gained worth and honor, that she took pains to take his love away from Clara and draw it to herself." Gaucelm Faidit is said to have loved and praised Maria de Ventadorn, while she only wanted the praise and renown through the world ("ella non amava lui, si no per cortezia e per las grans lauzors qu'el fazia de leis e per lo ric reso en qu'el l'avia meza per tot lo mon").[11] The *vidas* emphasize the advantage women patrons take of male poets, but one of the trobairitz, Isabella, makes the contrary case; when she asks her former lover why his songs have changed, he answers that he praised her not from love, but for the honor and profit he expected from it, as joglars do (Rieger, 2.10).

Occasionally, vernacular lyric poets wrote poems to women about subjects other than love, politics, war, nobility.[12] Some poets claimed to create new technical forms for them: Arnaut Daniel sent the sestina, a form he invented, to his lady "for her pleasure" (1.38). He implies that she has an interest in the technical aspects of his art, saying she owns the craftsman and the shop where he "files and planes his words" (10, cf. 21, 2).[13] Dante a century later also claimed that he created the double-sestina, inspired by Arnaut's poem, for the "donna pietrosa": "though she is stone to me, she gives me the courage to dare to make the novelty that shines through your form, that was never thought of before."[14] More interesting is his suggestion in the *Vita Nuova* (18) that he changed or tried to change the direction of his love poetry from self-pity to praise of Beatrice as a result of the incisive remarks of certain women. When one of a group of ladies asks him how he could love a woman if he could not bear to be in her presence, he answers that his "beatitude" had rested in her greeting, but now it lies in something that cannot fail; when she asks what that is, he says it is in the words that praise his lady. If that is the case, she says, those words you spoke about your own condition had some other point. Why, in other words, were you always talking about yourself? Dante is so ashamed that he determines to write only in praise of Beatrice. Although he does not entirely succeed in this work, he does begin to make the change. The very next poem he writes, according to the fiction of the *Vita Nuova,* is "Donne ch'avete intelletto d'amore," addressed to those ladies who understand love, and this is the poem he has the poet Bonagiunta cite in *Purgatorio,* 24.51, as the example of the sweet new style. The last poem cited in the *Vita Nuova,* "Oltre la spera," which looks ahead to the *Comedy,* was also written at the request of women.

Whatever the historic reality of Dante's claims about the role of women in his literary development, it is significant that he chose to make them. It is another indication of the recognized importance of women in the development of (romance) vernacular literatures, acknowledged by contemporary writers and modern scholars alike. M. Dominica Legge credits a series of queens of Anglo-Norman England with creating the demand for vernacular literature: Maud/Matilda and Adeliza, the two queens of Henry I, and the three Eleanors.[15] They commissioned or received a variety of religious and secular narratives. Benedeit's *Voyage de saint Brendan* was dedicated to Matilda, who asked him to write it in Latin and later had him translate it to French ("en letre mis e en romanz"); the work was popular and the author apparently rededicated it to Adeliza at a later date.[16] Adeliza commissioned a life of Henry I by David, which is not extant; we know of it from Gaimar, who mentions it in his *Estoire des Engleis,* offering to tell more about Henry than David had.[17] I will come to works connected with the first Eleanor in due course. In the previous chapter, I mentioned the translation of Aelred's life of Edward the Confessor for Eleanor of Provence, queen of Henry III.[18] Girard d'Amiens composed the romance *Escanor* for Eleanor of Castile, queen of Edward I; it will be discussed later.[19]

The taste for historical narrative with more than a touch of the exotic carries into the romances; indeed, the romances seem to reflect elements from virtually all the early histories in French and from some of the Latin histories composed for women as well. Gaimar's *Estoire des Engleis* was commissioned by a noblewoman, Constance Fitzgilbert, and written perhaps with an eye to a commission from another woman, as Gaimar implies at the end. He offers to tell more about king Henry's (romantic) activities, his hunting, his play, his loves, his feasts, his generosity, nobility, and rich assembly of barons, than was written in David's book or held in the hand of the queen of Luvain, who commissioned the book which his own lady Custance keeps in her chamber and reads often. Gaimar, not surprisingly, presents a number of women in significant roles, one whose Lucretia-like response to rape causes the rejection of a bad king and two queens who work to procure the throne for their sons.[20] Several are heirs to their lands, a frequent motif in romances written for women and not unknown to history. The work begins with one such heir, whose uncle married her apparently beneath her rank; but she motivated her husband, Havelock, to discover and claim his own inheritance. Elfled, the sister of king Edred, was his choice to succeed him as ruler of Mercia (3491-92); one of Edmund's sons, sent into exile, married the daughter and heir of the king of Hungary. Another heir is Elftroed (Aelfthryth), whose story is also told by William of Malmesbury (GRA 2.157), but here the story is expanded and modified with more romantic elements (3595ff.). She is presented as the only daughter of a rich old man, who let her do whatever she wanted; when the king's envoy saw her, she was playing chess, beautiful as a fairy—Gaimar later says he could not describe all her beauty if he spoke from morning to evening. When the king finally came to see her, she did nothing to attract him, but he recognized her beauty, removed her wimple, and fell in love with her; instead of having her husband killed directly, the king sent him north, where he was conveniently killed by outlaws, and the king quietly married her. But after the king's death, the romantic heroine gives way to the ambitious mother: though her stepson rules, she has the power of the kingdom through the courage of her lineage ("la force del regne aveit / pur la baldur de sun lignage," 3976-77), and she contrives to have her stepson replaced by her son, probably conspiring in his death, though not so obviously as in William's version.

But the works that do most to bring courtly elements into history and cultivate the audience for romance are Wace's translation of Geoffrey of Monmouth, dedicated to Eleanor of Aquitaine, and the adaptations of the classical stories, the *Roman de Thèbes,* the *Roman de Troie,* even the *Eneas,* probably written for the same court. And Eleanor's presence in the audience is felt to some extent in all these works. Wace dedicated his French translation of Geoffrey of Monmouth's *Historia Regum Britanniae,* the *Roman de Brut,* to Eleanor of Aquitaine, though it may well have been Henry who commissioned it as he commissioned the history of his Norman ancestors, the *Roman de Rou.*[21] The *Rou* nonetheless praises the queen and her generosity and gives a brief history of her life, including the significant fact that she was the only direct heir to her lands: "Eleanor is noble, of good birth, and wise. / She was queen of France in her youth: / Louis married her in a great wedding. / They went to Jerusalem on long pilgrimage; / there each suffered distress and pain. / When they came back, by counsel of their baronage / the queen left him with her rich kin. / She suffered no harm from this separation: / she went to Poitiers, her native dwelling; / there was no nearer heir than her in her line. / King Henry took her in rich marriage, / who held England and the coast land, / between Spain and Scotland, from shore to shore" (24–36).[22]

The dedication of the *Brut* no longer exists, but Layamon, who translated the work into English, says that Wace gave it to Eleanor: "A Frenchis clerc, / Wace wes ihoten. / þe wel couþe writen / & he hoe ȝef pare aeðelen / Aelienor þe wes Henries quene / þes heȝes kinges."[23] Wace added many courtly (and Ovidian) elements to his translation, presumably for Eleanor's taste: Uther's love for Ygerne, which began before he met her, the signs of love he gives her during the banquet, his suffering, and the physical symptoms of love. Arthur's qualities include not only generosity, a love of *pris* and *gloire,* and a desire for his deeds to be remembered but also the requirement that he be served "curteisement." Guenever is beautiful, courtly, generous, and well-spoken (*bone-parliere*). When Arthur calls an assembly there is much joy and kissing and recounting of *"avantures"*; people come for the king's gifts, for love and honor, to know his barons, to see his domains and hear his courtesies. The court includes singers, musicians, and minstrels (*chanteors, estrumanteors, tresgiteors*) who tell tales (*contes*) and fables. It has been suggested that the coronation of Arthur and Guenever may be modeled on the coronation of Henry and Eleanor.[24]

It is likely that Eleanor's tastes are reflected in the French renditions of the classical "histories" as well.[25] The *Eneas,* which appears to be the least structured to female interests, is nonetheless much more sympathetic in its presentation of women than Virgil's poem. Not only does it develop the love story of Lavinia and Eneas, which has no place in the *Aeneid,* and make Lavinia an active figure in it (writing a letter and having it shot at the hero's feet), but it plays up the roles of other women, including the queen consorts of both Latinus and Evander, and treats Dido (and Lavinia's mother) with greater sympathy. Dido, we are told, rules better than any count or marquis, and much is made of her cleverness in getting the new land and founding the city. Sibylla is an awesome (but not raging) and highly educated priestess who knows astronomy, necromancy, medicine, rhetoric, music, dialectic, and grammar. Camilla, a wise ruler as well as an impressive warrior, fights with enormous success until someone strikes her in the back, and then she is honored by the most marvelous tomb in the poem. The poet calls attention to her sex with a misogynist attack by an opponent whom she promptly kills, suggesting a battle of the sexes aspect which the woman wins. Even Lavinia's mother plays a far less negative role in the French version. It is true that she opposes Eneas, but she has good reason, from a woman's point of view: the Trojans are not trustworthy with women, Paris stole Menelaus's wife and the adultery led to the war, and Eneas deserted Dido after taking her hospitality. She does not want to lose her daughter or the land to an untrustworthy stranger, and since Roman destiny has no importance in the French version and the queen does not commit suicide in frustration when she loses, the audience—at least women in the audience—can be more sympathetic to what she says. Moreover, her view is echoed by Pallas's mother, who lost her son to Eneas's cause, which she opposed; in a long speech of mourning after her son's death, which has no counterpart in the *Aeneid,* she too accuses the Trojans of bad faith. Both women seem to have a voice in their husband's courts and to command respect even though their views do not prevail.[26]

It is possible that a compliment is intended to Eleanor in the enhanced and improved roles of the queen consorts; at the very least, the increased importance of female characters and the added love story would be to her taste. Certainly both are true in the *Roman de Thèbes* and the *Roman de Troie,* where I would argue compliments are certainly intended to Eleanor in the treatment of the wise and dignified queen mothers, Jocasta and Hecuba. There is no direct reference to Eleanor in the *Thèbes,* but there are several suggestive allusions: in the Constans edition, the author says that "the laughs and kisses of the daughters of Adrastus are worth more than London or Poitiers," 971-72; Bezzola points out that these are Eleanor's two capitals and asks who but Eleanor would have been touched by the lines ("qui, sinon Aliénor, devait etre touché par les vers?" 3.271).[27] Jocasta's past has serious blemishes (marriage with and children by her own son, who had killed his father, however unintentionally), blemishes that make Eleanor's past (divorce from the king of France after fifteen years and two children) seem inconsequential. Jocasta marries her son at the urging of her barons, because he has freed her land from a monster, knowing that he killed her husband in a general mêlée but afraid that without a husband or child to guard her honor, she will not be able to hold her land in need or war ("Se besoingne me sort ou guerre, / ne pourrai pas tenir ma terre," 261-62).[28] Like Eleanor (and Henry's mother), Jocasta is necessarily older than her second husband. Nothing is made of that fact at the time, but later in the story there is a subtle comment which is indirectly relevant. When Parthenopeu, who was engaged to Jocasta's daughter Antigone, dies, he sends a message to his own mother, telling her to remarry quickly to preserve her great land and honor; he mentions that she is still young, that she was only eleven when he was born and seemed more a sister than a mother (8793-8810). Eleven years was precisely the difference in age between Eleanor and her second husband, Henry.

In the *Roman,* as the men predictably make war while the women try to make peace or grieve for their losses, Jocasta becomes the voice of reason, trying to persuade her son to make peace with his brother, to share or risk losing all, not to perjure himself for possessions.[29] When the men fight over who will go to negotiate with the attacking army, Jocasta says "Je irai," sure that any who goes with her will be safe (4017-20). Since "you all fail the king," she will take her two daughters; "because of the lack of good men the message will be carried by women" (4024-26: "quant vos tuit en failliez le roi, / et pour soufraite de preudomes / ert cist mesages fez par dames"). The embassy fails, though her son is receptive to her message of peace and participation, because his colleagues refuse to share his trust (not without reason) and want to make war. She is more successful later in persuading Ethiocles, with the help of other women, to make peace with his man Daire, who is torn between loyalty to him and the safety of his hostage son. Daire's wife had persuaded him that his son's life was more important than his oath to his lord, with the unanswerable logic that since he swore loyalty to both warring brothers, he has perjured himself to one already; and Daire's daughter attracts Ethiocles, who is then persuaded by his mother to act with measure rather than right, to avoid war and act with *cortoisie*. Antigone pleads her case, the daughter promises her favor, and Jocasta pledges herself for Daire, as a good, chaste, and charitable lady (8064-68).[30]

Among the gods, Juno plays a similar role. She is the "dame de touz, / bele et bonne, cortoise et prouz" (9427-28), Jupiter's sister and wife, lady of her own kingdom ("dame de meismes mon regne," 9476), the "queen of the Greeks," honored by dukes, counts, and kings (9445ff.), and she pleads for her people in a council of the gods, threatening to have nothing more to do with her husband if he does not help the Greeks (who are, incidentally, presented as the just side in this story).[31] But Jupiter's sons by other women, Hercules and Bacchus, argue for Thebes against the Greek aggressors, and Capaneus's defiance tips the scales.

After the general destruction, the women are left to grieve; Ismene has already become a nun after the death of her fiancé, with money from her brother to build an abbey for herself and a hundred girls who take the veil out of love for her (6167ff.). But the Greek women react differently after the war. Though they wish only to die, they have a conference ("ont un parlement asemblé," 9926) and consult the two daughters of the king (his heirs, we were told at the beginning, 1021), who advise that all go to ask the help of the duke of Athens.[32] The women depart, a vast, grieving, barefoot, and disheveled, but nonetheless awesome army, "l'ost as dames" (10183), on a long hard journey which includes deserts and wild beasts; the beasts and the men who meet them on the road are frightened by them. When they get to Thebes, they join the duke of Athens in his assault on the city, breaking down the wall, bold because they do not care if they live (10457ff.). They retrieve the bodies and bury them. The statesmanlike and heroic actions of such women are interspersed with romantic tales of young lovers, all doomed to sad fates, but it is Jocasta and the woman's army who catch one's attention.

In the *Roman de Troie*, the emphasis shifts further toward the romantic stories, though here too there is an impressive queen mother, Hecuba.[33]

Assuming a date after 1165, I think one can see more specific identifications with Eleanor in this work. The author, Benoît de Sainte-Maure, acknowledges her presence in an aside of elaborate praise for a "riche dame de riche rei," who may blame him for his treatment of Briseida (13457ff.).[34] Benoît praises that lady for her goodness equal to her position, her qualities of "pris e valor / honesté e sen e honor . . . largece e beauté"; misdeeds of other women are extinguished by her good, all learning abounds in her, and she has no peer (13457ff.). Briseida is the negative exemplum; she is the daughter of a traitor, therefore perhaps fated to betray, which may explain why she is condemned for changing lovers when Helen is not condemned for leaving a husband. At the same time, Briseida is also a victim, distrusted by both sides.[35] Her position is not an easy one, and she does show some loyalty to Troilus, standing up for him to Diomede, though she is pleased to have Diomede's love, and presumably his protection. She is not, however, royal, like Helen or Hecuba, and it is unlikely that Eleanor would have identified with her.

Benoît is probably complimenting different aspects of Eleanor in his presentation of both Hecuba and Helen. The wise and long-suffering Hecuba, the queen of Troy, is described as a woman of great learning, without female desire, just, pious, and righteous (5509ff.). She is the mother of five sons and three daughters (Hector, Helenus, Deiphebus, Troilus, Paris, Cassandra, Polixenain, and Andromache [also listed among her daughters in Dares]); Eleanor had five sons and three daughters with Henry (William, Henry, Matilda, Richard, Geoffrey, Eleanor, Joanna, and John).[36] Certainly Eleanor would have identified with another queen who had accomplished such a feat. But it is equally if not more likely that Eleanor would also have seen herself in the beautiful Helen, who had been married to a king and carried off with her consent by a prince who placed her at the center of a court filled with poetry and learning. She might well have seen in Helen's alabaster chamber of art a compliment to her and her court, particularly since Helen is presented so sympathetically.[37]

The *Chambre de Labastre,* constructed by three poets, wise doctors learned in necromancy (14668-69), was given to Helen when Paris brought her to Troy; when Hector is wounded, he is brought there to be cared for, so it becomes the center of the court, attended by all the ladies and princes and people of greatest worth (14611-16). In the chamber are figures of women and men that seem to represent the powers of poetry and music: one holds a mirror in which people see themselves exactly as they are; one is constantly in action or creating the illusion of great actions (including a ship on the high seas, "nef siglant par haute mer," 14731, a metaphor Benoît uses for his own poem, "mout par ai ancore a sigler, / quar ancor sui en haute mer," 14943-44); one figure restores and dispels anger or grief with heavenly music of various instruments, and one scatters flowers, beneath an eagle who is repeatedly attacked by a satyr with a club (satiric verse). This last image, Benoît explains, shows people what each of them should do, without others being aware; that is, it gives a different and pertinent message to each member of the audience (14863ff.). The chamber of alabaster is both stone and transparent, representing perhaps the power and the mimetic qualities of poetry. Everyone who enters it is kept from villainy while there.

With the chamber, Benoît makes an explicit connection between magic and poetry which recalls his treatment of Medea at the beginning of the story as a figure for the artist. He had presented himself in the opening lines as one who has wisdom and learning, knowledge of the liberal arts; since anyone with such gifts should not hesitate to do good or to teach, he will translate the story to Romance for those who do not understand Latin (1–38). The first story he tells is of Jason seeking the golden fleece (a quest Dante will use much later as a figure for composing the *Comedy*), which he can get only with the help of Medea. Medea, like many heroines of romances for women, is the only child and heir of a king (1215), highly educated, learned in the arts and in magic ("de conjure et de sorcerie . . . astronomie e nigromance," 1218–21), so that she could make day night or waters run backward. She has had no interest in love before she sees Jason (1283–84), but as soon as she does, she is ready to give herself, her wisdom and her body. She teaches him all he needs to know about the dangers of getting to the fleece, and then, when he swears to keep faith with her, she gives him the necessary tools, a protective figure and ring, an ointment against fire, and a written ritual (1667ff.). The poet seems to suggest that Medea, like the poet, is doing the right thing by using her knowledge to benefit someone else, even if he betrays her; perhaps the poet, like Medea, can be ill rewarded for his service.[38] The betrayal is to Jason's shame and the gods will avenge her harshly, Benoît comments (2042), saying nothing of the part Medea took in the revenge that might put her in a bad light.

Many women in the poem are presented as victims of male violence or betrayal, even when they have extraordinary abilities, like Medea and Cassandra, who was wondrously learned and knew divine arts and secrets thoroughly ("merveilles ert escientose / des arz e des segreiz devins / saveit les somes e les fins" (5532–34). But there is one group of women who not only meet men as equals in their world of fighting but frequently surpass them, and they are the Amazons, whose actions dominate the twenty-first through the twenty-third battles. Theirs is a woman's fantasy, a world entirely controlled by women, who allow no men in and have children without husbands. To preserve their society, some of them meet men of honor and valor in a lovely island each spring, become pregnant, keep the females and reject the males (whom they send back to their fathers); other women remain virgins and train as warriors. Led by their queen, Panthesilee, who is brave and hardy, beautiful and wise, of great valor and birth, honored and renowned (23361-64), a thousand of them come to help the Trojans. In the first battle, Panthesilee does not strike without killing her opponent (23621-23); she unseats Menelaus, wrests Diomede's shield from him—if night had not stopped the battle, Benoît says, the Greeks would have had to give up their siege of the city. The queen alone killed more than the two best men together.

As the women fight, with war cries that Benoît calls beautiful to hear like something divine, a thousand women in the palace weep and grieve for their losses. Panthesilee, also called "la reine de Femenie" (a pun?), has a fierce joust with Telemon, on horse and on foot, but her most intense battles come with Achilles's son, Pirrus, whom she wants to kill to avenge Hector and who wants to kill her because she is a woman killing men (24079ff.). In one encounter, she bloodies his head, face, and chest and seizes his visor before they are separated; in another she thrusts her lance into his body, but finally he gets her when her helmet is not laced, cuts her arm off, and with the help of his company—he could not do it alone—unseats her. Then he knocks her brains out and in a fury, cuts off all her limbs (24312ff.), destroying not only her but also any pretense of honor for himself. Her women take revenge on the Greeks, killing more than ten thousand of them. Eleanor, who had to convince both her husbands to fight for her lands, must have been pleased by the picture of women doing it all for themselves so effectively, despite the violent end of their queen.

If he intended Eleanor to identify with the fertile older queen, the beautiful younger queen surrounded by art, and perhaps even the warrior queen, Benoît seems to identify himself with Medea, the artist figure. If that is so, he may also be suggesting a close identity between poet and woman patron, one which is suggested in other works composed for women which will be discussed. Even Chrétien de Troyes, who is so uncomfortable with his work for a woman patron, may at times identify with women characters, though perhaps not happily: Enide, who gives voice to her husband's fault and suffers for it, like the poet who calls attention to the faults of the chivalric world; Thessala, who creates illusion and confuses life and death, dream and reality, in the service of her hypocritical mistress in *Cliges,* while her male counterpart builds an elaborate but finally vulnerable refuge; and Lunete, who manipulates the actions of her mistress and the hero (not without risk) and tells of it for the amusement of others. Yet in the one story Chrétien admits to telling at the insistence of a woman, the *Chevalier de la Charrete (Lancelot),* the woman who manipulates the action is to be identified not with the poet but with his patron, Marie de Champagne.

It is likely that the story Marie, Eleanor's daughter by Louis VII, wanted Chrétien to tell, the story of a knight inspired purely by love, rescuing a queen imprisoned by the faults and failures of a male world of violence, lust, and a questionable sense of honor, is the story of her mother, Eleanor, imprisoned by her husband Henry II in 1174.[39] By rescuing Guenever (Eleanor) with the help of numerous women, Lancelot (Chrétien) would also rescue from those false values a good part of Arthur's (Henry's) circle. That the court of King Arthur in *Lancelot* is the Anglo-Norman court of Henry and Eleanor is suggested by the reference at the beginning of the romance to the ladies of the English court being eloquent in French ("bien parlant en langue françoise," 40).[40] It is possible that Chrétien's Guenever is modeled on Eleanor, not only in her imprisonment in this romance but throughout Chrétien's romances. Whether the poet wrote *Erec* and *Cliges* for the Anglo-Norman court or simply had that court in mind as a likely audience (the details about England in *Cliges* as well as the allusions to contemporary international politics suggest some connection), his treatment of Arthur's queen might be a compliment to the current queen of England before she had fallen out with her husband.[41] In the early romances Chrétien's Guenever acts for social harmony, arranges marriages, advises the king (though without much success) against disruptive action; but by the time of *Yvain* and *Lancelot*, after Eleanor has been imprisoned by Henry for inciting revolts against him, Guenever becomes more complex, even morally ambiguous, as she presses Calogrenant to tell the tale of his shame and makes a mockery of Lancelot's devotion in the tourney of Nouauz.[42] Though she retains some powers in the court—the king tells her Kay will do for her what he will not do for him, and she feels free to give Kay a promise in the name of the king—she also suffers from, indeed is imprisoned because of, Arthur's recklessness, Kay's egotism, and Meleagant's villainy. At the same time, when she has power, as over the hero, she exercises it capriciously and tyrannically. Chrétien seems to be sympathetic to women who are victims, trapped by male violence like Laudine and Lunete in *Yvain* and Guenever in the first part of *Lancelot*, but not to those who initiate action in their own interests, as Guenever does in the latter part of the romance or as Marie does in imposing an unwanted story on him.

It is difficult not to relate Guenever's treatment of Lancelot to Marie's treatment of the poet. Chrétien tells us at the very beginning that Marie imposed the content and the message of the story on him ("matiere et san li done et livre / la contesse," 26–27, with a probable pun on countess and storyteller), and later that he is so uncomfortable with it he refuses to finish it. It is tantalizing to wonder if Chrétien is not fighting Marie all through it. Even the dedication, though complimentary, is rather grudging. When Lancelot turns to look at the queen in the tower, exposing himself to Meleagant's attack, or when he alternates between his best and his worst at her capricious command, is Chrétien suggesting that by following Marie's commands, he exposes himself to criticism and ridicule? When Guenever refuses to speak to Lancelot because of his brief hesitation to get in the cart and Lancelot attempts suicide, is Chrétien alluding to Marie's disfavor because of his rejection of other subjects or his hesitation to undertake this one, and his own thoughts of giving up poetry altogether? Are Lancelot's repeated attempts to find Gawain—who is connected throughout the romance with reason rather than love, perhaps meant as a male versus female value—a suggestion that Chrétien considered writing nonromances or even romances like *Perceval* that he would undertake for a man?[43]

Chrétien's open rebellion against his patron is unusual if not unique among romance writers who wrote for women. But it is not surprising in Chrétien, who, in most of his work, shows a distinct preference for themes and characters which I identify with romances written for male patrons or for general audiences, though women would have been part of the larger audience in either case.[44] Although I am drawing conclusions from a handful of texts, I think the coincidence of characteristics is striking enough to warrant comment. In the romances I will discuss which were commissioned by or dedicated to women, the heroine and other women characters are often highly educated, with powers like the poet's to manipulate characters and events; a woman is frequently the heir to her land and rules it effectively, raising the hero to her status by marriage after she has helped him to be worthy of it. In contrast, romance poets not writing for a woman patron prefer to have heroes rescue damsels in distress whom they raise in social rank by marriage; their heroines rarely control the action, they are not usually highly educated or heirs to their own lands, and when they are, there are extenuating circumstances which detract from their prestige.

The education of Chrétien's heroines is not emphasized, and with the exception of Guenever, they do not manipulate the hero, though he may act in response to them.[45] They do not enhance the hero's status; on the contrary, Erec bestows castles on Enide's impoverished father and asks his own father to give Enide half of his lands for life if he dies. Yvain takes over the widowed Laudine's land, but he is himself the son of a king. Both heroes of Cliges are heirs to the Byzantine empire. Perceval seems to be moving away from a courtly world dominated by women; there is no indication that he will return to Blanchflur; and Gawain, whose adventures involve service to women, is ridiculed.[46]

Chrétien's *Erec* and *Yvain* were adapted into German by Hartmann von Aue, not as far as we know for women patrons. Like Chrétien, Hartmann focuses on the knight's development in his *Erec* and *Iwein,* though he goes further in making the women gentle; Laudine even acknowledges her fault and asks the hero's forgiveness at the end. In his other poems, the women are foils for the men's stories. In *Arme Heinrich,* a child who wants to be a martyr is made instead to marry the hero, whom her willingness to be sacrificed has saved; the marriage raises her secular status considerably from that of a serf and frees her parents. In *Gregorius,* the heroine is of royal birth, but the victim of her brother's incest; she is left to rule her land only as the result of the incest when her brother has to leave, and in order (for the needs of the plot) to cause more incest and prepare for the awesome penance of her son, Gregorius. When both retire from the world to a religious life, he ascends to a higher throne, the papacy. Though both women inherit lands which they give over to their husbands, neither she nor Laudine is presented as the heir carefully educated to the role.

In other German romances, the possibility of women inheriting and ruling is also played down. Gottfried von Strassburg's Isot is a highly educated heroine, with musical and poetic gifts, which are refined by the hero (suggesting that his gifts are greater), gifts which put her in conflict with her society and her marriage; as an only child, she might well be the heir to her land, but that point is barely mentioned. Her father had taken Ireland by force and married the sister of the previous duke who should be the source of his legitimacy, but the author makes Rome the validating authority. Ireland should be Isot's heritage, as Mark's men point out, but that is not referred to at the betrothal, and in any case she would bring the land to Mark, not to the hero. Her mother's medical powers cure the hero but that feat is countered by her magic powers which backfire badly when the potion she designed for Isot's happy marriage traps her in an adulterous affair. Isot's artistic talents are extraordinary, but they are developed to make her a suitable partner in love for the hero, not to prepare her to rule. Wolfram's Parzival rescues and marries Cundwiramur, who has ruled her own land in a desperate situation; he is, however, destined to a greater heritage, the grail kingdom. His claim to the grail kingdom is through his mother, but she cannot inherit it herself. The mother, Herzeloyde, apparently had control of her first husband's lands, but rather than govern them, she held a tourney to give herself and the lands to the winner, and after the death of her second husband, Parzival's father, she retires to a forest to raise her son. In the early part of the story, before the hero's birth, two other women hold lands and want to bestow them on Parzival's father along with themselves, but they fail and they fade out of the story very quickly. One of them, like several other women in the poem, has gone too far in testing her lover and lost him, an obvious lesson that women should not try to control their men's lives.

Women fare no better in French romances that are not written for women patrons. The heroine in Raoul de Houdenc's *Meraugis de Portlesguez* begins as the heir to her land who governs well, whom girls come from far and wide to hear and see (123), but she very quickly becomes the object of male competition and exercises no control over the plot except to establish when the men will fight for her.[47] Women play a small role in the story and are belittled when they assert themselves. The hero and Gawain both love her and fight for her; her preference is not considered, and she can only delay their battle while she goes to Arthur for judgment.

At the court, Kay ridicules her problem, suggesting that each man have her for a month, and the queen aggressively demands that she be the one to preside, bringing in ladies to hear the case because judgments of love are hers (887ff.). The division between love as a woman's concern and fighting as a man's is quite clear, since neither man accepts the women's judgment; a fight is scheduled and meanwhile the men go off for a year to have adventures. In the course of the adventures, both men are imprisoned: Gawain by a woman who makes him fight and kill whoever comes or be killed himself, from whom the hero rescues him by pretending to be a woman but carrying a sword under his cloak; and Meraugis in a garden where one can do nothing but dance, until he is able to kill his captor and escape. In both cases, the hero is temporarily involved in womanish behavior but succeeds only when he takes manly action.[48]

Hugh of Rutland is more overt in his misogyny. In *Ipomedon*, he wrote what seems like an anti-Lancelot, certainly a story which presents women unfavorably and humiliates the arrogant heroine.[49] Though she is heir to her land and said to be wise, good, and beautiful, she is so proud that she will take only a man who has conquered all. She is called "la Fiere Pucele," and she gets her comeuppance by falling in love with a hero who refuses to fight, who makes himself an object of ridicule, acting like a coward not at the lady's command or to prove his devotion, as Lancelot does, but by his own choice and to punish her for her pride. The poet underscores his attitude at the end of the poem with an address to (male) lovers from the god of love, telling them to love loyally and warning that they will be excommunicated if they withdraw before they have done their thing ("devant ço ke il ait sun bon fait," 10566) but absolved if they have full leave to enjoy ("plener cungé [probably a misogynist pun] de enveisir," 10568-69). Any lady, Hugh says, who does not believe him can come and he will inscribe the charter, hanging the seal on her rear ("se li seaus li pent as nages," 10580). That is the last line of the poem as we have it.

Hugh's later romance, *Protheselaus,* was written for a male patron, Gilbert of Monmouth, son of Baderon, who ordered him to translate it from a Latin book he had (12701-2).[50] Hugh's poem is a model of the romance written for a man, in which women are either helpless or treacherous, men put their loyalties to other men over all others in a male world in which fighting alternates with mutual support, and war, not marriage, achieves the solution. In his adventures, Protheselaus keeps making male friends from among allies of his father and even allies of his enemies who are won over by his heroism. The hero is the son of Ipomedon and la Fiere; as the younger brother, he is heir only to his mother's land at the beginning, but he looks like his father, fights like his father, and ends winning his father's heritage as well. It is only after he is established as king of his father's land that he finally sends to the heroine to marry her.

The heroine is Medea, a woman who had loved his father. The widowed-queen of Crete, she rules the land not as her father's heir but as her husband's relict.[51] She sends him an offer of aid and love when his inheritance is usurped by his brother, but the wrong message is substituted, so he spurns her aid and mistrusts her love for most of the romance. He also holds against her that she did not give him a double reward as promised when he saved her dog, although she did not know who he was, and she is obliged to put herself through public humiliation at the end to make it up to him. Other women in the romance fare no better. One falls in love with the hero and tries to win him, committing a double betrayal of her husband and her lover, who happens to be the hero's treacherous enemy. Yet another imprisons him when he refuses her advances, to the distress of some of her own men. There is a Pucele Salvage, in whose service a knight fights all comers and tricks them into falling into a sleep from which they awake as lepers.[52] A girl who had been unfaithful to her knight is publicly humiliated once a year: the bloody head of her lover is set before her and she is beaten and dragged off by the hair; the hero reconciles her with the knight but only after she has begged forgiveness. And the poet interjects remarks about women throughout; bad women trouble a whole kingdom, 80-81; you have to be careful with women who do not get their way in love, 1752ff.; a woman's cleverness can lead to the death of many good knights and trouble for many lands, 6186-89; clever women deceive wise men, 6447.

Marie de Champagne, who commissioned Chrétien's *Lancelot,* also encouraged Gautier d'Arras, a poet who seems to have worked for men and women patrons, sometimes on the same project. What Marie's role was in Gautier's *Eracle* cannot be determined, but it is possible that she influenced him to moderate the misogyny inherent in the story (of the wise child who reveals the infidelity of all women). Gautier says he began *Eracle* for Thibaut of Blois and for Marie, Thibaut's sister-in-law: "Li quens Tiebaus . . . me fist ceste oevre rimoiier; / par lui le fis, . . . et par le contesse autressi, / Marie, fille Loey" (6523-28), though he finished it for Baudouin V of Hainaut (6559-61).[53] *Eracle* is a curiously conflicted work, which seems to fluctuate between saint's life and romance, between misogyny and philogyny, and which could be read as a cautionary tale for jealous husbands. The nominal hero is conceived with divine help and born to a devout mother who literally gives away all her wealth for the father's soul and finally sells her son, with his enthusiastic agreement, in order to give more. The heroine is brought up by an aunt, who protects her from the world and sends her off to marry the emperor with injunctions to give generously, saying those to whom God grants power should give more.

Despite these examples, the author and his hero mouth traditional antifeminist "truths" and unmask a series of women candidates for empress who hide their vices under the appearance of good. When the virtually perfect heroine is found, she becomes a model empress, praised by all, helping any who come to her, aiding churches, caring for orphans and the poor, establishing abbeys; "the Holy Spirit works in her" ("oevre en li sains Esperis," 2928). Nonetheless, the emperor is afraid to leave her unguarded when he goes away; he ignores Eracle's strong advice to let her guard her own virtue so she will love the lord from whom her honors come, rather than show her the way to misbehave by punishing her for nothing. As Eracle points out, the emperor is making a serious mistake in ignoring his advice, since he has never been wrong, but the emperor closes the empress up in a tower, guarded day and night by twenty-four men—again the motif of the imprisoned queen. She has impressive monologues on the injustice of her situation, monologues which may express both the poet's view and Marie's and which justify her decision to take a lover, an action for which she takes full responsibility when it is discovered.

In what might well be a statement about women and courtly culture, the empress, having been wronged by the highest representative of patri-archal power, turns to art for comfort, to a young man who plays the harp beautifully. When the emperor returns and discovers the affair, Eracle tells him it was all his fault and persuades him to give her up, though he is sad to lose "la dame de le millor vie, / le plus vaillant, le plus senee / qui onques fust de Rome nee" (5076–78). She goes off happily with her (well-born) musician-lover, but Rome has lost an exemplary empress. The romance ends with Eracle's conquering the pagan who took the true cross, which had been discovered by another holy empress, Helena. But the apparently perfect Eracle cannot enter the sepulchre where the cross is buried because of his worldly pride until he repents and asks God to pardon him as he had pardoned the Magdalene, identifying himself with a woman in his sin. Thus the hero who began by revealing the vices of so many women ends being saved by identifying himself with a woman sinner. The misogyny that is expressed within the romance is in fact belied by the exemplary actions of the women who frame the story—Eracle's mother, the empress's aunt, the historic Helena, even the empress herself when left to act as she chooses—while both the emperor and the hero make serious mistakes and the only man worthy of the empress is a musician.

Gautier's other romance, *Ille et Galeron,* which is more conventional in its plot, was also begun for a woman, Beatrice of Burgundy, wife of emperor Frederick Barbarossa.[54] Though he finished it for Thibaut of Blois (Marie's brother-in-law), Gautier acknowledges Beatrice's support even at the end: "do you think I would have undertaken this without him or her making me? But the work is well employed whichever of them it is sent to" ("Cuidiés, se il ne me feïst / et ele ausi, que jel deïsse, / ne en tel painne m'en meïsse? / Mais l'uevre est molt bien emploïe / au quel d'ax qu'el soit envoïe," 6592p–t). His praise of Beatrice here is brief but strong: "la meldre qui soit nee" (6592g). At the beginning of the poem he praises her lavishly as an example to all women, a model of "savoir ... proece ... bonté ... largece"; counseled from infancy by "cortoisie et porveance" and accompanied by "sapience," she adorns the court of Germany as she brought honor to Rome, where she was crowned. She has power but even greater will; anyone can come before her and she will hear them (1-129).

The story of *Ille et Galeron* is filled with themes I associate with romances for women. Its hero is vulnerable on many levels: socially, he is inferior to both his wives—raised by the first to a dukedom, by the second to an empire; emotionally, he lacks confidence in himself and therefore in Galeron's love; and physically, he loses an eye because he tries too hard to prove himself, and he lacks vision—like the emperor in *Eracle,* he worries without cause about the fickleness of women, trusting to theory rather than to his own experience. Both the women he marries are the only heirs to their lands: Ganor, as the only child, inherits her father's empire, but Galeron, rather surprisingly, is the chosen heir of her brother's land. He chooses not to marry so that she will inherit (1395-98), and after her death, her husband divides her land among their three children, two sons and a daughter, reinforcing the tradition of female inheritance. Both women go on quests to find the hero because their lands need his service. It is rather disconcerting that Galeron abandons her land for several years, letting it go to wrack and ruin while she looks for Ille to come back and save it, but Gautier seems to be emphasizing her singleminded devotion—all her companions in the quest die, while she carries on and succeeds. Both women prefer nobility of character to high birth, and both refuse husbands of their own rank in favor of the hero: Galeron rejects counts and dukes, Ganor the emperor of Constantinople, preferring to rule alone if she cannot marry Ille.[55] Ille is the son of count Eliduc, and the story may owe something to the *lai* by Marie de France which tells of another man with certain limitations caught between two women, both of whom seem to be too good for him. If *Ille* was inspired by *Eliduc,* and there seems no way to prove which way the influence went, we would have a woman encouraging a poet to write a work based in part at least on the work of a woman poet.

A sister of one of Gautier's patrons, countess Yolande (Yolent) de Pol, the sister of Baudouin V of Hainaut for whom Gautier finished *Eracle,* commissioned a romance by an unknown poet that shares motifs with Gautier's *Ille.* Yolande was an aunt by marriage of Philip Augustus, therefore related by marriage to his half-sisters, Marie de Champagne and Alix de Blois, both patrons of romance poets. Yolande was also the mother of two daughters, one of whom inherited her father's lands (Fourrier, 118-19). The romance written for her, *Guillaume de Palerme,* like *Ille,* has a hero who is lower born than the heroine, though not by as much as it appears through most of the story, since he is the grandson of the Greek emperor *through his mother;* a heroine who is the only heir to the Roman empire; and a woman who rules a major land on her own.[56] In addition, and this is unusual in romances commissioned by women, it has educated women who misuse their powers, though instead of being punished at the end, as happens so often in the prose romances, they are saved.

The story, according to the poet, is about both Guillaume and his mother, Felise, and women manipulate the plot for good and ill. Felise is a good and loyal lady (like the countess Yolent, 9623, 9656), daughter of the emperor of Greece, who puts two educated Greek women in charge of her son's education. Unfortunately, they plot with the king's brother to murder him and his father, but the child is rescued by a werwolf. The werwolf is himself the son of the king of Spain, transformed by his step-mother, another educated lady ("sage a merveille et bien letree," 7305) gone astray.[57] The werwolf cares for the child until he is taken into the household of the emperor of Rome, where he and Meliors, the emperor's daughter and only heir, fall in love. Guillaume, apparently fatherless, thinks the love is impossible. Meliors, like so many heroines of romances for women, is not concerned about his birth; she thinks he must be well-born, and in any case gold is gold wherever you find it. To avoid an unwanted marriage, she suggests they flee, disguised at the suggestion of her cousin-companion in bearskins. Under the care of the werwolf, they eventually get to southern Italy, now ruled by Guillaume's widowed mother, who is fighting off an attack by the king of Spain because she refused to let his son marry her daughter. Unrecognized, Guillaume fights for his mother and sister, saves their land, and using his poverty as an excuse, refuses the queen's offer of herself and the land.

Queen Felise presides over the final scenes of reconciliation and resolution. As she makes peace with the king of Spain, the werwolf sheds tears at the king's feet and the king remembers hearing that his second wife had transformed his son. Threatened with burning and the imprisonment of her son, his wife asks the wolf's forgiveness and turns him back into a man. When he is embarrassed at his nakedness, she throws her mantle over him, a protective gesture that suggests her rehabilitation. Even the women who plotted against Guillaume and his father are pardoned and allowed to retire to a hermitage, while the younger characters are united in marriage. Though Felise gives the traditional advice to the young brides to serve their husbands and keep peace, her life remains one of power and independence. Guillaume's marriage to Meliors puts him in line for the empire and they return to *her* land, leaving his mother still ruling as queen of southern Italy. When her son becomes the emperor of Rome and her daughter the queen of Spain, the vision she had had of *her* destiny is fulfilled.

Even when romances purport to be addressed to women the poet was courting rather than to named patrons, as with three other romances from the late twelfth century, *Bel Inconnu, Partonopeu de Blois,* and *Florimont,* they share many of the themes I have been tracing. Renaut de Beaujeu wrote a romance for the lady who, he says, taught or inspired him to write *cançons,* and he did so with the same objective, to win her love. He uses the story of the Bel Inconnu to get what he wants in a charmingly direct way, one that tells us something about audience involvement with romance. Renaut suspends the story with the hero committed to the wrong woman, gambling that his lady outside the romance has so identified with the heroine that she will be kind to the poet in order to make him restore the hero to the right woman: "if you show him a kind semblance, [Renaus] will make Guinglain find again the love he lost . . . but if you delay, . . . he will never have her" ("mais por un biau sanblant mostrer / vos feroit Guinglain retrover / s'amie, que il a perdue . . . se de çou li faites delai, / . . . ja mais n'avera s'amie," 6255-61). A clever ploy, it suggests that audiences could sometimes influence the outcome of a story, as they did later with serial novels, and it gives support to the idea that a poet might expect a patron to identify with and be complimented by his treatment of a character in his story.[58]

The heroine of this story, who is simply called the Pucele-as-blances-mains, is a woman of extraordinary education and talent.[59] Her father was a rich king, and she is his only child and heir (4933ff.); he had her taught the seven arts (with magic replacing music) and much else, so she can read the future and work enchantments. She does, in fact, use her powers to manipulate the hero and the action of the story, at least up to the point at which they consummate their love; then her power over him fails, or she refuses to use it, and the hero is free to stay or leave.[60] Though he wants to stay, he is torn by his commitment to chivalry, which is part of his attraction for her, not to say his heritage as Gawain's son; the other woman, Blonde Esmeree, lures him away with a tourney of which she and her huge land are the prize. The Blonde is also the only heir to her land, and it is so large a land that it will make the hero quite powerful (5283-84), a point which weighs heavily with his uncle Arthur later. Blonde Esmeree was the victim of evil enchanters, who seized her city by illusion and, when she would not marry one of them, turned her into a dragon by hitting her with a book. I have somewhat facetiously suggested that this might represent the dangers of education for women—"hit them with books and they turn into dragons"—but one might also say it represents the dangers of refusing a literary lover, since poets are magicians—"refuse me, and I will make you a monster with my words." The hero is again a young and unproven unknown for a good part of the romance, who is drawn through a series of adventures and tests by the heroine's magic powers; and all the action of the romance is set in motion by the two women.[61]

The magic powers of women in these romances addressed to friends of the poet are positive and perhaps complimentary to the lady to whom they are addressed.[62] Like the poet, the women in *Bel Inconnu* and *Partonopeu* create action and illusion, but only to help or at the very least to amuse; there is no hint of these heroines misusing their learning for harm. Melior in *Partonopeu* is the empress, educated to her position as her father's only heir—or so he had been assured by augurs, though in fact she has a sister, who plays an important role in the plot.[63] She learned the seven arts thoroughly, then all of medicine (including cures), then religion (*divinité*, old law and new), and finally "nigremance et enchantement"; by fifteen she had surpassed all her teachers, and she had had more than two hundred (4573ff.). Her powers enabled her to entertain her father by making his chamber grow to encompass the country, fill with light and armed knights who fought and disappeared, or wild beasts, or castles of a thousand people (4635ff.); she is also able to draw the hero to her, to keep him invisible to all but herself, to entertain him with the deeds of ancient times (1868) by her sweet words ("douce et soëf a le parole," 1871). She has, in other words, a poet's powers, which do finally prevail in this romance, although they are countered for a time by the demands of the conventional world in the person of the hero's mother, sister to the king of France. The mother, understandably worried, exerts her own magic powers with a love potion to free the hero from what she thinks is a demonic love and a lantern to enable him to see his love as she is.

The light reveals, of course, that the heroine is human not demonic, but it also seems to put an end to her magic. Because she is the empress, however, she can still exert some control over the action of the story: she holds a tourney to determine the best of her many suitors, which is interestingly inconclusive, but then she makes the contenders go through a beauty contest, with a distinctly feminist tone. Saying "I care a lot about beauty" ("je tir molt a la belté," 10388) and telling the men "you shouldn't be surprised, since that's the way you choose among us" ("si ne vos en mervellies mie, / car si choisit chascuns de vos / quant doit prendre une de nos," 10392-94), Melior has them disarm and parade in their robes. The hero is embarrassed, but he wins this contest without challenge. The scene makes many points, not the least of which is that the strongest fighter is not necessarily the best man, at least from a woman's viewpoint. Although she is an empress in her own right and can manipulate so much of the action, Melior continues to worry about a woman's plight in love, afraid she will seem frivolous unless she hides her feelings, while men have the best part, the freedom to speak their feelings (9045ff.).[64]

Partonopeu is another hero who is manipulated by the women in his life, his love and his mother—one might even say that Melior acts like his mother when he departs, giving him money and telling him to help the poor—and he needs the nurturing and plotting of the heroine's sister to bring him back to health and to his lady. The poet, whose powers are certainly reflected in the heroine's, claims to identify with the hero or at least to compare himself favorably with Partonopeu, who is luckier in his love if not as loyal as the poet. The poet complains periodically about his own devotion and her failure to reward him and warns her that chastity poisons beauty (6281). Like Renaut, he stops before the end of his story, saying there is more to tell (about the other characters), but he is in such pain for his lady that he can only weep. However, if she would wink at him, he could go on.[65]

Florimont, the hero of the romance by Aimon/Aymes de Varenne, is another young hero who must be helped by a series of women and occasional magic to get through adventures: he is nurtured at the beginning by a fairy who gives him a ring that will make people grant what he asks, a protective ointment, and a special sword; another woman gives him a magic ointment at the end that enables him to get past a gate and lions in order to rescue his father and grandfather; and the heroine raises his status, bringing him the kingdom of Greece. Florimont falls in love with the fairy, heir to the Ile Selee, who heals his wounds after he kills a monster; she offers herself and her land to him, but he hesitates because of his parents, afraid they will die of grief if he leaves them. She gives him her love secretly as long as he tells no one, but his mother follows him and sees the fairy, who must cut herself off from him or die.[66] This rejection weans the hero from his parents. He gives away everything he has, including his identity; he departs as the "povres perdus," leaving them and their land vulnerable to a devastating war. He will come back at the end to rescue and restore them, needing the help of yet another lady and her ointment. Meanwhile, he goes away and serves the heroine's father, quickly winning her love and eventually the father's support, despite his poverty, and becoming, through his marriage, heir to the Greek kingdom.

The heroine, Romadanaple, who is introduced in the story before the hero, is the only child of the Greek king who had himself inherited the right to the throne from a woman, his mother.[67] He has his daughter taught letters by a woman master from Cyprus, who is "mout bien letree" (1009) because of her "bien letrez" father. The governess teaches her the art of conversation and grammar; Romadanaple reads about battles and love, but she is more interested in love (1027–38). At the hero's first sight of her, he forgets his fairy love and agrees to serve her father. Romadanaple argues with herself about her feelings, justifying her love both by etymology—the syllables of her name turned around mean "full of love," "plena d'amor" 7760ff.—and by proverbial wisdom and logic. Her arguments may well express the views of a dependent poet as well as a woman facing an unwanted marriage: a good poor man is better than a bad baron (7887–88); there is no use adding wealth to wealth (7917–18); an apple is a better fruit than an acorn, though it comes from a smaller tree

(8975-82); if I married a king or emperor he would be a lord rather than a friend, this one would be lord and friend (9013-16).

The motif of a woman seeing value in a man of lower birth recurs through these romances. Certainly hypogamy favors a woman, though hypergamy may benefit her family. The position of a woman who marries above her has something in common with the dependent poet's and may explain why poets are so sympathetic to its opposite. It is impossible to know if the woman character is asserting her own rights to choose when she prefers someone of lower status, or if the poet is making a plea for himself when he has her argue for quality despite lower birth. It is certainly not coincidental that shortly after Romadanaple resolves her doubts and invites Florimont into her bed, the poet digresses about the "fine amor" that existed in their time and the meaning of his own name, Aymes, which like his heroine's destines him for love, 9217ff. Like Renaut and the poet of *Partonopeu*, Aymes claims to write for the lady he loves, "Aymes por amour *anulli*" (8, which Hilka interprets as an anagram for Juliane, xcviii). Aymes says that he put the story which came from Greek to Latin into writing as "fine amors" advised him, composing the romance for his "amie" Vialine, another anagram for Juliane (9207-16).

I have concentrated on romances composed for women in the late twelfth century because this was the beginning, and in some ways the climax, from our point of view, of the genre, though romances were still composed for women and dedicated to them in the succeeding centuries.[68] I will conclude with two from the second half of the thirteenth century, *Escanor* and *Cléomadès*, which in different ways combine many of the motifs discussed here. Both were composed at the command of queens, and both are based on stories told by women. Gerard of Amiens wrote *Escanor* "at the command of a noble, lovely, and wise lady . . . the worthiest queen ever born in Spain . . . wife of the King of England" (8-29), that is, Eleanor of Castile, queen until her death in 1290 of Edward I, himself a descendant of the Eleanor in whose court it all seems to have begun. Adenès li Rois composed *Cléomadès* at the command of two ladies, whose names are inscribed at the end of the poem, Marie, queen of France, wife of Philippe le Hardi, and Blanche de France, widow of Ferdinand of Castile and sister of Philippe.[69]

Gerard says Eleanor told him the story of *Escanor* ("de qui li contes est venus . . . le conte que la gentiex dame m'a dit," 19, 48-49) and he rejoices to follow the will of such a lady, to tell the tale as the "matere" has it (50-60).[70] His response to his patron's material is quite different from Chrétien's to Marie's version of *Lancelot*, though the hero of this story is equally unusual if in quite a different way. The women who told him the story, like the woman the hero falls in love with, have the power to turn a very ugly duckling into a swan. The main protagonist of the story is Kay, Arthur's seneschal, well known to romance audiences. He is a working

seneschal throughout the romance, ordering food, organizing meals, returning to court at his lord's summons, and through it all he continues to
exchange the insults he is known for in Arthurian romance: "your tongue
should be banished and thrown into the latrine," Arthur tells him early on
("tel langue devroit on banir / et jeter en une longaingne," 298-99). But
in this romance, he falls in love and struggles through most of its almost
26,000 lines to be worthy of the lady. His transformation into a courtly
lover, both courageous and humble, is very appealing, perhaps because he
is constantly struggling with his old self. Inspired by love for Andrivete,
he fights well, amazed at the force love has given him—"I wasn't worth
two nuts before" ("ainc mais ne valui II nois," 4274)—but afraid there
are too many good knights for him to be able to win her. Though he is
never at a loss for words with others, he cannot bring himself to declare
his love to her; he resolves not to bring ridicule on himself any more, but
when he thinks he has lost her, the venomous tongue takes over. He wishes
the same misery to the king and all who make fun of him in very uncourtly
language: "now I see that your courtesy is shit . . . I've been pissing into
the wind" ("or voi bien que devenue / est vo courtoisie la merde . . . j'ai
pissie contre le vent," 22536-37, 22544).

Fortunately, his lady is equally sharp-tongued; as Dynadan notes, they
suit each other.[71] Andrivete is a woman of spirit, gracious to those who
please her but cruel to those who do not; she is cultivated and charming
enough to delight Gawain but harsh to Dynadan, who presumably deserves it for his misogyny. Like Romadanaple in *Florimont,* she is the first
main character whose story is told in the romance. The only heir of the
king of Northumberland, well educated, with no interest in marrying, she
is determined and able to follow her own will. After her father dies, her
uncle tries to marry her to someone unsuitable whom he can control, but
she refuses. He imprisons her and usurps her land, but Andrivete escapes
and goes on a quest for aid to Britain to recover her land. She does not
simply ask for aid, she gets it by locating and helping to rescue Gawain's
brother, Gifflet, a situation she manipulates to her advantage, gaining the
gratitude of Gawain and their uncle Arthur.

Gifflet's love story is a subplot of this romance. He too is a hero with
problems, though they are practical rather than personal: he is imprisoned
for a good part of the romance until he is rescued by the heroine. The
woman he loves is the queen of Traverse, and he is not of her status ("pas
de la hautece, / du pooir ne de la justece," 18381-82). She shares many
of the characteristics of the heroines I have discussed: we are told that she
is of much higher rank than Gifflet, a reigning queen, learned, full of honor
and good, who inspires the women in her company and has restored her
whole country with her goodness; she offers her land and her wealth to
help Andrivete win her land back. The queen has no desire to marry until
she meets Gifflet, and though she marries him, she leaves him and returns

to the celibate life in grief when her brother dies. The sad story of her brother, Escanor, the titular hero of the romance, and his wife, their deep mutual love and deaths, is told very briefly. It includes, however, an interesting detail: when the wife dies, Escanor decides to become a hermit, but first he has to find an heir for her land as well as his own, because she is yet another woman who inherited her land.

There are several women in the romance with extraordinary powers of one sort or another: a cousin of Escanor's mother, who knew astronomy and magic and prophesied a great future for Gawain; a girl who is able to cure a drugged horse by taking a sachet of powder out of its ear and to end a war by putting her body between two fighting knights to make them stop, berating Arthur so severely for letting the fight go on that his barons support her, the fight stops, and the siege is lifted; and queen Esclarmonde, who made a mechanical bed for her lover that suggests (as in *Partonopeu*) a woman's ability to create fantasy and art through love. The bed sits on lions who seem to be attacking until a viele plays by itself to calm them, with a tree of gold with flowers and fruit and birds that can be made to sing sweetly or be silent, and an angel above it with a trumpet that sounds a melody that can not be imagined (15832ff.). I do not know if this kind of art by magic in a chamber goes back to Benoît's *chambre de labastre*; if it does, Gerard has changed the woman's role from the inhabitant of the chamber to the creator of it. The poet also reveals a sympathy for women's interests through remarks like Arthur's, that a man should never marry his daughter to a bad man for wealth (252ff.), echoed later by Kay; and indirectly, by showing up the men's attitudes, in the custom that women are not allowed to show their grief at tourneys because it spoils the men's pleasure (6148ff.) and in Kay's cursing all women because he has been persuaded, wrongly, that Andrivet betrayed him.

Cléomadès is another long romance in which women are models of loyalty, courtesy, and wisdom and their interests are paramount, even if most of them do not rule countries or control the action of the story. Though the plot turns on magic, the tone is more sentimental, perhaps even more realistic, less dramatic or heroic, than the other romances. Instead of active, powerful women fashioning their own lives, the focus is on the ability of women to work together and within a male world. Nonetheless, the two women patrons might well have taken satisfaction in the presentation of women in the poem, queens of exemplary behavior, a beautiful, wise, and talented heroine, beautiful, loyal, and loving sisters and companions, all supportive and protective of each other. The women are not exceptionally educated—only the (male) villain is learned—and they do not manipulate the action, but they often guide it with counsel and moral support. Queens are always consulted and seem to be always present when decisions are made; they advise mercy and support, building friendship through marriage rather than fighting. Though the heroine must wait to be rescued, she uses clever ruses to protect herself meanwhile. A major portion of the romance (more than 3,500 of its 18,688 lines) is devoted to preparations for the marriage of the hero and heroine, which leads to eight other marriages, emphasizing woman's social and political role as peacemaker.[72]

The poet and his characters are concerned about women's needs and feelings: the hero's three sisters sneak a look at their future husbands and worry who will get the ugly one; their brother, worried his sister will die of sorrow, tries to talk their father out of the rash promise that set up the marriage; the father himself had hesitated to betroth all three at once and lose the joy of marrying each separately. The heroine, worried about her companions who concealed her elopement, makes the hero promise to send for them and find husbands for them. When the heroine finds herself in a strange place, she takes heart at the sight of other women, who befriend and protect her; and when she describes the hero to her mother, she says she has never seen such a courtly thing, "ains si courtoise riens ne vit" (3578). Men grieve like women and take comfort from them: when the hero temporarily loses his love, he faints often in his sisters' arms and they keep him from killing himself. The heroine's father comforts her for the loss of her mother. Her mother dies of grief when she disappears, just as the hero's father dies of grief when he disappears.

The serious mistakes and misdeeds in the story are committed by men: the hero's father makes a rash promise in reward for extraordinary gifts, which threatens the happiness of a daughter; the villain plots with some success against hero and heroine; the hero foolishly underestimates the villain's capacity to harm, and equally foolishly leaves the heroine completely alone in a park outside the city walls. And there is virtually no misogyny in the story. Even when the poet tells us that many women can not keep secrets, he belies his own comment: the secret is first told by a woman, but the chain includes as many men as women, going from a companion of the heroine to her cousin, who tells her brother, who tells his mother, who tells her husband, who tells his companion (10485ff.).

As in so many romances written for women, the main women, the hero's mother and the heroine, are both heirs to their lands, though in this case the fact is more important in the descriptions of them than in the action. His mother, Ynabel, is heir to all Spain, and wise in word and deed ("hoirs fu de trestoute la terre / d'Espaigne et de tout le pays. / Sage fu en fais et en dis," 106–8). She cares for poor noble girls, orphaned maidens, and defenseless ladies (189–92). The heroine, Clarmondine, is also "un tout seul hoir" (2744), who composes and sings songs while she waits for the hero. She is tender toward her parents, insisting on seeing them before she elopes, and anxious enough about her meeting with the hero's family to ask to freshen up and rest from the wind, after a long ride on a magic horse. This leads to a kidnapping by the villain, but the fault is the hero's who left her alone. The tension in the story focuses on her plight, first in the hands of the villain, then of a noble king who insists on marrying her. She preserves herself from both by extracting promises that they will not touch her before the marriage, and by creating clever fictions about her identity and experiences.[73] Finally, she pretends to go mad, with such violence that she has to be physically restrained, though she is gently cared for by the king's mother and sister, and she persists in this fiction until the hero rescues her, so all through his quest we are worried about her. The hero does not win the heroine by fighting, though he fights and helps people as he goes; but he finds and rescues Clarmondine by art not violence, with the aid of a magic horse and only when he too adopts false identities in the company of a loyal minstrel who points him in the right direction. Since the minstrel, Pinchonnet, may be a stand-in for the poet (see van Hasselt, *Cléomadès*, xxiv), some connection may be implied between the hero and heroine, who use the minstrel's art of creating fictions so successfully, and the source of the poet's fictions, the women who told him the story.

Adenès acknowledges their part in his composition twice: at the beginning, after listing his other works, one of which was addressed to the same queen Marie,[74] he says he is nervous about undertaking such a diverse and marvelous story, but he is comforted by the fact that two ladies commanded him to listen to it and put it in rhyme, two ladies who are the flower of sense, beauty, and worth. They are, like the ladies in the story, "sage et courtoise et debonaire," a model of all good, but he will not name them, for fear of annoying them, until the end. At the end (18519ff.), he says he can tell no more, because that is all the ladies who told him the story said. He works their names into an acrostic, LA ROINE DE FRANCE MARIE, MADAME BLANCHE ANNE (18531-69), in the course of which he recalls their command, hopes he has pleased them, praises their goodness and wisdom, and assures us there is nothing but truth in his story. Then he tells something about himself and his other patrons and finally sends the book to the count of Artois. A miniature in the manuscript on which the van Hasselt edition is based shows Marie on a bed of state, Blanche and the daughter of the count of Artois on cushions, and Adenès half-kneeling before them, as Blanche tells a story and the others listen (described, xxvii). The appeal of the story is indicated by a Froissart poem van Hasselt mentions (xv-xvi) in which the poet sees a girl reading a romance she describes as "bien fais / et dittés amoureusement"; it turns out to be *Cléomadès*, which they then read to each other.

This is a far cry from the somewhat petulant testimony to a taste for courtly literature a century earlier by Denis Piramus in the prologue to *La Vie Seint Edmund*. Denis calls works like *Partonopeu*, which are popular at rich courts, fables and lies, like dreams which cannot be true ("fable . . . menceonge. / La matire resemble songe / kar ceo ne poüst unkes estre,"

29-31). He says Dame Marie (Marie de France) makes rhymes and composes *lais* which are not at all true, but are loved and praised; that men (kings, princes, counts, barons, and vavasours) and women love them, women because they are according to their desire.[75] Such works make people forget their thoughts and their troubles, unlike the useful material he is about to offer, which cures their souls. The reference to women's desires might mean simply that fantasies about love are what women want to hear, or it might refer to their commissioning such works from other poets; it is tantalizing to wonder if Denis had any reason to suspect a hidden political agenda, though he gives no indication of that. In any case, his words testify to women's place as significant members of the audience for courtly literature.

It would seem from this brief survey of romances composed to please specific women, whether patrons or friends, that certain motifs did appeal to those women: the vulnerable hero who needs the help of women at least as much as he serves them, in contrast to the overpowering heroes of epics; the heroine in a position of power and wealth, who controls the action by her superior education and special powers, who has more to give the hero than to receive from him, in magic gifts or land. The vulnerable hero is characteristic of the romance, whether written for male or female patrons, but I would suggest that he evolves in that direction because of the influence of women patrons and audience on the genre. The gifted heroine, on the other hand, is primarily a feature of romances dedicated to specific women, who might identify with and be complimented by such a heroine and be persuaded to value the poet as the heroine does the hero. Whether the poet expresses his feelings or his patron's through these impressive heroines is a question I cannot answer, but I think it is not unlikely that their intentions might coincide. It is at least possible that for many poets a world in which women had power to control the political and the cultural scene might have seemed a more welcoming world for them.

Part Three
Women in Control

5 Women's Visions of Women

"DO NOT THINK THEY ARE THE FIGMENTS OF WOMEN"

After the letters that show women exercising authority in the secular and religious worlds or participating in the scholarly and intellectual lives of friends and colleagues, after the histories and romances that reveal how interested women were in the accomplishments and adventures of other women, it is not surprising to find women writers presenting women characters who are intelligent, forceful, and courageous. Women in narratives by women take an active part in their own and others' lives, as the last chapter will show, but even in visionary literature, where there are no heroines to fashion or plot lines to shape, where the major purpose is to receive and convey God's message, one finds women concerned with the problems women face and looking for female models with power and knowledge.

Hildegard of Bingen and Elisabeth of Schönau were public figures whose advice was sought by men and women of some standing in the religious (and in Hildegard's case also the secular) world. They were consulted because they were known to have visions which gave them a direct line to divine truth; the written records of those visions were also consulted, and it is as the well-known authors of the visions that they command a chapter in this study. Both Hildegard and Elisabeth were Benedictines with some authority in the ecclesiastical world, Hildegard as abbess, Elisabeth as magistra, but as visionaries they were known and respected well beyond their administrative spheres.[1] Though both claimed to be untutored (though not illiterate), to be the blank tablets on which God's finger wrote, because the voice of God did speak through them they were widely consulted even about doctrine, their advice and information requested on a wide range of subjects. Whereas Heloise sent forty-two questions to Abelard for his answers, Hildegard received sixty-nine questions from the monks of Villers for her (God's) answers. Both Hildegard and Elisabeth were given a divine mission to correct the church and clergy and to fight the Cathar heresy, and despite some initial reluctance, they did so resoundingly.[2]

The decision to preach God's word publicly, by spoken or written word, was not an easy one for either of them. Hildegard looked to Bernard of Clairvaux for validation before she made her revelations public; Elisabeth turned to Hildegard when she needed courage to continue. Both suffered physically and psychologically from the strain of conveying the divine message to a corrupt world, which often cast them in the (male) role of public opposition to the male hierarchy. But along with the voice of God which spoke through them, they both had a sense of their own nobility, their position in the worldly hierarchy which balanced the assumed humility of a religious and gave them a certain confidence in dealing with the religious hierarchy.[3] Though both spoke forcefully as God's tools, they also felt the need for women models to support them in their visions, Elisabeth looked to unusual historic women like Mary and certain saints and martyrs as well as to Hildegard, Hildegard to abstract figures like Ecclesia and Wisdom and female aspects of the divinity. There are hints in the visions that both felt the deprivation of sacerdotal powers, Elisabeth more acutely than Hildegard, but their visions set them above priests by putting them in direct contact with God.

Hildegard, the older of the two, was already known for her visions and her criticism of major ecclesiastical and secular leaders when Elisabeth revealed her visions and looked to Hildegard as a model and source of moral support. Hildegard had shown concern for Elisabeth in her letter to the Schönau magistra, and she answered Elisabeth's own letter to her with sympathy and encouragement. Her *Scivias*, written in 1151, a year before Elisabeth's visions began, was the acknowledged model for Elisabeth's *Liber viarum dei*, with divine sanction: in a vision, an angel showed Elisabeth a pile of her books and told her she would receive the revelation contained in them after she visited Hildegard, which she did in 1156. Anne Clark points out that Elisabeth and Hildegard had to create new literary genres to express their experiences, so this vision may be Elisabeth's acknowledgment that Hildegard's work offered her the mode she needed. They shared not only the unusual experience of their visions and a public following for them but also other interests, the dangers posed by the Cathar heresy, the corruption of the clergy, and Ursula and her army of eleven thousand virgin martyrs (on which Hildegard's poems may owe something to Elisabeth's visions). And certainly Hildegard's prestige made it easier for Elisabeth to make her messages public. A contemporary chronicle pairs them and their powers: "in these days, God shows signs of his power in the frail sex, in his two handmaids, Hildegard in Rupertsberg near Bingen, and Elisabeth in Schönau, whom he filled with the spirit of prophecy, and revealed many kinds of visions to them, writings which are considered gospel."[4] Because Hildegard is the better-known figure, her range of works broader, and her productive years extending before and after her younger contemporary's, I will end with her and take up Elisabeth's works first.

"I CHOSE YOU BECAUSE YOU ARE FRAGILE"

Elisabeth's visions began when she was a young adult, after she had spent more than a decade in the convent at Schönau, which she entered at about twelve. Her fellow nuns knew and kept a record of her visions for more than a decade before Elisabeth made them public in 1154, when she told her abbot in the story she related to Hildegard. In 1155, her brother Ekbert, persuaded either by a message in his sister's visions or by his sense of their importance or both, and certainly at her urging, entered the monastery at Schönau and began to record and probably to edit the visions, which found a large audience.[5] The first three books, as Ekbert arranged them, are the "visionary diary" (Clark's phrase from Kurt Köster's "visionäre Tagebuch"); they include autobiographical details about the visions and how they came about, the questions she put for herself and others, and the answers she received. A brief piece on the assumption of the Virgin, which had been very popular on its own, appears now as part of the second book.[6] The fourth, the *Liber viarum dei*, sermons on the roads/ways of God, was widely read and circulated in Germany, France, and England and continued to be copied and later printed and translated for several centuries.[7] The book on Ursula's army, elicited by requests to validate recently discovered relics, became the accepted version of the legend.[8]

In the autobiographical books, Elisabeth reveals the inhibitions she feels as a woman, but also the comfort and support she receives from other women, her fellow sisters and their magistra in her daily life, the Virgin Mary and women saints in her visions. She reveals doubts about herself and her religion and tensions in her relation to the priesthood, but also a trusting and good working relationship with her brother, her angel, and male saints.[9] She looks to her brother, whose judgment she trusts, and her abbot for guidance in revealing the visions, worried that people will either think her more holy than she is or will dismiss them as a woman's imaginings ("muliebria figmenta") or the devil's creations, but she makes it clear that God wants them revealed. When she talks to her brother, she describes the physical distress that resulted from her trying to keep everything hidden and the relief when she told. Once when she was in torture over her visions, she says, the sisters pressed her to reveal them—the sisters, in fact, kept notes of the visions all along—and she recovered (*Visionen*, 1.21). Even when Ekbert joins her and they work together, she controls certain aspects of the visions, either by keeping some of them to herself (2.5) or by deciding when and how to put questions in them; indeed, she seems to get answers for the questions others raise only when she has made them her own.

In the beginning, her psychological distress is considerable, relieved only by the Virgin Mary, who appears as both queen and priest, offering her a female model for the highest forms of authority. Though her sisters tended her in her physical sickness "with maternal affection," her anguish of spirit, which we would call deep depression, seems to have been a lonely experience. She speaks of a darkness of spirit ("obscuritate animi"), of being unable to cast the sadness (*tristicia*, very close to despair) from her, when even the prayers that usually delighted her bothered her, when she threw the psalter far from her after reading only one psalm. She doubted Christ: who was he, who so humbled himself for mankind (*homines*)? Could everything written about him be true? Yet he was good, whoever he was, about whom so many good things were written. She doubted even "our blessed advocate," presumably the Virgin. Unable to eat or drink, she thought of suicide to end her suffering, but "in this worst temptation he who keeps Israel did not sleep over me" (1.2).[10]

This state of mind continued from Pentecost to the end of May. Then, with the magistra and the sisters praying with her and helping her to read because she was so weak, she withstood visions that came from Satan (1.3–4) and was rewarded with two visions of Mary. During a mass for the Virgin, Elisabeth collapsed in ecstasy and saw a royal woman, the queen of heaven and mother of the savior, accompanied by Benedict, who comforted her, though she could not hear the words (1.5).[11] Elisabeth came out of her ecstasy, took communion, fell into it again, and saw Mary at the altar in a priestly garment, wearing a diadem with Hail Mary on it so there could be no doubt of her identity.[12] The vision of the woman Mary as priest, countered shortly by the devil as priest (1.8), presumably representing the corrupt clergy, and the fact that Elisabeth so often goes into ecstasy during the mass, where she sees not only God and the saints ("everything *read* in the gospel was *shown* to me," 1.50) but the actual blood and flesh of the Eucharist (1.27, 28) with some regularity, all this while the (male) priest is dealing with symbolic reenactments, is very suggestive. It may well mean that Elisabeth has a perhaps unconscious but nonetheless strong desire to be a priest, to consecrate the host (not an unusual desire for devout girls and women though not often articulated or recorded in the Middle Ages), and that frustration is part of her suffering until the telling of her visions gives her a voice and public role as prophet that transcends the priest's. The visions, too, give her a power priests do not have, while they are exercising one she does not have.[13]

Mary comes several more times to comfort Elisabeth (1.7, 11, 18, 21, 23), sometimes alone, sometimes with other saints, the four evangelists, or a multitude of crowned women martyrs. Perhaps because Mary opens the way, perhaps because she simply gives her confidence, Elisabeth begins to see other saints, often on their feast days, men like John the Baptist and Peter and Paul, and women who are good models for her, Margaret, who fought with devils and monsters (1.16), Christina who debated pagans (1.18), Mary Magdalene, the first to see the risen Christ and to announce it to the disciples (a scene Elisabeth witnesses several times, 1.17, 50).[14] One senses the common interests in the society of the holy women in heaven and on earth. Mary seems to share Elisabeth's concern for her sisters, descending to be near when they pray for a nun of Dirstein who had just died (1.56) and appearing briefly as they do a litany for a dying sister (1.54), whose soul is carried off by angels three days later. She helps Elisabeth win her brother to the priesthood, telling her to comfort him in his fear and ask him to do it for her (Mary's) service (1.59). And Mary is in Elisabeth's thoughts when "these words flowed from my mouth: He descended from heaven . . . entered through the ear of a virgin . . ." (1.57). Is it possible not to make some connection between the words that are divinely inspired in Elisabeth and the Word that is divinely inspired in the Virgin (a connection that becomes much stronger in Hildegard's imagery)?

Mary (the first human who gave flesh to Christ, as the priest does with the Eucharist) is a silent presence when the angel sends Elisabeth to take communion though she had felt herself weak and unworthy (1.66).[15] Elisabeth's tendency to judge herself unfit is a recurring theme, presumably because it is necessary to remind others (as well as herself) that grace is the source of her visions, especially as she takes on a more aggressive role.[16] After she receives communion at the angel's command, Elisabeth has a vision independent of formal services which seems to impose a male role on her; standing alone in the oratory just before vespers, she is struck by a sudden light and falls in a "mentis excessum" from which the angel tells her to rise, act virilely, and give Christ's message to the sinners of the world: "As people crucified me, so I am daily crucified among those who sin against me in their hearts" (1.67). Elisabeth tells the sisters, who had run up to support her, to bring tablets and write down the words.[17] When Elisabeth objects that she does not know what to say or do because she is unlearned in divine scripture, the angel tells her his grace is sufficient (1.68), and the lord puts words in her mouth (1.69).[18] The male role is made more explicit on another occasion when Elisabeth is alone in the chapter and the angel addresses her as "son of man" ("fili hominis," 1.70); again Elisabeth demurs, saying she does not know how to speak, she is slow in speaking, but the angel assures her if she opens her mouth, he will speak.[19]

Elisabeth's interests and her visions expand in the course of the first book. She sees souls in purgatory, a subject that will recur; she sees the events of Christ's and Mary's lives from the epiphany to the ascension and assumption on appropriate days; she worries about sinful clerics and nuns, and her angel comes and tells her what to say to them (1.58). She prepares for visions by reading and meditation, and she begins to ask questions during the vision and to get and report answers. She is bold enough to ask John the Evangelist to let her see some of the things shown to him on earth, and he does (1.60). Some visions become more complicated in

Hildegardian fashion, including symbolic figures like a white wheel, moving swiftly, with a bird and then a ladder (1.40), and when she asks the meaning, she is told to ask doctors who study scripture, because she cannot understand on her own, so she asks her brother to seek the interpretation in his readings.

But Elisabeth is still not comfortable with the visions and they continue to be physically taxing. She tries but fails to avoid one, provoking the angel to say that others would accept much worse if they could see the visions. By the second book, when Peter and Paul ask Elisabeth if she would rather have vexations with her visions or not have either, she answers that she prefers to have the visions and they promise her less suffering in the future; when she asks why she has to undergo the suffering, she is told so that her health will appear a more glorious miracle (2.9). The next to last scene of the first book and one of the most important begins with Elisabeth in a secret place of prayer, from which the angel carries her up until she can see all the ends of the earth and the fiery arrows of God's wrath. Then he asks her why she hides gold in the mud, the word of God which was sent through her mouth to earth, not to be hidden but for the glory of God and the salvation of his people. He beats her, leaving marks the sisters could see, and she finally has the magistra, the only one who knows her secret, show the abbot the books of her visions which she keeps hidden under her bed (1.78).[20] The book closes with the Virgin, as queen of heaven, comforting Elisabeth and getting the lord to rid her of the devil that was tormenting her (1.79).

The second book shows a more confident Elisabeth.[21] Though both she and her brother seem to feel the need to defend themselves against those who are "scandalized that God deigns to magnify his mercy through the frail sex"—Ekbert by pointing to the holy women who prophesied and governed in the Old Testament, Holda, Deborah, Judith, and Jahel (2.1), Elisabeth by evoking a more traditional male presence in her visions, male saints who intercede with Mary for her and requests for masses and indulgences from the abbot—in fact the female presence is if anything more exalted. If the male roles are required, they are made subservient to the female: the saints intercede with Mary, who is approached like a queen by her ministers; and Mary speaks of the priest, who says a mass for her as "my servant" ("servus meus," 2.13). Elisabeth may take communion during mass to have her vision, but she then converses with Mary and the saints in heaven, while the priests on earth cannot always carry out their role properly: Elisabeth describes one case in which the priest handles the eucharist carelessly and Elisabeth turns to Mary to undo the damage (2.25).[22] When she does not see the Virgin for some time, the angel tells her to get an indulgence from the abbot; then "our most glorious lady" comes and converses at length with her (2.5, cf. 2.12), the abbot serving as an intermediary between the two women. The conversation is not recorded because, Elisabeth says, the words have gone from her memory for her sins—perhaps, but this is also a way to keep parts of her visions to herself.

There is a certain tension between the powers of the (male) mass and of (female) prayer in a vision Elisabeth has of three dead nuns who professed at different ages (to make it clear that the problem is the same for any nun). They are all unable to enter heaven because no one thinks they need prayers so no one prays for them. They ask Elisabeth to have her abbot say masses for them, which he does, and when Elisabeth tells her sisters, they also immediately take on various "afflictions" and prayers for them (2.7). The three women are later told by a young man to thank Elisabeth for her intercession with her abbot, but Elisabeth asks them to requite what she and the nuns did when they die, that is, pray for them, as if she at least thought the women's prayers for the dead were also important (2.14).[23]

I do not mean to suggest that Elisabeth shows or even feels hostility for the males she deals with, priests or saints; on the contrary, she seems to have a good relationship with all of them, and her visions are a model of male-female balance, women accompanying men, men accompanying women. What I am suggesting is that as a woman she feels a perhaps unconscious frustration that she cannot play the male role of priest, particularly in relation to the eucharist, and that is what underlies the continuing tensions in the visions. However, she does seem to become more confident as she progresses through the second book. For one thing, God does not hold her sex against her. In a vision in which God speaks directly to her, not through the angel, he tells Elisabeth, "I chose you, though you are small in your eyes because you are fragile, and I made you a sign to those stronger than you . . . because I am good and do not consider the person [implies the sex?], but who seeks me in his heart and loves me, I love and show myself to him." And then God gives a unisex summary of the fall: "I created mankind [*hominem*, male and female] in my image and similitude and made him (*eum*) conscious of me so that he might be more prudent than other creatures, and he (*ille*) did not wish to remain so, but was inflated by the counsel of the poisonous serpent to scorn me. . . . And he [the serpent] taught him to rise higher while he descended lower. . . . O man [*homo*, to Elisabeth], hear and understand the words . . . for I have made you to be my servant [*domesticus meus*, masc.], and I have consecrated you, and illumined you, and opened your eyes that you might see not by other vision but through the knowledge which I opened to you" (2.18). The *hominem* at the beginning suggests that God is speaking of Adam and Eve as one, and the masculine pronouns make it clear that he holds Adam at least equally if not more responsible for the fall.[24]

Elisabeth herself is cast in one of her visions as a positive female model of fidelity, in direct contrast to Peter's failure. On Easter, Elisabeth has a vision of three men, one of them Christ, who asks her if she believes that he was resurrected from the dead on this day, true God and true man, and she answers that she does, but asks him to help her to believe perfectly if her belief is imperfect. He asks her the same question three times and three times she affirms her belief (2.27). Since the next vision she has is of Peter crucified upside down, the contrast between the apostle who denied Christ three times and the woman who affirmed him three times is glaring.[25] One cannot help wondering if Elisabeth ever questioned the choice of men as apostles (and priests), when women remained loyal while men (Judas, Peter) betrayed, or if she simply accepted the role imposed on her and Hildegard to clean up the mess the male clergy had made.

Although Elisabeth asks an occasional question for others, she asks more and more questions of her own, in sharp contrast to her passive reception of the early visions at the beginning of the first book, questions that seem more like the investigative reporting she will do on Ursula's army. On the feast of the division of the apostles, she asks why Peter and Paul stand apart from the others and is told it is because their bones were divided on this day; why then, she asks, do they all appear (2.30)? The last episode of visions in book two, on the bodily assumption of the Virgin, is controversial because of the uncertainty in the fathers.[26] When Elisabeth first asked about it at the request of "one of our elders," perhaps but not necessarily her brother (2.31), the Virgin said she could not know at that point but would be told in the future. A year later, with that same unnamed person urging her to pray for the revelation and Elisabeth lying sick in bed unable to go to mass, the full vision of the Virgin's resurrection and assumption appeared to her, so she knew the answer from her own eyes. But for two years Elisabeth hesitated to tell of it, for fear of being judged a "[female] inventor of novelties" ("inventrix novitatum"), until the Virgin appeared to her again, on the feast of the assumption, told her the word was not for the public, which might be misled, but neither was it "revealed to be deleted and forgotten, but to enhance my praise among those who especially love me." When Mary appears again, for a long conversation, Elisabeth asks for more details of her life, how long she lived after Christ's ascension, if she was assumed in the same year, if the disciples were at her burial, and later, how old she was at the time of the annunciation (2.32), as if Elisabeth were conducting historical research by interviewing an eyewitness.

By the third book, when Ekbert is living at Schönau, the questions take up even more space, some of them coming from him but many from her, as if his presence roused certain interests in her, or simply gave her the courage to pursue things she did not dare to ask on her own.[27] And she often puts them in a series of questions, which suggests that she is following her own line of inquiry. It is in this book that Elisabeth has the striking vision of Christ as a beautiful and female virgin whom the angel identifies as the sacred humanity of Christ, and the sun in which she sits as the divinity which possesses and illumines the humanity of the savior (3.4). Her brother prepares her for the next vision with an obvious question, which she puts to John the Evangelist: "Why was the humanity of Christ shown to me as a virgin and not in virile form?" His answer adds a dimension without canceling the original interpretation: "the lord wishes it to be done so that the vision might more aptly also signify his blessed mother," which seems to emphasize an identity between Christ and his mother, rather than deny the possibility of Christ in female form. John goes on to glorify Mary, speaking of her as born from the seed of kings, ruling with royal power in heaven and earth. On another occasion, Mary appears in full majesty as queen and Theotokos, first with a child, then without, and Elisabeth asks another awkward question for her brother, this time whether Origen, who was condemned by the church for heresies but had so praised Mary, was saved. Mary explains that Origen is not suffering too much because, though he looked too hard for divine secrets, he loved scripture; she assures Elisabeth that he has a special light on days on which she is celebrated, though his fate cannot now be revealed (3.5). This is a comforting answer for those who are themselves probing into delicate questions.

Another question which pertains indirectly to her is suggested to Elisabeth by "one more learned," about the three heavens of Paul (3.8). At first the angel refuses to answer, but as Elisabeth thinks about it, she prays the lord to give her divine understanding (*intellectum*), and it comes whole (*totam intelligentiam*) to her mind, in words she says she did not know before, which the angel spoke in her heart. He tells her that she had experienced Paul's heavens. It is as if the angel refused to take questions that came from Ekbert, until Elisabeth had made them her own, which may mean that when she gets answers to others' questions, the issues are important to her as well. Certainly the bodily assumption of Mary, an event which raises Elisabeth's special protector, a woman, above the apostles and all other humans, has special significance for Elisabeth as do Paul's visions. In the latter case, the details are important enough for the angel to reappear to Elisabeth, while she sits dictating it to a sister, to bring everything back to her memory. Later, when she asks Paul a prepared question about the fate of Greeks who did not believe in the procession of the spirit from father and son (3.9), she picks up a distinction he makes between faith here with hope, and there with knowledge, making a distinction of her own, asking whether we should call it faith when it is certain (3.10).

Before she puts a question to her dead uncle, bishop Ekbert, about a subject that has long interested her, the efficacy of prayers for the dead, she asks him if he knows about the grace the lord conferred on her and how he deigned to operate through her (3.11), perhaps a natural desire to show that she too has achieved some distinction in the religious world, but also a clear indication that she is becoming more comfortable with her situation.[28] Nonetheless, she continues to ask questions that defend the verisimilitude of her visions: she asks the angel how an angel could be seen by the women at the tomb of Christ, when they are invisible, and is told that spiritual creatures can take on forms to be seen by men, as the Lord transfigured himself so Abraham could see him in three persons (3.15). The brother's question about the knowledge of angels, though it arises from Pseudo-Dionysius, is also relevant to her, since it confronts the issue of how angels know and how much they know; her angel says he receives the words from the heart of the living God, through the mediation of the higher orders of angels, and speaks them to her heart (3.13). Similarly the question about how long the first apostate angel was in glory, pertains to Elisabeth in that his fall was caused by pride, the attempt to be equal to God (3.16).

Having gotten information about her superhuman guide, Elisabeth turns to her human model, the nun who also had visions and who had shown some compassion for her, Hildegard. Elisabeth's two letters to Hildegard mentioned earlier are included at this point, toward the end of the autobiographical books, just before Elisabeth begins to preach God's messages to sinners, particularly the corrupt clergy; they allow Elisabeth to justify herself and give her the added sanction of a respected figure who was doing the same thing. The rest of the third book is devoted mainly to God's message to sinful mankind, homicides, adulterers, Cathars, hypocrites, and shepherds who allow their sheep to perish (3.22–27), a message Hildegard was also carrying. When Elisabeth questions the meaning of some aspects of the later visions, the angel refers her to learned people who read scripture, and she turns to her brother to find the appropriate interpretations. She does not expect him to know the answer, but asks him to find it in his books. They work as a team, Elisabeth getting the word directly from heaven, Ekbert finding human interpretations when needed. Elisabeth certainly relies on his support, probably more than the works now show, since he deleted references to himself (Clark, 47), but she does not suggest that he is in any way responsible for her visions, nor that he provides a literary form for them.[29] The only human source Elisabeth acknowledges for any of her work is Hildegard, whom she has to consult before she can dictate the *Liber viarum dei*.

The *Liber viarum dei,* the book of God's ways or roads (or roads to God), the fourth book of visions, follows naturally on the third. Once Elisabeth has accepted the roles of conveyor of God's wrath to sinful mankind and instrument of conversion, she has to provide models for behavior. She begins quite confidently: "It happened in the fifth year of my visitation, with Pentecost [the feast of the visitation of tongues on the apostles] approaching, I Elisabeth saw in a vision of my spirit a high mountain. . . ." Her angel is now an "instructor," a "doctor," a formal teacher rather than a guide, which may mean that Elisabeth is admitting to more learning than she has in the past. She also acknowledges a literary model for her work in an unusual way: the angel reminds her of a vision a year ago in which he showed her a tent filled with books, all to be dictated before the last judgment. He raised one of them and said "This is the book of God's ways, which will be revealed to you when you have visited sister Hildegard and heard her" (4.6).[30] Hildegard provides a model of visions which are directed at a wide audience with the avowed intent of moving that audience to reform itself.

Elisabeth sees ten ways or roads and describes each of them in a separate sermon. Most are concerned with the religious life, though there is one about marriage, which is traditional in its views (4.13).[31] The way of the continent (celibates, 4.14) includes a discussion of the will being taken for the deed in relation to the temptation of lust, related to the problem of intention which concerned Heloise and Abelard. The discussion culminates in a graphic demonstration in which the angel has Elisabeth immerse her hand in filth to see that only the outside, which can be cleansed, is affected, while the inner part, the soul, must consent to temptation to be stained (4.14).[32] The sermon on the way of prelates does not come to her for some time, because of her faults, Elisabeth fears. But having a sense now of the importance of her work, she prays, helped by the prayers of her sisters, for the sermon to be given to her, an interesting situation in which women religious pray for the words to correct male clergy: "do not consider my merits, . . . but carry out what you began through me. Deign to open to us a fitting discipline for the way of rectors of the church, which you showed me in a mystery, from which some fruit of correction may come, as you know is necessary to your people" (4.15). The angel appears and gives her the "sermon I desired," which is a stirring attack on clerical sins and threat of eternal punishment. And in the last chapter, the angel tells Elisabeth to send the book to the bishops of Triers, Cologne, and Mainz, with a message to announce its contents to the Roman church and all the people and churches of God and to emend their own errors: "Read and hear the divine admonitions, and receive them with calm mind, and do not think they are the figments of women (*figmenta mulierum*), because they are not, but come from God the father omnipotent, who is the font and origin of all good" (4.20).

The remaining book of visions, on the sacred army of the virgins of Cologne, arose from questions that were brought to Elisabeth about bones discovered outside Cologne in 1156.[33] Abbot Gerlach of Deutz asked her to confirm the identity of the bones and the inscriptions which were found with them, suspecting people, not unnaturally, of forging them for profit. Elisabeth was being asked to do historical research with eyewitness sources, the saints themselves. Though she says she was compelled to it by others, the assignment clearly interests her, as it did Hildegard. It would be hard to imagine such women not responding to the story of Ursula, a woman who rather than marry gathered an army of eleven thousand virgins to go on a pilgrimage to Rome, determined to be martyred, a militant version of Christine's *City of Ladies* (which includes them, 3.10.2). Indeed, Elisabeth apparently was eager to take a small part in their martyrdom, saying she would willingly accept a tongue-lashing from "those who are opposed to the grace of God in me," since she hoped for some reward if what the lord revealed through her labors increased the honor of the martyrs (5.1).

But Elisabeth does not receive the information passively. She has her own doubts about the story and she keeps asking questions and pushing for explanations until they are satisfied. The main problem in identifying the bones as those of Ursula's army was that they included men and children, though they were supposed by legend to have been only women, and the inscriptions found with them named various men, including a pope who was otherwise unknown. The story clearly loses some of its appeal if the women who were supposed to have, as Elisabeth says, guided their own ships (5.6), had men to rely on, but she makes the best of the new information by emphasizing the honor God paid that holy society with the escort of such elevated people, an honor which should also be given them by Christians (5.4). In fact, it is probably because she thought the bishop-martyrs would bring prestige to the virgin army in the minds of contemporary men that Elisabeth gives such attention to their inscriptions. Certainly, there are a surprising number of men in her visions about an army of women, though it might be argued that their presence also shows the power of the women's movement to draw so many distinguished men with it.

Elisabeth's first source of information is a woman, St. Verena, whose bones were given by Gerlach to abbot Hildelin and brought back to Schönau, and who is later identified by Ursula as her cousin. Verena not only assures Elisabeth of her identity, and of her own intervention in correcting the spelling of her name (a small but important point, since it affirms the saints' control over the written evidence which was so controversial, 5.2), but she also reveals that Elisabeth was predestined to play a role in the story, explaining that certain things did not need to be expressed more clearly in the inscriptions because they were all to be manifested to Elisabeth in the future (5.11). She validates the bones that came with hers as her nephew's, who appears himself to assure Elisabeth that he was with the army because he was so attached to his aunt who gave him the strength to suffer martyrdom with her (5.3). Elisabeth is not convinced, believing still that the army was made up only of women. Verena gives a series of explanations, that the fame of the enterprise attracted people to them, that God ordained that bishops would accompany them and others would join them on the way; when Elisabeth objects that according to the story the women were alone on the ships when they were blown out to sea, Verena replies that Ursula's father was so concerned about her plans that he quietly arranged for men to be with her (5.6). A particularly serious problem is the presence, according to the inscriptions, of the most distinguished man of all, a pope, whose name did not, however, appear in the list of Roman pontiffs, which Elisabeth herself checked (5.8). Verena explains that he was British, that he had many relatives in the women's army, and had a divine revelation that he should leave the papacy and accompany them; the cardinals were so indignant that he gave up the papacy because of the "foolishness of little women" ("fatuitatem muliercularum," 5.7), that they deleted his name from papal records (5.8).[34]

Virtually all of the men who accompanied the women were drawn by their women relatives, nieces, sisters, aunts, even mothers.[35] Family affection is an underlying theme of the story, reflecting Elisabeth's own experience. One of the most striking figures in the story, whom Clark sees as a possible figure for Elisabeth (129–30), is Ursula's wise aunt, St. Gerasma, whose name appears in one of the inscriptions as the leader of the sacred virgins (5.15). Elisabeth comes to her identity in a roundabout way, but finally learns from St. Nicholas (perhaps introduced as an objective source?) that Gerasma was a queen of Sicily, sister of Ursula's mother, and a woman of such great wisdom that her brother-in-law asked her advice about Ursula's plans. Divinely inspired, she understood that God was behind it and decided to join Ursula; she left her country in the hands of one son and two daughters—that is, she was ruling it, as heir or regent—and went to Britain with the other four daughters and younger son, who wanted to come out of love for his sisters. Gerasma oversaw the gathering of the army which she led through the pilgrimage and joined in martyrdom (5.15).

Elisabeth continuously questions discrepancies in names (5.14) and dates (5.16, 21), as well as unexplained details (5.19, 21). She asks why the angel calls one of the virgins Constantina, when others call her Firmindina, and is told that it was customary in ancient times for people to use their parents' names as well as their own (5.14). She asks Verena who was responsible for the martyrdom, which some lay to Attila though he lived much later (5.16); she asks Ursula if the Clematius who reburied some of the bodies was the same Clematius who was said to have built her church, and Ursula says no, he came much later (5.21). After a year of investigation, when Elisabeth was almost finished, Ursula herself finally appeared on the feast of the eleven thousand, and Elisabeth asked her the questions that completed the story: who composed their bones so carefully and gave them such honorable burial in the midst of such persecution (5.19), what her enemies had against her, and how she actually died (5.21).[36]

Elisabeth's study of Ursula was her last big work. It shows her interest in historic women, strong and dedicated to their faith, prepared to die for it and to lead men by their example to the same kind of self-sacrifice. But it also shows her development as a scholar, as an investigator, as someone who wished to get at the truth, and was not willing to take even written evidence at face value, but went to the source and questioned it until she was satisfied. Though others may have presented her with many of the original questions, her concern for preserving the independence of the women and turning the presence of the men into a further argument for the women's success shapes the investigation and the final report. She was clearly moving in a different direction from her mentor, Hildegard, when she died at thirty-six in 1164 or 1165.

Ekbert described her death in a letter to three nuns in their family, grieving for his own and the world's loss: "our Elisabeth . . . who brought me into the light of unknown novelty, drew me to the familiar ministry of Jesus, whose mellifluous mouth gave me divine consolations and instructions, who made my heart taste the first fruits of sweetness hidden in God . . . the chosen lamp of heavenly light, the illustrious virgin honored by the abundance of God's grace, splendid jewel of our convent, leader of our virgin college, was taken from this light before her mature years." He takes leave of her directly, regretting her not only as a sister, but also as a source of the divine: "through you heaven was opened to earth and secrets hidden to the world flowed through the organ of your voice to us and your eloquence was more precious than gold, sweeter than honey. Through you angels spoke familiarly with us and we with angels. O happy woman, many kings and prophets wished to see what you saw and did not."[37]

"REJOICE THAT THE FINGER OF GOD WRITES IN YOU"

Hildegard of Bingen, who provided an important model as a respected visionary and successful abbess and author to the younger Elisabeth, lived through eight decades of the twelfth century (1098–1179) and a wide range of experiences. Like Elisabeth, she was revered for her visions and locally celebrated as a saint, but she alone among women religious writers was given a volume of her own in the *Patriologia Latina* seven centuries later. Like Elisabeth, Hildegard received revelations of divine truth from God and was hesitant to reveal them until God forced her to, and then became a popular author; the published versions of the visions were widely sought after—though perhaps less widely read than Elisabeth's because more abstruse. Hildegard's visions supplied interpretations of scripture and mysterious prophecies more than answers to direct questions, but her prophecies were taken seriously at the highest levels.[38] Her work went far beyond her visions, into medicine, music, and poetry, and in all areas, though her major subjects are the reform of the world and the church and the parameters of the good, devout life, she shows concern and sympathy for women. I will limit myself here to comments about her presentation of herself and other women and women's roles across her work.[39]

Like Elisabeth, Hildegard suffered physical pain, which both accepted as part of the price they paid for their extraordinary experiences, and which was probably at least in part a manifestation of the tension they felt as women impelled by God into the not only unusual but prohibited role of teaching men, indeed the clergy, about religion. Hildegard's relation to the sacerdotal role is not as obviously troubled as Elisabeth's, but there are suggestive moments, as when she blesses water to restore the health of a young woman (and coincidentally cures a young man's mortal illness), blesses bread to cure a woman's lust, and exorcises a demon from another woman.[40] She does not see Mary directly as priest, as Elisabeth did, but she makes a similar if more complex connection: God speaks to her traditionally of the church as the bride of Christ in the *Scivias* but cast in the male role of offering the gift of bread and wine on the altar (2.6.11), and then describes the priest as reenacting the role of the Virgin Mary, "as my son miraculously received humanity in the Virgin, so now this oblation miraculously becomes His body and blood on the altar" (2.6.15).

Certainly there is some satisfaction to a woman whom priests "scorn because of Eve's transgression" being told by God that she must stir them to action because they are lukewarm in God's service (Sciv.1.Preface). Though she accepts the authority of the male over the female in theory (both in the church and in marriage), God's word gives Hildegard a higher authority in whose name she can and does oppose the will of the male hierarchy. She turns her professed weakness, her "feminine frailty," into a strength by inverting traditional imagery: because men who should be strong and virtuous are corrupt, the world has fallen on womanish times, so it is to a weak woman that God turns to set it straight.[41] Similarly, if man is the stronger figure, then it is Adam, not Eve, who should be held accountable for the fall, and Hildegard emphasizes the male role in the fall, and the female (Mary's) in the redemption.

There were men who doubted Hildegard—she tells of a philosopher who doubted her gift, but examined her written visions and was so won over he helped adorn her convent and asked to be buried there (*Vita*, 2.12)—and there were men who opposed her even when she invoked God's will, the monks of Disibodenberg who tried to prevent her leaving them, the bishops who transferred Richardis, and those who laid an interdict on her convent when she buried a once-excommunicated nobleman. But she does not seem to have had a problem with men generally; she had three male secretaries who were apparently devoted to her, and many male friends who corresponded with her and sought her advice and comfort. She identified herself with historic men, Moses (who had trouble leading his people into the wilderness as she did her nuns in the new convent), Paul (in his love for Timothy), John (receiving revelations directly from

Christ), Joshua and Joseph (who were the object of envy), Laurence, Job, and Jeremiah (for their physical sufferings, all in the *Vita*).[42] She did, however, compare herself to Susanna, whom God saved from false witnesses (*Vita*, 2.3), when speaking of the difficulties she had with sisters who resented her imposition of the rule, though others stood with her through all her sufferings.

Guibert and other men who wrote about her usually identified her with women, the bride of the Canticles, the Virgin Mary, Miriam, sister of Aaron and Moses, Deborah, Judith (Gb16). Godfrey compared her to Leah and Rachel, for her ability to be effective in the active as well as the contemplative life, Theodoric to Deborah, "challenging women not to despair because of the weakness of their sex, but to be capable of prophetic grace, a grace merited by purity of mind, not diversity of sex." Like Elisabeth, she also relied on the women around her, the nuns in her convent, for support; she had women friends among her fellow abbesses, and she glorified the Virgin's role and some women saints (including Ursula) in her poetry. But in contrast to Elisabeth, Hildegard does not seem to have looked to historical women for models of authority; in her visions she sees symbolic rather than historical women, Ecclesia and a series of personified virtues rather than Verena, or Ursula, or Mary.[43] At the same time, Hildegard recognized the role of women in her life, her mother and her nurses, Jutta who trained her, Richardis who helped in her work, Richardis's mother who supported her move to Rupertsberg, the nuns who stayed with her; and in her writings, as in her life, Hildegard was very concerned with the problems of living women, physical, psychological, and social.[44] And she often saw the female side of God: when Hildegard saw herself as Moses in the wilderness, she felt God caring for her like a nurturing woman, "a mother giving milk to her crying infant," and she explained her own role as the voice of Wisdom, the female personification of God in the OT (cited by Theodoric, *Vita*, 2.2: "Wisdom in the name of charity teaches and orders me to speak").

Since Hildegard furnished much of the information we have about her in her letters and visions and through her biographers, to a great extent she shaped our view of her. She presents herself as a woman of noble birth who had early religious training with a devout and noble recluse, Jutta, in poetry (psalms) and music (notation and playing the lyre).[45] Her visions began in early childhood and embarrassed her when she realized others did not have them, but she was encouraged first by a woman (presumably Jutta), then by her teacher (presumably Volmar) and finally by the pope.[46] She alludes to the skepticism of other men in a vision of three towers: in the first, young noblewomen listen to the word of God from her mouth with great hunger, stable and wise women embrace the truth of God in their hearts, and strong armed men from the common people approach them in wonder and desire. In the second tower, two of the rooms are dried up and there are men who question the words "that woman speaks as if they were from God," and are unwilling to change (*Vita,* 2.15). Presumably they represent men of the church who rejected the message Hildegard carried, while religious women and the common people accepted it, the former with greater understanding.[47]

Hildegard's bouts of oppressive illness may reflect her own suppressed doubts about her visions or, perhaps more likely, the strain of confronting the doubts of others. She juxtaposes an account of her illness which followed the overwhelming experience of the vision explaining the gospel of John, an illness that lasted for a year (*Vita,* 3.20), with her cure of a noblewoman who was possessed by the devil, as though recognizing that she too was possessed, and using her power of exorcism to emphasize the divine source of her own "possession." She approaches the problem scientifically: after seeing the woman's condition in a true vision, she wondered how a demonic form entered a person ("Et me cogitante et scire volente, quomodo diabolica forma hominem intraret," 3.20.27–30); the answer she received, colored perhaps by her observations of mentally ill people, was that the devil does not in fact enter the person, but hovers over, causing the body to act in a certain way, while the soul is as if in a deep sleep (in sharp contrast to Hildegard's visions in which she is fully awake). The woman had been taken to many other holy people to no effect, when the evil spirit (expressing the woman's unconscious desire?) identified Hildegard as the source of the cure, first as "a certain old woman from the upper Rhine, through whose advice he would be cast out," then mockingly as "Scrumpilgard" (an unpleasant detail which is inserted by Theodoric, 3.21.12). Hildegard sent an exorcism ritual which was only temporarily successful; the spirit returned to the woman and declared that it would leave only in the presence of the old woman, so the abbot sent the patient herself to Hildegard. Hildegard reports that she and her companions were terrified by her arrival, but God calmed them and they found a place for her in the sisters' dwelling "without the help of men" (3.22.14). Hildegard describes her analysis of the case ("I saw that he [the spirit] had suffered three tortures in the woman . . ."), and her treatment (the prayers and fasting of the nuns and their neighbors, her control of the spirit's speech, refuting its lies, but allowing it to speak truth freely), but she attributes the victory over Satan to God.[48] After this episode, Hildegard was again beset by physical pain, and she remembered the evil spirit's derisive prophecy of her death; but instead of dying she made another tour, preaching the word of God to congregations of men and women and settling dissensions among them. When she finished the tour, a very beautiful and loving man (Christ?) appeared to her and cast out "those who afflicted me" (3.24), which suggests that on some level Hildegard did identify with the possessed woman she had cured.

Hildegard was able to preach, publicly, to clergy and laymen despite the injunctions of Paul, because she presented and no doubt saw herself as a *tabula rasa* on which God could write his message, without complications from human learning. She speaks of herself as a timid, poor little thing, who exhausted herself speaking before masters and doctors and other wise men in whatever major places they lived ("ego autem timida et paupercula per duos annos valde fatigata sum, ut coram magistris et doctoribus ac caeteris sapientibus in quibusdam majoribus locis ubi mansio illorum est, vivente voce ista proferrem," VA15r to bishops of the church), forced by God to deliver his message.

Just how blank a tablet she was is open to argument. Though she often speaks of herself as uneducated, she means in the sense of formal logical and rhetorical training: she does not know how to dissect a text ("non in abscissione textus," VA 1, to Bernard); she has not been taught by philosophers, ("indocta de philosophis," VA 2, to Eugene); and the visions do not teach her to write as philosophers write (to Guibert, Dronke, *Women Writers,* 250-54, "sicut philosophi scribunt scribere in visione hac non doceor"). She says her Latin is not polished ("latinis verbis non limatis," ibid.), but the visions come in Latin and she dictates them in Latin; indeed she speaks and writes what the visions teach her (DB 3).[49] In answer to questions from Guibert, Hildegard makes it clear that she controls the written versions of the visions he and others admire; she describes them as waking visions, not through any of her five senses but only in the soul and never with loss of consciousness, always with her physical eyes open (Dronke, *Women Writers,* 250ff.). "I see, hear and know simultaneously, and learn what I know as if in a moment. But what I do not see I do not know, for I am not learned. And the things I write are those I see and hear through the vision, nor do I set down words other than those that I hear; I utter them in unpolished Latin, just as I hear them through the vision" (Dronke, 168). Despite her lack of formal training, Hildegard might well have been acquainted with sophisticated texts she had never been taught. The monastery she founded at Rupertsberg included a scriptorium, where the sisters worked hard at copying (Gb38). It is at least possible that her visions reflect written sources, perhaps without conscious awareness, and probable that they reflect oral sources, the conversations of learned men who came to her for divine words and coincidentally brought her human learning.

The self Hildegard chooses to present to the audience of her visionary works, the way she introduces herself to the literate world—a frail being of simple education—does not differ from her autobiographical memories, but the description of her experiences emphasizes her role as a divine instrument. Though she was trembling with fear, timid in speech, simple in exposition and uneducated in writing, the vision she describes at the beginning of the *Scivias* (at age forty-two), gave her understanding of the old and new testaments, as an exegete but also as a prophet. For all the

avowed and no doubt deeply felt humility, Hildegard recognizes the visionary gift as a power of secret mysteries ("virtutem . . . mysterium secre-
tarum") which are not dreams or delirious fantasies, but received fully
awake with her mind alert, so she is a willing but conscious tool. God,
through a feminine attribute, "the living light" ("lux vivens"), addressing
her as a frail being (*homo*, the sexually neutral term that she prefers), says
he has shown her secrets beyond what ancient people saw in him, and
commands her to speak and write what she saw, not with human understanding or composition, but as she perceived in heaven.[50]

To write the visions, Hildegard needed the support of two companions,
"the noble girl of good conduct" (Richardis) and the man "she had sought
and found" (Volmar, the monk who was her first formal teacher). That
God is presented through a feminine attribute, Hildegard as sexually neutral or androgynous, and her co-workers as a sexually balanced team
cannot be coincidental. Particularly since God reminds her that she is to
speak out and stir to action those priests (who "see into scripture" but
"are lukewarm in God's service") who scorn her because of Eve's transgression ("qui te propter praevaricationem Evae volunt contemptibilem
esse"). The point is repeated at the beginning of the second book even
more strongly, presumably in case the audience had forgotten or missed it.
After a vision of Christ (described as *homo*), the voice (from the living fire,
masc.), addresses Hildegard as a woman by name ("in nomine femineo"),
saying she is trampled by men because of Eve's transgression ("quamvis
conculcata sis per virilem formam propter praevaricationem Evae," 2.1.Pref).
Hildegard embraces the connection with Eve, making it work for her as
she does the traditional weakness of women. She contrasts herself "in the
softness of a fragile rib" with strong lions and their learning, while the
vision shows Adam (like the priests in 1.1) failing to act. In an inverted
view of the fall, Adam errs by omission, by turning away from the flower
offered to him to taste or touch, a subtle hint of Hildegard's tendency to
put the responsibility for the fall on the stronger partner, Adam, which
runs through her works (see below). The voice, though it plays to Hildegard's humility, reminds her that God sent Christ into the purity of the
Virgin and through that humble girl deceived death, the destroyer of
mankind. Thus Hildegard, like the Virgin Mary, receives the word of God
and manifests it to mankind, both reversing the role of Eve.

There is less intimate biographical detail and less self-effacing humility
in the preface to the second book of visions, the *Liber vitae meritorum*
(LVM).[51] At sixty, in 1158, as she notes, Hildegard is more matter-of-fact,
more assured in her role. She mentions other texts she has produced in
between, in natural science, music, and poetry, the language she invented,
biblical commentaries, and the same pair of helpers.[52] The book ends with
God's declaration of the truth of the visions, and dire warnings to any who
would tamper with them. Hildegard is God's (musical) instrument, the

person (*homo*) who sees and does not see, who proffers the visions like a string of the cithara, the sound coming not by itself but from another's touch, yet part of the work of salvation.[53] Reminding the audience that Adam (*homo*, but "de limo factus," made from mud, 6.44) was deceived by the devil and therefore we can see the mysteries of God only through a veil, God speaks in the person of Christ, who redeemed Adam's sin, the son of God and Mary, "I came from the supernal father and took the flesh of viridity from the virgin mother" (6.45). He declares Hildegard's visions true and threatens "any who would add anything to them in opposition to what they say, will deserve the penalties described in the visions, or if any take away in opposition, he will deserve to be obliterated from the joys shown." The last word is from God as the living voice (fem.) of the living and unfailing light (fem.) confirming what it said as faithful and to be heeded and remembered by the faithful.

The preface to the third book of visions, *Liber divinorum operum simplicis hominis* (LDO, PL197, cc.741ff), goes even further in its assertion of their importance as a complement to and explanation of scripture, though it also emphasizes her frailty as an old woman. The voice from heaven says: "O little form (fem.), the daughter of many labors, dried up by many grave infirmities of body, but yet imbued with the depth of God's mysteries, commend what you see with the interior eyes and hear with the interior ears of the soul to stable writing (*stabili scripturae*) for the use of mankind, so they can understand their creator through them, and not refuse to worship him with worthy honor. So write not according to your heart, but according to my testimony, who am life without beginning or end, things not invented by you nor by the premeditations of other men, but preordained by me before the beginning of the world." The true and living light here is *lumen*, masculine, as God is the eternal father at the end, as though Hildegard, still a poor little female form ("pauperculam femineam formam"), were now comfortable in her role as the spokesman even of the God of the patriarchy, though here too God is not exclusively male; he retains feminine attributes: "Ego summa et ignea vis," "I am the highest, fiery force," the source of life (1.1). Hildegard's inspiration has come from the Holy Spirit, as it did to the writers of scripture, and anyone who dares to add to or subtract from it commits a sin against the Holy Spirit, which will not be remitted (10.38).

The combination of self-effacement and self-assurance that comes of being the conscious tool of the divine is of course related to Hildegard's sense of herself as a woman, weaker in strength, lower in prestige than a man, but chosen by God to do what men have failed to do, or to right the wrongs they have committed. This sometimes contradictory view of women runs through Hildegard's writings in different ways. I will look briefly at her use of symbolic female figures, her presentation of historic women, and her discussions of social conditions in her visionary works, the poems of the *Symphonia,* and the medical text known as *Causae et Curae,* leaving to the end a discussion of her complex treatment of Adam and Eve, who are for her as they have been for so many women not only an ur-myth of human existence, in particular of male-female relations, but also a source of conflict between standard teachings and her sense of justice and moral responsibility.

Hildegard's moral teachings are not usually directed at men and women separately, but she does occasionally speak of distinct social roles. In the first book of visions, the *Scivias,* she speaks of an equality in the sexes within marriage, woman created for the sake of man and from the man, man for the sake of woman *and from woman,* to work in unity to produce children (1.2.12). She uses Paul's words (1 Cor. 11:8–12), but changes his meaning: Paul said "Man is not from woman, but woman from man; man is not created for the sake of woman but woman for the sake of man." Newman discusses this passage, noting that Hildegard so accentuated Paul's reminder of mutual dependence, "as woman was made from man, so man is now born of woman," that she inadvertently denied the first point (*Sister of Wisdom,* 99).[54] Paul is arguing for the superiority of man, not for equality in marriage. Hildegard focuses on the biological area in which cooperation is essential. But she also uses a biological difference to make a point of religious equality: circumcision is not needed by women, since the tabernacle within is touched only in the embrace of the flesh, and women are subject to their husbands (2.3.21) and feel desire less strongly (2.3.22), while "the foreskin is the crime of Adam's transgression" which Christ removed ("praeputium est crimen transgressionis Adae, quod Filius meus abstulit," 2.3.24), replacing it with baptism, which is a circumcision for all men and women (2.3.29).[55]

Though a woman cannot be a priest, Hildegard suggests that her chosen virginity puts her in a more intimate relationship with God than a male virgin; hers is marriage ("in sanctissima desponsatione . . . coniunctam . . . in consortio suo," 2.5.10), his fellowship ("sodalitatem eius accipiet," 2.5.9). Hildegard does not say a woman is not suitable for the priesthood because she is not made in the image of God, but because she is made to bear and nourish children, giving her physical "weakness" a positive function (2.6.76), and implicitly raising a question about women like Hildegard who chose not to bear physical children.[56] Even the natural image she uses for conception implies a latent power in women: woman cannot conceive by herself just as the earth cannot plow itself (ibid.)—but things can grow without plowing, if nature or God seeds them, while a farmer cannot grow things without fertile earth. As Hildegard frequently says, the Virgin Mary was impregnated with Christ without the help of a man, that is, through God woman can do what man cannot.[57] Though woman cannot be priest and consecrate the body and blood of my son, God tells Hildegard, she can sing praise of the creator, as the earth can receive rain to water its fruits, and as the earth brings forth all fruits, so in woman the fruit of all good works is perfected because she as virgin can receive the (highest) priest and all the ministry of God's altar as spouse and with him possess all its wealth.

If women cannot be priests, they can nonetheless represent God in Hildegard's visions. She sees the first woman containing symbolically within herself the whole human race (figure 3, 1.2) reflecting the beauty of the most high (3.13.16), at least as foreshadowing such reflection in Mary, through whom God was made physically visible.[58] In the parable of the ten pieces of silver (Luke 15.8), a woman represents God, while the coins stand for the orders of the heavenly hierarchy and the man who fell (3.2.20). Christ is symbolized by a woman in the baptismal rite, standing "in the sweetness of a nurturer" (2.3.32). God is sometimes presented as androgynous, not only in the feminine aspects of the living light which so frequently speaks to Hildegard, but also in his jealousy, which appears as a human head, that does not have hair like a man nor a veil like a woman, because it has neither masculine anxiety about being conquered by one of greater strength, nor feminine weakness of a timid mind afraid it cannot conquer its opponents, though it is more manly than womanly because the power of God resembles manly virility more than it does womanly weakness (3.5.13).[59]

The virtues are normally seen as women, appearing in the drama at the end of the third book, where all the characters (virtues and the soul) are female except the devil and all but the devil sing. In the old psychomachic tradition, the virtues are often warriors, but Hildegard's are sometimes androgynous. Sanctity (feminine noun) is seen with three heads, of such brilliance that one cannot see if the faces are male or female, though the one on the left is veiled like a woman (3.9.3).[60] Modifying the traditional view of the body as represented by woman, the soul by man, Hildegard speaks of them both as female, the soul as mistress (*magistra*), the flesh as handmaid (*ancilla*, 1.4). Few "historic" women are mentioned in the *Scivias,* apart from Mary (and Eve, though she seems more mythic than historic).[61] Judith is mentioned at the end, as the instrument of God's conquest of Holofernes, like the boy (David) against Goliath (and perhaps implicitly like Hildegard against the corrupt church). But Mary is the figure of greatest importance to Hildegard here and elsewhere, often spoken of as if an equal parent of Christ with God: Christ is the only begotten of the father before time, the only born of the mother in time (2.2.8). God speaks of Mary conceiving Christ without male power ("sine virili fortitudine," 2.6.26),[62] and acknowledges her role in the incarnation: "my son born of the Virgin," 3.1.6, 3.5.19; "I put my son on the breast of mercy when I sent him into the womb of the Virgin Mary," 3.3.8.[63] There is an implicit connection between the Virgin and Hildegard, both women in whom God chose to form his word, so that it might be manifest to mankind, through much of Hildegard's writing: "The most High Father sought for a Virgin's candor, and willed that His Word should take His body in her. For the Virgin's mind was by His mystery illumined" (*Scivias*, 3.13.1); "the Virgin bore/produced (*genuit*) pure man (*hominem*) in pure virginity, when the ruler of all destined his word with sweet mission to believers" (LVM 2.28).[64]

In the LVM, which is primarily concerned with virtues and vices, the hierarchical order that underlies the work has a traditional sexual component: all creatures look to God as woman to man (5.31), the female genus is subject to the male as other luminaries are to those with masculine strength like the sun (4.16), and cosmological and social harmony depend on such an order. The fragile works of women do not have the strong marrow, the inner core, of men (2.54), and a man who wishes to be faithful should reject womanish levity and grasp virile fortitude (4.28). The treatment of sins is for the most part sexually neutral, the virtues traditionally female and the vices mixed (pride has a womanish face and a virile chest, 3.2). Fornication is a sin against nature for man or woman, and should be expurgated with a hairshirt, fasting, whips, genuflections and prayer. Adultery, on the other hand, may be worse for men, since God made man and took woman from his side so the two became one flesh; therefore, a man who violates the legal pact of marriage loses his strength (*robur virtutis*), is debilitated in his powers (*viribus*), 3.76. When Hildegard discusses particularly female sins, it is with a leniency that suggests she understood the problems that led to them. The penance she gives to women who abort their fetuses ("oppress and dissipate their conceptions [*conceptus suos*], the matter of the figure of mankind in themselves," 1.114) is harsh fasts and scourges. It is clearly a less severe sin than infanticide for Hildegard; those who kill their own infants sin more than bestially, but they too can avoid damnation if they punish themselves with very severe fasts and dire scourging and harshness of dress in anguish of solitude (1.115).[65]

In the last book of visions, the LDO, the scope is cosmological.[66] The social comments are few and traditional, but usually made in connection with moral lessons, which are not so traditional. A woman is said to adorn herself to the honor and glory of her husband and to seem more beautiful to him (10.9), not to criticize her worldly vanity but to present a model for mankind to learn how to adorn the soul for the highest kingdom.[67] A woman, being weak (*debilis*), looks to a man to care for her, is subject to him and ought to be ready to serve him (4.65), not just because she is subject to him, but implicitly in return for his protection and care. Humility, which is natural to woman in her state of subjection, is also essential in the human relation to God, giving woman an edge over man. In an exposition on the gospel about the birth of Christ (Pitra, 245ff.), Hildegard comments that God wished Mary to marry Joseph so that he would care for her, and she would be subject to him, because every woman who has a child should have a man caring for her (*procurantem*); the explanation for this is that humility follows subjection, and there would have been danger of pride if Mary had managed on her own. This implies that Mary might well have managed on her own, but that it was more important to preserve her as an exemplar of humility. (It is significant that Mary's obedience in the LDO is prefigured by Abraham's [1.17], not therefore a sign of purely female subjection.) Is it stretching too far to suggest that Hildegard consciously chose the exemplary role of the female in the salvation of mankind over her independence? The subjection to a specific man is, of course, only relevant in secular marriage—those who, like Hildegard, choose Christ as their husband, do not submit to it. In a later passage in the LDO, the virgin who calls Christ her husband repudiates man (*virum*), the human husband (8.4). Such virgins are technically subject to the church hierarchy, but in Hildegard's case, her heavenly husband often superseded the worldly authority.

Hildegard frequently associates Eve's creation with Mary's conception, so that she appears to be one of the tools in the redemptive process, rather than the agent of the fall: God created man from earth and changed him to flesh, but woman from the man's flesh not to be changed, and they knew through the spirit of prophecy that woman would give birth through the inspiration of the Holy Spirit to the son of God (7.3, cf. 7.13: Eve was created not from seed but from the flesh of man, God created her by the power with which he sent his son into the Virgin).[68] God's words describing the incarnation suggest that Mary avenged the devil's deception of Eve: "when the time of full justice came through my son, the ancient serpent was astonished, since he was completely deceived by a woman" (5.16). Moreover, her mediation, giving human form to Christ, is crucial to human knowledge or love of God: "when woman enclosed/surrounded (*circumdedit*) this son of God, men who saw him in the similitude of their image loved him more than if they had not seen him, since what men see in the shadow they cannot fully know" (7.3).

In her medical writings, Hildegard gives women a more active role in the production of a child, even more influence in conception, and implies that each conception and birth imitates the annunciation and incarnation. The medical works, *The Book of Compound Medicine* (*Liber compositae medicinae*, called *Causae et curae* by its editor) and *The Book of Simple Medicine* (*Liber simplicis medicinae*), are the product of Hildegard's experience and observations of the women (and men) she knew and treated.[69] She was not unorthodox in her pronouncements but extraordinary in the extent of her concern with issues of gender and reproduction and in her treatment of women as different from men, not only in the obvious ways but also in their temperaments; she does not treat them as opposites or lesser parallels of their male counterparts but notes their characteristics separately.[70] Where she particularly differs from other medical writers, even those, like Trotula, who wrote on the diseases of women, is in her interest in sexual behavior and gender characteristics; and she differs from theological writers on women in her objective descriptions of those characteristics without moral judgments.

Hildegard attributes an influence to both parents in the kind of child that is conceived, in its gender and character: plump women have sufficient heat to overcome the force of the man's seed so the child looks like the mother, while the children of thin women look like their fathers (2.36). The love the parents have for each other determines the child's sex and strength: if they love each other, with the righteous love of charity ("in recto amore caritatis"), they will have a virtuous male; if the woman does not love the man, it will be a weak and not virtuous male; if his seed is thin, but they love each other, they will have a virtuous female; and if he does not love her, it will be female if his seed is thin, male but bitter if his seed is strong (2.35-36).[71] Though the woman's blood has very little seed and thin spume (the foam that contains seed), her heat is necessary to conception, and to the nourishment and continuing development of the fetus: "when the seed of the man falls in its place, then the blood of the woman receives it with the desire of love, and draws it into itself . . . and the man's flesh is cooked from the heat and sweat of the woman inside and out . . . his blood, from the very powerful force of will is liquified and . . . receives something from the spume and sweat of the woman, and his flesh is mixed with the woman's, so they become one" (2.67-68). Her role in conception is active: "when the seed falls in its place, the powerful heat of the brain draws it and holds it . . . all the members which are open in the menstrual period shut, just as a strong man holds something in his hand; and then the menstrual blood mixes with the seed and makes blood and flesh ("sanguineum facit et *incarnat*," 2.104). As in the incarnation, God works with the mother to give life to the child. God enters the woman's body first to infuse life (and soul) into the fetus like a strong hot wind (2.61-62), reminiscent of the annunciation, and again at birth "the power of eternity, which took Eve from the side of Adam, comes and overturns all the corners of the habitation of the woman's body." All its connections meet that force and receive it and open and contain it while the infant comes out, and then return as they were, and the soul of the infant feels the power of eternity and rejoices (2.66).

Hildegard recognizes that women as well as men can take pleasure in sex, though less, and that most people fare better when sexually active than when not, indeed abstinence can produce general weakness or illness in women.[72] But she does not connect her own ill health, as Cadden notes, with a tension between religious vows and normal health ("It Takes All Kinds," n.76); if she made the connection with her own state, it would have been as a physical fact to be accepted, a result of the fall. Nothing in Hildegard's writings suggests that she would have preferred a noncelibate life. On the contrary, she implies that left to themselves, women might prefer to be celibate, but since sex is necessary for the human race to continue, women have the capacity to be aroused: the periodic "fluid of fertility with heat" that a woman experiences enables her to receive her husband, but a woman is not inflamed into desire unless she has previously been touched by a man, because a woman's desire is not as strong as a man's (*Scivias*, 2.3.22). That is indeed why a woman must submit to a man's will; if she were not subject to man, she would not necessarily engage in sex and there would be no procreation.[73] Her natural impulse is to look to God not to man, as Hildegard told the nuns of Zwiefalten: a woman who has chosen God "ought to remain as Eve was before God presented her to Adam, when she looked not to Adam but to God. So a woman does who refuses a carnal husband for love of God; she looks to God and not to another man whom previously she did not wish to have" (VA, 250r).

Mary and the other women celebrated in the poems of the *Symphonia* reject men in their devotion to God, at most making use of their services in a holy cause.[74] Holy virgins who were born in the crime of Adam turn away from it to Christ as their spouse, repudiating human husbands ("repudiantes virum," 57.6); widows, who were constructed in the rib of the first mother, who followed her in exile and suffered her pain, also turn to Christ, choosing spiritual marriage over carnal (58). Ursula, the leader of a golden army ("aureus exercitus," 60) of virgins, rejects her husband but is accompanied by religious and wise men who minister to her army, because God signed in the first woman that women were to be nourished by man's care ("Deus enim / in prima muliere presignavit / ut mulier a viri custodia / nutriretur." 63.4), as if man were appointed to serve woman, rather than woman to be subject to man, and in a sense that is the reversal achieved by the choice of virginity. The church, Ecclesia, is adorned by Ursula and her virgins, its precious stones, but their beauty is an active force, as Hildegard shows in one of her most powerful images: "the throat of the ancient serpent / is strangled / in these pearls / from the matter of the Word of God" (64.10). In the poems to Ecclesia, Hildegard addresses her as a virgin (66), as bride of God (66, 69) and as a mother (67); like Ursula and Hildegard, the church is modeled on Mary.[75]

Mary is the center of a cycle of poems which come between those to the Father and those to the Holy Spirit, as though she represented her son in the trinity; Newman entitles the first two cycles "Father and Son" and "Mother and Son," following Hildegard's tendency to speak of Christ as the son of both.[76] Mary is the form in which God's word took on flesh (1), the authoress of life (*auctrix vite*, 8), the supreme blessing in feminine form before all creatures (12). She is also Eve, both countering and fulfilling, the form that was taken from Adam (1), the unguent to the wound that Eve constructed (10); she raised man from their (Adam and Eve's) fall

(14), and embellished heaven more than the other woman disturbed the earth, when the king entered her subject female form (16). Mary is the fulfillment, the perfection of God's creation of mankind in his image: "O how great / in its powers is the side of man / from which God brought forth the form of woman, / which he made the mirror / of all his beauty / and the embrace / of his whole creation" (20.4a). Mary is also implicitly a special model for Hildegard, as the woman God chose to embody his word and manifest it to mankind (in the visions): "you are that luminous matter / through which this very Word breathed forth / all virtues" (10); "the supernal Father . . . wished his Word to be incarnate in her . . . in the mystical mystery of God, / as the Virgin's mind was illumined" (21).[77]

Hildegard's poems were set to music, and the music is as extraordinary in its composition as the poems are in their imagery and form.[78] The music, as much a product of her revelation as the words, departs from rules and conventions in its expanded space and disjunct motion, the extended scope of its melodic registers and the leaps both upward and—more radical still—downward. Holsinger suggests that music is one of the ways in which Hildegard reacted to the constraints of the male-dominated church, "constructing powerful alternatives to patriarchal traditions . . . centered around the female body . . ." (116). The female body has particularly melodious qualities, for Hildegard, who describes it as "open like a wooden frame in which strings have been fastened for strumming" (*Causae et Curae*, 105). If the female body is like a musical instrument, is it not then also more receptive to God's harmony than the male? Hildegard describes her own body as a trumpet (*tuba*), through which God blows. Despite Cistercian objections to womanish sounds and wide ranges (Holsinger 103, 106), Hildegard seems to flaunt the possibilities of the female range: the music of "Ave generosa" (*Symph* 17.5) reaches its highest point on the word *symphonia* ("for your womb held joy, / when all the celestial harmony resounded from you"), the music resonating from the Virgin's womb.[79] The Virgin's flesh, "anything but a passive receptacle for the Word, blooms in fertility and song"; the (female) body of Ecclesia resonates with the same sounds two verses later (17.7), and the music of both Mary and the church is heard through the voices of the women singing Hildegard's words and music, creating a bond between the female bodies of the earthly women and the Virgin and Ecclesia (Holsinger, 102, 109).

Music counters the effects of the fall by making people more receptive to the Holy Spirit (*Scivias*, 3.13.14). In the letter Hildegard wrote to the prelates of Mainz, when their interdict prevented music in her convent, she argued that God wants mankind to praise him with music, explaining that we can "transform and shape the performance of our inner being towards praises of the Creator" and strive for "the voice of the living spirit which Adam lost through disobedience" (VA23).[80] Adam had rejoiced in the sweetness of angelic praise before he fell, and the prophets, taught by the

Holy Spirit, composed psalms and canticles to recapture that sweetness and stir mankind to that praise, and invented musical instruments so that "the songs could be expressed in multitudinous sounds, so that listeners, aroused and made adept outwardly, might be nurtured within by the forms and qualities of the instruments, as by the meaning of the words performed with them." Adam's voice before the fall had contained "the sound of every harmony and the sweetness of the whole art of music," which the frail human body can no longer endure, but wise men strive to work back to. They imitate the prophets, inventing different kinds of harmonies with their human art which the devil tries to disrupt, lest man, transformed by the music and its memory of the sweetness of songs in heaven, escape his machinations. Music is thus a key instrument for the salvation of mankind and the prelates, by denying it to the nuns, are doing the devil's work. While, one might add, woman's body, functioning in harmony with the divine will like a musical instrument, does God's work.

It is not surprising that the creation and fall of Adam and Eve is a constant theme through Hildegard's works, since their story underlies Christian attitudes toward woman in all their complications, and Hildegard believed the hostility she encountered from men arose from their identifying her with Eve (in the prefaces to books one and two of the Scivias). Hildegard tends to put much of the responsibility for original sin on Adam, presumably because as the stronger one he should have been better able to resist. But she also turns the traditional male view of the fall on its head by opposing it with the traditional male view of sexual hierarchy: if woman is weaker and man stronger, then the man must be ultimately responsible for the fall. Being weaker, Hildegard says, Eve fell first, which was just as well, since Adam's sin would have been stronger, more obdurate, incorrigible, and salvation would not have been possible (CC, 2.47), though of course woman plays a key role in salvation, through Mary. Hildegard speaks of corrupt times as "womanly," that is, soft and given to vice, but she does not blame that softness on women; indeed, it is because of male deficiencies, that women have to assume the male roles of preaching and guidance.

In the medical work, Causae et Curae, where Hildegard is more concerned with the physical and social consequences of the fall than with moral judgments, Adam's fall changes the universe and human physiology: after Adam sinned (seduced by the demon who deceived him and called him lord of the earth, 2.58), night began, all the elements darkened (2.46), and the firmament, which had not moved or revolved before the fall, began to move as it would do until the last day (1.10). For mankind, the immediate results of the fall are death, sex, and physical weakness, which Adam and Eve would not otherwise have known (2.47). Adam's flesh incurs weakness and frailty ("debilitatem et fragilitatem," 2.81), the words Hildegard so often applies to herself; by the fall, man is reduced to a kind of female fragility.[81] In Adam's transgression, the power of man moved to his genitals in a poisonous spume, while woman's blood went into contrary effusion (2.60). Menstruation is a result of the fall—when the flood of cupidity entered Eve all her veins opened in a flow of blood—but it also serves a useful purpose in purging blood and humors, which is necessary to prevent illness (2.102). Woman incurred the pains of childbirth, man the problems of lust, which Hildegard emphasizes perhaps because many women's problems follow from it. In his transgression, man's virile power went into exile and fled furtively into his genitals (2.70); he changed in body and mind, his blood ejecting spume, which we call seed, in the ardor and heat of desire (2.33). In man, such desire is like the fire of burning mountains, hard to extinguish, while woman's is more easily extinguished, like burning trees, and has a positive side, like the soft heat of the sun which produces fruit (2.136-37).

Adam was affected psychologically as well as physically by the fall. Since he knew good and did evil, when he ate the apple he became subject to melancholy, to sorrow and despair which arise from the suggestion of the devil (2.143). Before Adam transgressed, what now is bile shone like crystal in him, what is melancholy shone like dawn and he had knowledge and perfection of good works in him. When he transgressed, the splendor of innocence was darkened in him and his eyes which at first saw heavenly things were extinguished, bile changed to bitterness and melancholy into the blackness of impiety, and his soul contracted deep sorrow (*tristicia*) and sought its excuse in wrath (2.145-46). Before his transgression, Adam knew the songs of angels and every kind of music; after, from the cleverness of the serpent, a wind twisted itself in his marrow and in his thigh, and from the wind spleen grew and inept rejoicing and laughter and noise (2.148-49).[82]

Most of what Adam suffered from the fall applies to Eve as well—Eve's sight and hearing for heavenly things was extinguished when she looked at and listened to the serpent with consent (2.103). But what Hildegard emphasizes is Eve as the mother of mankind: just as air holds all the stars in itself, so she had the human race in herself whole and uncorrupt without pain (2.104, cf. *Scivias*, 1.2). When Adam looked at Eve, he was filled with wisdom, since he saw the mother through whom he should procreate children; as she was brought forth from man, so every kind of human life proceeded from her (2.46). When, however, Eve looked at Adam, she looked at him as if she saw heaven and as the soul tends upward which desires heavenly things, since its hope was in the man. One might say he looked to the earthly future, she to the heavenly source.

In the creation of Adam and Eve, there was a basic difference, which continues to affect their postlapsarian lives: Adam was formed from mud which is stronger matter than the flesh from which Eve was formed (2.35). God created man from all the elements, holding the earth together with water, sending fire and air to give life to his form (2.42, 45); Adam was virile from the viridity of earth, powerful from the elements (2.46). Eve formed from his marrow was soft and had an airy mind and a keen or intelligent (*acutam*) and delightful life, since weight of earth did not press her. Since man's creation involved an essential transformation from clay to flesh, he is the cause and dominator of what is created, and his labor (at which he sweats, 2.46) now involves essential transformation, making the earth bring forth fruit (2.59); while woman, who did not change, who was flesh formed from flesh, now does the artificial and artistic work of the hands, reworking previously existing material. It is hard to imagine that the aristocratic Hildegard did not consider the latter, whether the sewing of garments or the illumination of manuscripts, a higher form of labor than farming, albeit less necessary to existence.[83]

In the *Scivias*, the moral aspect of the fall dominates, though it is still connected to the physical. God's voice identifies Hildegard with Eve, but only to show up the hypocritical attitude of the male clergy, descendants of Adam, one might say, who fail to see their own faults. Hildegard's interpretation of Eve is complex: she is both the innocent cloud that contains the stars of the human race (1.2.10), and the susceptible victim of the devil's seduction, chosen because more easily conquered than Adam, and because Adam's love for her would make him follow her lead—she has such power over him because she was part of him, "made from his rib." So, the voice comments, woman can overthrow man if instead of shunning, detaching himself from her (*abhorrens*), he easily accepts her words (ibid.). There is a strong sense in the passage that man, like Adam, is led by woman when he chooses to be. The following sentence, "a mature woman was not given to a little boy, but to a mature man," may well be a comment on Adam, even though it begins a new section, which points out that "Adam might have blamed his wife because her advice brought death," but he did not dismiss her because he knew she was given to him by divine power (1.2.11).[84] That is, he tried to shift the blame to her, but he could not separate from her, because she was part of him, by his choice as well as God's will. In a later passage, Hildegard makes the shifting of blame explicit: one should confess one's sins "as the old Adam did not; for he concealed his transgression instead of confessing it. How? He did not confess it by repenting, but concealed it by accusing the woman" (2.6.82).

A woman is now under the power of her husband because he is the sower and she receives the seed to bring a child into the world, because the strength of man is to the susceptibility of woman as the hardness of stone is to the softness of earth (1.2.11). Stone is a curious image for the source of seed, making for a startling contrast with the warm, moist earth, teeming with life. God announces that he inflicted the pain of childbirth on Eve when she conceived sin in the taste of the fruit, but adds that woman should therefore be cherished in this time with "a great and healing tenderness" ("unde et mulier in hoc eodem tempore in magna medicina misericordiae habenda est," 1.2.20). This is consistent with Hildegard's slant on woman's subjection to man, which she usually presents as man's responsibility to take care of woman.[85]

Eve's sin is recalled from time to time through the *Scivias*, in connection with the positive female figures foreshadowed by Eve, the church (Ecclesia) and Mary: when Hildegard sees a priest at the altar, she hears "eat and drink the body and blood of my son to wipe out Eve's transgression" (2.6, preface);[86] in a passage that begins with Isaiah's words foretelling the virgin birth, we are reminded that the first woman fled from virtues by consenting to the counsel she heard from the serpent and the whole human race fell in her, but only after we have heard at length what the virgin birth meant for mankind (3.8.15). The drama at the end of the *Scivias* begins with a joyful reminder of Mary's role in countering the effects of the fall: "It is His sole Word, by Whom He created the world, / The primary matter, which Eve threw into disorder. / He formed the Word in you . . . The Most High Father sought for a Virgin's candor, / And willed that His Word should take in her His body. / For the Virgin's mind was by His mystery illumined, / And from her virginity sprang the glorious Flower," 3.13.1. Mary returns to the condition Eve had lost of being illumined by divine mysteries, in which she foreshadows that other daughter of Eve, Hildegard. It is in woman (Mary, Hildegard, and Eve) that God chooses to reflect his beauty: "praise God . . . for the miracles God has wrought in the frail earthly reflection of the beauty of the Most High; as He Himself foreshadowed when He first made Woman from the rib of the man He had created" (3.13.16).

Adam's sin, on the other hand, is consistently and frequently condemned by God's voice.[87] When he transgressed God's command Adam was afraid and hid himself (1.4.4); harmful poisons, the corruption of vice, were instilled in the soul (1.4.5); the bitter foreskin is the crime of Adam's transgression (2.3.24); his fall closed heaven (2.3.26); the old Adam transgressed the command of life and was driven out into the calamities of the world (2.5.38); the crime of Adam which brought death to man aroused his senses to fornication (2.6.62); God's grace made Adam, the devil drew him away from innocent deeds (3.2.10). The same pattern of acknowledging the sin of both Adam and Eve but putting more weight on Adam's role by referring much more frequently to it and even partially excusing Eve's actions, obtains generally through the other visionary books. In the *Liber vitae meritorum*, Eve's faults are to have seduced the first man (*hominem*) many times, after the devil first deceived him (1.34); the belly of the ancient serpent swallowed Eve and vomited through Eve many filths (2.2);[88] the devil conquered her through pride, which is the mother of vices as Eve is the mother of the whole species (3.49). But much more is said about

Adam: having transgressed the precept of God, Adam rushed into death (1.59); the first angel fell and made the first man fall (1.118); the serpent drew man from paradise, after he had seduced him with food (2.41); death entered man in the fall of Adam, the serpent deceived him, he (Adam) took his counsel and lost the knowledge of the voices of animals (3.80); in paradise, through the serpent, man accepted the knowledge of evil in the taste of the apple (6.16).[89] In one case, the voice from the living light implies that a woman (Mary) restored what a man had lost: "after man was deceived by the devil's counsel, I came flaming, rested in the womb of the virgin, was incarnate from her flesh, that never sweated with any filth like the flesh of Adam" (6.32).

In the *Liber divinorum operum*, Hildegard gives Eve both more and less responsibility: the devil attacked God's work, mankind, in her because seeing her, he knew her to be the future mother of the great world; when Eve, tasting the apple, felt herself to be different, she gave it to her husband, so both lost their heavenly vestment (1.14). But the devil was able to deceive Eve since she was without deception; he covered himself so Eve did not know his craftiness, and his deception could not be seen (4.37). Despite her fall, which is repaired by Mary, Eve is necessary to complete all the works of man according to God (4.66); and Mary, in God's words, seems to avenge the devil's deception of Eve by deceiving him: "when the time of full justice came through my son, the ancient serpent was astonished, since he was completely deceived by a woman" (5.16). The other references to Eve in the LDO are connected with the Virgin: Abraham's obedience contrasting with Eve, who desired to have what she should not have, foreshadowed the Virgin's (1.17); the first woman who lost paradise and the name "daughter of Sion" because of her transgression of the divine precept was redeemed when our redeemer arose in virginal nature (3.11); God created Eve (virgin and mother) without pain or seed from the sleeping man as he sent his son into Mary (mother and virgin), an analogy in which Eve is the Christ figure (7.13).[90]

In her letters, Hildegard is often concerned with rebellion against authority, the authority of the abbesses and abbots who write to her for advice, and she frequently speaks of Adam's fall in those terms, but rarely of Eve's part in it. She cites Adam frequently in her letters to male clergy: Adam derided obedience at the beginning of the world and times perished (VA38r, to a bishop); he was driven out of paradise and none of his sons/children saw paradise bodily (VA125, to an abbot); his disobedience was restored through punishment (VA70r, to five abbots); man was blinded by the fall of Adam and cannot see with carnal eyes (VA149r, to a priest); Adam received God's command in good will, but defaulted by the devil's counsel, lost paradise and his clear vestment and went into dark earth and vestment of mourning (VA15r, appendix 1, to clergy); bright day turned to night through disobedience in the fall of Adam (VA43r, to a bishop); lust of the flesh was the cost Adam paid for the apple (VA109r, to monks).[91] To women Hildegard wrote less frequently but no less forcefully of Adam: Adam scorned his lord, *listened to the filthy worm*, and so threw off his honor and angelic dress (to an unnamed "daughter of Adam," DB 4); to former palatine countess Gertrude, God turned back the days of your nobility and wealth lest you be seduced by Adam's fall (VA232); to a matron who wanted to leave her husband, she says that a man who turns to other women is as guilty as Adam was when he transgressed the precepts of God through the counsel of woman and the serpent, and will be expelled from paradise until he is washed in penance (Pi95).[92]

Hildegard uses the fall of Adam very personally, in connection with her own situation, identifying her enemies with God's, as the rebellious Lucifer or the disobedient Adam. When Helenger, abbot of Hildegard's old monastery, Disibodenberg, expresses the hope that the hatreds and hostilities of many years have ceased and asks her if there are still hidden dissensions to reveal them (VA77), she responds with a sermon about the fall of Lucifer who did not praise God, and makes much of God foreseeing that a work would be done in female nature that not angels or men or other creatures could carry through. The Virgin in the light of the sun of ancient counsel turned the fall of woman into good, which God brought about to the confusion of the devil who had deceived woman, not knowing what would come through her as God knew (VA77r). The analogies are obvious between Lucifer and the monks who opposed her, on the one hand, and on the other between herself who sees normally "in the light of the sun of ancient counsel" and the Virgin, destined by God to help man repair the fall.

As she does in her poems, Hildegard links the fall with the redemption through Christ's incarnation in the Virgin, so the Virgin seems to take Eve's place: "Eve brought forth every kind of human; she truly is the rod that repaired anew in her greenness when the son of God came out of her womb, while "Adam fled life in pride and found exile" (VA220r, to monks of St. Eucharius); more conventionally, Eve was of sterile life, but Mary conferred greater grace than Eve harmed (VA15r, app.1).[93] Indeed, Hildegard implies that Adam was responsible for Eve's fall, since left to her own resources, Eve would have preferred God to Adam (VA250r).[94] This might well be Hildegard's projection of her own view—as an Eve, she prefers God to a human husband.[95] In an address to her nuns that accompanies her life of their patron, St. Rupert (Pi p.358ff), Hildegard says God knew that "the devil wanted to suffocate life through a woman and so, in his wisdom, prepared a great tower so that He might offer another life through another woman in the chastity of innocence," as though God refused to give up on women because of Eve, but gave the whole sex a new start with Mary. Hildegard then addresses God as Wisdom (a female figure), praising her for finding another woman whom the serpent could not delude, who crowned the *whole human race,* so that the devil now could not delude man (*hominem*) as he had before.

In Hildegard's poems, in contrast to the other works, Eve is given much more attention than Adam. Here Hildegard seems to be emphasizing and strengthening the female role: as Christ brought life, reversing the death that is Adam's heritage, so Mary's advent changes the heritage of Eve— women are henceforth agents of salvation rather than of damnation. Adam's fall and guilt are alluded to negatively in connection with the devil and Christ (29, 50.3a, 57.9-10); his responsibility for man's fallen state, our birth through mixed blood and exile because of his fall, are contrasted with the joy Mary brings to the elements (13). Mary counters both Adam and Eve:[96] "you [Mary] blossomed / in another way / than Adam gave rise / to the whole human race. / . . . from your womb / came another life / of which Adam / had stripped his sons. / . . . how great / in its powers is the side of man / from which God brought forth the form of woman, / which he made the mirror / of all his beauty / and the embrace / of his whole creation. / . . . how greatly we . . . mourn / because sadness flowed in guilt / through the serpent's counsel / into woman. / For the very woman / whom God made to be mother of all / plucked at her womb / with the wounds of ignorance / and brought forth consummate pain / for her kind. / But, O dawn, / from your womb / a new sun has come forth, / which has cleansed all the guilt of Eve / and through you brought a blessing greater / than the harm Eve did to mankind. / Hence, O saving Lady, / you who bore the new light / for humankind: / gather the members of your Son / into celestial harmony" (20).

Hildegard casts Mary, a new Eve in the role of Christ, so a woman reverses Eve's legacy of death and conquers her enemy, the devil, bringing mankind to greater heights than Eve had descended from: "Hail Mary, / author [fem.] of life (*auctrix vite*) . . . who confounded death, / and crushed the serpent / toward whom Eve stretched / erect . . . with pride" (8); "you poured / ointments / through your holy Son / on the sobbing wounds of death / that Eve built / into torments for souls. / You destroyed death, / building life" (9); "today a closed gate / has opened to us, / which the serpent choked in a woman" (11), recalling Christ's harrowing of hell; "because a woman constructed death, / a bright virgin has demolished it, / and so the supreme blessing is / in feminine form / beyond all creation, / because God was made man / in the most sweet and blessed virgin" (12); "humility ascends over all . . . malice / which flowed from woman, / this woman erased / and . . . adorned heaven / more than she formerly troubled earth" (16).[97]

One of Hildegard's most enthusiastic followers, her last secretary, Guibert of Gembloux, connects her with Mary as a counter Eve: "O wondrous piety of the benign Redeemer to be preached to human kind, who through that sex by which death entered, life was restored in his mother; from whose hand the pestiferous drink of perdition was offered to us, from that hand the antidote of recovery was poured out for us in you with salutary doctrine" (Gb16 to Hildegard); and "with the exception of her from whom the sun of justice arose . . . harbor of perpetual light and star of the sea, with her exception it is not heard in the world that the female sex through which the shadows of death are spread over the world is signed in any other [person] with the privilege of greater gift, or irradiated with such splendor" (Gb18 to Hildegard).

Hildegard, a woman chosen by God to carry his word to the church and all its members, was listened to with respect rather than ridicule by powerful men in the secular and church hierarchies. She was a woman who had overcome her physical limitations—her illness as well as her sex, the one a more extreme manifestation of the other—to become not only a respected visionary, writer, preacher, and international correspondent but also an effective administrator of the convent she founded. Godfrey describes her negotiating for the property by purchase and exchange, ensuring its protection from local interests by the diocese, and the right of the sisters to choose their priests from their old monastery of Disibodenberg, under whose spiritual protection they remained, but insisting on removing from the control of the monks the land and possessions that had been left to the nuns (*Vita*). He balances his description of her successful negotiations with her own description (from a letter to Guibert of Gembloux) of herself as a feather borne on the wind, carried as God wills through her visions. Guibert describes the ample buildings she had built, with plumbing, the many guests, the work of the scriptorium, and her own tending to others, giving the requested counsels, comforting those who come to her (Gb38). She was a woman in a position of authority who understood and sympathized with the problems of women, physical, social, and psychological, and treated them with medical advice and spiritual and practical counsel. When Elisabeth of Schönau needed the support of another woman who had presented her visions to the world, she could look to Hildegard and say: "your words enflamed me as if fire touched my heart . . . you are blessed since the lord chose you and placed you . . . that you might go and bear fruit and your fruit remain." The abbess of Bamberg expressed a pride I like to think many contemporary women took in Hildegard: "Christ made us particularly happy in this, that he not only foresaw and predestined you for this from the female sex, but illumined many through doctrine by his grace" (VA61).

Both Hildegard and Elisabeth were women of vision in the literal and figurative sense. They communicated directly with God or the saints, and they relayed the messages they received to their fellows. But they also helped to focus those messages in ways that bear on perceptions and problems of women. Elisabeth was concerned with historical problems, Hildegard with mental, moral, and medical problems, with women's roles in the religious and the biological process. Both played male roles, teaching and answering theological questions, but both relied on the women around them for support. Both looked to female figures for authority, Elisabeth to Mary and the saints, Hildegard to female aspects of God. Elisabeth looked to other women, the saints and Hildegard, as her models, while Hildegard provided a model for other women, like Elisabeth and the many abbesses who corresponded with her. Their preferred models are women of authority and action, the Virgin Mary, queen of heaven and an active force in the redemption, Ursula the leader of an "army" of virgins and martyrs. Like Mary and Ursula, Elisabeth and Hildegard were figures of some authority in their world, actively working to fight corruption and guiding others through their writings.

6 *Women Representing Women*

Women who wrote in the narrative genres of courtly romances or who
wrote lives of saints for court audiences were also attracted by intelligent,
courageous, and effective women, women who take an active role in their
own and others' lives, women who overcome constraints of the patriarchy
and defeat its representatives, who have or find the courage to live or die
as they choose. Like Elisabeth and Hildegard, these writers are concerned
with human not just women's social and moral issues, but like them they
are also particularly alert to problems women face. Though none of the
writers deny that women can be weak or evil, they show that men can be
equally so. Though most of them struggle with the concept of themselves
as women and writers, all of them present women whose virtue and
nobility, learning and self-sacrifice, are implicit if not explicit answers to
misogynist charges.

Among the narrative poets I consider here, I include Hrotsvit of Gandersheim and Clemence of Barking, who wrote saints' lives for court as
well as convent audiences and whose works say something to secular as
well as religious women. Saints' lives by women is an enormous subject in
itself, which I do not address, except insofar as the issues and approaches
seem to coincide with those of secular women writers. Hrotsvit wrote plays
modeled on Terence as well as narrative poetry and had an audience in the
imperial court, and the nun(s) of Barking wrote (translated and adapted)
lives of royal saints in Anglo-Norman for a royal court; she composed in
the form (and the time) of the early courtly romances and the works of
Marie de France, probably for the same court in which courtly narrative
seems to have begun, that of Eleanor of Aquitaine and Henry II.

I will look briefly at the lyric poems of the trobairitz, in connection with
both male-female debates and the expression of women's voices. The trobairitz present problems of genre and identity, but they warrant mention
not only because of the existence of so many women poets composing
secular, courtly lyrics in the same tradition and the same century, who were

admired enough for (some of) their poems to be preserved, but also because they do seem to speak differently from their male counterparts. Most of the writers I am concerned with, Hrotsvit, the trobairitz, Marie de France, Christine de Pizan, are by now as well known to modern scholars as they were to their contemporaries. Much has been written about all of them in recent years because there is much to be said about them, but I shall confine myself to the way they present themselves as women authors and the way they present their women characters. My choice for inclusion is determined primarily by the popularity and importance of the writers in question, because it gives a sense of what audiences responded to and what women who had an audience wanted to say to them. Though Christine falls outside my time frame, she brings together so many of the elements I have been discussing and she is such a major figure that she must be included.

However diffident most of these writers may be about their own talents or their right as a woman to take the initiative, the women they speak through—personifications, saints, historic and fictional heroines, or lyrical personae—are articulate and active figures who accomplish something the audience, male and female, can admire. The authors take pride in women's achievements as, I think, they expect the women in their audience to do, but they tell a good enough story to hold a male audience as well. Indeed they all seem to have male patrons and male readers or listeners. Hrotsvit sent copies of her works to learned men and she was respected enough as a poet to be asked to write the first life of the emperor Otto I by a member of the royal family; both the subject and his son Otto II asked for a copy. The nun of Barking makes a pointed reference to the court of Henry and Eleanor in the Life of Edward the Confessor, and addresses herself frequently to "Seignurs" as Clemence does in the Life of St. Catherine.[1] The poems and *vidas* of the trobairitz are included with men's in manuscript collections for performance. Marie de France dedicated the *lais* to a noble king, the fables to a count William. She was popular enough with men and women to inspire Denis Piramus's pointed envy, cited at the end of chapter 4.

Christine de Pizan, who was known and admired in France, England, and Italy, was described by a friendly poet, Eustache Deschamps as a "muse eloquent among the nine, without equal today in acquired wisdom and all doctrine, science, philosophy, knowledge."[2] The chancellor of the University of Paris, Jean Gerson, spoke admiringly of her as an "insigni[s]" and "virilis femina," a "virago."[3] Martin LeFranc, in *Le Champion des dames* (written in 1440, presumably after her death), devotes a long passage to Christine, praising her learning in letters and Latin, and her style, ranking her above her famous contemporaries, Froissart, Machaut, and Alain Chartier, calling her Tully (Cicero) for eloquence, Cato for wisdom.[4] In her time, people read not only her works on love and on women, but also on political theory, and warfare. The treatise on arms and chivalry continued to be read for several centuries, though her name and her sex were suppressed in some versions for fear men would not want to read a woman on warfare.[5] Christine dedicated only a few of her works to women: the debate on the *Roman de la Rose* (to queen Isabel), the *Trésor* (to Marguerite, daughter of the duke of Burgundy), *L'épistre de la prison de vie humaine* (to Marie de Berry); a two-volume manuscript of collected works was commissioned by the queen, but individual lyric poems and other works in it are dedicated to important men.[6] Christine also wrote a letter to the queen, imploring her to work for peace in France among the warring factions of the royal family, since pity, charity, clemency and benevolence are naturally found in women, particularly in princesses; she cites the examples of queen Esther, who appeased the wrath of the king so he revoked the sentence against her people, and of Blanche, queen of France, who carried her young son among the quarreling barons to shame them into peace. Christine's other major works were either commissioned by or presented to men—presumably one would not present a work that did not either interest or flatter the recipient. Even the *Cité des Dames* was presented to two dukes though it is undisguised propaganda for women. The life of Charles V was requested by the king's brother, Philip, duke of Burgundy, after she sent him the *Mutacion de Fortune*.

Though like Christine all the women discussed here appealed to a mixed audience, I am concerned with what they say in particular to a female audience, whether medieval or modern. Hrotsvit, a canoness writing at the imperial abbey of Gandersheim in the tenth century, chose the stories of saints and martyrs or miracles of the virgin as her material, until she was asked to write two historic epics, one on the life of Otto I, another on the foundation of her abbey. She collected her works in three large parts, consisting of eight short narrative poems, six dramas, and the two epics.[7] Hrotsvit frequently uses diminutives and deprecating terms to speak of her own work—*libellum, opusculum, fronticula, carminula, sordidola camena, versiculos, dictatiunculae*, "the rusticity of my poor speech," "the vileness of my labor"—and of herself—*feminea fragilitas, talentum ingenioli, nesciola, mea inscientia, vilis mulierculae, meum posse licet minime*. But she uses this humble stance in order both to forestall criticism, as she admits ("humility of confession breaks the force of reproof"), and to disguise the boldness of her enterprise.[8]

Even in the prefaces to her earliest works, the short narrative poems, where she seems most hesitant, Hrotsvit's daring and stubbornness, her determination to write as she chooses, appear. Virtually every humble self-depreciation is countered by an opposing assertion: there is little ornament in her work, but not little diligence; it is to be corrected by the kindness of the wise, not those who delight in and disparage errors—in other words she is open to constructive criticism, not to ridicule. She is not expert in the techniques of prosody or composition, but she has been instructed by most learned teachers, whose training must lend some authority; she did not consult experts *before* she finished, lest she be stopped because of her "rusticity." But she knew enough to edit her own material: "in secret, even furtively, I labored sometimes composing, sometimes destroying what was badly composed." She has since found that some of her material is considered apocryphal, an error she excuses as ignorance rather than presumption, but she will not retract the material because what seems false might be true; that is, she does not accept learned opinion on its authenticity. If her poems are uncultivated, they are also new, original with her ("carminulis novis," *Historia Nativitatis,* 18, "versiculos novellos," *Basilius,* 1); even one of her sources is new, an eyewitness account is the basis of *Pelagius.*

The strongest defense of all is God's support. The metrical mode (dactyls) might *seem* (*videatur*) difficult for feminine fragility, had she relied only on her own strength, but she had divine grace. She cannot let her talent rust out of negligence since it comes from God.[9] She asks her abbess Gerberga not to scorn her poems, however poor they are, but to praise the deeds of God with a kind breast, implying that the poems as well as the events described in them are acts of God, the same claim made by Elisabeth of Schönau and Hildegard of Bingen, but here in defense of a literary production. She breaks into the stories from time to time to pray for help or ask for the readers' prayers: let whoever reads this say with compassionate breast, "Pious king, spare poor Hrotsvit, let her continue with divine odes to praise your stupendous deeds." This serves both to remind us of the author and implies that since she has continued to write, God has willed it. She seems even to identify her work with God's, describing the creator as "painting" heaven with the stars ("qui caelum *pingis* sideribus variis," *Gongulf,* 2), and herself in the same poem as painting characters ("this one, whom our hand began to paint," "hic quem nostra manus coepit iam pingere," 69) and events ("let us paint what we began with a frail pen," "pingamus coepta nos fragili calamo," 338).

In the preface to the second book, the dramas, Hrotsvit speaks with more assurance. She translates her name into Latin, interpreting it as *Clamor validus,* the "strong call" or "loud noise" of Gandersheim, using it to counter the "sweet speech" of Terence's plays, beautiful in style but tainted with unspeakable matter. She says she will replace the unchaste acts of lascivious women with the laudable chastity of sacred virgins, but in fact two of her plays are about the redemption of prostitutes, with scenes set in brothels.[10] This is titillation with a redeeming social value. Hrotsvit insists that she has to use what is "not suited to our hearing" in order to satisfy her purpose (*proposito*) which is clearly not just to provide holy examples for the nuns—they presumably should have been satisfied with the graphic descriptions of martyrdom that dominate some of her plays—but to replace Terence in the court, where he is so popular. She is glorifying God through the victories of her subjects, "especially when feminine fragility triumphs and virile strength is subject to confusion" ("praesertim cum feminea fragilitas vinceret et virilis robur confusioni subiaceret"), apparently referring to the martyrs and their pagan prosecutors, but applicable also to herself and Terence, whom she clearly hopes to replace.

Hrotsvit still worries about her style, but she presents her limitations in a more aggressive way, as a debate: "I do not doubt that there will be objections to the vileness of my composition, inferior, more limited, deeply dissimilar to what I propose to imitate; I concede that (*concedo*) but I answer (*denuntio*, a juridical term indicating an official declaration or testimony), that I cannot be rebuked as if I wished to be compared . . . even to the least disciples of such authorities, but only that I give back my wit (*ingenium* here, not the self-deprecating *ingeniolum*), accepted, to the giver. The message supersedes the style, as in the gospels. She is in some way God's tool. "I am not so loving of myself (*amatrix mei*), that to avoid censure I would cease to preach the virtue of Christ that worked through the saints, *however* [not *if*] he gives me the ability." She even seems to excuse the "rusticity of my badly flawed (*vitiosi*) speech," with the importance of her development as a writer: "it is good for me to have done it, since the earlier work was in a heroic metre, this is dramatic."

Hrotsvit sent the plays to certain learned men and she includes her letter to them. They have encouraged her, as the *truly* learned do, without envy, men nourished in philosophical studies and perfected in learning; of course, the more she humbly exalts them, the more she in fact exalts her own work which they support, though she calls it the "little work of an abject little woman" ("opusculum vilis mulierculae"). Again she says she has hidden the work up to now, when she sends it for their correction; this both tells us that she did it all on her own, and implies that since we have it [in the collected works] they have corrected or approved it. She asserts her own wit and even learning more confidently: "I am a being capable of instruction" ("animal capax disciplinae"); "I know God gave me a good mind" ("perspicax ingenium divinitus mihi collatum esse agnosco"); though limited by laziness, "I have tried to rip pieces from Philosophy's dress," presumably an allusion to Boethius. She does, indeed, show off her learning in logic, in music, and in mathematics, in various passages in the plays. "The bestower of wit will be praised so much the more in me as woman's sense is *believed* to be slower" ("quanto muliebris sensus tardior esse creditur").

Finally, in her prefaces to the epics, though she continues to deplore her uncultivated style and inferior learning, and to be humble in expression ("the less [the work] is supported by authority, the more it lacks defense"), she also asserts the ground-breaking quality of her work and its prestige.

It is the first life of Otto, for much of which she had no written sources, and it was commissioned by a member of the imperial family, a point that is made often, supposedly to excuse her temerity in undertaking the project.[11] She sends it to her abbess Gerberga, who commissioned it, and at her urging to a friendly archbishop, for their judgment, which was presumably favorable, since she also sends it, with individual poetic dedications, to Otto I and to Otto II. She interrupts the poem in various places to say she does not have the wisdom, or does not think it right for a fragile woman to do what she then does, such as talk about war. In the opening of the Gandersheim epic, she expresses her enthusiasm for the work unequivocally: "the suppliant devotion of my humble mind burns to reveal the foundation of happy Gandersheim . . . the order of things demands that the illustrious construction be recited with a suitable poem" (apto carmine). The poem traces the devoted perseverance of women in the foundation of the abbey.

Throughout her works, Hrotsvit emphasizes the devotion and the strength of the women she portrays and frequently shows them standing up to patriarchal authority.[12] Of the eight shorter poems, four are about men, four primarily about women, with the stories of the Virgin and St. Agnes framing all the others. The first poem, on the nativity of the Virgin, praises the women, Mary and her mother, Anna, by contrasting their devotion with the arrogance of the priests and the limited faith of their husbands, Joseph and Joachim: Joachim has difficulty bearing scorn and answering God's summons—he disappears for five months when he is scorned for his sterility and hesitates to return even when summoned by an angel—while Anna prays for knowledge and appropriate action, bears the taunts even of her maid with patience, and accepts the angel's message, going out to meet Joachim. Mary climbs the fifteen steps of the temple for her dedication at age two without looking back, and though forced by the priests to marry at age fourteen, she remains a virgin. She accepts her role as Christ's mother, while Joseph is upset at the announcement of her pregnancy and later skeptical about the possibility of fulfilling her desires for fruit and water. Mary has royal stature: the Pharaoh prostrates himself before her to ask her son's grace, and it is through her parents, Anna and Joachim, that Mary is connected to the royal family of David, not through her husband Joseph as in the Gospels (Matt. 1:20, Lk. 3:23-32).[13]

A poem about a miracle of the Virgin, Theophilus, an early Faust story, tells of a male sinner saved by Mary, who is called a powerful ruler of heaven and of earth and mother of God, "eadem mundi dominatrix" (208), "sancta dei genitrix eademque potens dominatrix / caelorum" (333-34). In Basilius, the compact with the devil is also made by a man, but the story focuses on the woman for whom he makes it. She is her father's only child, whom he has promised to Christ for her soul. The devil makes her servant burn with love for her and sends his ministers to do the same to her, so she persuades her father to let them marry rather than let her die; it is a marriage, Hrotsvit says, carried out with Satan's fraud. But when Christ lets her know that her husband is not a Catholic, she takes over, questioning him, insisting that he come to church to prove his faith. When he refuses and confesses the truth, she "puts down womanly weakness and assumes virile strength" ("*molli*tiem iam deponens *muli*ebrem et sumens *vires . . . viriles*," 168-69, with plays on the key words to emphasize the contrast); she goes for help to a holy man, the Basilius of the title, who saves them both.

The last poem is about the martyrdom of St. Agnes, who has a series of confrontations with non-believing males, the young man who loves her, his father, pontiffs, and a judge. Making it clear at the beginning that she would rather be killed than corrupt the beauty of virginity, she boldly faces any danger they present, secure in her faith. When she is put in a brothel, Christ makes her hair grow to cover her naked body and angels clothe her; the fire of martyrdom divides around her, only a sword can kill her. Though she rejects all requests from men with unbending firmness and praise for her nobler spouse, she shows tenderness toward parental love: she weeps and prays for the man whose son died for love of her until he is converted, and she appears in a vision to her own parents at her tomb, reassuring and comforting them. She is not indifferent to human feeling, even if she cannot be tempted by lust or worldly love.

In the six dramas, Hrotsvit focuses almost exclusively on women. Only the first play, *The Conversion of Gallicanus,* has a male protagonist, and even he is converted by a woman, Constantina, who dominates the action of the first half. Having taken a vow of virginity, but not wanting to put her father, the emperor, in an awkward position publicly since Gallicanus is his major general, she agrees to marry him and then plots to avoid it. She has his daughters come to her so she can convert them, and sends two of her male servants to Gallicanus to convert him. Daughters precede their fathers in religion in this play, Gallicanus's daughters in their conversion, Constantina in her devotion. (Constantine is not only the father of the heroine, he is also the son of a major figure in religious lore, Helena, who found the cross.)

The Resurrection of Drusiana and Calimachus is about a chaste wife, Drusiana, who attracts the unwanted love of a young man, Calimachus. She too worries about public consequences, fearing civil discord if she tells, and she asks God to let her die rather than cause ruin to a young man. But Calimachus, urged on by an evil servant, almost rapes her corpse, and both men are killed by a serpent, which seems to be an instrument of divine justice here. Calimachus, whom God wants to save—perhaps his love for Drusiana indicates good in him—is resurrected by a holy man, repents, and asks him to resurrect Drusiana. She, in turn, resurrects the servant, but he—lacking the inspiration of love for her?—cannot be saved;

he prefers to die rather than to face "such an abundant spread of the power of grace."[14]

Two of the plays tell of the conversion of a prostitute through the offices of a holy man, but in both cases because the woman is ripe for conversion. In *Abraham*, Maria begins as a virgin, an orphan under the care of her uncle, but she is deceived and seduced by a man disguised as a monk, and then she is neglected when she might be saved by the uncle who misinterprets a vision of her danger, thinking it refers to the church rather than to her. She falls into despair and gives herself over to prostitution; when he goes to visit disguised as a lover, she recognizes the odor of sanctity in him, regrets her fall, and returns to a life of strict penance, of hairshirts, vigils and fasting, to be an example to those she helped to sin. The prostitute in *Pafnutius*, Thais, does not begin as a holy woman, but she knows about God and his justice, and responds quickly to the teachings of the holy man who comes again disguised as a lover—this must have been an intriguing motif to the audience. He gives her hope and she submits, though not without some hesitation, to a terrible penance, enclosed in a cell in which she must do all her bodily functions. She is uncertain if she can live with the stench and upset that there will be no place pure enough to call on God, but she survives to be purified and die in holiness. In this play, too, a holy man misreads a vision, assuming that it has to do with a man, not with her. Hrotsvit seems to be making a point, however gently, about men in the church neglecting the needs of women. In contrast, Thais is put in the care of an abbess, who instead of being shocked at her life worries about the tenderness of her delicate mind in such harsh suffering, and promises to watch over her with maternal affection.

Thais suffers a harsher penance than Maria because she was more committed to her sinful life, but both women have lived successfully as prostitutes and been in charge of their own earnings; both are shown in suggestive scenes with supposed clients whom they are ready to serve, and yet both are saved with much more emphasis on the holiness of their new lives than on the sinfulness of the old. Hrotsvit does not shrink in horror from the notion of the whore any more than the abbess in her play does, but describes her situation and her conversion with as much zest as she does the martyrdom of young virgins. Indeed, Hrotsvit is not fanatic about bodily integrity; she has several of her virgin saints face the threat of a brothel with confidence that there is no guilt without consent, that it is better for the body to be stained with injuries than the soul polluted with idols. Hrotsvit's heroines may be mainly virgins or whores, but they are finally all saints. What matters to her is the strength of their faith and the courage to live by it. Or to die by it—the remaining two plays (*Dulcitius* and *Sapientia*) are about the martyrdom of trios of virgins, who seem from their names (Agapes, Chionia, Hirena, and Fides, Spes, Karitas) to have some allegorical significance, but their bodily tortures are described in realistic detail. In both, the pagan emperor and his officers are ridiculed by the innocent young virgins, and the virgins are put through horrible tortures until they finally die. The time and effort it takes to kill them makes the patriarchal establishment look ineffectual as well as violent and cruel.

In *The Martyrdom of Faith, Hope, and Charity,* there is an added social context of a Christian women's movement. Roman women are reported at the beginning of the play to be following Sapientia, the mother of the three virgins, and threatening civil concord by refusing to eat or sleep with their husbands; at the end, Roman matrons join Sapientia in caring for the bodies of her martyred daughters, burying them, watching over them with her, and then waiting with her until she dies so they can bury her. Her prayer and their response ends the play, and the collection of dramas. It is difficult not to see the community of women in this play as an image of Hrotsvit's convent, or the figure of Sapientia as a reflection of Hrotsvit herself. Sapientia and her daughters are spoken of in the same patronizing way Hrotsvit speaks of herself: when their advent is announced by an imperial officer as a threat to the state, the emperor refuses to take it seriously: what harm can the coming of these little women do to the state ("Numquid tantillarum adventus muliercularum aliquid rei publicae adducere poterit detrimentum?" 1.3)? He tries to coax them by flattery and kindness, assuming with his officer that the fragility of the female sex is easily softened by flattery. Sapientia rejects his paternal advances and answers his attempts at small talk with insults and overwhelmingly learned discourses. When he asks the ages of her daughters, she decides to "fatigue this fool with an arithmetical disputation" and launches into a technical discourse about numbers which he cannot follow, though he tries valiantly: "what a long and perplexing lecture has come out of my question."

Hrotsvit's own learning is seen in the display of arithmetical knowledge in this play, in the logical categories in *Drusiana,* and in the lengthy discourses on the macro and microcosm, on harmony and music in *Pafnutius.* Here the disclaimers of the learned man about his ignorance echo those of the author: "I who am clearly ignorant and no philosopher . . . I was eager to share the tiny drop of knowledge which I drank from the overflowing cup of philosophers." If his learning despite his protests of ignorance seems appropriate to a male character, one must remember that behind his learned words is a woman author, who for all her protestations of ignorance has the learning and skill to set up as Terence's rival and corrector. And one cannot help wondering if Hrotsvit is being even more daring in allowing her female characters to take on and make fools of the emperor and his court, even if they are pagans, since she is writing, at least in part, for a court which bolstered its imperial status by drawing on ancient Roman practices.[15]

St. Catherine is, like Sapientia, a figure of great knowledge and skill in debate, who does not hesitate to teach men in public, whether emperors or scholars or the people. Her life by Clemence, a nun of Barking, also comes out of a royal convent.[16] Whether Clemence, like Hrotsvit, also wrote a life of a king, Edward the Confessor, we do not know. But such a life was composed at Barking by a nun some years before the life of Catherine, perhaps by Clemence. The editor dates the life of the English saint between 1163 and 1170 because of the enthusiastic references to Henry II and his wife and heirs, arguing that this is likely to predate the family problems and the conflict with the church.[17] The mention of the queen and their heirs was added by the author, in the passage on the meaning of Edward's prophecy of English history: she traces the kings of England from Edward through the foreigners, who had no relation to Alfred, to the "good Henry" (Henry I) who chose Edward's (great-grand) niece, the "good Matilda," as his companion, not for need or fear but only for love (4967-78). Through her the land was again held by its rightful heirs ("dreiz eirs," 4982). When the empress was born from them, the tree flowered, and it bore fruit that comforted the land in the "glorious Henry," born from the empress (4985-90). Now the land has returned to the lineage of Edward, "God's friend," and the author wishes God's grace for his heirs to reign as long as the world endures, to keep "our king, their father, and our queen, their mother, in true holiness, peace, joy, and plenty, and the power to defeat their enemies" (4993-5006). This sounds very much like the hopes one voices early in a regime.

The author disclaims her part in the interpretation of the prophecy: "Jo n'en dei los ne blasme aveir, / Kar n'istrat pas de mun saveir / E quanque de l'historie ai dit, / Altre de mei l'out ainz escrit. / Mais en romanz l'ai translaté / Certes cuntre ma volenté, / Kar ne sent en mei sens ne grace / Que jo sulung dreit le parface." "I should have neither praise nor blame, for it does not come from my knowledge, and whatever I have said of the history, another wrote it before. But I translated it into romance, against my will, since I do not think I have the sense or the grace to carry it out properly," 4921-28. It may not be coincidental that these remarks come near the end of the poem. At the beginning, at least in what remains of the prologue, she only apologizes for her French, "a false French of England," "un faus franceis sai d'Angletere," 7, in which she cannot keep the order of the cases, and she asks those who have learned it elsewhere (presumably including the king and queen) to amend it where necessary (9-10). Like Hrotsvit, she may believe that the "humility of confession breaks the force of reproof." But it is only toward the end of the poem that she reveals her identity as a nun of Barking, a handmaid of Jesus, who translated it for love of Edward, in case anyone wants to know who did it, which I take to mean she had not revealed herself in the missing part of the prologue. She does not want to give her name because she knows it is "*not yet* worthy to be read where such a holy name is written" ("Mais sun num n'i vult dire a ore, / Kar bien set n'est pas digne unkore / Qu'en livre seit oï ne lit / U si tres saint num ad escrit," 5308-11). She asks all who hear *her* romance ("cest soen rumanz") not to scorn it because a woman translated it, or to reject the good that is in it (5312-17). She asks forgiveness for her presumption in translating the life, blaming her inability for its defects, not her will (5318-23), and asks prayers that she who "made this *new* life" ("ki fist ceste vie nuvele," 5327) and her companions join St. Edward after this life. I like to think that the author put all this at the end hoping that the audience would already have appreciated and accepted the poem.

In the story, a certain importance is given to Edward's (and Henry's) descent from the Norman dukes through his mother Emma; she is noble and beautiful, her father, nephew, and brother, men of holy life, high birth, and renown, 95ff. Eldred (AEthelred) showed wisdom in choosing a wife from such a lineage, 131-32, even if her subsequent history is not ideal. Her role as Cnut's wife—he married her to get the Normans on his side and neutralize the threat of the rightful heirs, 583ff—is played down; Edward makes one reference to it in a prayer to God, saying that his mother had abandoned him and made his enemy his stepfather (657-60). Edward's wife, in contrast, is a model of perfection though she is the daughter of an evil man who killed the king's brother. She is a rose born from a thorn (1257), with the same virtues as Edward, wisdom, goodness, no love for worldly things, and perfect chastity.[18] She is talented and trained, like the product of an elegant convent: she does beautiful embroidery with silk and gold, she can reproduce anything in painting, and when she is not working, she takes pleasure in beautiful books (1279-84). She is all the more to be honored for coming from evil and being good.

What is most important about her is that like Edward she wants to be a virgin, something which neither knows until their wedding day, and which both keep secret from then on. Edward has been described as chaste, humble, lacking in pride, good to the poor and sick, devout in religion, and determined to maintain his chastity. His virtues are monkish, and similar to those of holy women, and his fears about losing his chastity sound very much like a woman's: he worries about the treasure of chastity being stolen if he marries, because it is in a "feeble vessel," his body (1105-7). Even his prayers have feminist elements in the examples of those God saved: Joseph, from the woman who so loved him but got only his cloak—an extraordinarily sympathetic view of Potiphar's wife; Susanna, the female equivalent of Joseph; and Judith, who never faltered in her mission and whose story receives the most attention (1148-77). Much is made of Edward's devotion to God and to God's mother (see 917-18, 1025), who is his model for chastity. He asks God, who "made your mother from your daughter," who was both mother and virgin, handmaid on earth, queen in heaven, who maintained her chastity in marriage

(1185-93), to give him the same sort of marriage (1198ff.), and he asks in the name of "my lady, your mother." Then he asks Mary, "my lady, sweet flower," for a marriage in which the lady will not deceive him nor his chastity be abused. The marriage is all he hoped and more: when he is ill, she takes on the burden of the dedication of a church and does alone what both should have done together (4611-24). Her grief at his death is beyond description, and her ladies ("dames" and "dameiseles") share it with her (5123ff.).

In the death scene, the author shows awareness of the needs of secular widows. The king takes leave of his wife and his friends, asking the princes to be good to her for love of him, to honor her, preserve her rights, and let no one do her wrong in her dowry, commanding them to confirm whatever he gave her (5067ff.).[19] The queen's dowry also comes up in the life of St. Catherine. When the pagan tyrant promises Catherine that if she sacrifices to his gods, she will be second only to the queen at court, with power to raise or lower others in honor, he says she can claim any of his possessions except the queen's dowry, "in which I do not want to wrong her" ("fors sulement de sun duaire, dunt jo ne li voil pas tort faire," 1271-72, a consideration that is not in the Latin life but that was of prime concern to contemporary royal and noble women).[20]

Clemence's concern for women is apparent in her choice of topic and in the way she treats it. She makes clear in the prologue that she is translating the life of Catherine, a true friend/lover of God, because she wants to, not because another has requested it: "A cel ovre que *vuil* traitier / D'une sue veraie amie, / De qui *voil* translater la vie," 30-32. She did it, she tells us at the end, for love of God (2692). She speaks with authority in the work, beginning like Marie de France: "one who knows and understands good, should show it wisely, so that by the fruit of that goodness others can be admonished to do good and to wish good," 1-5.[21] Clemence is translating a life from Latin to Romance which has already been done, but in a form that no longer pleases. The rhyme is considered poor (probably because it is irregular assonance, MacBain suggests, xiii), but Clemence seems to have sympathy for her predecessor, suggesting that the problem may be with the audience which is more given to evil and envy than it used to be, meaning I assume more desirous of novelty than of value. Any praise for the revision should go not to her, but to the one from whom her poor knowledge comes—it may be poor, but like Hrotsvit's, it comes from God. Nonetheless, Clemence does seem to take some pride in her achievement, when she names herself at the end and asks for prayers from those who hear the book with good hearts: "Jo ki sa vie ai translatee, / Par nun sui Clemence numee. / De Berkinge sui nunain. / Pur s'amur pris cest oevre en mein" ("I who have translated her life am called Clemence. I am a nun of Barking. For his [God's] love I took this work in hand," 2689-92).[22]

The joy Clemence takes in her writing is, I think, reflected in one of her additions to her source. When the emperor offers Catherine almost anything if she will sacrifice to his gods, including a statue of herself to be worshipped in the palace and the temple, she refuses, saying if the statue lacks the senses, the power to speak and hear, the body is worth little, and more important, "its knowledge is little use if it can not hear or speak" ("Poi li valdra sun saveir, / Quant oir ne puet ne parler," 1327-28). The passage on the statue and Catherine's rejection and ridiculing of the idea suggests that Clemence may be commenting on women who are worshipped (in courtly lyrics?) but not allowed a voice, as well as arguing for women with knowledge to be able to use it. Clemence interjects a long speech of her own addressed to the "Segnurs" of her audience after the martyrdom of the learned men converted by Catherine's speeches, underscoring the meaning of their death and the goodness of the God who protected their bodies from the flames (1159-1238). Like her heroine, Clemence is not afraid to preach to men in the hope of converting them.

Catherine is presented, like the heroine of so many romances written for women, as a beautiful noble girl, the only child of a king, who has her educated to oppose others and defend herself, so no dialectician in the world can defeat her (141-44, Clemence's addition); though she knows a great deal about secular matters, she is only interested in religious. Nonetheless, her father leaves his kingdom to her and she governs it wisely and generously, dispensing treasure. Like many romance heroines, she takes the initiative, investigating the laments of Christians who are being forced to sacrifice to pagan gods, going to the emperor to show him what is wrong in his law. Impressed with her looks and her learned speech, he tries to persuade her, and when he fails, he sends for the most learned masters in his realm. Before the debate begins, Catherine again takes the initiative, saying it is unfair of the emperor to pit fifty against one and promise them honors if they succeed but nothing to her; she demands some reward and asks only that he will serve God if God gives her victory, but the emperor refuses (645ff.). Then she begins the debate, challenging the masters to dispute with her and test her sense (671-76). Though they are offended to be summoned to argue with a "plaideresse," the equivalent of a lawyeress, saying any poor clerk "clerjastre" could defeat her, they are finally overwhelmed by her arguments and converted by them.[23] Never since a mother bore us, they say, did we hear a woman speak or dispute so wisely, so full of truth that she cannot be contradicted, 1078ff.; it is no small thing, what this "lady" argues ("dame" here, 1094, a term of respect, no longer "pucele" or "plaideresse"). When they are led to the fire to be martyred, they call for her, wanting to be baptized, and she comforts them, saying they are washed in the blood of God, apparently baptizing them with her words.

Catherine's arguments convert the learned men, God's miracles the populace, but the emperor is impervious to both despite her attempts ("par sermuner e par preier / s'ele [le] poust ja fors traire / del mal," 1374–76) and those of the empress ("fierement le met a raisun," 2127), both women trying do what early popes urged believing women to do, persuade the unbelieving husband. The empress is converted by instinctive faith from what she heard of Catherine and a dream vision she had, while her husband's chief counsellor is converted by the disputes and miracles, by reason but also by what he can hear and see for himself, lacking that capacity for faith that is so often connected with women.[24]

The role of the empress, more typically a woman's role than the heroine's, highlights the compassion that binds women in the poem. Though men and women weep for the empress when she is killed, the women of the palace have a particular grief because they have lost their lady, with which Clemence sympathizes ("bien en pout aver pité / ki unkes vers femme eust amisté," "anyone who has loved a woman [as friend or lover] might well feel pity," 2351–52, Clemence's addition). When Catherine faces the final tortures, all grieve for her for different reasons, the rich for her nobility, the poor for her generosity, the well-born for her lineage, the low-born for her troubles, but it is the women's grief Clemence focuses on. They grieve for her beauty, her sense, her breeding, and her youth, weeping and beating their breasts, lamenting the lovely Catherine as their companion and their neighbor, as one of them, and they are the ones she stops to comfort, the "gentils pulceles" and "nobles barnesses beles," telling them to rejoice with her because she is going to her king, her husband, her lover (2519–44, much expanded by Clemence).

Clemence's added attention to women in the story seems to be part of her sense of a balanced role for women in heaven and earth. She speaks of Mary, the "beautiful queen of the city of God," in terms that suggest equality between her and God: she is mother and maid, who carried her maker in her chaste body; he is her son and her father, she is his daughter and his mother; she alone is empress, lady, and queen, crowned beside her son (like a dowager regent, 1745–68). All the while, the heroine is playing the unusual role of learned teacher, publically preaching, converting, perhaps even baptizing. And she identifies less with Mary than with Christ. When she is put in prison, she rejoices that she can experience what he did when he put himself in prison in a womb to take on our humanity (Clemence's addition); what he did for her she will happily do for him (1441–52). Thus the life suggests both the community of women in compassion and faith, and the extraordinary possibilities of an intelligent and highly trained woman to compete with men in an intellectual battle and to defeat them, to be an imitator of Christ not only as martyr but also as teacher and converter.

Like Hrotsvit, Clemence seems to take pride in the learned woman's ability to argue as an equal or better than men, even if their heroines are

God's instrument, fighting in his service. In secular literature, too, in the time of Clemence, the late twelfth and early thirteenth century, women debate men and hold their own. The debates are usually about love and sex and the demands of life, and the debates can be written by men or by women, or perhaps by men and women together. That lyric debates are frequently fictitious and that it is virtually impossible to determine who is responsible for a given poem there is no question. There is evidence, however, in medieval letters, that when women felt strongly they were not afraid to argue with popes or kings, and we have at least one poem in which a woman, Gormonda de Monpeslier, answered a poem by a man, Guilhem Figueira. In response to the Alibigensian crusade, Guilhem attacked Rome, the church and the pope, for leading the world into war, for deceiving and betraying, for selling its people and sacraments out of greed. Gormonda answered his poem stanza for stanza, using the same rhyme sounds and many of the same rhyme words, but turning his words against him in defense of Rome and orthodoxy, blaming arrogant secular leaders for the world's troubles and criticizing the errors of the heretics.[25]

There is also good reason to think women debated with men in the course of their lives at court, in a lighter vein as well. Andreas Capellanus warns that a man of the higher nobility should be careful what he says because women of the nobility and the high nobility are very quick to censure and ridicule the words and deeds of men of that class.[26] Though the debates in Andreas, like the debates in most Provençal pastorelas and Italian lyrics, are written by men, the voices of the women have a realistic ring. The women in these works are in fact so ready to show up the hypocrisy of the male rhetoric of courtly love and so much more concerned with practical realities, that I think they owe a lot to actual discussions between men and women. That is, men choose to voice their own criticism of their rhetorical postures through women, because women were in fact critical of them. That same sort of partly serious partly playful debate which must have gone on at courts where such literature was performed is reflected in the debate poems included in the new and comprehensive edition of women poets in Provençal, the trobairitz, though the identity of most of the authors may never be known.[27] The *razo* of one of the few women poets whose historical identity is known, Maria de Ventadorn, says she was arguing with her lover about seignory in love, in the presence of Gui d'Ussel, a poet who had often sung her praises but had stopped singing because of a great sorrow. In order to get him started again and to comfort him, she wrote a stanza putting the question to him and drew him into the debate.[28] Though this story cannot tell us who wrote the poem, it is yet another indication that love debates were a part of court life.

Because the question of authorship is so vexed, I will not go into detail about the debates and dialogues, but I do want to mention a few points that are consistent with what I have seen of women's views of themselves elsewhere. Whether they are discussing with other women their love affairs, advising men in love, or arguing with their own lovers, the women are often concerned with the fitness of such a love for them, and the man's tendency to fail or betray them: "a mi no's taing," "it is not fitting to me," unless he repents his deception, N'Almucs tells N'Iseuz who is arguing the man's case (2); "m'amors no'l tanh," "my love is not suitable to him," he is so foolish and fickle, a *domna* tells a *donzela,* who has accused her of letting the man die, "I am not wrong to deny him my love, since I don't want my worth to decline because of him" (3). Alamanda tells Giraut de Bornelh she will do her best for him, but the lady says she was right to be angry when he courted someone else, and he had better behave from now on (4).

Women are very aware of the hypocrisy of male rhetoric: Maria de Ventadorn asks Gui if a woman should treat a lover equally in what pertains to love, and he predictably says there should be no dominance between lovers, when they have "made one heart of two." But she points out that a man should pray as to a lover and a lady, but a woman should honor him as a friend, not as a lord, that if he offers his service as her man, it would be a betrayal to act as an equal when he claimed to be a servant (9).[29] Ysabella asks Elias Cairel why he has turned his love elsewhere, though she never failed him; he says in an unusually frank admission (if he is the author, or a strong indictment if she is) that he sang her praises not out of love but for the honor and profit he expected from it ("s'ieu en dizia lauzor / en mon chantar, no.l dis per drudaria / mas per honor e pron q'ieu n'atendia," 10.12-14). Probably the most blatant contrast between the rhetoric of courtly love and the language of daily life is found in the poem by Raimbaut de Vaqueiras, in which he speaks the courtly clichés in Provençal, and the lady undercuts them in Genoese, not valuing his "proensalesco" any more than German or Sardinian, and rejecting his rhetoric, "no vollo questo latì" (21.71-73, 81), because she has a handsome husband, Provençals are not to be trusted, and he is just a minstrel ("iuiar," the last word of the poem).

There are only four poems in which one woman advises another, three of them mediating for a man (2 and 3 mentioned above, another by Azalais d'Altier in the form of a letter, 43, which I shall come to), and one which rejects worldly love altogether. One woman asks advice from another for herself and her sister, whether to take a husband or remain a virgin (1), knowing that having children is hard on her body, but life without a husband is very difficult. The solution Na Carenza offers is to take a husband appropriate to her (their?) education, worth, beauty, youth, fresh color, courtesy, and merit, with whom she can remain a virgin and bear "glorious children." The list of qualities suggests that she (they?) might expect to be the object of courtly love, so the poem is not just a traditional religious contrast between the pains of married life and the glories of virginity, but also an implicit criticism of the hyperbole of courtly love: the only lover who could be worthy of the kind of woman described in courtly poems is God.

When the trobairitz write about their own love, in *cansos*, they write about the joy and the suffering of love, about betrayal and frustration, about the problems posed by *lauzengers*, as the trobadors do, but there are differences. Women address their lovers directly more often and more intensely than men do, and are far less apt to turn to the audience, or to Love, or to the singer. They use many more negatives, sometimes to express strong feelings ("ni anc no fo qu'eu non agues talan," "never have I been without the wish," 39.4), but usually to describe frustration or despair ("vas lui no'm val merces ni cortesia / ni ma beltatz ni mos pretz ni mos sens," "nothing serves me with him, not favor, nor courtesy, nor my beauty, nor my prestige nor my sense," 35.4–5).[30] And they use contrary-to-fact constructions, and the past tense more frequently, confronting a reality that is not as they would wish, or that no longer is.[31] But they do not wallow in self-pity, nor are they any more "masochistic" than male poets in their suffering.[32] They speak forcefully about their love, their need and even their right to express it, and they are aware of themselves as women, speaking to or setting examples for other women.[33]

Among the trobairitz whose names we know, there are only two for whom we have both a *vida* and more than one poem (Castelloza and the countess of Dia), though the *vidas* tell little more than that the names were recognized. There is one poem by Azalais de Porcairagues (27), who also has a *vida*, and single poems attributed to women about whom we know nothing else: one by Azalais d'Altier (43), to a Clara who may be a fellow poet, Clara d'Anduza (33), and one by Bieris de Romans to a Maria (28). Azalais de Porcairagues may have known Raimbaut d'Aurenga and the countess of Narbonne. Her one extant *canso* is sent through a joglar to a woman at Narbonne who is "the guide to joy," and it mentions a terrible loss which seems to have nothing to do with her love, and which may refer to the death of Raimbaut (27).[34] The poem expresses her grief, but also her defiant joy in love. It begins with a winter scene, that corresponds to her mood of severe distress, then shifts to her love which is going well though she has set it too high, on a man of great worth who does not have a false heart; he has promised his love to her and it suits her, she says, cursing those who disagree. She is ready to put herself at his mercy, *but only if* he does not say or ask anything outrageous.

Azalais d'Altier also sends her poem to a woman; it is in fact a verse letter in couplets, addressed to a Clara, whom Azalais has learned to love from the reports of the man who loves her. Azalais writes to persuade Clara to give up her excessive anger against the man, warning her that other lovers will think she is being fickle, like Briseida (perhaps an allusion to the fact that women's actions can easily be misinterpreted), assuring her that he acted out of too much love, and that she, Azalais, will be surety for him, if Clara, being true to her name, pardons him for love of her (43).[35] Clara's poem blames the *lauzenger* for sending her love away, but they cannot change her mind. Asserting that she loves him more than anything in the world, she insists no one can change her mind, not if a hundred ladies begged her to, would she change him for another lover (33).

It is possible to read the *canso* by Bieris de Romans in this same tradition of women writing to other women either pleading for the love of a man or trying to dissuade from an inappropriate one. I do not argue against the possibility of a lesbian love in Bieris's poem, about which so much has been said, but like Rieger ("Was Bieris de Romans Lesbian? Women's Relations with Each Other in the World of the Troubadours," Paden, *Voice*, 73-94) I think one has to consider the kind of language used to express love in contemporary writing, which sounds erotic to us but may not have been to them. The same language can be used for any strong human love, as for human and divine love. Indeed, Azalais says in her poem to Clara that Clara's semblance is written in her heart from what she has been told about her, that she never loved a woman with such deep love ("amor coral") without seeing her, that there is nothing she would not do to please her, that she has a very great desire to see her and tell her what is in her heart and learn what is in Clara's. Then she argues for the man who loves Clara. Her intensity is not markedly different from Bieris, who writes in praise of Na Maria's qualities and beauty, so fine that she is without peer and draws Bieris toward her; Bieris hopes for comfort and joy with "fin'amors" from Maria, but she also begs her not to love a faithless (male) lover ("non ametz entendidor truan," 28.20). Though there is evidence of attachments that seem to involve more passion than friendship as we think of it, such as Hildegard's letter to Richardis of Stade, and Bieris's poem may well be one of those, it is also possible that it expresses only a deep attachment and admiration in emotionally charged language.

The tendency to love someone who may not be suitable or may seem suitable but not be receptive is a topos in courtly love poetry, by women or men. Castelloza says "he is a fool who reproves me for loving you, since it suits me so well" ("Assatz es fols qui m'en repren / de vos amar, pois tant gen mi conve," 29.25-26). Castelloza, who has recently received most critical attention among the trobairitz, shares both the emphasis on suffering in love and the need to sing about it with Bernart de Ventàdorn, also a favorite among critics.[36] Castelloza may be ambivalent about the object of her love ("s'ie.us trobes avinen, / humil e franc e de bona merce, / be.us amera," "*if* I found you charming, humble, open, and compassionate, I *would love* you well," 29.1-3), but not about her singing ("e fauc chanssos per tal q'eu fass'auzir / vostre bon pretz; don eu no.m puosc sofrir / que no.us fassa lauzar a tota gen," "I compose songs to make your worth known; and I can not keep from having you praised by all," 29.5-7). She is careful to keep herself above reproach in her emotional attachments, to give him no reason to complain about her (29.13-16), but is more than ready to incur the disapproval of those who think women should not court men: "I know that it is good for me, even if everyone says it is not fitting for a lady to ask a knight or keep him asking a long time," 29.17-20, that is she rejects the woman's double role as object, at once passive and submissive.[37]

Castelloza also casts doubts on the effectiveness of the man's asking: "I know that knights do themselves harm when they ask ladies more than ladies do them, for they have no other wealth or seignory; if a lady loves, she *should* ask a knight, if she finds worth and chivalry/service (*vassalatge*) in him" (30.46-54). Whether it is men or women who have no other resources is not specified; the ambiguity suggests the importance of words for both. Castelloza addresses the first envoi of this poem to another woman, probably a poet: "Lady Almucs, I love what is a source of harm to me, for he who maintains worth, has a fickle heart towards me" (30.55-59), as though asking Almucs to dissuade her, but her second envoi, presumably to the man, reasserts her need to love for her own well-being: "I do not renounce loving you, for I live in good faith, goodness and good heart" (59-62, cf. 31.19-20). Though her speaking out will have set a bad example for other women who love ("mout aurai mes mal usatge / a las autras amairitz," 31.21-22), since it is usually the man who sends the message in carefully chosen words ("e motz triatz e chausitz," 31.24, perhaps implying the hypocrisy of courtly love language), she also declares that it suited her ("aissi.m cove") and that she is "healed" ("garida") by it, which suggests that other women might well want to follow her example.

Castelloza's poetry, or singing, seems to have two main aspects: the relief and satisfaction that come from expressing herself ("I would rather ask than let myself die, because I am restored by the asking," 29.22-23); and the implied threat or retaliation of public exposure (not only the reports of his bad behavior toward her, of the sin he will incur if he lets her die, 29.46-47, but also a reminder of her ability to embarrass him).[38] Castelloza had stolen his glove, but returned it so he would not be harmed by the woman who retains him (30.37ff); she says "if it helped I would remind you in my song," as if she had not, but since that is what she is doing, and telling the world besides, she may well be implying that she can do him a lot more damage, both in word and in deed. At the same time, she can be generous about the other woman ("I know well that a woman of higher rank is fitting for you," 30.26-27), and even offer to share him with her ("I do not ask him not to love or serve her. Let him serve her, but come back to me, not let me die altogether," 32.19-22). This is reminiscent of Bernart de Ventadorn's "Lady, love the other one openly and me secretly, so I get all the benefit, and he the good words" (6.57–60). It is conceivable that she wants to retain enough of him to enable her to keep singing.[39]

The countess of Dia can also suffer for love, but she sees no good reason to and prefers not to: "A chantar m'er de so q'ieu no volria, tant me rancur de lui cui sui amia," "I have to sing about what I would rather not, I am so distressed by him whose lover I am" (35.1–2). She deserves and expects joy in love, having all the requisite qualities: "Valer mi deu mos pretz e mos paratges / e ma beutatz e plus mos fis coratges," "My prestige and my rank, my beauty and more my true heart should avail" (35.29–30), and therefore she sends the song as her messenger, even though she had said at the beginning: "vas lui no'm val merces ni cortesia / ni ma beltatz ni mos pretz ni mos sens," "nothing serves me with him, not favor, nor courtesy, nor my beauty, nor my prestige nor my sense" (35.4–5).[40] She does not worry about what is fitting for her, but tells him how he should behave: "it is not right that another love take you from me," "non es ges dreitz c'autr'amors vos mi toilla," 35.17, and warns him in the very last line, that "many people have been harmed by too much pride" (35.37).

The problem is in him; he does not love as she does and she takes pleasure in conquering him in love, though he is more valiant (35.11–12). She frequently asserts her own constancy, and reveals her doubts about his: "since I am true to him, he should be true to me" (34.5–6); she begs him to have faith in her and not in what others might tell him, for she will never be false to him, as long as she finds no falseness in him (34.29–32). She expects him to treat their love with the same respect she does, but she implies that unless he does, she will not either.[41] Though she understands that other women could not help loving him, he should know enough to recognize (and therefore love) the finest one ("la plus fina" 35.27), and remember their agreement (35.28). That is, he owes her love, both because she is the most deserving and because he made a commitment to her.

There is nothing self-effacing about the countess. She declares that "a woman who understands about worth should set her understanding on a worthy valiant knight . . . and dare to love him openly" (34.17–21); if she does so, worthy and friendly people will speak well of her, which defines any opposition as unworthy and hostile. In the envoi, she offers herself: "the worthy and valiant know your worth, therefore I ask you forthwith, if it please you, for your acceptance" (34.33–36). She declares her longing for a knight she had ("per un cavallier q'ai agut," 36.2, implying a physical relation), but he has betrayed her because she did *not* give him her love, and she regrets it. She tells the world that she wants to hold him naked in her arms, and promises her heart, love, sense, eyes, life to him. She wants to lie with him and kiss him, have him "in a husband's place," but it is not clear who will play the husband's role, since she asks "when will I have you *in my power?*" (36.18) and makes it all contingent on his promising to do "all that I might want" (36.24). She is so confident that not even false, treacherous *lausengier* with their evil words can disturb her joy and happiness; they are like a cloud that keeps out the sun, but they will not stop her: "You, jealous evil speakers, do not think that I will hesitate to let joy and youth please me" (37.17–19).

Marie de France also had trouble with envy and slander, but she too refuses to let it stop her. And like the countess of Dia, but quite different from other women writers, Marie does not feel a need to assume a humble posture. If Marie had doubts about her abilities or her accomplishments, she does not betray them to the audience. She does not, like Hrotsvit, pretend to be humble and ignorant. On the contrary, she wants us to know that she knows Latin (she had considered translating from *latin* to *romaunz, Lais,* 28–30), as well as English (from which she claims to translate the fables), and some Breton (she gives an occasional Breton word and its meaning), and she begins the prologue to the *lais* saying that anyone with God-given eloquence should not hide it, but show it, use it to spread the effect of good.[42] Marie chooses for the most part to work with oral sources in the *lais*—even in the Tristan story, for which there were already written sources, she chooses to tell an episode that exists nowhere else in the extant versions—and apparently in many of the fables as well. That is, though she could work with learned sources if she chose to, she prefers to work with material that has no written form, that she can mold (or even invent) to her purpose.

Marie makes an implicit connection between her works and those of ancient writers who hid their learning so others would search for it and be bettered in the attempt. If she chooses to tell the *lais* so the adventures will be remembered, there is presumably something to be learned from those adventures. *That* is, I think, the truth she so frequently claims for them, perhaps in answer to Denis Piramus's attacks on the *lais* as not at all true, "ke ne sunt pas de tut verais." Marie is concerned with different perceptions of truth particularly in the fables, best illustrated in the one in which a man shows a lion a painting of a man killing a lion. The painting is man-made as the lion points out, whereas the lion shows the man the real execution of a man by a lion, and comments: "you showed me a painting . . . but I showed you a greater truth, which you saw uncovered / as it was" (37.55–58). The moral she draws is that one should not heed fables which are lies nor paintings which are dreams ("fable, ke est de mençuinge, / ne a peinture, que semble sunge," 37.61–62), but believe only the work one sees that reveals the truth ("ceo est a creire dunt hum veit l'ovre, / que la verité tut descovre," 37.63–64).[43] She is presumably making a distinction between what others do and what she is showing in her stories, perhaps also between the male realm of authority and hers of experience (as Christine de Pizan does in the *Mutacion de Fortune*). She insists on the truth of the wise as opposed to the lies of the evil or the folly of fools.

Marie makes a strong statement in the prologue to *Guigemar* criticizing those who envy and slander anyone, *man or woman* of great worth ("hummë u femme de grant pris, / cil ki de sun bien unt envie / sovent en dïent vileinie," 8–10), calling them "evil, cowardly dogs, who bite treacherously" (13–14). But the spiteful slanderers who would turn her accomplishments against her (17) will not stop her: "Nel voil mie pur ceo leissier" (15). This means that she has already had success in her story-telling, perhaps with individual *lais* which she now collects. She reminds her audience of her presence at the beginning and the end of virtually every lai, of her control of the material, sometimes directly "this happened as I have told you" ("issi avient cum dit vos ai," *Equitan*, 311), sometimes indirectly "from this story that you have heard, the lai of Guigemar was composed" ("de cest cunte ke oï avez / fu Guigemar le lai trovez," 883–84). In the middle of the collection, Marie gives another prologue, reminding us of the project: "Since I have begun the lais, I will not stop, I will tell all the adventures I know in rhyme" (*Yonec*, 1–4); and yet another at the beginning of *Milun*: "who would tell different tales should begin differently and speak reasonably to be pleasing to people" (1–4).

The self-consciousness of the writer becomes even more pronounced in the last part of the collection.[44] *Milun*, a lai in which a woman writes her son's story in a letter, ends "and I who have put the lai in writing take much delight in telling it" ("e jeo que le [lai] ai mis en escrit / al recunter mut me delit," 535–36). *Chaitivel*, a lai in which a woman composes a lai about her four lovers, begins, "Desire has seized me to remember a lai I have heard of. I shall tell you the adventure" ("Talent me prist de remembrer / un lai dunt jo oï parler. / L'aventure vus en dirai," 1–3); it ends "Here it ends, there is no more; I have heard no more, I know no more, I shall tell you no more" ("Ici finist, [il] n'i ad plus; / Plus n'en oi ne plus n'en sai / ne plus ne vus en cunterai," 238–40). *Chevrefoil*, the unknown (perhaps invented by Marie) episode from a story with known written sources, Tristan, begins "It pleases me and I very much want to tell you the truth of the lai people call Chevrefoil and why it was composed and where. Many have told it to me and I have found it in writing" ("Asez me plest e bien le voil / del lai que hum nume Chevrefoil / que la verité vus en cunt / e pur quei il fu fet e dunt. / Plusurs le me unt cunté e dit / e jeo ·l'ai trové en escrit"). It ends "I have spoken the truth of the lai I have told here" ("Dit vus en ai la verité / del lai que j'ai ici cunté," (117–18). In the last three lais, Marie also calls attention to herself and her material by offering different names for the lais: *Chaitivel* is either "the four sorrows," or "the unfortunate one," depending on the perspective of the woman or the man; *Chevrefoil* is "Gotelef" in English, "Chevrefoil" in French, with the same meaning in both; the last lai was first called *Eliduc* but was renamed *Guildelüec ha Gualadun,* because it happened to the women ("kar des dames est avenu," 25). For such short tales, Marie gives an unusual amount of space to her authorial comments.[45] She also alludes indirectly to her role with the large number of women characters who tell or write stories, in *Fresne, Lanval, Deus Amanz, Yonec, Laustic, Milun,* and *Chaitivel.*

In the *Fables,* there is a moral to be drawn from each story, which gives Marie ample opportunity to make what are sometimes quite surprising points about them. In the prologue to that collection, she places herself among the educated from the first line ("Cil ki seivent de lettruüre," 1) and her reference to philosophers' moral writings, defending the fables (and perhaps the *lais*): "there is no fable of folly where there is not some philosophy" (23-24). She also mentions that the work was commissioned, that is there are those who value what she does (27-37). She is not happy with all the material—one wonders if the misogynist tales are among those she does not care for, particularly since she draws quite unexpected morals from them—but she has agreed to do it (for count William who is named in the epilogue) and will put effort and pain into it. At the end she says she has translated the fables from Alfred's English, a claim that cannot be substantiated; no such collection exists, and we have no way of knowing whether Marie was working with written texts for all her fables. It seems more likely that many are oral again, leaving her even more room to draw her own morals.[46] Whatever her sources, she wants to be sure no clerks claim her work as their own, which they might well do ("put cel estre que clerc plusur / prendreient sur eus mun labur," epilogue, 5-6), so she names herself: "I shall give my name for remembrance: Marie is my name, I am from France" ("Me numerai pur remembrance: Marie ai num, si sui de France," 3-4). She adds that he is a fool who lets himself be forgotten ("il fet que fol ki sei ublie," 8).

Marie is an extraordinary woman, but her characters for the most part are not. Despite the supernatural elements, the *lais* are mostly concerned with ordinary people coping with the problems of ordinary life, unhappy marriages, possessive parents, inadequate reward for services, frustrated desires, the limitations of people and of society. Like the trobairitz, Marie's women know suffering in their personal lives, but they find outlets for it in their love, even in the suffering if they have chosen it, and sometimes in art. Marie gives a balanced picture of good and evil, of women and men, but she does seem to have more concern for the problems of women, for their need to take control of their lives as we say, and for female bonding. She may even be giving messages to women that men in the audience will not notice. Good women in the *lais* help each other, nurture rejected children, supply the emotional and physical needs of men and other women, and present a woman's world of love and caring which contrasts with the man's world of selfishness, possessiveness, and violence.

That is not to say there are not good men and bad women, but they are there to make the world of good women all the clearer by contrast. Even the bad women assert themselves for self-protection and self-advancement, the right instincts in the wrong context or the wrong intensity.

Since the *lais* are probably arranged as Marie wanted them, I will follow their order in my remarks, but touch only on the motifs I am concerned with. Instead of looking at the *lais* from the perspective of a general audience, seeing the balance of positive and negative examples, I attempt to look from the perspective of a woman in Marie's audience, to imagine what she might have identified or sympathized with.[47] *Guigemar* sets out the basic contrast between a male world of fighting and hunting outside the home (the only interests of the narcissistic hero), and oppressive marriage inside (the possessive old husband of the heroine and the younger but equally possessive rescuer, Meriaduc, who will not give her up without a fight). Marie offers a further contrast between male possessiveness in personal relations and the female world of loving and caring, represented by the young wife and her companion. There is great love between them ("entre les deus out grant amur," 250) as there is not between husband and wife. The two women rescue the young hero, nurse his wound, feed him, and supply the love he has lacked in his life. At the same time, his love gives the wife the strength to free herself from her marriage; she escapes hoping only to die, but that action enables her ultimately to be reunited with her lover. In a way, this *lai* suggests Marie's intent in the collection: the hunt, the violent pursuit of prey, is the male pursuit of *pris* through fighting, while Marie pursues *pris* through writing, and the cure of the wounded man by women and love is her attempt to heal social ills with her words.[48]

In *Equitan*, there is no female bonding; the woman adopts the male values of the king, self-indulgent and self-serving. Her first response to his advances is understandably self-protective, she worries that his status and wealth give him an advantage—power to compel—but he promises to be her servant, in the language of courtly love debates. Maria de Ventadorn says men promise to serve while they are courting, but want to assume lordship once they have what they want (Rieger, *Trobairitz,* 9). In this case, the king remains loyal to her, and she takes advantage of the opportunity to become queen by attempting to murder her husband. She plays the male game of power politics, protecting herself until she is sure of the king, then using his love to further her ambitions. It was not unknown for men to get rid of their wives by divorce or death if a better match presented itself. Since the husband in the *lai* seems to be beyond reproach, the wife's act is condemned and she is punished, but one wonders if some women in the audience did not applaud her initiative?

It would be more difficult to applaud the actions of the mother in *Fresne,* a lai which takes place almost entirely in a female world, contrasting the many good women with the <u>bad mother who gratuitously slanders</u> <u>another woman and then finds herself in the same situation.</u>[49] The response to her slander is particularly interesting: women hate her for it, recognizing the virtues of the slandered woman, but the woman's husband, who ought to know better, hates his wife. The slanderer recognizes the justice of her plight in terms of her attack on other women: "<u>I condemned myself when</u> <u>I slandered all women</u>" ("jeo meïsmes me jugai: / de tutes femmes mesparlai," 79–80). Other women work together to save the child: they dissuade the mother from having her killed, one carries her off and leaves her near an abbey, where the widowed daughter of the man who finds her nurses her, and the abbess raises her as a niece. Finally, the girl's own generous gesture toward her lover and the woman who is to take her place wins her back her identity and her lover. But it is the mother who recognizes the tokens of her daughter, seeks the truth, and then makes a public avowal of her "villainy" (*vileinie,* 467). She is careful to obtain her husband's pardon before she tells him, but she accepts public shame to restore her rejected child to her rightful place. One might say that the mother began with the negative values of the patriarchal society, sacrificing even her child in order to avoid losing face, until she was moved by the example of her daughter's selfless love.

In *Bisclavret,* in contrast to the female world of *Fresne,* there is malebonding, recognition and solidarity with the man in the beast against the wife who had feared the beast in the man. Admittedly, her action seems worthy of condemnation, but if we look at the story only from her point of view, we might be more sympathetic. Marie begins with a description of the dangerous violence of werwolves, savage beasts, who devour people and do great harm while they are in that rage ("beste salvage, / tant cum il est en cele rage, hummes devure, grant mal fait," 9–11). Then she tells of a man who disappears three days a week, whose wife is not unnaturally suspicious and wants to know about his absence but very much fears his anger ("jeo creim tant vostre curuz," 35), a strong hint that he has a temper and that she has felt it. When she learns the truth, she is, again not unnaturally, frightened and turns for help to a man who had offered love. She uses that man without loving him, something Marie certainly does not approve, and she condemns her own husband to continuous life as a beast, and yet she does not destroy her husband's clothes, which would have made it impossible for him ever to be rescued. Did she love the man and hate the beast? Is she wrong to have feared the beast in the man—a side she as wife might well have known—while the king and his court recognize the man in the beast, the side that was shown to the outside or male world? Did she take his clothes in order to reveal him as she saw him, as an abusive husband? She and her children are the only victims we see of his anger. Marie does give examples of violent husbands, in *Yonec* and *Laustic,* so it may not be an anachronism to see in Bisclavret's wife an example of the abused wife who is blamed for her attempt to save herself by a society which sees only the good in the man, even when she has exposed him by taking away the veneer of civilization, a society which tortures her to restore *his* identity. And surely some abused wives in the audience would have recognized her plight.[50]

In the following *lai*, *Lanval*, Marie shows a society (the Arthurian court) that is unrelievedly corrupt: the king ignores the hero's service and forgets to reward him; other knights envy him and only offer friendship when he has wealth to share; the queen abuses her position, offers herself to him and attacks him violently in word and deed when he rejects her; and Arthur's barons are ready to condemn Lanval unjustly to please the king. The world of love, on the other hand, is one of nurture, generosity, and forgiveness, and it is made up entirely of women. When the lady comes to court with her female retinue to save Lanval, she drops her cloak, a sign of defiance in the male world of epic and perhaps here too, but for a woman it also serves as a revelation of beauty. The king in *Deus Amanz* is also less than exemplary, though with some excuse. He takes such comfort in his daughter after his wife dies, that he makes it impossible for her to marry, possessive love in the personal sphere causing negligence in the public, where an heir must be needed. The daughter is cast in a maternal role with both her father and her lover and, trying to satisfy both, turns for help to her physician aunt. The aunt supplies the needed potion, but the lover is too reckless to admit he needs help, too proud perhaps to accept it from women, despite the girl's plaintive "drink your medicine" ("bevez vostre mescine," 200). He dies, because his male pride is unwilling to accept the needed nurture of the female world. The father's possessiveness and the lover's ego condemn the girl they love to death.

In *Yonec*, the heroine is altogether without female support, and her story ends in death, implying that women need other women to survive in the world, though she does fashion a solution for herself in her mind. Her only companion is her husband's old and unsympathetic sister; the heroine is not allowed to speak to other women, not even to go to church, which understandably turns her against her husband. Left to her own resources, she creates a world of love in her imagination, willing an adventure, a lover to come to her from a world of dreams, of potential that must be actualized by desire, and she transforms him in *her* image. He even speaks of God and the fall from a feminist perspective, putting the blame on Adam: "I believe in the creator who freed us from the grief that Adam, our father, led us into when he bit into the bitter apple" ("Jeo crei mut bien al Creatur, / que nus geta de la tristur, / u Adam nus mist, nostre pere, / par le mors de la pumme amere," 149–52).[51] The strength she gains from this love and the pregnancy that results from it, or from her restored psyche, enables her to free herself from the worst aspects of her marriage, and to endure the rest until the son is old enough to replace or revenge his father, and then she can die.[52] The son's murder of his father or step-father, while it avenges the mother's suffering, also aligns him with the male world of violence that had destroyed his mother's bird-lover. In this lai, the world of love is a world of dreams that can only be fully possessed in death.

In *Laustic* as in *Yonec* the world of love is destroyed by the husband's violence, coupled with suspicion and gratuitous cruelty. Again, the marriage is less than perfect and there is a hint of abuse. But in this case the wife lacks the heart or the will to resist her husband. Her love or perhaps her need is not strong enough to confront the threat of violence, so she makes do with the memory of the love, elegantly preserved by art. But it is not the living art of song and poetry, it is a silent, static symbol, a dead bird sealed in a rich casket, unable to sing. It is perhaps the fate she has accepted for herself.

In *Milun and Chaitivel*, Marie returns to the larger male world of chivalry and honor through fighting, pitting it against the female world of love, but in rather different ways. In *Milun*, the woman sends for the man, attracted by his chivalric reputation, and he promises never to leave her, a promise he keeps in that he loves no other woman, but breaks in that he continues to go off fighting, leaving her to deal with her pregnancy and an unwanted and potentially dangerous marriage. That the dangers do not materialize is not thanks to him. The woman arranges first for her sister to care for the child, and later for communication with her lover—he provides the means, a swan that only moves when it is hungry, a perfect symbol for his love, but asks *her* to make a plan. It is only after the lover is defeated by their son—something he could have avoided had he sought his son before he sought his rival, put love before chivalry instead of the other way round—that he can be reunited with his love. Public defeat in the male world of fighting is the entry to residence in the female world of love.

The lovers in *Chaitivel* are killed before they can make that shift. They all choose to serve their love by violence and three of them die, fighting recklessly in the service of the same woman, while the fourth is so wounded that he cannot enjoy her love, even though he has her company. She provides female care, burying the bodies of the three, and nursing the fourth, and she takes considerable if selfish satisfaction from the honor of their service, even composing a *lai* to commemorate *her* loss (and her success). She wants to call it the "four sorrows," from her perspective, but the living lover insists it be called "the unfortunate one," from his. The pointless competition for priority in grief shows up the emptiness of the courtly love game, a male creation of which this woman takes full advantage.

Chevrefoil moves into a world of real love, in which the lovers despite their separation and frustrations, share a perfect understanding, and make the most of a moment of shared joy in solitude in the forest, removed from the hostile social world that exiled Tristan and imprisons the queen. The hero preserves that moment in art, a living art in contrast to the bird's casket in Laustic, a lai that can be heard and sung by others and give joy to them.[53] Instead of ending here, Marie concludes the collection with a lai that allows the female world of love and sisterhood to conquer definitively the male world of violence and betrayal. Marie emphasizes this point by noting that the lai was originally named for the hero, Eliduc, but has been renamed for the two women because it happened to them. That is, what interests her is their story. The hero serves two kings, both of whom harbor suspicions about him, both of whom need him, one apparently wrongs him, the other is wronged by him. The male hierarchic world of service is one with severe limitations, as Marie has shown in other lais. The hero's ambiguous position and morality in that world is reflected in his relations with the women: he betrays his wife by accepting tokens of love from another woman, and betrays the other woman by eloping with her without telling her of his marriage, compounding his sin with betrayal of her father and murder of a sailor who reveals the truth.

One might say that Eliduc is a man unhappy in his professional life who looks to a younger woman to assuage his ego, and it is only the nurturing generosity of his wife that saves them all. In contrast to husbands who spy on their wives to catch and hurt them, she spies on her husband to help him. She nurses the girl back to health, removes herself to a nunnery to enable them to marry, and finally takes the girl into her convent, where she treats her like a sister, and instructs her in a life that is implied to be more satisfying than either marriage was. It is the life of a community of women who support each other in love and a common service. He retains contact with them only by message, until he tacitly acknowledges the superiority of their life by following their example and retiring from the secular world.

In the Fables, Marie moves away from the emotional needs of the individual that dominate the lais, to more overtly social issues, giving a good deal of attention and criticism to the abuses of power by lords and judges who do not take their responsibilities seriously, or who are corrupt, greedy, treacherous, and who exploit the poor. But she is still concerned with women. The nurturing woman is present in the various goddesses of the animals, Destinee, Sepande, Criere, who were male in Marie's sources (see Spiegel, 11). Other females are praised for their cleverness (engin) in saving themselves and their offspring, even if it means lying (21). In two stories of women caught by their husbands with their lovers, the women convince the husband he did not see what he saw: in one she draws the lesson that sense and cleverness is a greater help than wealth or relations (44), in the other that clever and lying women know the art of tricking people better than the devil (45). In the first story (44), where the woman shows her husband his own image in a pot of water and points out that he is not in the pot, so his sight has deceived him just as it did when he saw her in bed with another man, one might ask if Marie is also implying against the literal level of the story that the wife let her husband see what he wanted to see (her innocence) while he had seen what he expected to see (her guilt). In the other (45), the woman does not deny what her husband saw, but treats it as a vision which portends her death as it did her mother's and grandmother's. She insists he summon her relations, that she and he divide their possessions, and she retire with her part to an abbey to prepare for death. This threat of taking her portion away, combined with an implied assertion of her innocence, makes him say he was lying, swear to it before her family perjuring himself, and promise never to bring it up again. She uses his greed as well as his gullibility to strengthen her own position.[54]

Marie does not draw the obvious misogynist moral in these or in other stories: in one, the woman lends the body of her dead husband to be hanged in place of a thief who asks her advice and offers his love; she saves him, asserting that "one should use the dead to free the living, from whom we can have comfort" (25.35–36). Marie comments simply that the dead can have no faith in the living, because the world is false and fickle. In another (57), a wife foolishly wastes two of her husband's three wishes; from this Marie concludes that one should not believe the word of someone else or take the counsel of the clever (but rely on oneself). In the tale of the scissors versus the scythe, the story of the arguing couple shows that if a fool talks folly and is shown sense, *he* (*fols,* 95.31, *il,* 95.34) will only get angry and refuse to be silenced. In the story it is she who stubbornly refuses to give up the wrong position; the story has a female subject, the moral a male. Yet another tale of a contrary wife ends with the message that people fight their lord without thinking of the consequences, but eventually he will take his revenge (96), shifting the moral away from marriage where the woman is apparently at fault to a social situation where the man is. The point is the folly of opposing someone with greater power, whether people against their lord or a wife against her husband. In some fables (87, 92, 103), the wise advice of a woman is not heeded. Only in one, in which the wife counsels her husband to kill the snake that has been the source of their prosperity, does Marie draw a moral directly criticizing the woman: many women counsel what goes against their men, wise men should not listen to foolish women as this peasant did (73). In fact, as the story goes, he is the fool, taking her bad advice in the first place, and then coming back to her for more despite the disasters caused by the original advice.

In a fable that has no women characters (53), Marie nonetheless makes a point in defense of women through Adam and Eve. A peasant asks a hermit why Adam ate the fruit that destroyed people ("Pur quei Adam manga le fruit, / par quei le people aveit destruit," 5–6); the hermit teaches him that all men partake of the same curiosity, that it was the devil who counseled Adam and deceived him through his wife. The moral Marie draws is that one should blame oneself, not others. The peasant, who instinctively blames Adam, reenacts his sin, while the hermit gives the official (religious) interpretation, blaming Eve and the devil, but Marie counters his lesson with her own, suggesting that all (men and women) should take responsibility for their own acts. Marie's fables offer a rather subtle counter to misogynist moralizing.[55]

Christine de Pizan, writing two centuries later, offers far more direct and aggressive defenses against misogyny. She uses examples of extraordinary, indeed superhuman women, often from male authors and sometimes against their own misogyny, but within settings she has created, a universal history of fortune's effects or the building of a city of ladies, and from the mouths and under the control of female personifications, who have higher than human authority but are sometimes only thinly disguised stand-ins for her.[56] Christine's mental world is populated like Hrotsvit's, with spectacular heroines, as Marie's is not. But though her presentation of herself is also cast in the same humble, self-deprecatory mode as Hrotsvit's, she fashions a self-confident voice for herself through the personifications, the allegorical women who speak for her and make the arguments for women and against misogynist men Christine pretends to be unable to make in her own voice.

This is true of Christine's larger works, like the *Mutacion de Fortune*, the *Cité des Dames*, and *L'Avision Christine*. That is not to say that she cannot argue forcefully in her own voice, as she does in the early debate over the *Roman de la Rose*, where she takes on Jean de Meun's defenders, including royal secretaries and chancellors and renowned scholars. She did have the support of the chancellor of the University of Paris, Jean Gerson, but she was the focus of hostility. Her opponents attempted to intimidate her by exalted praise of the author she was attacking, or condescending requests to her to correct her folly, the presumption of an impassioned woman (*Débat*, 1.6.14–15), a woman not lacking in intelligence insofar as a woman can possess it (2.154.7–8). They speak of her reputation for wit and melodious eloquence in her letters and other "little things" ("chosettes," 3.3.6) and warn her not to get above herself, like the crow who when praised for his song sang still louder and lost his food (3.3.735–38). They are shocked that she should "dare and presume to correct" such an "excellent and irreprehensible doctor of holy divine Scripture and high philosophy" (1.6.20–23). But they do not silence her. Though she takes the humble stance, admitting to womanly ignorance, she pits her small knowledge against their lovely eloquence ("femmenine ignorance," "petit sçavoir . . . respondant a leur belle eloquence," 1.2.26, 42). She begins as a woman ignorant and light-weight, with little arguments, asking pardon for her womanly weakness (1.5.6–10), but she asserts the justice of her

cause, the harm Jean's work can do, all the worse because of its knowle
and eloquence, the dishonorable language and shameful and horrible end
(the rape that concludes the poem), and the abuse of religion in the
suggestion that paradise can be achieved through sex (1.5). She criticizes
the excessive praise of the author, as though he were on a level with Christ
or Mary or Paul (3.4.40-43), wonders why if he were so great he did so
little (3.4.202-03); she may be a "simple little woman," but she uses the
doctrine of the holy church to correct their errors (3.4.539-40). She reminds Gontier Col that a little point of a knife can pierce a sack filled and
swollen with material objects—she is clearly the little knife, but whether
her contemporary opponent or Jean de Meun is the stuffed sack is perhaps
intentionally ambiguous (1.7.44-47). She notes that many wise and learned
doctors agree with her, and she suggests that if her opponent wants to
learn about Hell and Paradise, presented in more subtle terms, in higher
expression of theology, more profitably and poetically than Jean's poem,
he should read the book of Dante—or have it expounded for him, since it
is superbly written in the Florentine language which she can read and
apparently he cannot (3.4.868-76).

Christine is particularly distressed by the harm Jean can do women: not
only that he teaches men how to take the castle, instead of teaching women
to defend it (3.4.717-20), but also that he incites men to abuse women.
She tells of a man who had the same faith in the *Roman de la Rose* he
had in the Gospel, and when he was in a fit of jealously, he would read it
to his wife and then beat her, saying Jean knew what women were like
(3.4.803-09). It should not, she insists, be considered folly or presumption
for her, a woman, to take on such a subtle author, when he, a single man,
dared to defame without exception an entire sex. She knows that there
"have been, are, and will be many valiant women, more honorable, better
in their habits, even more learned, from whom the world has had greater
good than ever from him, even in secular policy and virtuous customs"
(1.5.230-34). She cites a series of women from the Bible (Sara, Rebecca,
Esther, Judith), and from modern France (queens and duchesses, women
of beauty, chastity, honor, and learning, even valiant women of lower
rank); she does not defend them, she assures him, because she is a woman,
but because as a woman she has truth and knowledge, whereas he lacks
experience of women and speaks only by conjecture (1.5.238-58), a position she will expand in her attacks on the misogynist tradition.

Experience is her answer to male authority. When she sets out to construct a larger edifice, she again adopts the posture of inadequacy for the
task: in the *Mutacion*, she is simple and with little sense or understanding
to speak of such high matters ("moy simple et pou sensible," "a si petit
sentement comme j'ay," "selon mon povre entendement," "combien que
mon sens petit monte / pour parler de chose si haute") but Fortune has
given her so much experience that she has enough material.[57] In the life of

Charles V, which she was commissioned to write by the king's brother because he had been impressed with the *Mutacion,* she both demurs and justifies: "ignorance encumbers my sense, I, Christine de Pizan, a woman under the shadow of ignorance as to clear understanding, but endowed with God's and nature's gift"; she says she wanted to do it "to the extent of my small wit ("selon l'estendue de mon petit engin"), and that she needs God's help to speak of such high matter as wisdom, but she does it. In the *Cité,* she does not doubt her ability, but she is so disturbed by her meditations on misogynous texts that she begins to doubt her own experience— "I relied more on the judgment of others than on what I myself felt and knew," 1.1.1—and to question God—how could such a worthy artisan make such an abominable creature?—even to defy him—a servant who receives less owes less. She comes to hate herself and the whole sex as a monstrosity in nature, until she is comforted and inspired by the figures of Reason, Rectitude (Droiture), and Justice, who frequently cite her earlier writings. In *L'Avision,* faced with the awesome figures of France and Philosophy, she speaks of herself as "your poor unworthy servant" ("vostre pauvre indigne serve"), but France (Libera) calls *her* "chiere amie," or "belle douce amie," to whom God and nature gave a love of study beyond the common order of women. France asks Christine to ghost-write her history, saying how much her writings have comforted her and her children, begging her to save France (which she will attempt to do much later in the *Ditié de Jehanne d'Arc*). Philosophy calls her "my very loyal handmaid" ("mon ancelle tres loialle") and offers her treasures too heavy for Christine's "weak female body" ("mon corps femmenin et foible"). Christine calls herself a servile mercenary in contrast to Philosophy's child, Boethius, but she plays the Boethius role in the third book.[58]

Christine tells her biography in a long lament to Philosophy in *L'Avision,* expanding things she had said in earlier works like the first book of the *Mutacion,* where she gave an allegorical biography, a description of how Fortune turned her into a man so she could cope with the problems of her life. In the *Mutacion,* she insists that the changes to her body and face are true, though her description of the event is metaphorical or fictional. Her early life, she says, was favored by Fortune, with her father, a renowned philosopher, invited to the French court, her mother a figure of greater prowess than the Amazon Panthasellee (which suggests that Christine identifies herself with the Amazons to some extent). She is speaking not of her natural mother, but of Nature, who wanted her to be female, like herself [cf. *L'Avision* 1.3, a sense of her destiny to champion the sex?], though Christine resembles her father in all but her sex. She was named for the most perfect man who ever was, Christ, in a feminine form. But she is unable by custom, a custom she deplores as unfair to women, to inherit her father's goods; that is, she loses for lack of training his great treasure of knowledge, despite her good will and inclination for it. She is sent off on a voyage to Ymeneus, marriage, a happy voyage for ten years until a storm destroys her husband and she is left to pilot their ship alone, unprepared and untrained, and it is wrecked. But Fortune saves her by massaging her limbs until they become stronger, her voice deeper, her heart bolder; she stops weeping, repairs the boat and pilots it successfully. By the time she writes the *Mutacion*, she has been a true man ("vrays hom") for thirteen years; though she would prefer to have remained a woman with her husband, she must and will continue to be a man (1295-1411).

Christine drops the metamorphosis imagery but makes an even stronger statement about herself as a male in spirit, in the first chapter of the *Cité*, when she berates God for making her inhabit a female body. In the *Cité* she shows herself working alone and apparently happily in her study, surrounded by books, until she is called to supper by her mother. She mentions later that her father encouraged her to learn while her mother wanted her to spend her time spinning, so it is ironic that Christine's learning and writing is the main financial support of her mother after her father's death. Finally, in *L'Avision*, she tells her whole story in a Boethian lament to Philosophy beginning with her heritage of learning on both sides, and her marriage to a noble and virtuous young scholar. Then, a series of deaths, the king's which affected her father's financial position, her father's, and her husband's, plunged her into what would be a difficult but valuable experience of the external world. A widow at twenty-five with three children, a mother and other relatives to support, she was suddenly faced with false claims of debts, theft of the money she had invested, long bureaucratic hassles to obtain money owed her father and her husband without any knowledge of the family's affairs—the only complaint she makes of her husband is that he did not entrust her with that information—mistreatment by officials, even rumors about her loose life because she had to go about so much in public to settle her affairs, and no help from the nobles who are "obliged" to help widows and orphans. It is no wonder she had to become male to cope. But her distress led her to write, first to express her grief for her husband in ballades. She returned to the life that most naturally pleased her, of solitary meditations on Latin, the disciplines of learning, and rhetoric; she desired to so fill herself with study that no woman born for a long time would pass her. When a man told her that learning is not suitable for women, however little it is, she responded that ignorance is even less suitable to men, however great it is: "une fois respondis a un homme qui repprouvoit mon desir de savoir disant que il napertient a femme avoir science comme il en soit pou et lui dis que moins apartient a homme ignorance comme il en soit beaucop" (59v).

Nature, using a distinctly female image, wants Christine's learning and her experience to give birth to new writings, like a woman who forgets the pain of labor when she hears her child cry, writings that will keep her memory before princes (60r).[59] Nature makes babies herself in a rather unusual way at the beginning of *L'Avision:* she takes matter from the (male) figure of Chaos, mixes it, moulds it, and puts it back into Chaos to bake (2r); the female Nature fashions the child, the male Chaos incubates it, a striking reversal of sex roles. For Christine, Nature implies, it is as natural to write books as to have babies. She has produced fifteen volumes not counting her short poems and gained a reputation in France and abroad because, she says modestly, it is unusual for a woman to write; she does not claim to be alone, only that it has not happened for a while ("pour la chose non usagee que femme escripse comme pieca ne avenist," 61r). But her life is still plagued by death, now of her patrons: the duke of Milan who had invited her to come to his court, the duke of Burgundy who asked her to do a life of Charles V. Christine is comforted as Boethius was by Philosophy, though Christine's Philosophy is the abbess and superior of a convent, suggesting that true learning is a female realm like the city of ladies not like the male-dominated university she visits in the second book. Philosophy reminds her of the prosperity she has enjoyed, and implies that the death of her husband was a good since if he had lived, Christine would not have been able to study as she has, or enjoyed the delights of learning and the solitary life. Her body has been changed from weak and feminine to that of a man to meet her needs (71r). The tribulations test her patience, refine her virtue, help her earn salvation, and, perhaps most comforting of all, her persecutors will be punished.

Earlier in *L'Avision*, Lady Opinion, who is described as the daughter of ignorance and the desire to know, rather like what Christine says of herself, had talked about the public reception of Christine's works. She said that some people assumed they were written by clerks or priests in her name, that they could not come from a woman's "sentement," a somewhat backhanded compliment, while others said her style was too obscure. But Opinion says that the foundation of her works is truth by the witness of experience, of reason and true feeling, that different judgments come from envy which blinds people to truth. She reassures Christine that in the future her works will be talked of more than now—a self-prophecy of fame that like Dante's proved to be true. Opinion also tells Christine that once you attain truth by study, opinion departs (46v), so when she takes her leave of Christine, we can assume that Christine has attained truth. It is not irrelevant that the first survey of Greek philosophy in the vernacular is given in *L'Avision*.

L'Avision also presents a bleak view of French history and contemporary politics, heavily veiled in allegory. History is a major part of Christine's work. She wrote a life of Charles V at the request of his brother after he had seen the *Mutacion*. In this work, which is straight history, she cannot rely on personifications to speak for her, so she has to present her own research from chronicles, from the reports of people still living who served the king, and from her own memory of him. Like Hrotsvit's life of Otto, this is the first commissioned life of Charles V. Like Hrotsvit, Christine is aware that there are those who might object to a woman speaking about arms, to whom she answers that builders do not make the stones they use but assemble the materials, embroiderers do not make silk but work with it. Moreover, she claims, Hugh of St. Victor said a wise man learns willingly, even from a child—if the doctrine is good he retains it, if not he lets it go. And like Hrotsvit, Christine gets in a certain amount of material of concern to women, though it is only a small proportion of the whole: a description of Charles's queen, Jeanne de Bourbon and of her death (much longer than the passage on the death of the pope or the emperor); the king's punishing a rapist by death, driving away anyone who dishonored a woman, and discouraging husbands from locking up their wives. She commends the duke of Bourbon for comforting poor noble women and helping them in the Council with their needs, as he did Christine, and twice mentions the fact that the duke of Burgundy held Flemish lands because of his wife, Marguerite, heir of the count of Flanders. She mentions and names the good and wise woman in whose care the king's second son was placed, and the holy woman he summoned to speak with him and asked to pray for him, noting that such women should be loved and honored by notable men, just as Jerome wrote "belles escriptures" for Paula and her daughter Eustochium (3.23).

In the *Mutacion,* she offers a universal history, ancient and biblical, moving back and forth between the two, but she also gives a picture of contemporary history, corruption in courts, oppression of the poor, and mistreatment of women by slander and physical attack (book 3). If people wonder why she does not speak of women's vices, it is because the worst of their vices do little to make the world worse, since they are little involved in affairs of government, though a lot is said about them in books (*livres*); indeed, many authors say two pounds (*livres*) of evil about women for every ounce of evil in them (6636–38). But in fact as she goes through her history, women play a substantial role in it. The Amazons, an early city of ladies, are featured. Christine, like other writers writing for women, notes that the Amazons allow no men in their kingdom and go abroad to take lovers to perpetuate their lines without marriage, a direct attack on the patriarchal system. She brings them in four times: in book 5, Thamyris, queen of the Amazons, defeats Cyrus to avenge her son; at the beginning of book 6, she describes their history and customs in some detail, at the end, Panthasellee's exploits and death in the Trojan war; and in 7, Alexander asks the Amazon queen Candace who had never been conquered by arms to yield but settles for a friendly meeting. What these passages have in common is praise of the fighting skills and strategies of the women, the fear they inspire in other peoples and in great warriors or heroes, like Cyrus, Hercules, and Theseus, and the apparent harmony of their kingdom, which she says in the *Cité* lasted over eight hundred years. They are ruled by two queens at a time, a fact we are told just after the story of Thebes, where the two brothers bring a devastating civil war on the land precisely because they are unable to share the rule. In the last major episode Christine describes, Panthasellee and her women wreak such havoc among the Greeks that they vow to kill her; they surround her, cutting her off from her friends, and then two "heroes" attack her together, Achilles's son, whom she could have killed if others had not rescued him, and Ajax. Christine thus carries the shameful conduct, which would not be acceptable against men however threatening, further than the *Roman de Troie*.

The history is filled with impressive women. Semiramis is praised at length, for her adventures, her fighting skills, extending her kingdom to cover a third of the world, constructing buildings and defenses for her cities (while her husband is reported only to have built a temple to his father), her wisdom and ability to govern over forty-two years (5.9088ff.). She marries her son because she wants no other crowned women in the land—a desire to retain power which Christine does not criticize—and because there was no law against it (V). The heroic deeds of Judith and Esther are praised: Judith takes Holofernes's head back to her people saying "by me, a woman, God has saved all the land of Jewry" ("par moy femme, a Dieu garie / toute la terre de Juirie," 5.10311-12); the Jews are brought out of slavery by Esther, the valiant and wise ("le peuple des juifs . . . mis furent hors de servage / Par Hester la preux et la sage," 5.11679-82). An army of Greek women comes to Thebes to avenge the death of their men with engines of war; they storm the city, pierce the wall with stones, mount by ladders, enter and kill all they meet (5.13165ff.). Medea's story is told with great sympathy, as a love-story but with a twist, the agony of the intellectual who knows better but cannot keep herself from the folly of love, a story that is frequently told of men, rarely if ever of women (6.14301ff.); she warns Jason early on that if he deceives her she will take revenge, which to some extent justifies what she does. Briseida is briefly mentioned, because Christine does not approve of her, dismissing her as a traitor like her father (6.16105-6). Penelope is mentioned as a valiant lady, and "preudefemme," though Christine has little use for Ulysses; she describes his staying two years with Circe, having a son by her, and then returning to Penelope, who instead of turning her back on him—presumably as he deserved—received him with joy.

Most of the women Christine features in the *Mutacion* are of course included in the *Cité*, but here Christine goes further still, rewriting the history of the world as the product of women's actions and thoughts. Reason, Rectitude, and Justice help Christine build this city, peopled by ladies of the past and present, as a refuge and defense for ladies of the past, present, and future, another "civitas Dei," as Justice calls it at the end, making the identification with Augustine's city of God explicit. Augustine contrasted his city of God with the city of man, which is the city of the devil; Christine's city of ladies is *not* the city of man, but the city of God. That is, women left to themselves create a better civilization than men. First they dig out the dirt of misogynist lies about women, which include the idea that the creation of man in God's image refers to his material body—this cannot be, Reason says, because God had not yet taken a human body. It means the soul, the intellectual spirit, and God placed "wholly similar souls, equally good and noble in the feminine and in the masculine bodies."[60]

Once such misconceptions have been cleared out, the stones can be placed, the foundations and walls built of women who governed in their own name or as regents, women who fought, women who established laws, who wrote poetry, who painted, who invented alphabets and grammar, numbers, cloth-making, agriculture, even armor. Christine makes women responsible for civilization in all its parts. Once the walls are up, they build houses, with women who play more traditional roles, but with unusual intensity and self-sacrifice, divinely inspired prophets, and devoted wives, daughters, and friends. She emphasizes their virtue and chastity, their abhorrence of rape, with examples of women who kill their attackers or commit suicide, and the wonderfully practical ploy of the women from Lombardy who wore rotten meat on their breasts to discourage the rape of invading soldiers. Finally, the city is ready for its queen, the Virgin Mary, a figure of authority, who accepts with pleasure as the "chef du sexe femmenin." She brings in her entourage the famous saints, among them the scholar-martyr Catherine, the heir of her kingdom, highly educated, who defeats the wise men of the land in debate and converts them before she is martyred, and a series of others who preach as well as convert by example, including the author's namesake, Christine, who is defended by a mob of women. Ursula is there with her eleven thousand virgins.

The work ends with advice to married women, to accept their positions in marriage, since it is not always good to be independent—Christine had known the worst of an independence thrust on her—to cherish good husbands, have some gratitude for those in between, and endure the bad, trying to bring them back to a reasonable life, and taking some comfort in the fact that their patience would lead to paradise. She gives the passive role an active twist, counselling all women to be so virtuous in their actions that they make liars of the men who accuse them of vice, so the vices of the evil will fall on their heads. This is a passage that disturbs some of Christine's readers, who see it as surrendering to the patriarchal mode. But one should not forget the world Christine was writing for.[61] She was a realist and she knew from her own experience and her observation what could happen to women. She knew it was not easy for women to get out of bad marriages or to survive outside them—many could not count on their families or gain or buy entrance to convents, so making the best of a bad marriage was all they could do, short of a life of prostitution. In the *Livre des Trois Vertus,* she advises women on action in the world if life gives them the opportunity, taking charge of courts or estates, being informed and involved in all the details, political, legal, financial, even agricultural. But she also tells them how to make the best of their lot if it is not happy—sometimes a bad husband repents at the end and leaves his long-suffering wife his whole fortune—and she advises those who are widowed, who are liberated by fate, so to speak, not to remarry but to seize their independence when it is given to them.

Christine had faith in women's ability to accomplish great things. It seems most fitting that the last work we have from her should be her poem in praise and support of another woman, a contemporary, Joan of Arc. The poem was written in 1429, after a long silence, during which Christine may have retired to her daughter's convent at Poissy. She begins with her joy after eleven years of weeping, not for herself but for the country, reminiscent of the figure of France in *L'Avision.* But now there is hope. France has been raised up by a virgin, la Pucelle, who supports the king (Charles VII) against his enemies, who captures castles and towns, doing what thousands of men could not do. She does honor to the female sex ("quel honneur au femenin / sexe," 265–66, the enjambment emphasizing the fact that she is a woman). She is an androgynous figure, a Moses, leading his people out of Egypt, a Joshua in war, a champion who gives the sweet nourishment of peace to France from her breast. Not Esther, Judith, or Deborah, women of great worth through whom God restored his people, can compare to Joan in the miracles God wrought through her. Not only will she save France and defeat the English, she will restore harmony to Christendom and the church, conquer the Holy Land, and save the faith. Christine presents Joan as the incarnation of the glory of the *Cité.* One can only hope that Christine died before her dreams of France being saved by a woman warrior-hero could be destroyed.

Though Christine never had a formal public position, she was able to work in a man's world as a professional writer, and to succeed in it. Like women who ruled lands or great abbeys, who strove for secular power, or committed their thoughts and conflicts to writing throughout the Middle Ages, she was fully aware that she was a woman, but she was able to assume a male role and perform it with ability that was recognized even by her enemies. She wrote and was read in the "male" spheres of history, of warfare, of political theory, of the education of a prince, but she also wrote in defense of women, and she won a male audience for those works as well. She lived a life of great accomplishment like her heroines. She was herself a model women could follow with pride, and for that she deserves respect and admiration.

Christine lived and wrote many centuries after the first women included in this study, women involved in political struggles like Judith, mother of Charles the Bald, women who wrote powerful poetry in convents, like Radegund and Hrotsvit. But she is part of the same tradition. It is a tradition not in the sense that the women necessarily knew of one another and could consciously imitate the actions or writings of earlier figures, but in the sense that all the women living public lives in whatever sphere faced the same kinds of challenges and prejudices as women, and looked to the same kinds of support in female figures, whether historical or allegorical. Christine is a fitting person to conclude this study of women of letters in the Middle Ages, women who engaged in all spheres of activity, political, intellectual, religious, even military, whom we know about because they were in one way or another involved in letters, some as correspondents, collaborators, instigators, or patrons of works written by men, others as writers of poetry and prose, secular and religious. All of them struggled to succeed in their worlds, not in small part because they were women, and most of them have for a time been deprived of their proper place in political, religious, or literary history because they were women. That place is slowly and not unpainfully being restored to them by the work of many scholars and critics, and I hope this study will do its part toward that restoration.

NOTES

1. The large correspondence of Catherine of Siena, the Paston family letters, and the letters of German mystics were well known. Even the recent *Dear Sister: Medieval Women and the Epistolary Genre,* ed. Karen Cherewatuk and Ulrike Wiethaus (Philadelphia: University of Pennsylvania Press, 1993), which includes a piece on Radegund, focuses on the better-known women (Hildegard and Heloise) and the later ones (Catherine, the Pastons, Christine de Pizan, Maria de Hout).

2. Misogyny is a complex subject, to which people react passionately; witness the recent controversies over the issue of *Speculum* dedicated to medieval women (volume 68, 1993) and over Howard Bloch's work, which erupted in the *Medieval Feminist Newsletter* (numbers 7 and 8, 1989 and 1990), to which he refers at the beginning of *Medieval Misogyny and the Invention of Western Romantic Love* (1991).

3. There is evidence of such involvement across the centuries and the continent, despite the differences in law and custom. The proof, of course, lies in the texts. For a detailed summary of those, I refer the reader to my guide to medieval women's correspondence, now in preparation.

4. Elaine Pagels shows how from the beginning of the Christian era, people used the story of Adam, Eve, and the serpent to express what they thought about sexual matters. See Pagels, *Adam, Eve, and the Serpent* (New York: Random House, 1988).

5. The use of feminine abstract nouns like *caritas* as attributes of God, which may or may not imply a feminine aspect to the divinity, is different, I think, from the feminine imagery that Bynum discusses in *Jesus as Mother: Studies in the Spirituality of the High Middle Ages* (Berkeley: University of California Press, 1982). In the identification of God or the self with "mother," the male is consciously cast in a female role.

6. Abelard, for example, in his *Expositio in Hexameron,* points out the universality of the masculine as in the passage "he created them *(eos)* male and female." Abelard says *eos* includes male and female, using the male gender for the dignity of the virile sex, just as today if there is only one man with many women, we speak of them in the masculine. See *Opera Petri Abaelardi,* ed. V. Cousin (Paris: A. Durand, 1849, 1859), vol. 1, 659.

7. On the Guglielmites, see Stephen Wessley, "The Thirteenth Century Guglielmites: Salvation through Women," in *Medieval Women,* ed. Derek Baker (Oxford: Blackwell, 1978), and Barbara Newman, *From Virile Man to Woman Christ: Studies in Medieval Religion and Literature* (Philadelphia: University of Pennsylvania Press, 1995). Newman's study came out after I had finished mine, so I have not been able to do more than acknowledge it. But I would like to think the two books are complementary. Our interests overlap, and our approach—to concentrate on the ways women cope with misogyny or assert themselves despite it—is similar.

1. WOMEN IN CORRESPONDENCE

1. For background on medieval letters, see Giles Constable, *Letters and Letter-Collections* (Turnhout: Brepols, 1976); also James J. Murphy, *Rhetoric in the Middle*

Ages (Berkeley: University of California Press, 1974) and "Anonymous of Bologna: The Principles of Letter-Writing (1135 A.D.)," in *Three Medieval Rhetorical Arts,* ed. James J. Murphy (Berkeley: University of California Press, 1971). I address the question of authenticity briefly in the guide. Since letters by men and women, cleric or lay, were usually dictated to a secretary and we do not know how much editing any secretary or scribe did at the time of transcribing or of collecting a letter, we cannot be certain which words are the author's. We can, however, barring outright forgery, assume that the contents represent the ideas of the sender, man or woman.

2. I do not mean to imply that this was true always or everywhere, or in the same way, but the letters indicate that in Europe and the Christian empires, either by force of character or circumstance or custom, women did participate, directly or indirectly, in the business of government.

3. Pauline Stafford, in *Queens, Concubines and Dowagers: The King's Wife in the Early Middle Ages* (London: Batsford, 1983), discusses many of the women whose letters I worked with, and their regencies. See also Edith Ennen, *Frauen im Mittelalter* (Munich: C. H. Beck, 1984), which was translated by Edmund Jephcott as *The Medieval Woman* (Oxford: Blackwell, 1989). I should note that I do not claim the women regents were in sole charge—they had to work with and through male officials—but that they were more than figureheads; they were in a position to make and influence decisions.

4. It was to Pulcheria that popes turned for help in battles against the heresies of Nestor and Eutyches, and Gregory used her as an example of zeal to a later empress, Leonia (MGH, GregI, *Reg* 13.42). Pulcheria took as her own model the Virgin Mary, not only in her ascetic life but also in her right to receive communion with priests in a sacred place, claiming her share of the priestly character of an emperor: "have I not given birth to God?" (cited by Kenneth G. Holum, *Theodosian Empresses* [Berkeley: University of California Press, 1982], 160). She also championed the view of Mary as Theotokos, mother of God, against Nestor, a battle in which she was supported by pope Leo I; PL54 includes eleven letters from Leo to Pulcheria.

5. An unusual number of letters to and from Brunhild have been kept and published, exchanges with emperor Maurice (MGH, MK, EpAustr. and HGF, 4) and pope Gregory I (ten extant letters about church governance and personnel, MGH, GregI, *Reg*). Gregory also wrote to her son and grandsons, but a comparison of his letters to them with his letters to her makes it clear that while they have the title, she has the power.

6. For an analysis of Adela's politic maneuvers to enhance the Thibaudian family, see Kimberly LoPrete, "The Anglo-Norman Card of Adela of Blois," *Albion* 22 (1990), 569–89.

7. Stafford, who calls the tenth century "a century of women" (141), identifies the *colloquium dominarum* as the site of the final resolution of Henry of Bavaria's struggle for the regency, which he lost to the empresses (*Queens,* 142). C. W. Previté-Orton, in *The Shorter Cambridge Medieval History* (Cambridge: Cambridge University Press, 1953), 1.444, attributes a key role in the resolution to Gerbert of Aurillac, but Gerbert himself wrote to Beatrice commending the excellence of her acumen for the peace that has been established among princes (MGH, BDKz2 ep.63). Ferdinand Lot notes the big role Beatrice played in the negotiations and in the conclusion of peace; see *Les Derniers Carolingiens, Lothaire, Louis V, Charles de Lorraine* (Paris: Bouillon, 1891), 141. Gunther Wolf lists the men who take an oath to support the succession of Otto III but does not mention the women's meeting; see "Theophanu und Adalheid," in *Kaiserin Theophanu, Prinzessin aus der Fremde—des Westreichs Grosse Kaiserin,* ed. Gunther Wolf (Cologne: Böhlau, 1991).

8. Eleanor was eleven years older than her husband, as his mother, the empress Matilda, had been ten years older than her husband Geoffrey of Anjou. Both women had been married before and so brought political and marital experience to their marriages, as well

as high birth and holdings, giving them at least a level playing field in their relations with husbands who were not hesitant to assert themselves. For Eleanor's role in the development of vernacular literature at Henry's court, see chapter 4.

9. Eleanor's letters to Celestine III are included in the collection of Peter of Blois, who may have been responsible for some of the language in them but probably not for the views expressed. It is unlikely that the queen of England, not to say duchess of Normandy and countess of Anjou, as she refers to herself in the letters, would have allowed herself to be represented to the pope in words she did not approve or did not wish to have publicly connected with her.

10. Churchmen write to women about the cause of the church being committed to their hands, either by God or by their husbands. Anselm asks queen Matilda to care for the churches of England, to warm the orphans of Christ under her wings like the chicken in the gospel, a figure that in fact refers to Christ; see *Sancti Anselmi Cantuarensis Archiepiscopi Opera Omnia*, ed. F. S. Schmitt (Edinburgh: Thomas Nelson, 1946), ep.288. On clergy in the high Middle Ages encouraging wives to influence their husbands, see Sharon Farmer, "Persuasive Voices: Clerical Images of Medieval Wives," *Speculum* 61 (1986), 517–43.

11. Gilbert of Foliot wrote in a similar vein to the countess of Leicester when she was very ill, trying to persuade her not to give herself over to thoughts of paradise, where they do not lack examples of goodness, but to think how needed she is in this world as an exemplar of virtue; see *The Letters and Charters of Gilbert of Foliot*, ed. Z. N. Brooke, Dom Adrian Morey, and C. N. L. Brooke (Cambridge: Cambridge University Press, 1976), ep.120.

12. Note the emphasis on the regent's authority, "when you were ruling *alone,*" perhaps meant to flatter, but certainly also an acknowledgment from an authoritative source of the real, not nominal, power of her position. Nicholas also commended the empress Eudocia for "fortitude of mind in womanly weakness," a "virile breast surpassing the zeal of men in the cause of piety" (MGH EpKar 4, Nic, ep.96).

13. Peter encouraged Adelaide to be "a virago of the Lord" and asked her help in dealing with priests who lived openly with women; though he knew the clergy would object to her interference, he trusts her to do something "since virile strength rules in her feminine breast."

14. Cited by Marjorie Chibnall, *The Empress Matilda* (Oxford: Blackwell, 1991), 113.

15. Ewald Könsgen, *Epistulae duorum amantium* (Leiden: Brill, 1974), ep.50.

16. In such usage, the word *virile* seems to be the equivalent of "virtuous," which was connected in medieval etymology with the word for "man," *vir*: St. Desiderius's mother encouraged him to follow his course "virilely" (cited in MGH, SRM 4, *Vita Desiderii*, 569–70). But when Guibert of Gembloux uses it to argue that women usually need the discipline of "virile judgment" and the service of men to take care of external business for which "womanly softness" does not suffice, he clearly means "male" as opposed to female. See *Guiberti Gemblacensis, Epistolae,* ed. Albert Derolez CCCM 66 and 66a (Turnholt: Brepols, 1989), hereafter cited as Gb, ep.26.500ff.

17. Christina's biographer, who probably learned her story directly from her, uses "virile" of her in another interesting context: when she and a cleric were struggling with their passionate feelings for each other, she pretended to be untouched, but he gave in to them and said she was more like a man than a woman, though, the author comments, "she with her more masculine qualities might more justifiably have called him a woman," and praises her for behaving "manfully" in the danger (C. H. Talbot, ed., *The Life of Christina of Markyate* [Oxford: Oxford University Press, 1959], s.43–4, p. 115). It is, as it happens, men who succumb to lust in this story.

18. The Virgin portrayed as an Ottonian queen in a contemporary gospel has been interpreted as a compliment to Adelaide and Theophanu. See Rosamund McKitterick, "Women in the Ottonian Church: An Iconographic Perspective," in *Women in the*

Church, ed. W. J. Sheils and Diana Wood (Oxford: Blackwell, 1990), 88. Stafford points out that the iconology of Maria Regina crowned in heaven and ruling with her son was available in the tenth century (27), and Chibnall speaks of the growing cult of the Virgin in England during the reign of Henry I, with the first known carving of Mary's coronation at Henry's abbey of Reading, and Matilda's patronage of Cistercian houses, dedicated to Mary (181).

19. Peter Damian writing to Agnes, to keep her thoughts from returning to her old life, mentions that the humble innkeeper Helena, who became an empress, has churches named for her, which is rare among queens (ep.149); he makes the same remark to "duke" Beatrice (ep.51).

20. The letter was in the papal archives and was certainly written with papal encouragement, if not dictation, but it is cited as the words and authority of a woman. Medieval queens were also cited as models for persuading husbands. Bishop Nicetus of Trier used the example of queen Clothild, who converted her husband Clovis I, to encourage her granddaughter Chlodosuinda (Brunhild's sister-in-law) to persuade her husband to the faith: "proclaim incessantly, incessantly sing" (MGH MK EpAustr 8), but she was not successful. The role of women in converting their husbands to the faith or to orthodoxy is a constant theme of early popes to queens; in later centuries they ask queens to persuade their husbands to defend or support the church.

21. Peter also used Judith as an example of a retiring widow, in a letter to his sisters, though her heroic deed could not fail to have come to mind (ep.94); in fact, he pairs her with Ruth, the one a model of devotion in prosperity, the other in adversity, a contrast between action and suffering.

22. Women like Hildegard of Bingen and Elisabeth of Schönau also felt that God had called on women to correct the church because men were failing it; see chapter 5.

23. Radegund's letter is cited by Gregory of Tours in his *History of the Franks*, 9.42.

24. She includes a political message from the divine voice, condemning papal corruption and preferring the antipope Victor IV ("the one chosen by the emperor") to pope Alexander III (6.4). On Elisabeth's interest in the schism, see Anne L. Clark, *Elisabeth of Schönau: A Twelfth-Century Visionary* (Philadelphia: University of Pennsylvania Press, 1992), 121-22. The letters are in *Die Visionen der heiligen Elisabeth und die Schriften der Aebte Ekbert und Emecho von Schönau* (Brünn: Studien aus dem Benedictiner- und Cistercienser Orden, 1884), most of them in book 6, some within the visions. Another letter was published by P. Schmitz, "'Visions' inédites de sainte Élisabeth de Schoenau," *Revue Bénédictine* 47 (1935), 181-83.

25. A personal question can lead to a religious answer. One letter reports that the Virgin refused to tell her about the soul of a dead brother, but did (apparently) send John the Evangelist to tell her about Origen's soul, that God would do whatever Mary wanted for Origen on the last day, a strong suggestion that he would be saved (6.22).

26. Elisabeth says she heard of Hildegard's compassion from the words of her consoler *(consolatoris)*, but she gives no hint who that is. She might have heard about Hildegard's letter to her magistra showing concern for her, though it would be more appropriate to speak of her in the feminine, and Hildegard's letter does not mention a revelation. What Hildegard does say about Elisabeth, singling her out among the nuns in the magistra's care is: "hold that daughter of God, Elisabeth, in your heart with ardent love, so that you may always nourish her with the milk of consolation" ("filiam Dei Elisabeth cum ardenti amore in corde tuo habe, ita quod lacte consolationis eam semper nutrias," VA95). See also L. Van Acker, "Der Briefwechsel zwischen Elisabeth von Schönau und Hildegard von Bingen," *Instrumenta Patristica* 23 (1991), 416.

27. We are finally to have a complete modern edition of Hildegard's huge collection of letters by Lieven Van Acker. Two volumes have been published so far, *Hildegardis Bingensis Epistolarium*, CCCM 91 and 91A (Turnhout: Brepols, 1991, 1993), which go through letter 250r, cited here as VA. Though questions of authenticity may still

arise about particular letters, much has been done by Marianna Schrader and Ad-elgundis Führkötter, *Die Echtheit des Schrifttums der heiligen Hildegard von Bingen* (Köln: Böhlau, 1956). For other letters, I have relied on the nineteenth-century editions of the PL197, and J. B. Pitra, *Analecta sacra*, v.8, *Analecta Sancte Hildegardis opera* (Typis Sacri Montis Cassinensis, 1882), cited as Pi, and Führkötter's German transla-tion, Hildegard von Bingen, *Briefwechsel* (Salzburg: Müller, 1965). Peter Dronke edited unpublished letters from the Berlin MS, in *Women Writers of the Middle Ages* (Cam-bridge: Cambridge University Press, 1984), cited as DB. The letters in the first volume of Van Acker have been translated by Joseph L. Baird and Radd K. Ehrman, *The Letters of Hildegard of Bingen* (New York: Oxford University Press, 1994), but the translations given here are my own, done before the *Letters* was available.

28. Guibert of Gembloux, her last secretary, warned Hildegard shortly after he met her to pray until God gave her the answers, reminding her of what Gregory testified about holy prophets, that they sometimes said things from their own spirit, believing them to come from the spirit of prophecy (Gb19). Either Guibert is being sanctimo-nious or he has reason to suspect that some of her pronouncements reflect her own views rather than God's. It is indeed sometimes hard to tell where God's voice stops and hers begins.

29. Peter Dronke translates passages from several of the relevant letters and tells the story in *Women Writers*. Sabina Flanagan discusses the relation between the two women in "Spiritualis Amicitia in a Twelfth-Century Convent? Hildegard of Bingen and Richardis of Stade," *Parergon* 29 (1981), 15–21. See also Ulrike Wiethaus, "In Search of Medieval Women's Friendships: Hildegard of Bingen's Letters to Her Female Contemporaries," in *Maps of Flesh and Light: The Religious Experience of Medieval Women Mystics*, ed. U. Wiethaus (Syracuse: Syracuse University Press, 1993).

30. Hildegard reminds Hazzecha of her duty with a stirring "Who sees all things says, 'You have eyes to see and to look around. Where you see mud, there wash, and what is dry, make green. But the spices you have, make them savory. If you did not have eyes you could excuse yourself, but you have eyes, and why do you not look through them?'" (VA159r).

31. Hildegard puts much of the weight for the fall on Adam, who had the primary responsibility (see chapter 5). She wrote to a nun who had left the cloister, claiming she entered unwillingly, about the horrors of Hell, which Adam took on when he scorned the Lord to listen to the worm (DB4). She also exalts the life of chastity over marriage and childbearing with the Pauline idea that the single woman has more children than the one who has a husband (Gal.4:27, VA73), an idea often echoed by male writers on virginity, but which has more resonance coming from a woman.

32. One of her correspondents, Berthold, abbot of Zwiefalten, complains that though he is "often made happier by the consolations of your words, yet by their obscurities, because they almost do not lie open to my intellect, I am made sadder," and asks for solace suitable to "the capacity of my little wit" (VA244).

33. She answered these, then Ralph of Villers sent thirty-four new questions, which she never finished answering. For the first thirty-five questions, see Gb19. The thirty-eight answers (she handled multiple-part questions separately) are in PL197, c.1037–54; Ralph's additional questions are in Gb25. The monks continued to press her for answers to these and further questions until she died, and hoped to find the answers written somewhere even after her death. Apparently she had written some, but they disappeared. For that intriguing story, see Gb26. For a brief discussion of some of Hildegard's answers in relation to contemporary monastic versus scholastic approaches to theology, see Anne C. Bartlett, "Commentary, Polemic, and Prophecy in Hildegard of Bingen's *Solutiones Triginta Octo Quaestionum*," *Viator* 23 (1992), 153–65. On friars turning to women for revelation and religious information because of their privileged relationship with the divine, see John Coakley, "Gender and Authority of

Friars: The Significance of Holy Women for Thirteenth Century Franciscans and Dominicans," *Church History* 60 (1991), 445-60.

34. Van Acker numbers the letters about demonic possession 68 and 68r but does not print them in his edition because they are included in Monika Klaes's edition of the *Vita Sanctae Hildegardis* (Turnholt: Brepols, 1993). The problem, Hildegard's suggested exorcism, and her more effective therapy are described in the life. The PL edition of the life, c.91-130, was translated by Anna Silvas in "Saint Hildegard of Bingen and the Vita Sanctae Hildegardis," *Tjurunga*.

35. Hildegard had the help of devoted secretaries and assistants, but she wrote down some things herself. The secretaries corrected her grammar but not her content, though her last, Guibert, pushed her to let him do more editing with Augustinian arguments for clothing the truth in eloquence and she may have been tired or busy enough to let him. But as Newman points out, she had already published her major works before he arrived (*Sister of Wisdom*, 23-24).

36. By substituting "the speech of your mouth" for "the fruit of your womb," Guibert suggests the same connection between Mary and Hildegard that Hildegard herself seems to imply to often (see chapter 5). Both women gave human expression to the Word of God.

37. Marsilia, abbess of Saint-Amand de Rouen, wrote to Bovo II, abbot of Saint-Amand d'Elnone, to announce a miracle performed by "our common patron" in 1107, "in our presence, in our church." Since, "though not similar by sex, but equal by vocation," they serve the same eternal king under the same patron, she feels they should rejoice in common over the manifestation of their saint's power. It is interesting that after this assertion of equality, she should refer in her story to Eve in stereotypical terms, telling of a woman driven to despair by another woman's false tale of her husband's affair, "seduced like Eve by the serpent in her credulity." For the text, see Henri Platelle, "Les Relations entre l'abbaye Saint'Amand de Rouen et l'abbaye Saint'Amand d'Elnone," *La Normandie bénédictine au temps de Guillaume le Conquerant, XIe siècle* (Lille: Facultés Catholiques, 1967), 83-106. For a detailed study of male and female monastic relations which made me aware of this exchange, see Penelope Johnson, *Equal in Monastic Profession: Religious Women in Medieval France* (Chicago: University of Chicago Press, 1991).

38. There were exceptions, of course, and even more often suspicions about male-female friendships within the church, but among those who corresponded—or whose correspondence is extant—the relations seem to have been chaste, however deep the affection or flirtatious the language. In the case of Abelard and Heloise, the physical affair was over well before the extant letters were written. For instances of disapproval, suspicions, and scandal, see Sharon K. Elkins, *Holy Women of Twelfth Century England* (Chapel Hill: University of North Carolina Press, 1988).

39. See Jo Ann McNamara, "Cornelia's Daughters: Paula and Eustochium," *Women's Studies* 11 (1984), 9-27, on the tendency of Roman women in the early centuries of the church to leave their blood families and create Christian families with like-minded women and sometimes men, families which might also include blood relations.

40. Peter Brown says that Ambrose chose to speak to Rome through Marcellina; see *The Body and Society: Men, Women, and Sexual Renunciation in Early Christianity* (New York: Columbia University Press, 1988), 343.

41. There are a few examples of family letters between laymen, e.g., the now well-known letter of advice from Dhuoda to her distant son, written also to keep her memory alive in him, and a letter from Beatrice of Aquila to her uncle, encouraging him to return to the crusade in Spain and die there in God's service (HGF 15.318).

42. Jerome's letters name Paula's daughters, Eustochium, Blesilla, Paulina, her granddaughters Paula, Principia, Lea, Asella, Laeta, Furia, Geruchia, Celantia, Juliana,

Proba, Demetrias, Hedybia, Algasia, Fabiola. On the friendship between Jerome and women, see Elizabeth A. Clark, *Jerome, Chrysostom and Friends: Essays and Translations*, Studies in Women and Religion, 1 (New York: Edwin Mellen, 1979).

43. Mary McLaughlin analyzes Abelard's affirmative though sometimes ambiguous feminism in ep.6 in terms I find both elegant and convincing. See her "Peter Abelard and the Dignity of Women: Twelfth-Century 'Feminism' in Theory and Practice," *Pierre Abélard—Pierre le Vénérable: Les Courants philosophiques, littéraires et artistiques en Occident au milieu du XIIe siècle* (Paris: Editions du Centre National de la Recherche Scientifiques, 1975), 317. One might note that there is a distinct difference in tone between what Abelard says to justify his work with the nuns to a male friend in the *Historia calamitatum*—that the weaker sex needs the stronger, that abbesses should not rule men—and what he says when he is speaking to women, defending the role of women in the church in his history of nuns.

44. "Soror mea Heloissa, quondam mihi in saeculo chara, nunc in Christo charissima"; the text is in PL178, c.375-78, and Cousin, 1.680-81. The translation is from Betty Radice, *The Letters of Abelard and Heloise* (Harmondsworth: Penguin, 1974), 270-71.

45. Hugh's letters are in *Sacrae antiquitatis monumenta*, ed. C. L. Hugo (Saint-Die: J. Charlot, 1731), vol. 2, 348-49, epp.16, 17.

46. It is quite possible that Heloise and Abelard exchanged love poems, but no texts are extant. Heloise speaks of Abelard's love poems and reveals her own training in classical poetry, and Hugh Metel says that Heloise surpassed her sex in writing verse and prose, so an exchange seems likely.

47. Whether she sent poems to him we do not know, but since we know she sent letters which are not extant and since Ennodius acknowledges her technical knowledge, it is at least possible. For his works, see *Magni Felicis Ennodi Opera Omnia*, ed. William Hartel, Corpus Scriptorum Ecclesiasticorum, 6 (Vienna: Geroldus, 1882). His letters are in MGH, AA 7 and PL63.

48. The third poem is praise to the emperor Justinus and empress Sophia, who had sent her relics of the true cross. The poems were published in an appendix to the edition of Fortunatus, *Venanti Fortunati Opera Poetica*, ed. Fridericus Leo (Berlin: Weidmann, 1881), 271ff. The poems to Hamalafred and Artachis were translated by Marcelle Thiebaux, *The Writings of Medieval Women* (New York: Garland, 1987). For a study of the poems, see Karen Cherewatuk, "Radegund and Epistolary Tradition," in *Dear Sister*, ed. Cherewatuk and Wiethaus. The poems were attributed to Fortunatus, who was thought to have written them in her name; but there is no reason to deny her authorship, since we know from Fortunatus that she wrote poetry and she inscribes her name in each of the poems.

49. They became his family. To Agnes he wrote: "Mother to me by honor, sister sweet by love . . . Christ is witness . . . holy Mary sees that you were to me not other than you would be a sister from the womb and as if in one birth mother Radegund had given birth to both with chaste womb [*viscera*] and as if the dear breasts of the blessed one had struck the two with one flowing milk" (11.6). For the text, see *Venanti Fortunati Opera Poetica*, ed. Leo. Dronke notes that the only poems Fortunatus published in his lifetime are those in book 8. The poems in book 11, which includes most of those to Radegund and Agnes, were collected after his death and may have been essentially private. See Peter Dronke, *Medieval Latin and the Rise of European Love-Lyric* (Oxford: Clarendon, 1968), vol. 1, 202. Two lives of Radegund, one by Fortunatus and one by Baudonivia, a nun in her convent, have been translated in *Sainted Women of the Dark Ages*, ed. and trans. Jo Ann McNamara and John E. Halborg, with E. Gordon Whatley (Durham, N.C.: Duke University Press, 1992). McNamara's study of Catholic nuns, *Sisters in Arms: Catholic Nuns through Two Millennia* (Cam-

bridge, Mass.: Harvard University Press, 1996), also discusses Radegund, along with many others from the Middle Ages.

50. Bede, in his *Ecclesiastical History,* tells the story of an earlier poetic collaboration between an illiterate poet and a famous abbess. Caedmon had a miraculous gift of poetry and Hilda of Whitby had him taught all of sacred history so he could put it into verse (4.24).

51. Marbod of Rennes (1035–1123) was also a cathedral-trained poet and churchman, a bishop comfortable with classical as well as Christian texts, divided like Hildebert in his view of women as dangerous snares or holy models, who wrote poems to numerous women. See Walther Bulst, "Liebesbriefgedichte Marbods," *Liber Floridus, Mittellateinische Studien Paul Lehmann Gewidmet,* ed. Bernhard Bischoff and Suso Brechter (St. Ottilien: Eos, 1950), 287–301. At least one of these poems suggests an exchange, though we cannot know if the letter was in verse: "I read rejoicing, dearest, what you sent me, / for there it is held that I please you / . . . Happy the tablets, happy the stylus and the hand / the right hand when your letter was made" (290). Dronke, in *Women Writers,* 85, notes that three of Marbod's poems are called *Rescripta,* which also suggests answering verses.

52. Dronke (*Medieval Latin,* 213ff.) connects the women with the convent of Le Ronceray in Angers, where girls who were not nuns also went to be educated. Marbod and Baudri studied in the cathedral school of Angers. Dronke says the Muriel to whom Baudri wrote had been educated and lived at Le Ronceray, a convent in Angers, but had not taken vows; see Peter Dronke, *Women Writers,* 85. However, both Hildebert and Baudri call her "virgin" in their poems, which certainly suggests a religious dedication. Serlo calls her "soror" (see *The Anglo-Latin Satirical Poets and Epigrammatists of the Twelfth Century,* ed. Thomas Wright [London: Longman, 1872], vol. 2, 233–40), praises her choice of husband, God, and compares her life favorably to the cares of married women. Sharon K. Elkins says Muriel came from a rich Norman family and became a nun at Wilton (*Holy Women,* 6). Gerald Bond, in a book I saw after I had finished this text, discusses Muriel, Constance, Baudri, Marbod, and Adela of Blois, and gives text and translation of the exchange between Constance and Baudri, *The Loving Subject: Desire, Eloquence, and Power in Romanesque France* (Philadelphia: University of Pennsylvania Press, 1995).

53. For Hildebert's poetry, I used A. B. Scott's edition of the *Carmina Minora* (Leipzig: Tübner, 1969), when I could; references are to the numbers of the poems in his edition. For the letters and other poems I used PL171. Scott suggests identifying Hildebert's Cecilia with the daughter of William I who was an oblate in 1066 and an abbess in 1113; she died in 1127.

54. For Baudri's poems, see *Le Epistole metriche di Baldericus Burguliensis,* ed. M. Teresa Razzoli (Milano: SAEDA, 1936); since the poems are not numbered, references are to page numbers. The poems were edited earlier by Phyllis Abraham in *Les Oeuvres poétiques de Baudri de Bourgueil* (Paris: Slatkine, 1974 [1926]), along with the one answering poem from Constance, 344–49. Baudri also wrote a brief life of Robert of Arbrissel (PL162, c.1043–58) for Petronilla, abbess of Fontevrault, which begins very diffidently with praise for her and her work with poor women and hesitation about his own capacity.

55. The occasional greeting to others may be a way to allay suspicions about the intent of the poems, like the encouragement to persevere in virginity. Cf. to Agnes: the one thing Christ, who can do anything, cannot do is restore violated virginity.

56. Dronke (*Women Writers,* 107) speaks of the exchange between Baudri and Constance as a "fiction of eroticism which is also a guarantee of freedom, for Constance as for Baudri." Stephen Nichols emphasizes the erotic tension between reading and sexuality in the exchange, his page a metaphor for the body, her body "eroticized by the mutual interaction of reading and writing"; see Nichols, "An Intellectual An-

thropology of Marriage in the Middle Ages," in *The New Materialism*, ed. M. S. Brownlee, K. Brownlee, and S. G. Nichols (Baltimore: Johns Hopkins University Press, 1991), 83-85.

57. This poem is found in *Les Oeuvres poétiques de Baudri de Bourgueil*, 196-231; the shorter one is in *Le Epistole metriche di Baldericus Burguliensis*, 69-70. Perhaps Benoît's Chambre de labastre in the *Roman de Troie*, which seems intended as a compliment to queen Eleanor (see chapter 4), owes something to this poem dedicated to the king's aunt.

58. Marie was married to Henry of Champagne, grandson of Adela and Stephen of Blois; her sister was married to his brother Thibaut V of Blois. Poems in honor of their illustrious ancestor might well have been known to her family.

2. RELIGIOUS TEXTS

1. I am not speaking of the formulaic disclaimers, such variations on the humility topos as "you asked me to do something I am not capable of but rather than disobey I send my unworthy effort," though they also occur. I am concerned in these chapters with works the man felt called upon to write by the woman's request coinciding with his interest, or by his concern for her needs.

2. See Gertrud Simon, "Untersuchungen zur Topik der Widmungsbriefe mittelalterlicher Geschichtsschreiber bis zum Ende des 12 Jarhhunderts," *Archiv für Diplomatik Schriftgeschichte Siegel- und Wappenkunde* 4 (1958), 52-119, and 5-6 (1959-60), 73-153. The basic topoi which may be included are: the occasion of the work, the writer's hesitation to take it on and humility before it, justification of the work by the request or commission, the form, sources, and purpose of the work, and the reader's judgment.

3. We know, for instance, of one dedication of a life of Anselm of Lucca to Matilda of Tuscany by Rangerius, because Donizo cites the dedication in his life of Matilda. The dedication does not appear in the published edition because it was not in the manuscript on which the edition was based. See Donizo, *Vita Mathildis*, ed. Luigi Simeoni (Bologna: Zanichelli, 1930-34), vol. 2, 389-438, and n. on 69, in which Simeoni says that Donizo's dedicatory epistle was also omitted by copyists. I am limiting myself here to works in which some connection between the author and the patron is explicit. With saints' lives, which I do not discuss here, the original impetus may come from a convent, indeed the first life might well be written by a nun, but a male author may ultimately be preferred for the official life; see Jane Schulenberg, "Saints' Lives as a Source for the History of Women, 500-1100," *Medieval Women and the Sources of Medieval History*, ed. Joel T. Rosenthal (Athens: University of Georgia Press, 1990), 290-91.

4. Jerome speaks of religious women as the equal of men. To Lucinus, when he and his wife Theodora decided to embrace chastity, Jerome commented: "before you had a partner in the flesh, now you have one in spirit, a sister from a spouse, a man from a woman, an equal from a subject" (ep.71.3).

5. Peter Brown, *Augustine of Hippo: A Biography* (Berkeley: University of California, 1967), 342. Brown says Demetrias is Proba's grandniece, but E. Clark and George de Plinval (*Pélage: Sa vie, ses écrits et sa réforme* [Lausanne: Payot, 1943], 214-15), speak of Demetrias as her granddaughter. J. N. D. Kelly (*Jerome: His Life, Writings, and Controversies* [New York: Harper and Row, 1975]), without naming them, speaks of a mother and grandmother, and Jerome's letter mentions a grandmother, *avita*.

6. For Augustine's letters, see *Sancti Aureli Augustini Hipponiensis Episcopi Epistulae*, ed. A. Goldbacher, 4 vols. CSEL (Vienna: Tempsky, 1911), and PL33. For a

translation, see Sister Wilfrid Parsons, *Saint Augustine Letters,* 5 vols. (New York: Fathers of the Church, 1951-56).

7. Kelly says that people made fun of Jerome's "habit of dedicating his writings almost exclusively to women"; see Kelly, *Jerome,* 169. For the letters, see *Sancti Eusebii Hieronymi Epistulae,* ed. Isidorus Hilberg, 3 vols. (New York: Johnson, 1970, reprint of 1910). For translations of some, see F. A. Wright, *Selected Letters of St. Jerome* (London: Heinemann, 1933).

8. Of Augustine's nine basic texts on the rule, four addressed to men, five to women, it may be impossible to determine which came first; see George Lawless, *Augustine of Hippo and His Monastic Rule* (Oxford: Clarendon, 1987), 65-69. Lawless includes ep.211 among the documents that "constitute the basic dossier for the Regula," x, though he thinks the male version is older. J. C. Dickinson called ep.211 the "best known and the only one whose Augustinian authorship is all but universally acknowledged"; see Dickinson, *The Origins of the Austin Canons and Their Introduction into England* (London: SPCK, 1950), 257.

9. The parallels in monastic existence between men and women may be most evident in the early double monasteries, particularly when headed by women. Aldhelm wrote his *De virginitate* in the seventh century for the nuns of Barking, a double monastery, expecting the monks to hear it as well; see Janemarie Luecke, "The Unique Experience of Anglo-Saxon Nuns," *Medieval Religious Women,* vol. 2, *Peaceweavers,* ed. Lillian T. Shank and John A. Nichols (Kalamazoo: Cistercian Publications, 1987), 61. A manuscript from the eighth or ninth century of Aldhelm's *De virginitate* shows him presenting it to the abbess of Barking; see Karl J. Holzknecht, *Literary Patronage in the Middle Ages* (New York: Octagon, 1966), 165.

10. Peter also wrote a work on nuns for former countess Blanche (*Institutio monialis ad Blancam ex comitissa sanctimonialem,* PL145, c.731-50).

11. For his letter, see *Un Maitre de la vie spirituelle au XIe siècle, Jean de Fécamp,* ed. Jean Leclercq and Jean-Paul Bonnes (Paris: Vrin, 1946), 211-17.

12. For a detailed discussion of the text and excerpts, see André Wilmart, "Eve et Goscelin," *Revue Bénédictine* 46 (1934), 414-38, and 50 (1938), 42-83; Wilmart dates the work circa 1080. I am indebted to Professor Megan McLaughlin for this reference. Goscelin wrote several lives of royal women of Barking and legends of abbesses; see Elkins, *Holy Women,* 6-7.

13. This is perhaps the same Benedicta for whom Baudri of Bourgueil wrote an epitaph. There was another woman recluse at St. Laurent where Eve had retired, Petronilla, and Wilmart suggests that the three might have shared the life of sacrifice, reinforcing each other (fn.1, p.75). There was also a male recluse, Herveus, at least later, who shared Eve's life and grieved for her after her death. Their close connection is suggested by a letter to them, "Herveo et Evae inclusis," from Geoffrey of Vendôme (PL157, ep.48) and by Hilarius in a poem in praise of Eve, *Hilarii Versus et Ludi,* ed. John B. Fuller (New York: Holt, 1929), 46-53. Hilarius, who seems to have exchanged poems with nuns, gives some biographic details about Eve and plays on her name: "she was not the Eve who gave the seeds of sin to the world (18). . . . The first was perdition, the second sacred action (21-22) . . . predestined by God to be without sin in the future" (25-26).

14. A number of rules were written for women by well-known churchmen in the twelfth century. Aelred of Rievaulx did a *De institutione inclusarum* for a "soror" who requested it; St. Francis wrote one for Chiara; and Bernard of Clairvaux wrote on virginity for a virgin, Sophia (ep.113). The *Ancrene Wisse* was written at the request of three women recluses, and Osbert of Clare wrote a work on virginity, probably in the late 1150s, inspired by a visit to Barking, where two of his nieces, the dearly loved Margaret and Cecilia, were nuns. According to Armitage Robinson, Osbert had two clear successes in his career, both involving women: he was instrumental in the foun-

dation of a woman's house, Kilburn, and in the restoration of the Feast of the Conception of the Virgin Mary. See the introduction to *The Letters of Osbert of Clare,* ed. E. W. Williamson (London: Oxford, 1929).

15. Linda Georgianna analyzes Heloise's request in terms of the critical and independent position she takes in the debate among Cluniacs, Cistercians, and regular canons about rules and religious life and her problems with regulating the exterior as opposed to the interior life; see Georgianna, "Any Corner of Heaven: Heloise's Critique of Monasticism," *MS* 49 (1987), 221-53. Eileen Kearney argues that Heloise has her own program in mind, which she sets out for Abelard when she requests the rule from him, using the then-modern techniques of discursive inquiry in scriptural commentary but also relying on her own experience and her knowledge of women; see Kearney, "Heloise: Inquiry and the *Sacra Pagina,*" in *Ambiguous Realities: Women in the Middle Ages and Renaissance,* ed. Carole Levin and Jeanie Watson (Detroit: Wayne State University Press, 1987), 66-81. Both Georgianna and Kearney note that though Heloise begins by saying women and men are not equal, therefore they need different rules, she in fact implies that if women follow the gospel—the only norm they have, since the fathers did not impose a rule on them—they are equal to men. Mary McLaughlin commented that in the works he wrote for the Paraclete, Abelard "was to formulate most comprehensively his approach to the ideals and problems of contemporary monasticism" ("Peter Abelard and the Dignity of Women," 317).

16. The personal letters and letters of instruction were edited by J. T. Muckle in *Medieval Studies* 15 (1953), 47-94, and 17 (1955), 240-81, and the *Historia Calamitatum* in MS 12 (1950), 163-213. They were translated by Betty Radice, *The Letters of Abelard and Heloise,* cited as R. For a recent, detailed, and to me persuasive review of the much-discussed authenticity of the letters, see Barbara Newman, "Authority, Authenticity, and the Repression of Heloise," *JMRS* (1992), 121-57, reprinted in *From Virile Woman.*

17. Indeed, Nature gave women certain advantages, greater sobriety and less need for nourishment, which would make them less of a burden to monastic orders than men are, an answer to those who complain about attending to the needs of idle nuns, as Georgianna points out ("Any Corner of Heaven," 244). Heloise also argues that Paul and Christ exalted the life of the mind, Mary sitting idle to listen to Christ's words while Martha worked for her as much as for Christ.

18. For the text of the rule, see "Abelard's Rule for Religious Women," ed. T. P. McLaughlin, MS 18 (1956), 241-92. For a translation, see Radice, *Letters of Abelard and Heloise,* 183ff.

19. The rule is intended to be generally applicable to later generations and other houses, not just to the original Paraclete, since it allows for an abbess who may need instruction from the lettered (T. P. McLaughlin, ed., "Abelard's Rule," 253; Radice, *Letters of Abelard and Heloise,* 201). But the abbess was also to be chosen for her preeminence over the others in her life and learning *(vita, doctrina),* mature in age, taking the office to serve, not to exercise authority. Because biblical and conciliar authority makes woman subject to man, Abelard declares that monasteries of women should be subject to monasteries of men, but in practice he says the abbot should be like a steward in the king's palace, serving the women who are the brides of his lord, and the men are not to impose anything against the will of the abbess, but do everything at her bidding. Heloise's Paraclete was not subject to a male monastery.

20. Abelard makes the weakness of the nuns' sex an argument for their studies, to keep them out of trouble: since nuns can sweat less than monks in hard labor, they can therefore fall more easily into temptation from leisure and the weakness of their nature.

21. Abelard's covering letter to Heloise ends with an acknowledgment of the range of their relations—"Be well in the Lord, his handmaid, dear to me once in the world,

now dearest in Christ: wife then in the flesh, sister now in spirit, and consort in the profession of holy purpose" (Cousin 1.350, R 34)—as if embracing their common responsibility and purpose. The sermons are in Cousin 1.350ff. and PL178, c.379ff. I will come back to them at the end of the chapter, where I take up the other works Abelard wrote for the Paraclete, as part of the overall view of women he offered the nuns at Heloise's inspiration.

22. Ambrose's three letters to Marcellina are in PL16, ep.20, c.994–1002; ep.22, c.1019–26; ep.41, c.1113–21.

23. Adam de Perseigne, *Lettres*, ed. Jean Bouvet (Paris: Editions du Cerf, 1960). I have seen only the first volume. Some of the letters are also in PL211. Marie of Champagne was his protector, according to Bouvet, but I know of nothing that he wrote for her. She died in 1198; the letter to Blanche of Champagne is after 1201.

24. The tone of Adam's letter to a countess who requested guidance for a moral life of piety and good works within marriage—"you compelled me to describe this formula to you"—is more didactic (ep.15). She apparently had chosen to marry when she might not have: "Otherwise your marriage cannot be excused, especially since it was agreed to not by command but by indulgence." While it is necessary for her to please her husband, he is the carnal husband of her flesh, God the spiritual husband of her soul; and while God cedes the law of her body to her carnal husband, he claims her soul for himself. Adam attacks the vanity of "women of our time" who have long tails like little foxes from the plunder of the poor and advises her to adorn the part of her which married Christ with virtues.

25. To Furia, a relative of Paula and Eustochium, he said: "if only men would imitate the accomplishments of women" ("utinam praeconia feminarum imitarentur viri," ep.54.2).

26. On the importance of this translation, see Henri de Lubac's introduction in Origen, *On First Principles*, trans. G. W. Butterworth (New York: Harper and Row, 1966), xlii, xlv. The translation was not then made public, but it survived and is now the only source for correction of Rufinus, since the original is not extant. Jerome also addressed to Pammachius (Paula's son-in-law) and Marcella one of his counterdefenses to Rufinus's subsequent attack (PL23, c.415–514), making no particular distinction of audience between his closest male and female friends. Butterworth cites a letter of Jerome to Hedybia (120.10) to elucidate a passage in Origen about souls before birth, 228. And Brown says Jerome's translation of Origen's *Homilies on the Song of Songs*, which was dedicated to pope Damasus, was in fact intended for his "new circle of female spiritual charges"; see Brown, *The Body and Society*, 367. On Jerome's version of Origenism and on the role of women in the controversy, see Elizabeth Clark, *The Origenist Controversy: The Cultural Construction of an Early Christian Debate* (Princeton: Princeton University Press, 1992).

27. Jerome mentions Paula and her daughter and granddaughter by name in the prefaces addressed to them: the younger Paula and Eustochium in the prologues to his commentary on Nahum, CCSL 76A.526, Haggai, 76A.713, Sophonias, 76A.655, Daniel, PL28 c.1360, and Esther, PL28 c.1503. Even in those addressed to Pammachius, Paula's son-in-law, Jerome tells him that Paula had requested them twenty-two years before (Prologue to Hosea, CCSL 76.5) and asks him to accept as a pious heir what he had promised to "your holy and venerable relative Paula" (Joel, 76.160). Jerome does not distinguish between the scholarly needs of men and women in this circle. In the preface to Joshua, Jerome says that after the death of Paula he could not deny these books to Eustochium, particularly since the admirable and holy Pammachius also urged him to do it (PL28 c.506).

28. *Origenes Werke*, vol. 9, *Die Homilien zu Lukas in der Übersetzung des Hieronymus und Die Griechischen Reste der Homilien und des Lukas-Kommentars*, ed. Max Rauer (Berlin: Akademie Verlage, 1959).

29. Jerome began his commentary on Ecclesiasticus for Blesilla but finished it five years after her death; see Kelly, *Jerome,* 146. For Paula, whose fluency in Hebrew Jerome admired—he had struggled over it from adolescence, he says, while she could sing the psalms and speak it without a Latin accent (ep.108.26)—he did a commentary on Hebrew letters in the psalms for her to consult if she forgot anything (ep.30).

30. Kelly assumes from the preface that it was begun while Paula was still alive, though finished after her death, 284. Incidentally, we know that Jerome sent his recent translation of Job to Marcella, because he told Pammachius to borrow it from her (Kelly, *Jerome,* 189).

31. Cf. Kelly, *Jerome,* 283-84. In the preface to Joshua, Jerome says: "After the death of holy Paula, whose life is an example of virtue, we determined to take pains with these books, which I could not deny to Eustochium, virgin of Christ, while the spirit rules these limbs . . . especially when that admirable and holy man Pammachius importunes with his letters" (PL28, c.506).

32. The remaining three were sent to bishops Chromatius (Habakkuk), and Exsuperius (Zechariah) and to Minervius and Alexander (Malachi), CCSL, 76A, putting the women as audience and patron of his works on the same level as the church hierarchy.

33. In book 2 on Micah, Jerome complains that envy never ceases and begs Paula (the younger) and Eustochium by name to close their ears to its barkings and help by their prayers to open his mouth to be suited to speaking about scripture. He defends his use of Origen against those who complain that he contaminates the writings of the ancients "when I imitate him who, I do not doubt, pleases you and all the prudent"; if it is a crime to translate Greek "benedicta," let them accuse Ennius, Virgil, Plautus, Caecilius, Terence, Cicero, and other eloquent men, even "our Hilary" would be guilty of theft for his thousands of verses from Origen on the psalms (CCSL76, p.473). It is tempting to wonder how many of the people who object to his use of Origen are also the ones who object to his writing for women.

34. Popes too enlisted women in the fight against heresy in this period, particularly women of the imperial family. Pulcheria was deeply involved with pope Leo I in the struggle against Nestor and was particularly opposed to Nestor's denying the Virgin Mary the title Theotokos, mother of God. In the course of the controversy, Cyril of Alexandria sent her and her sisters a treatise adducing more than two hundred New Testament texts to prove that Mary was the mother of God.

35. Augustine wrote to a priest asking him to follow up on the debate in case Italica was "too modest to undertake that sort of controversy on someone else's objection" and to be sure those who disagreed with what he wrote to her write directly to him (ep.92a). That is, the letter to Italica is a key statement of Augustine's views and the priest is to make sure others see it. Chrysostom had encouraged Italica to fight publicly for her faith, telling her that while in secular affairs women and men had separate spheres, women the home, men the outside world, this was not the case in divine battles and the labors undertaken for the cause of the church. There, he says, women could overcome men (ep.170).

36. On the relation of the letter to Paulina—"which is really a treatise," according to Dewart—to Augustine's views on vision and the resurrection, see Joanne E. McW. Dewart, *Death and Resurrection* (Wilmington: Michael Glazier, 1986), 177-81.

37. The related works which Alcuin says Augustine mentioned in his retractions are about the nature of the soul, the immortality of the soul, the question of two souls, and the origin of the soul. For the letters, see *Alcuini Epistolae,* ed. Ernestus Dümmler (Berlin: Weidmann, 1895), MGH, EpKar, 2.

38. The biographer of Bertila, the first abbess of Chelles, claimed that "kings from across the seas from various parts of Saxony beseeched her to send her disciples as teachers and to establish similar monasteries for men and women" (*Vita Bertilae* 6,

MGH SRM 6.106; cited by Wemple, *Women in Frankish Society: Marriage and the Cloister, 500-900* [Philadelphia: University of Pennsylvania Press, 1981], 177).

39. This topos of intellectual humility can also be used by men. The abbot of Zwiefalten wrote to Hildegard, asking for a simpler expression of her wisdom suited to "the capacity of my little wit" ("pro capacitate ingenioli mei," VA 244), and Abelard offered his hymns to the nuns with requests for their prayers, now that he had done what they asked, despite their small wit *(ingenioli)*.

40. The empress Judith fought hard to assure her son a heritage despite the claims of his older brothers, her stepsons, and wielded considerable influence over her husband despite the opposition of others. She was blamed for the conflicts between her husband and his three older sons and was the object of fierce antifeminist attacks. Stafford notes, "The virulence of the abuse is a tribute to her importance" (*Queens,* 19); see also Elizabeth Ward, "Agobard of Lyons and Paschasius Radbertus as Critics of the Empress Judith," *Women in the Church.* In the preface to Esther, Rabanus says, "God who excited the mind of that queen to loose the calamities of her people, deign to lead you, working with similar zeal, to eternal joys" (PL29, c.635). Both commentaries are in PL29, Judith, c.539-92, Esther, 635-70.

41. The prophet Maria (Miriam), sister of Aaron and Moses (Exod.15), is brought in in connection with Judith singing the Lord's praises (ch.16, c.584). Semiramis is frequently mentioned positively in histories written for women; see chapter 3.

42. The reader referred to ("studiosus lector") may be any reader, but the knowledge of divine mysteries is specifically referred to the queen: "Tu autem, o nobilissima regina, cum sacramenta divina in expositis bene agnoveris." Rabanus later rededicated the commentary on Esther to empress Ermengard, adding a poem in which he compares her care for others directly to Esther's (ep.46), which suggests that he was seeking favor in both cases rather than responding to requests, but in Judith's case he seeks it by encouraging her in her cause as if it were God's will.

43. I find it particularly interesting that a man who though he engaged in it himself considered philosophy inadequate at best for learning the important truths should encourage intellectual investigation in a woman. For his letters, see *Die Briefe des Petrus Damiani,* ed. Kurt Reindel MGH, BDKz4 (Munich: MGH, 1983), projected 4 vols.

44. Abelard's language in the *Historia* suggests that he is virtually in despair, a very dangerous moral state in medieval theology: "quanta desperatione perturbarer . . . proferre non possum" (MS 12.196), "penitus desperatus" (198), "profugus ac iam desperatus" (201), "in tantam lapsus sum desperationem" (203), "desperabam penitus" (205).

45. It is interesting that Heloise admits to guilt about her current frame of mind, though she later speaks of her innocence, presumably while the love affair with Abelard was going on. There is no one, she says, even those who envied her once for being the object of his poems and songs, who does not feel compassion for her loss, because, though very guilty, she is also very innocent, if one considers not the act but the intention, "the spirit in which it was done" (R 115).

46. Penelope Johnson suggests that Heloise asked Abelard for the Rule in order to manipulate him into renewed contact, rather than to obtain his help, since she continued to run the Paraclete herself though his Rule specified that an abbot should preside over the nuns (*Equal in Monastic Profession,* 244). Abelard does put the convent under the supervision of a man, unlike Fontevrault, which was run by the abbess, but he also suggests that the man should be like a steward in a king's palace, serving the queen, doing nothing without consulting her, responding swiftly to her requests; the monks in the brother house were to profess their vows and promise obedience to her as well (MS 18, 259-60).

47. Mary McLaughlin notes that in the works Abelard wrote for the Paraclete, he

"was to formulate most comprehensively his approach to the ideals and problems of contemporary monasticism." She also suggests that "his insistence on the dependence of the Paraclete on him, and more generally on the need of women for the care of 'spiritual men,' may seem only to underscore the extent of his dependence on them, and this in turn makes more understandable the lengths to which he was prepared to go in exalting their sex and life, in exhorting them to assume the elevated and exemplary role for which he had cast them." See Mary McLaughlin, "Peter Abelard and the Dignity of Women," 317.

48. See note 17.

49. Abelard's responses are published with the questions (Cousin, 1.237-94). M. Cipollone discusses the similarity of mental outlook in Heloise's letters and the *Problemata*; see "In margine al *Problemata Heloissae*," *Aevum* 64 (1990), 227-44. For a learned analysis, I look forward to Mary McLaughlin's study of the *Problemata* in her forthcoming *Heloise and the Paraclete: Ductrix et Magistra.*

50. Eileen Kearney notes that this is Abelard's only extant commentary on the Old Testament; see Kearney, "Peter Abelard as Biblical Commentator: A Study of the *Expositio in Hexaemeron*," *Trierer theologische studien* 38 (1980), 199-210. Kearney also points to Abelard's attention to theological questions of sin and personal salvation as a unifying theme in the commentary.

51. This is particularly tantalizing given the philosophical discussions of the (feminine) *anima mundi* and its inevitable connections with the third person of the trinity in the twelfth century. See Tullio Gregory, *Anima Mundi: La filosofia di Guglielmo di Conches e la scuola di Chartres* (Florence: Sansoni, 1955) and B. Newman, *From Virile Woman*, ch. 6. Abelard's sermon on Pentecost (18, 1.484ff.) emphasizes the sisters' devotion to the holy spirit, wishing they could praise God in all tongues as the apostles did, but at least they are inspired to the three principal languages of doctrine (490).

52. The hymns have been reedited and published by Joseph Szövérffy in Peter Abelard, *Hymnarius Paraclitensis* (Albany: Classical Folia, 1975), 2 vols. A rather free translation into rhymed English verse was done by Sister Jane Patricia, *The Hymns of Abelard in English Verse* (Lanham, Md.: University Press of America, 1986). Szövérffy notes that for Abelard women are "the strong personalities, the superior beings who often surpass and put man to shame"; he suggests that the way women overcome the handicap of their part in the fall makes Abelard a "near-unique phenomenon in medieval hymnody" (vol. 1, p. 114). Since Szövérffy does not give line numbers, my references in the text are to poem and stanza number, all in vol. 2.

53. The phrase is "illarum sanctarum, quae virgines vel martyres minime exstiterunt," Szövérffy, 10, which Jane Patricia translates as "those women who as virgins and martyrs were less conspicuous," Radice as "saintly women who had been neither virgins nor martyrs." Like Radice, I take *minime* to mean "not at all."

54. He composed them so there would be one melody and one rhythm for the nocturnal hymns, another for the diurnal; the nocturnal tell the events of the days, the diurnal their meaning (allegorical or moral), so the obscurity of the night's story is removed in the light of the day's exposition.

55. Abelard makes the same connection in an Easter sermon, 13. It is interesting that he celebrates Miriam, a woman who had saved her brother Moses when he was a baby but whose role as a prophet and leader is played down in the Old Testament and indeed snuffed out when she corrects Moses, while Aaron, who did the same, is barely rebuked. Mary Magdalene's role was also played down after the gospels.

56. Jephthah's daughter was also a victim of her father's rashness. Abelard wrote a *planctus* on her, the lament of virgins of Israel for the daughter sacrificed by her

father; he also wrote one on Dina, a victim of rape (Cousin, 1.334, 335-37). Peter Dronke argues persuasively for the connection between the emotions Abelard describes for these figures and events of his and Heloise's life; see Dronke, *Poetic Individuality in the Middle Ages: New Departures in Poetry* (Oxford: Clarendon, 1970), 114ff.

57. The sermons are in Cousin 1.350ff. and PL178, c.379ff.

58. In the sermon on the purification of Mary, Abelard says that when woman was created from man's rib and flesh was put in place of the bone, woman was made stronger, man weaker (397).

59. In the (third) sermon on the circumcision (370-81), Abelard speaks of circumcision as the despoiling *(exspoliatio)* of the flesh, signaling a violent giving up of the old man and putting on the new, while baptism sanctifies both women and men by a gentler washing away of sin. Abelard seems to imply that taking flesh from the male member symbolically conquers lust, since human lust is based in that member—his own castration making him painfully aware of the fact. He also saw his own lust as a much stronger drive than Heloise's.

60. There is, perhaps, a hint of Mary's militancy in Abelard's later comment on her persistence as a mediator with her son: she keeps asking until she gets what she wants, whether at the marriage of Cana or in the salvation of Theophilus (526).

61. Abelard is very sensitive to the ignominy that comes to a woman who bears a child out of wedlock. He mentions this need to have Mary married to protect Christ and her from infamy in the sermon on the birth of Christ (368).

3. WOMEN AND THE WRITING OF HISTORY

1. When the direct male line dies out in a family before the female, women can trace their ancestry to earlier kings, a claim they can pass to their sons, whose fathers' families may well be relative newcomers to their position, having power but little prestige.

2. Cf. the "planned colloquy of ladies" ("institutum colloquium dominarum") mentioned earlier. Even when men were available, they sometimes sent their wives to negotiate for them, perhaps because they could compromise in ways the men could not without losing face, perhaps because they were on better terms or had connections with the others involved.

3. See *The Alexiad of Anna Comnena*, trans. E. R. A. Sewter (Harmondsworth: Penguin, 1969). Anna wrote, she said, because her father did not deserve to be forgotten, but she was also dissatisfied with the current regime.

4. Janet L. Nelson, "Perceptions du pouvoir chez les historiens du haut moyen âge," *La femme au moyen-âge*, ed. Michel Rouche and Jean Heuclin (Mauberge: Maulde et Renou-Sambre, 1990), 75-83, argues for the possibility that women wrote certain anonymous works. Elisabeth van Houts, "Women and the Writing of History in the Early Middle Ages: The Case of Abbess Matilda of Essen and Aethelweard," *Early Medieval Europe* 1 (1992), 53-68, argues for the authorship of Nordhausen nuns for the two lives of queen Matilda, and the instigation of their abbess Richburga behind both. Jane Schulenberg, "Saints' Lives as a Source for the History of Women, 500-1100," in *Medieval Women and the Sources of Medieval History*, ed. Joel T. Rosenthal (Athens: University of Georgia Press, 1990), 290-91, notes that the first life of a female saint was probably written by a nun of the same convent, but a male author was often preferred for the official life; see also Rosamund McKitterick, "Frauen und Schriftlichkeit im Frühenmittelalter," *Weiblicher Lebensgestaltung im Frühenmittelalter*, ed. H. W. Goetz. I am not covering saints' lives as a genre, an enormous subject in itself, though a few turn up in later chapters.

5. See Bernard Guenée, *Histoire et culture historique dans l'occident médiévale*

(Paris: Aubier Montaigne, 1980), for a detailed view of the nature, sources, and purposes of medieval histories and distinctions between historic genres. He notes that clerics who wrote them were (ostensibly) concerned with the care of souls, therefore more intent on effectiveness than on truth, and sometimes cited less reliable sources precisely because they would be more effective. Guenée also points out that history was used for legal claims and propaganda as well as for instruction and entertainment, and was more likely to be based on written sources than on direct experience, which could be discounted as aberrant.

6. Bede does say that the Picts got wives from the Scots on condition that in case of a dispute, they would choose their king from the female rather than the male royal line (*Historia ecclesiastica* 1.1), an ethnic rather than gender ploy, and the issue does not come up again.

7. I stop with Latin histories in the twelfth century, but of course from the late twelfth century on there was a flood of histories translated into French for women or composed in the vernacular at the request of women. I will mention some in the next chapter. Others include Aelred of Rievaulx's life of Edward, translated into French by a nun of Barking perhaps for her abbess and again later for Eleanor, queen of Henry III; Gaimar's *Estoire des Engleis,* commissioned by a noble woman, Constance Fitz-gilbert; Wace's *Roman de Brut;* an anonymous history which I have not been able to find, the *Estoire de Waldes,* probably from the 1190s, perhaps translated from English, done apparently for a woman (the orders of a "dame" and the request of a "duce amie" are described by M. Dominica Legge, *Anglo-Norman Literature and Its Background* [Oxford: Clarendon, 1963], 143-44). Later chronicles dedicated to or requested by queens include Froissart, who says he carried his chronicle to England and presented it to the queen, Philyppe of Hainault, who received it "to my great profit and advance-ment" (prologue, cited by Karl J. Holzknecht, *Literary Patronage in the Middle Ages* [New York: Octagon, 1966, first pub. 1923], 158); Joinville's memoirs of Louis IX at the request of his queen and dedicated to her son (Holzknecht, 134–35); and the French chronicle by the Dominican Nicholas Trevet for Mary, daughter of Edward I and a nun of Amesbury, which was used by Chaucer (M. Dominica Legge, *Anglo-Norman in the Cloisters* [Edinburgh: University Press, 1950], 77). Berenguela de León, sister of Blanche of Castile, daughter and heir of Alfonso VIII (granddaughter of Eleanor of Aquitaine and Henry II through her mother), commissioned a history of Spain *(Crónica de España)* from her friend and confessor, Lucas, bishop of Túy, in the 1240s; see Miriam Shadis, "Motherhood, Lineage, and Royal Power in Medieval Spain and France: Berenguela de León and Blanche de Castile," (Ph.D. diss., Duke University, 1994), for a very useful study of these two queen mothers and the power they exercised in Castile and France.

8. For a discussion of Paul's relations to Adelperga and her family and his histo-ries, the *Historia Romana* and the *History of the Lombards,* see Walter Goffart, *The Narrators of Barbarian History,* A.D. *550-800* (Princeton: Princeton University Press, 1988). Goffart, 432, suggests that the two histories would have constituted a "contin-uous history of Italy from pre-Roman to Frankish times," interpreting the Lombard segment so as to "suggest the course he thought best for the future of Italy at large and Lombard Benevento in particular." Adelperga was still alive when the *History of the Lombards* was written; it was apparently aimed at her son Grimoald, though there is no dedication.

9. Paul's first extant poem is a brief (thirty-six line) history of the world from the beginning to the Lombard present. It praises the peaceful reign of Adelperga's father and brother, the strength of her husband and her royal birth, and wishes them a happy end. It is structured as an acrostic, spelling out "Adelperga pia." For the text, see Karl Neff, *Die Gedichte des Paulus Diaconus,* Quellen und Untersuchungen zur lateinischen Philologie des Mittelalters 3 (Munich: C. H. Beck, 1908), 6-10.

10. *Pauli Diaconi Historia Romana*, ed. Amedeo Crivellucci (Rome: Tipografia del Senato, 1914).

11. Paul did eventually write the *History of the Lombards* but did not carry it beyond Liutprand, who died in 744. Goffart argues that Paul intended to write two more books but probably died before he could complete them.

12. Ernesto Sestan, "Qualche aspetto della personalità di Paolo Diacono nella sua 'Historia Romana,'" *Italia Medievale* (Napoli: ESI, 1966), 66, suggests that the anecdotes about women are all to suit a "gusto tipicamente femminile." Goffart, 351, noting that there are many women in the *History of the Lombards* and epitaphs of Carolingian ladies in Paul's book on the bishops of Metz, thinks the taste may be as much Paul's own or the public's. It is impossible to know, but I think it not unlikely that the attention to women in the HR and the HL owes something to Adelperga's presence; it is also not inconceivable that his connections with Carolingian women led him to note them even in the history of the bishops.

13. The phrase may indicate disapproval of the suicide and murder (Paul uses "arte muliebri" negatively in the history), but at the same time he shows admiration for the women's courage in battle, perhaps even in death. Pagan suicide is not a sin; indeed, in the case of Lucretia it can be high virtue, or of Hasdrubal's wife, heroic devotion, when she throws herself and her children "femineo furore" into the fire of the burning temple, where her husband had taken refuge after his defeat by Scipio (HR 4.12). Paul does not criticize the beautiful Digna, who threw herself from a tower into the water below rather than be mocked or dishonored by the conquering enemy (14.10). On the other hand, Cleopatra's suicide seems more like cowardice, after she fails to seduce the emperor, as she had others, in her desire to rule Rome "cupiditate muliebri" (7.7).

14. The elder Galla Placidia is a respected figure, not only in Paul's history but also in historic documents. Contemporary popes trusted her as a defender of the faith, and a later pope quoted a letter of hers as a model for a later empress to follow. The letter may have been dictated by a pope or member of his staff, but it is quoted as hers, a pope citing a woman's words as an authority. For this and other correspondence involving women mentioned in this chapter, see my forthcoming guide.

15. Amalasuntha's letters, announcing her choice of her cousin to Justinian and the Roman senate, and his, first praising her learning and her gifts for government and later excusing himself, as well as responses from Justinian and his empress, are included in the collection of Cassiodorus, who was her secretary (and perhaps her father's).

16. See Elizabeth Ward, "Caesar's Wife: The Career of the Empress Judith, 819–29," in *Charlemagne's Heir: New Perspectives on the Reign of Louis the Pious (814–40)*, ed. Peter Godman and Roger Collins (Oxford: Clarendon, 1990), for details of Judith's patronage and her son's political position.

17. For Ermold's text, *In Honorem Hludowici Ermoldi Nigelli Exulis Elegiacum Carmen*, see *Poème sur Louis le Pieux et épitres au roi Pépin*, ed. and trans. Edmond Faral (Paris: Champion, 1932). For Walafrid Strabo, see Ernestus Dümmler, ed., MGH *Poetae Latini*, 2.

18. Louis died in 840, and Judith did bring an army to support her son's cause at the decisive battle of Fontenoy in 841. But she had a falling out with him and died in 843 before the division she had worked for was accomplished, making Charles king of the West Franks.

19. Michael D. Reeve, "Freculf of Lisieux and Florus," *Revue d'Histoire des Textes* 19 (1989), describes Freculf's compilation as "the first medieval history of the world," 385. The work ends in the seventh century with pope Boniface and the "six universal synods."

20. In the first book of his *Chronicon*, Freculf mentions women from the Bible, including Eve and Sara, Deborah, Esther, and Judith; figures from classical myth, like

Procne and Philomela, Proserpine, Europa; women who, like the Amazons and Heli-carnis, fought, and who helped Xerxes (joining his principal leaders, so that female caution was seen in man, virile boldness in women, *Chronicon* 1.4.2); women like Lucretia and Hasdrubal's wife who chose death; even Alexandra, queen of the Jews, who cleverly manipulated the succession of her younger son (1.6.14). Whether Freculf included the women because he intended to dedicate the second part to Judith from the beginning, added them later when he decided to, or included them because of his own interests it may be impossible to determine.

21. Freculf relates several stories that Paul also told, about Placida, who was sent with her son when he was made caesar in Italy by her relative the Eastern emperor (2.5.8), and about Amalasuntha, chosen regent by her father but murdered by the cousin she had associated in her rule (2.5.21).

22. Even more extreme is the story from Josephus about Mary, who killed and ate her own son during the famine and destruction of Jerusalem; she is presented as a self-conscious exemplum, a frenzy for the pillagers, a fable for the ages, the only one so far missing in the destruction of the Jews ("praedonibus furor, saeculis fabula, quae sola deerat cladibus Judaeorum," 2.1.23).

23. For an overview of women in the imperial family and the monasteries con-nected with them, see K. J. Leyser, *Rule and Conflict in an Early Medieval Society, Ottonian Saxony* (London: Edward Arnold, 1979), chapters 5 and 6.

24. Widukind's monastery, Corvey, was an establishment of noblemen, so it is probable, as his editor suggests, that Widukind was related to the royal family. He certainly seems to take pride in the history of his namesake, who brought such military glory to the Saxons. For the text, see *Quellen zur Geschichte der Sächsischen Kaiserzeit,* ed. and trans. Albert Bauer and Reinhold Rau (Darmstadt: Wissenschaftliche Buch-gesellschaft, 1971).

25. Comparing Widukind's concerns with those of his contemporary Hrotsvit, Ernst Karpf notes that Widukind is interested in the roles of the people and of the institutional church in relation to kingship, while Hrotsvit emphasizes the royal family and consecration without reference to the clergy. See Karpf, *Herrscherlegitimation und Reichsbegriff in der Ottonischen Geschichtsschreibung des zehnten Jarhhunderts* (Stutt-gart: Franz Steiner, 1985).

26. The text of the *Annales Quedlinburgenses* can be found in MGH, SS 3.22–90, printed together with the *Annales Hildesheimenses,* the *Lamberti Annales,* and the *Annales Weissemburgenses,* which give much less attention to women in the same period and the same story. Only the AQ mentions the deaths of various women in Charlemagne's family and of duke Otto's mother, Oda (913), or gives most of the details about the Ottonian women and their political participation. There is implied criticism of Amalberga, daughter of the king of the Franks, who brought a costly war on her husband by refusing to surrender her claims to her lower-born half-brother, a story also told by Widukind (1.9), but one wonders if the AQ version does not also suggest the unfairness of ignoring women's legitimate claims.

27. It might be mentioned that Adelaide's connections with royalty were extraordi-nary, even for an empress. As Stafford points out in *Queens,* 116, she was the daughter, sister, and aunt of three kings of Burgundy, the wife, mother, and grandmother of three emperors of Germany, sister-in-law, mother-in-law, and grandmother of three French kings, not to say widow of a king of Lombard Italy.

28. Sophie's predecessor as abbess of Essen was Matilda, the granddaughter of Otto and his first wife, Edith, by their son Liudulf, who also commissioned a history of her family.

29. For the text of Hrotsvit's epics, see *Hrotsvithae Opera,* ed. H. Homeyer (Pader-born: Schöningh, 1970), and *Hrosvithae Liber Tertius,* text and trans. M. B. Bergman (Covington, Ky.: Sisters of St. Benedict, 1943). Abbess Gerberga was educated in Saint

Emmeram and may well have been tutored in Greek; see Katharina Wilson, *Hrotsvit of Gandersheim: The Ethics of Authorial Stance* (Leiden: Brill, 1988), 150. Theophanu, the wife of her cousin Otto II, was Byzantine, and there were various contacts with the eastern empire. Wilson, 114, notes that Hrotsvit is the only Saxon/Ottonian historian to depict female members of the dynasty in some detail and the first historian to provide intimate details of Adelaide's escape.

30. I should note that histories written by men for abbesses, such as Widukind's for the abbess of Quedlinburg and AEthelweard's for the abbess of Essen, give less attention to women in secular authority than the histories written for secular women. It may be that although abbesses may have a great deal of secular authority, they do not normally have to fight to get or hold it in the way secular women do, and therefore they do not need the same kind of propaganda. But it may also be that two examples are simply not enough to go on.

31. A number of women, queen Matilda, Hathumoda, Oda, Edith, and Adelaide, were reputed to be saints, and in a later generation, both Henry II and his wife Cunegund. For a study of these "saints" and their place in Ottonian history, see Patrick Corbet, *Les saints ottoniens: Sainteté dynastique, sainteté royale et sainteté féminine autour de l'an Mil* (Sigmaringen: Jan Thorbecke, 1986).

32. Corbet, 46–47, points out that this marriage was a coup for Otto, allying him with the most prestigious dynasty in western Europe at the time, giving him a distinct edge over his brother Henry, who was favored by their mother.

33. This episode of the two sisters being sent for the king's choice is repeated in many of the histories discussed in this section.

34. Oda's death at 107 years is mentioned in the AQ: "Domina Oda, mater scilicet ipsius [duke Otto], obiit anno 107 vitae suae" (913). Corbet points out (117) that Oda was probably a nun, since she is described as "in sanctimoniali habitu constituta" in an official document. He conjectures that Hrotsvit never mentions it because it might have interfered with Oda's more prestigious position as patron; it is perhaps more likely that she could expect her audience to assume that Oda became a nun during her retirement in the monastery without having to tell them.

35. See Van Houts, "Women and the Writing of History," 57. Van Houts says the list is only known from an entry in the memorial book of St. Gall, but it is an important source, "the only evidence for the names of the mother and sisters of Queen Matilda, wife of King Henry I. Thus, the nuns of Gandersheim were interested very early on in the women who, through marriage, joined the Liudolfing clan."

36. The *Vita Mathildis reginae antiquior*, ed. Rudolf Köpke, is in MGH, SS, 10 (1849), 573–82; hereafter cited as VMRA. The *Vita Mathildis reginae [posterior]*, ed. Georg H. Pertz, is in MGH, SS, 4, (1841), 282–302; cited as VMRP. The older, shorter life was a source for the later one. See Gerd Althoff, "Causa Scribendi und Darstellungsabsicht: Die Lebensbeschreibungen der Königin Mathilde und andere Beispiele," in *Litterae Medii Aevi: Festschrift für Johanne Autenrieth*, ed. Michael Borgolt and Herrad Spilling (Sigmaringen: Jan Thorbecke, 1988), for an explanation of the two lives in connection with the arrival of new empresses. Corbet discusses the place of the two works in Ottonian hagiography and their likely authorship. He considers abbess Richburga the likely author of the shorter life, and leaves open the authorship of the longer, noting that it might be a nun or a cleric, 156–57, though he favors someone from the clerical élite with royal connections, 232. Van Houts, 59, attributes both lives to nuns, though as she says, there is no definite proof.

37. See VMRA, 8, "few of either sex could imitate her," and VMRP, preface, recommending the deeds of his ancestors, particularly his great-grandmother Matilda, whose shining life is to be imitated and whose virtue is all the more praiseworthy in that her sex is more fragile. Matilda's life is to be read as both hagiography and Ottonian history, as Corbet points out, 121. Corbet also notes (265) that royal mon-

asteries for women taught women not only spiritual things, but their social role and family responsibility as well.

38. The VMRP notes (10) that she was so modest in her life as a widow that many thought her a virgin. But there was no question of abstinence in her married life. Indeed, both lives tell a probably spurious story of her abduction from the convent where she was being educated under the care of her abbess grandmother by Henry, who went to look at his father's choice for him secretly and was so taken by her he could not wait. The literary elaboration is obvious (Henry was not a romantic youth but a previously married man with a son, Thangmar), but the intent seems to be to emphasize the strong love that bound him to her.

39. For the text and identity of the principals, see *Chronicon AEthelweardi: The Chronicle of AEthelweard*, ed. and trans. A. Campbell (London: Thomas Nelson, 1962). AEthelweard follows the *Anglo-Saxon Chronicle* closely up to 892, then adds and omits more freely; see Van Houts (64), who argues, convincingly it seems to me, for Matilda's active role in having the work done, in opposition to those who read AEthelweard's dedication as implying it was his idea.

40. Campbell, the *Chronicon*'s editor, notes (xix) that AEthelweard is the only independent authority for the identification of the wife of Baldwin II of Flanders as a daughter of Alfred the Great (William of Malmesbury repeats it) and for the names of her two daughters, though she and her sons are named elsewhere. The counts of Flanders were also descended from Charlemagne, through his great-granddaughter Judith, who married Baldwin I.

41. A number of letters are extant in the correspondence between Matilda (and her mother Beatrice) and Gregory, and others are alluded to, which show the extent and intensity of their relations, his reliance on their support, and the resulting hostility of the German bishops. When Matilda thought of entering a monastery, Gregory insisted she was needed in the world; see ep.1.47, dated 1074 (*Das Register Gregors VII*, ed. Erich Caspar, MGH Epistolae Selectae, 1920-23). Matilda continued to support the papacy under Urban II and Paschal II.

42. The marriages, to Godfrey/Geoffrey of Lorraine, son of her stepfather, whom she left, and to the much younger Guelph who left her, were both political and short-lived and do not seem to have impeded Matilda's official roles. The child, a son who was born of the first marriage, did not live. Matilda made her own choice of heir: first she chose the son of one of her supporters, Guido Guerra, and finally the young emperor, Henry V. She had donated her entire allodial inheritance to the apostolic see, though reserving the rights of disposal during her lifetime and that of Henry V. That donation was to play a part in imperial-papal conflicts for centuries; Dante's contemporaries, his earliest commentators and the chronicler Giovanni Villani, speak of the Matildine lands, and Dante invokes her memory in the Matelda of the Earthly Paradise, according to his early commentators. She would thus incarnate Dante's ideal of a secular leader guiding to the ideal life on earth, which he expounds at the end of the *De monarchia*.

43. *Vita Mathildis, Carmine Scripta a Donizone Presbytero*, ed. Luigi Simeoni (Bologna: Zanichelli, 1930-34). References will be given by book and line number.

44. Donizo may also have known some of the Carolingian poems in praise of their rulers, or even Hrotsvit's *Gesta Ottonis*. He tells the story of Adelaide's escape, though with differences.

45. Tedaldus is one of three sons, and he in turn had three sons, a motif that contributes to the sense of divine favor to the family.

46. According to Simeoni, the *Vita*'s editor, Beatrice's grandfather Theoderic was the son of Beatrice, Hugh Capet's sister, herself the daughter of Hedwig, daughter of Henry I of Germany and sister of Otto I. Beatrice's parents were Frederick, duke of Upper Lorraine, and Matilda, daughter of Herman, duke of Swabia. Beatrice and her

sister Sophia were brought up by her godmother and aunt, the empress Gisela, her mother's sister, wife of Conrad II, after the death of their father in 1033.

47. Simeoni notes (56, note to 2.35) that besides the normal diplomatic contacts, the second wife of Henry IV, who took refuge with Matilda, was Russian, and returned to her family in Kiev, that Henry's mother Agnes was from Poitiers, that Matilda's first husband's lands included Frisia, and both she and her mother held lands in Lorraine through marriage.

48. Donizo certainly emphasizes Matilda's role in organizing this meeting, perhaps exaggerating it, as Simeoni suggests (58, notes to 2.67–70, 71–75), but her importance as a supporter of the papacy was recognized by contemporary historians; see below, n. 50.

49. There would be a misunderstanding later between Matilda and Conrad, which Donizo feels obliged to mention but which was resolved before his death (2.917ff.). Hostile sources attributed the death to Matilda, which Donizo does not mention.

50. Ekkehard called her the wealthiest, most famous woman of his times and most distinguished in virtues; see *Ekkehardi Chronicon*, MGH SS 6, 249. Hugh of Flavigny said she "alone at this time was found among women, who scorned the king's power, who countered his cunning and force even with military conflict, so was deservedly called 'virago,' who surpassed even men by the virtue of her spirit" (*Chronicon*, MGH, SS, 8.463). Bardone in his life of St. Anselm said: "The single and only one who remains in the faith, with zeal for God and obedient to pope Gregory, is the duke and marchioness, Matilda" (MGH, SS, 12.16).

51. I owe this reference to Megan McLaughlin, from a paper she read at the International Congress on Medieval Studies at Kalamazoo and shared with me, "Rethinking the Politics of Reform: Sex, Gender, and Power in the Eleventh Century." See also Walter Berschin, in *Bonizo von Sutri, Leben und Werke* (Berlin: de Gruyter, 1972); the text is in MGH, LL, 1.568. Both McLaughlin and Berschin also point out, however, that a later work of Bonizo's, *Liber de vita Christiana*, declares that women should not hold military or judicial powers, offering examples from classical and medieval history and noting that if Paul did not want women to teach, he certainly did not intend them to rule. It is assumed that the later work is an attack on Matilda, but what caused the break between them is not known.

52. *Encomium Emmae Reginae,* ed. and trans. Alistair Campbell (London: Royal Historical Society, 1949), Camden Third Series, vol. 72.

53. The author mentions the parents' special love for Harthacnut, whom they kept with them as the future heir of the kingdom, while they sent the other legitimate sons ("alios liberales filios," ibid., 2.18.5) to be educated by her brother in Normandy, as if all three were the children of Cnut and Emma. Even if this is meant to imply that Cnut adopted Emma's sons by AEthelred and therefore they could also be considered his heirs, it involves a radical twist of history and gives a false impression of the sons' relative ages. Harold is said to be not the son of a concubine, as is generally thought, but the son of a handmaid, furtively placed in the concubine's room (3.1).

54. The political nature of the work has been accepted since 1964, when Sten Körner raised the issue, according to Felice Lifshitz, who gives a useful summary of different arguments offered in the quarter century since in "The *Encomium Emmae Reginae*: A 'Political Pamphlet' of the Eleventh Century?" *Studies in Medieval History, Journal of the Haskins Society,* 1 (1989), 39–50. See also Eleanor Searle, "Emma the Conqueror," *Studies in Medieval History Presented to R. Allen Brown,* ed. C. Harper-Bell, C. J. Holdsworth, and J. L. Nelson (Woodbridge: Boydell, 1989); Eric John, "The Encomium Emma Reginae: A Riddle and a Solution," *Bulletin of the John Rylands Library,* 63 (1980), 58–94; Miles Campbell, "The *Encomium Emmae Reginae*: Personal Panegyric or Political Propaganda?" *Annuale Mediaevale,* 19 (1979), 27–45.

55. "Qua ex re mihi etiam, ut praecipis, memoriam rerum gestarum . . . posteritati mandare gestio" (Prol.7–8). "Quoniam vero, quin scripturus sim evadere me non posse

video, unum horum quae proponam eligendum esse autumno, scilicet aut variis judiciis hominum subiacere, aut de his quae mihi a te, domina regina, praecepta sunt, praecipientem negligendo conticessere" (Prol.23–26).

56. John (see n. 54) argues that an English audience would have known the truth, that it did not need to be told what the author leaves out, and Lifshitz that a Flemish audience would have had to take Emma's word for most of it. I think recent history has proved that effective propaganda can quickly take the place of historic fact and Emma might have gambled that her version, since it came from an eyewitness, would eventually be accepted as the truth.

57. What is particularly striking about Emma's terms is that she had already been married to AEthelred and had sons by him, one of whom, Edward, would eventually succeed her son by Cnut; of course, as the second wife to her first husband, AEthelred, who already had a son with a claim to the throne (Edmund Ironside, Cnut's rival), Emma had had experience of the problem. A. Campbell, editor of the *Encomium,* suggests (xlv) that she probably made a similar concession, which is not mentioned in the *Encomium,* that the claims of her sons by Cnut would take precedence over those of her other sons. Campbell adds that Cnut probably decided to marry Emma in order to forestall any attempt on her brother's part to support the cause of her sons.

58. Alfred was captured by Godwin, who would become the father-in-law of Emma's son Edward, a man of great power in England and certainly a threat to Emma's position. His part in Alfred's death is treated ambiguously in the *Encomium,* but he was considered an accomplice. Godwin's role in Alfred's death is denied in the anonymous life of king Edward written for his widow, Godwin's daughter Edith, but it probably would not have been brought up if it had not been widely believed.

59. The sojourn in Flanders and Emma's departure give the author the opportunity to describe the devotion of a nation to Emma, which he could not very well do with her English subjects, 3.11–12.

60. This is at the very least a telescoped view. Harold reigned from 1035 to 1040, dying conveniently as Harthacnut returned. Harthacnut succeeded him, 1040–42, and when he died, the English chose Edward, who had remained in Normandy. A. Campbell points out (xliii) that Emma's support of Harthacnut was a matter of political expediency, since Edward had no party in England, and that it does not mean she had no feeling for him. The four lines of verse about Emma quoted from the chronicle of Thomas Rudburn at the end of the life notes her relation to four kings, two husbands and two sons: "Duxit Etelredus hanc et postea Cnutus. / Edwardum sanctum parit haec et Hardecnutum. / Quattuor hos reges haec vidit sceptra gerentes. / Anglorum regum fuit haec sic mater et uxor" (c.1397–98).

61. *Vita AEduuardi Regis qui apud Westmonasterium Requiescit,* in *Lives of Edward the Confessor,* ed. Henry R. Luard (London: Longman, 1858), RBMAS, 3, or Chronicles and Memorials of Great Britain and Ireland during the Middle Ages. Aelred of Rievaulx also wrote a life of Edward (1163), which was translated into French by a nun of Barking, perhaps for her abbess (see chapter 6); another translation from Latin to French verse was done for Eleanor, wife of Henry III (*La Estoire de Seint AEdward le Rei,* included in the Luard volume). The author of the French life takes a position not at all sympathetic to Edith's family. He praises his patrons, Eleanor and her husband, and traces Henry's claim to the throne through women; Henry is a descendant of empress Matilda, daughter of the queen Matilda who married Henry I giving the Normans a legitimacy they had not had (3828ff.), through her relation to Edward, the last legitimate English king. (Edward was half-brother of Matilda's great-grandfather Edmund, son of king AEthelred and briefly king before Cnut took over.) The author praises Edith and attributes a mutual vow of chastity to her and Edward on their wedding night (1223ff.), insisting on this explanation of their childlessness, and denouncing others as slanders. He describes Edith as beautiful, wise, and good, a rose from a thorn. The poem ends with the defeat by the Norman William

of Edith's brother Harold, who had usurped the throne, the first in a series of illegitimate kings until Henry I's marriage to Matilda.

62. Kenneth E. Cutler, "Edith, Queen of England, 1045-1066," *Mediaeval Studies,* 35 (1973), 222-31, notes that other sources indicate Edith was loyal to her family and served their ends rather than Edward's, probably in opposition to Emma and Edward's Norman advisors. He also accepts Frank Barlow's dating of 1065-67 for the life. Barlow will not go so far as to say Edith commissioned the life to justify Harold's succession, although he does think it was intended to "prepare the English magnates for the implementation of a 'Godwinist' plan on Edward's death," *Edward the Confessor* (Berkeley: University of California Press, 1970), 227, 241. Barlow thinks she may have preferred Tostig over Harold to succeed Edward, 242.

63. The life says Godwin was married to the king's sister; in fact, his wife's brother was married to Cnut's sister. In any case, the point is to establish that Godwin had royal connections, before the marriage of his daughter to Edward.

64. Edward, who was in France, received embassies from the kings of Europe, all related to him through women, according to the author: the Roman/German emperor Henry, married to his half-sister Gunhild, Emma's daughter by Cnut; Henry, king of the Franks, said to be closely related by blood, presumably through his sister Adelaide, who was married to a duke of Normandy. The subsequent marriage with Godwin's daughter is explained by Cutler (223) as advantageous to both sides: Godwin's position as earl was appointive, but as father-in-law of the king, perhaps grandfather to the heir, he and his sons would be much stronger; Edward had lived most of his life in Normandy, and marriage to the family of one of the more powerful English earls might give him more security on the throne.

65. It is likely that Edith was working for the advancement of her brothers from at least 1046 (Cutler, 226-30) and continued to do so after the deaths of Godwin and his oldest son, since her four younger brothers all had earldoms by 1058.

66. "Nusquam quoque credidit elemosinam magis iri salvam, quam ubi infirmus sexus et minus in aedificiis efficax altius penuriarum sentit angustiam, et minus per se ad hanc proficit pellendam" (1029-32). Barlow suggests (233) that the monk Goscelin, the author of the *Liber confortatorius* for Eve mentioned in chapter 2, who was present at the dedications of Westminster and of Wilton, is a possible author of the *Vita AEduuardi.*

67. Early on in the story, the bishop of Wilton has a vision of St. Peter consecrating the king and designating a celibate life for him (184-85).

68. Barlow notes (252) that William of Poitiers, writing in support of William of Normandy ("the Conqueror"), twice admitted that Edward bequeathed the throne to Harold on his deathbed.

69. Eleanor of Aquitaine, wife of Henry II, carried on the double tradition, but as far as I know, the works written for her and her court were French versions of Latin histories and historic epics, and romances which will be discussed in the next chapter.

70. Stephen, who wrote letters to Adela about his experiences on crusade, returned after a cowardly retreat, but Adela urged him to go back, an episode that is reported by Orderic Vitalis in the *Historia Ecclesiastica,* 10.20.

71. Kimberly LoPrete, in "The Latin Literacy of Adela of Blois," read at the International Congress of Medieval Studies, Kalamazoo, May 1991. LoPrete analyzes Adela's political maneuvers to enhance her husband's family in "The Anglo-Norman Card of Adela of Blois," *Albion* 22 (1990), 569-89. I am grateful to Professor LoPrete for sharing her work on the countess with me. I draw on her paper read at the Medieval Academy meeting in March 1992, "Exemplary Women Rulers in Hugh of Fleury's *Historica Ecclesiastica* Written for Adela of Blois," for my discussion of that history, which has not been published since 1638 and which I have not seen. I understand that Martin de Ruiter, University of Groningen, is preparing an edition. The dedicatory letter and epilogue to Adela and selected passages are available in MGH, SS 9, 349ff.

72. Baudri of Bourgueil's poems were mentioned earlier; Ingelram wrote a poem for her about her father, William the Conqueror, which is cited in part by W. Wattenbach, "Lateinische Gedichte aus Frankreich im elften Jahrhundert," *Sitzungsberichte der Akademie der Wissenschaften,* Berlin (1891), 97-120, see 105. Ingelram claims that William rose from count to king because of his daughter ("filia causa fuit"), so that the "royal virgin might have a royal father." Adela also commissioned a life of her brother Henry I by David, which is not extant; we know it existed because Gaimar says Constance Fitzgilbert gave him a silver mark for that book, which she kept and read in her chamber; see Geffrei Gaimar, *L'Estoire des Engleis,* ed. Alexander Bell (Oxford: Blackwell, 1960), ANTS, 14-16, 6430ff. We do not know if the book Constance read was in French or Latin, or was a French translation of a Latin original; Constance commissioned Gaimar's *Histoire des engleis* in French.

73. The translation (except for the phrase in brackets, which is mine) is from LoPrete, "Exemplary Women Rulers."

74. Like many of the religious writers mentioned in the previous chapter, Hugh also gives more attention to Mary's positive role than to Eve's negative one: he speaks of Adam's being made from earth, Christ from a pure virgin, of God redeeming human nature by taking flesh from a woman, and the sorrow of death through Adam with no mention of Eve.

75. Since Adela continued to be involved in government after the majority of her son, there might be a veiled warning in the story of Semiramis. But the Amazons are presented as a shining example of women's virtues/strengths (*virtutibus*), equal to men's among the Scythians, so that one cannot tell which sex was more illustrious: "Itaque res gestas virorum mulierumque considerantibus incertum est, uter apud eos illustrior sexus fuerit" (MGH, SS 9.355). And the examples of women who extend their territory may well be a compliment to Adela's skills in administering the Thibaudian lands.

76. Hugh also gives some attention to the religious role played by empresses: Helena, the mother of Constantine, finding the true crosses and working miracles with them; Pacilla, the wife of Theodosius, caring for the sick and advising her husband on his moral responsibility.

77. *Sancti Anselmi Cantuarensis Archiepiscopi Opera Omnia,* ed. F. S. Schmitt (Edinburgh: Thomas Nelson, 1946); Anselm's letters are in vols. 3, 4, 5.

78. For the text of the life, see *Symeonis Dunelmensis Opera et Collectanea* I, ed. Hodgson Hinde (Durham: Andrews, 1868), Publications of the Surtees Society, 51, *Vita S. Margaretae Scotorum Reginae,* 234-54. Numbers in the text refer to chapters in this edition. Lois L. Huneycutt makes a strong argument for this longer and less hagiographic version of the life as the one commissioned by Matilda; see Huneycutt, "The Idea of the Perfect Princess: The *Life of St. Margaret* in the Reign of Matilda II (1100-1118)," *Anglo-Norman Studies* 12 (1989), ed. Marjorie Chibnall, 81-97. Huneycutt also notes similarities between the roles of mother and daughter as queens of Scotland and England and suggests that "through Matilda, this text became an important element in the shaping of high-medieval queenship" (97). Early works in Anglo-Norman were also dedicated to queen Matilda: Benedeit's *Voyage of St. Brendan* (later rededicated to her successor, Adeliza) and Philippe de Thaon's *Livre de Sibylle.*

79. Margaret is called another Helena, correcting the errors of others from scripture (8). Huneycutt notes (90) that R. L. G. Ritchie (*The Normans in Scotland,* 1953) was doubtful about the existence of these councils: "Turgot seems to represent Margaret presiding over a church council, which would have been unprecedented in all Christendom, and must be dismissed as well-intended hyperbole." But various letters from earlier centuries speak of women calling councils, sometimes presiding over them and participating in their discussions; so Margaret's role, while it might well be exaggerated, is not unprecedented. Her daughter Matilda, as Huneycutt points out, spoke at a council called by Anselm.

80. "Inerat enim reginae tanta cum jocunditate severitas, tanta cum severitate jocunditas, ut omnes qui erant in ejus obsequio, viri et feminae, illam et timendo diligerent, et diligendo timerent."

81. Letters sent by the monks of Malmesbury to David, king of Scotland, queen Matilda's brother, and to the empress Matilda, her daughter, presenting the work to the empress after her mother's death, emphasize the queen's role in its composition: "que hortatu domine nostre, sororis vestre, Mathildis regine scribere fecimus," and "hoc libro, quem iussu domine nostre de Anglorum regum gestis scribere fecimus." The letters were published by Ewald Könsgen, "Zwei unbekannte Briefe zu den *Gesta Regum Anglorum* des Wilhelm von Malmesbury," *Deutsches Archiv für Erforschung des Mittelalters* 31 (1975), 204-14. Much is made of the queen's love of letters, her piety, and her pride in her glorious ancestry, which the history serves. Her only error, which her daughter can rectify, was to leave the abbey without an abbot.

82. The text of the history is in *Willelmi Malmesbiriensis Monachi, De gestis regum Anglorum,* RBMAS 90, ed. William Stubbs (London: Eyre and Spottiswoode, 1887). It was translated by J. A. Giles as *William of Malmesbury's Chronicle of the Kings of England* (London: Bohn, 1847). The last three books, in Joseph Stephenson's translation, were reprinted by LLanerch Enterprise in 1989 as *A History of the Norman Kings (1066-1125)*. The numbers in the text are from the Latin edition.

83. The countess of Sicily, who married Baldwin of Jerusalem, restored his losses with her wealth; William comments that it was a matter of surprise whence a woman could accumulate such heaps of precious equipment (4.385).

84. Jean Dunbabin says Constance was opposed to Henry's accession, that she supported the third son, Robert (see Dunbabin, "What's in a Name? Philip, King of France," *Speculum* 68 [1993], 952-53). Has William confused the names, heard a different version, or been influenced by the similar situation (not to say similar names) in the Saxon dynasty, of a mother, Matilda, preferring the second son, Henry, to the first, Otto? It is interesting that in both cases, the father seems to favor primogeniture, the mother ostensibly ability.

85. In the same section, William mentions Adela of Blois, Henry's sister, as "celebrated for secular activity," but not her long and successful regency. Is William discrediting or playing down Henry's sisters in order to preclude any claims they or their children might have in opposition to Matilda's daughter? Though the history was begun while her son was alive, it was finished after his death, when the younger Matilda, to whom the book was finally presented, was her father's heir.

86. "Kenwalkius . . . regni arbitrium uxori Sexburgae delegandum putavit: nec deerat mulieri spiritus ad obeunda regni munia; ipsa novos exercitus moliri, veteres tenere in officio, ipsa subjectos clementer moderari, hostibus minaciter infremere, prorsus omnia facere, ut nihil praeter sexum discerneres: veruntamen plus quam foemineos animos anhelantem vita destituit, annua vix potestate perfunctam." AEthelweard mentions the same Seaxburh in his chronicle, 2.7.

87. "Militia Matildis marchisae, quae oblita sexus, nec dispar antiquis Amazonibus, ferrata virorum agmina in bellum agebat foemina; ejus suffragio Urbanus, posteriori tempore thronum indeptus apostolicum, securum per undecim annos actitavit otium," 3.289 (cf. 4.350). Matilda's forgetting her sex is presented positively, in contrast to Richilda, countess of Flanders, who, aspiring to things beyond her sex, stirs her people to rebellion by exacting new tributes from them (3.256).

88. Royal mothers also influence their sons. William tells the story of king Alfred's mother, who taught her son to read by a "game" (*ludo*), promising to give him her book if he could read it (2.123), and instilled an avidity for reading in him.

89. William says Ine's wife omitted nothing that might lead to his salvation. He had already told how Ethelburga had persuaded Ine to give up earthly things by arranging for the site of their recent festivities to be defiled with animal filth and a

sow put in their bed, then when he was amazed at the transformation, by drawing from it a lesson of the transitoriness of earthly wealth and luxury (1.35). In a similarly grotesque story, Ostritha, wife of Ethelred king of the Mercians and daughter of Oswy king of Northumbria, brought the trunk of her uncle's dismembered body to a monastery and persuaded the hostile monks, with the help of a miraculous light, to bury their former enemy (1.49).

90. See the letter to empress Matilda that accompanied the history: "Solebant sane huiusmodi libri regibus sive reginis antiquitus scribi, ut quasi ad vite sue exemplum eis instruerentur aliorum prosequi triumphos, aliorum vitare miserias, aliorum imitari sapientiam, aliorum contemnere stulticiam"; Könsgen, "Zwei unbekannte Briefe," 213.

91. Even when both sin, the woman may be more repentant: Philip of France, oppressed by lust, is lured by the beauty of Bertrada, countess of Anjou, into an illicit passion and excommunicated; though no lapse of time could stem his "mad excess," she acted with "better grace and greater success," retiring to a monastery long before he did (5.404).

92. Henry learned of the affair when snow threatened to reveal their tryst and the cleric talked the woman into carrying him out of the palace on her back so he would leave no tracks; the emperor saw them and sent both away from the court, making the man a bishop and the woman an abbess, with a veiled reference to the episode in the snow which they took as God's intervention so both thenceforth desisted from their sin (2.190).

93. In fact, it was Cnut's father who drove AEthelred out, but William's condemnation of Cnut may owe something to his role as the opponent of Emma's stepson, Edmund Ironside, the great-grandfather of William's patron, queen Matilda.

94. Perhaps the reference to her hoarding treasure is an attempt to excuse Edward's seizure of his mother's property.

95. For a detailed and fascinating study of her life and struggle for the throne, see Chibnall, *The Empress Matilda*.

96. Hugh presents the work as a supplement to the history he had collected for Matilda's aunt, Adela of Blois; see prologue, *Hugonis Liber qui Modernorum Regum Francorum Continet Actus*, MGH, SS 9.376-77. He also gives a brief summary of the longer history, noting the fraternal wars that divided France from the empire (now ruled by Matilda's husband), up to Charles the Bald with whom the new history begins. It includes relations between the Normans, Matilda's ancestors, and the Ottonians, ancestors of her husband, and stories of impressive queens, one who tried to free her husband from the Normans, another (Constance) who attempted to remain in power after the death of her husband, Robert (died 1031), with the support of many princes but finally ousted by her son Henry (10), a somewhat different perspective from William's.

97. "In eo etiam experiri potestis, quod nullus eorum, quorum liber presens continet memoriam, nec rex aliquis nec regina aliqua regalius vel splendidius vobis Anglorum regni hereditarii iura expectaverit"; Könsgen, "Zwei unbekannte Briefe," 214.

98. Unfortunately, Matilda and the legate fell out over his desire to have his nephew, Stephen's son, hold his father's lands while his father was in captivity, which Matilda refused (3.498).

99. The exception is Matilda's stepmother, who is said "through female inconstancy" to have broken faith with her, but we are not told how. Chibnall, however, says that Adeliza remained friendly to Matilda because she had interceded with the emperor for Adeliza's father many years before (80-1).

100. In the *Gesta Stephani Regis Anglorum*, favorable to Stephen, this Matilda is "a woman of clever breast and virile constancy" ("astuti pectoris virilisque constantiae femina"), while the empress is arrogant, lacking in feminine gentleness; cited by Betty Bandel, "The English Chroniclers' Attitude toward Women," *Journal of the History of*

Ideas 16 (1955), 113–18. Bandel makes a distinction between the treatment of women as competent human beings in preconquest English history and a general prejudice against women in postconquest works.

4. COURTLY LITERATURE

1. Despite the increase in government bureaucracies and the connected increased reluctance to recognize an official role for women in the late twelfth and thirteenth centuries, women did still inherit and occasionally administer lands, e.g., Ermengard, countess of Narbonne, and did continue to be chosen as regents by their husbands, e.g., Blanche of Castile by Louis VIII. Judith Weiss, noting that women can be powerful and powerless in Anglo-Norman romance as in life in this period, focuses on the powerful side, emphasizing the influence of "women of substance and authority" in the families of patrons or as patrons themselves; see Weiss, "The Power and the Weakness of Women in Anglo-Norman Romance" in *Women and Literature in Britain, 1100–1500,* ed. Carol M. Meale (Cambridge: Cambridge University Press, 1993), 7–23.

2. The statement is questionable on two counts. The evidence of the earliest extant poetry suggests that men wrote a lot of their poetry for other men. Though it has often been said that translations were made into the vernacular for women who did not know Latin, it seems unlikely that most of the laymen of a court in the early or mid-twelfth century were more comfortable in Latin than the women. There were probably some educated (Latin-literate) members of both sexes in the courts that encouraged translation and the development of vernacular literature, but entertainment in the vernacular would certainly reach a larger audience and, even more important, allow for greater freedom and play in the composition and in the exchange between poet and audience.

3. Questions have been raised about women's patronage of courtly literature; see E. Jane Burns and Roberta L. Krueger, introduction to *Courtly Ideology and Woman's Place in Medieval French Literature, Romance Notes* 25 (1985). In German literature, William C. McDonald (with Ulrich Goebel, *German Medieval Literary Patronage from Charlemagne to Maximilian I* [Amsterdam: Rodopi, 1973]) recognizes few women patrons, but Joachim Bumke (*Mäzene im Mittelalter: Die Gönner und Auftraggeber der Höfischen Literatur in Deutschland, 1150–1300* [Munich: C. H. Beck, 1979]), finds enough women patrons to devote a chapter to them, though he includes patrons of French and Latin. M. Dominca Legge (*Anglo-Norman Literature*) and Karl Holzknecht (*Literary Patronage in the Middle Ages*), of course, cite many women patrons for vernacular works. Most recently, Roberta L. Krueger, in a provocative study of misogyny in romance and women readers' possible responses to it (*Women Readers and the Ideology of Gender in Old French Verse Romance* [Cambridge: Cambridge University Press, 1993]), questions the influence of the women mentioned in prologues and epilogues, but she concentrates mainly on the romances written for male patrons or general audiences, where I too see misogyny and very different patterns of behavior.

4. For the texts, see *The Songs of Bernart de Ventadorn,* ed. and trans. Stephen G. Nichols, John A. Galm, and A. Bartlett Giamatti (Chapel Hill: University of North Carolina Press, 1965). Bernart's *vida,* historically inaccurate though it is, underscores his need for patronage and Eleanor's rank: it tells of his being sent away from Ventadorn and going to Normandy, to the duchess (Eleanor), who received him well, and of their great joy together until she married king Henry of England, who took her beyond the sea. For the text of the *vida,* see *Biographies des Troubadours,* ed. J. Boutière and A.-H. Schutz (Paris: Nizet, 1964), 6.A.5–14.

5. Raimbaut sent two poems to unnamed countesses, 19 and 28, though the latter is mainly a reassurance to men that he is no threat because he has lost his members.

For the poems, see W. Pattison, *The Life and Works of the Troubadour Raimbaut d'Orange* (Minneapolis: University of Minnesota Press, 1952). Bertran de Born was a nobleman who nonetheless had to rely on help from patrons, mainly those he supported in their battles. He wrote two poems for Matilda, daughter of Henry II and Eleanor and wife of Henry of Saxony, who was generous to him when she was in exile with her husband in Normandy; see *The Poems of the Troubadour Bertran de Born,* ed. and trans. William D. Paden, Tilde Sankovitch, and Patricia Stablein (Berkeley: University of California Press, 1986), 8 and 9.

6. Among the other lyric poets who wrote at some point for Ermengard are Peire Rogier, Peire d'Alvernh, Guiraut de Bornelh, and Azalais de Porcairagues (a woman). Other lyric poets connected to particular women patrons are Arnaut de Mareuil, who wrote for Adelaide, daughter of Raymond V of Toulouse, and Guiraut de Bornelh and Folquet de Marseille, for Eudoxie, Byzantine wife of Guillaume VIII of Montpellier. Marcabru included an envoy to the empress when writing to the emperor (Alfonso of Castile) about rewarding him, asking her to pray for him and offering to enrich her prestige. I have limited myself here to a very brief mention of Provençal poets, as the beginning of the tradition. French lyric poets can also be connected with specific women; see Holzknecht, 75-76. It is harder to connect German Minnesinger with particular women, though they were attached to various courts. For a discussion of women as patrons of German courtly literature, see Bumke, *Mäzene,* chapter 5. Italian poets, writing in Northern cities, Dante, Cecco, Guido Guinizelli, Guido Cavalcanti, Gianni Alfani, address women in their poems but do not have women patrons in a strict sense.

7. Raimbaut, in his "Escotatz, mas no say que s'es," boasts that he is doing something never seen done before by man or woman ("ia hom mays non vis fag aytal ad home ni a femna en est segle," 24.7), which is either a wild exaggeration or an indication that men and women composed poetry. There is a poem by a trobairitz, Azalais de Porcairagues, probably alluding to Raimbaut's death.

8. See Angelica Rieger, *Trobairitz: Der Beitrag der Frau in der altokzitanischen höfischen Lyrik* (Tübingen: Niemeyer, 1991), for a collection of debates between men and women which she assigns to the corpus of the trobairitz. I have suggested that the debates in the pastorelas and in Andreas Capellanus reflect court life in "Male Fantasy and Female Reality in Courtly Literature," *Women's Studies* 11 (1984), 67-97. I caution the reader that the debates in Provençal pastorelas, which usually end in a standoff, should not be confused with the French pastourelles, which often end in rape.

9. On the male game of courtly love, see E. Jane Burns, "The Man behind the Lady in Troubadour Lyric," *Romance Notes* 25 (1985), 254-70; Simon Gaunt, "Poetry of Exclusion: A Feminist Reading of Some Troubadour Lyrics," MLR 85 (1990), 310-29; and Frederick Goldin, "The Array of Perspectives in the Early Courtly Love Lyric," in *In Pursuit of Perfection: Courtly Love in Medieval Literature,* ed. J. M. Ferrante and G. D. Economou (Port Washington: Kennikat, 1975), 51-100.

10. Raimbaut addressed a number of poems in their entirety to women, which is unusual in Provençal: a verse letter (23), a debate with a woman about who suffered more in love (25), and two poems about his love for her (26, 35).

11. For the *razo* of Bertran de Born, see Boutière and Schutz, *Biographies des Troubadours,* 11.F.1,4; for Uc de Saint Circ, 33.B.3-11; for Gaucelm Faidit, 18.B.12. Linda Paterson cites Raimon de Miraval sending his poem to a lady, who will enrich his singing if she learns it, "since her praise gilds and her censure turns to lead"; see Paterson, *Troubadours and Eloquence* (Oxford: Clarendon, 1975), 180-81.

12. See, for example, Bertran, 30 (if it is his), and perhaps 17, though the editors suggest that Bertran often refers to Richard and Geoffrey in the feminine when he is attacking what they have done; in his poems for Matilda, Bertran praises her generosity to the detriment of his lords (7, 8). Also see Sordello, poems 20, 23, and 26 (the lament

for Blacatz), in *The Poetry of Sordello,* ed. and trans. J. J. Wilhelm (New York: Garland, 1987); he sent 22 to the king of Aragon, but in it he tells his lady that it is because of her that he despises evil and deception. Dante sent a canzone on virtue and one on nobility to women (Rime, 83 and 69); see *Dante's Lyric Poetry,* ed. K. Foster and P. Boyde (Oxford: Clarendon, 1967), 2 vols.

13. Raimbaut implies that his lady inspired the new form in the poem which foreshadows the sestina, "Ar resplan la flors enversa" ("Dona per cuy chant e siscle," 39.29), and the one which is both prose and verse, "Escotatz, mas no say que s'es" ("Dona, . . . ieu soy per vos gays, d'ira ples; / iratz jauzens me faytz trobar; . . . e soy fols cantayre cortes," 24).

14. "Canzone, io porto ne la mente donna / tal che, con tutto ch'ella mi sia petra, / mi dà baldanza . . . sì ch'io ardisco a far per questo freddo / la novità che per tua forma luce, / che non fu mai pensata in alcun tempo," *Dante's Lyric Poetry* 79.61–66.

15. Legge, *Anglo-Norman Literature,* 364. See also Legge, "La précocité de la littérature anglo-normande," CCM 8 (1965), 327–49, in which she calls Maud the first known patron of French letters ("Son nom est le premier connu d'un patron des lettres françaises," 329). In "Les Origines de l'anglo-normand littéraire," *Revue de linguistique Romane* 31 (1967), 44–54, Legge notes that patrons of Anglo-Norman were named earlier than their French counterparts and were not necessarily all of as high rank. In *Anglo-Norman in the Cloisters,* Legge connects a series of works by monastics with women patrons. She also points out that in some manuscripts, the name of the woman addressed was suppressed (33), in others the address deliberately altered from feminine to masculine (123).

16. Philippe de Thaon dedicated a French *Bestiaire* to Adeliza (Aaliz), including in it an allegory of her name (Legge, "La précocité," 333); this work was also rededicated, to Eleanor of Aquitaine. Hugh Shields argues that the *Bestiaire* was in fact dedicated to empress Matilda, also called Aaliz, to whom Philippe offered the *Livre de Sibylle,* at the time of her struggle for accession to the throne, 1139–43, and when Philippe says "reine est d'Engletere" in the dedication and "Deus li otreit majesté" in line 3157, he is supporting her claim; see Shields, "Philippe de Thaon, Auteur du Livre de Sibylle?" *Romania* 85 (1964), 455–77, esp. 472ff. He finds the rededication to Eleanor less shocking, since she is Matilda's daughter-in-law. Philippe had his own problems of accession to a heritage, in his case from his mother, which he mentions in both the *Bestiaire* and at the end of the *Sibylle* (474).

17. "Tels mil choses en purrad dire / ke unkes Davit ne fist escrivere / ne la reine de Luvain / n'en tint le livere en sa main"; cited by Diana B. Tyson, "Patronage of French Vernacular History Writers in the Twelfth and Thirteenth Centuries," *Romania* 100 (1979), 192. It is assumed that the book was in French from the connection with Constance, though that is not conclusive. For the text, see Geffrei Gaimar, *L'Estoire des Engleis,* ed. Alexander Bell (Oxford: Blackwell, 1960).

18. John of Hoveden, who was Eleanor's secretary, also did a French version of a verse life and passion of Christ, *Rossignos,* for her, in which he emphasized the life and death of the Virgin.

19. John Peckam wrote a French version of the heavenly hierarchy (*Jerarchie*), at the request of Eleanor of Castile. The variety of material that became available in French thanks to these queens is striking. But vernacular works were also provided for or through other women beginning in the twelfth century: Constance Fitzgilbert commissioned Gaimar's *Estoire,* Alice de Condet the *Proverbes de Salomon* from Samson de Nanteuil, and a lady Dionise *Le Romanz de Temtacioun de Secle* from Guischard de Beaulieu (Legge, *Anglo-Norman in the Cloisters,* 31–33). Abbesses of Barking had saints' lives and miracles of the Virgin translated into French (Legge, "La précocité," 348), and nuns of Barking wrote or translated the lives of Edward the Confessor and Saint Catherine (see chapter 6). An abbess of Barking who was the sister of Thomas

Becket helped Guernes de Pont Sainte-Maxence with his life of Thomas (Legge, "La précocité," 344). In the next century, a life of Thomas with pictures was sent by Matthew Paris to a countess of Arundel, Isabel, to whom he dedicated a translation of the life of St. Edmund (Legge, *Anglo-Norman in the Cloisters,* 26); Matthew also planned a book about saints with Latin text, French verses, and explanatory pictures for the countess of Winchester (ibid., 28). On works composed or translated for women in Flanders, mainly to French, see Mary D. Stanger, "Literary Patronage at the Medieval Court of Flanders," *French Studies* 11 (1957), 214-29.

20. Gaimar makes it clear not only that he did the work for Custance ("Ceste estorie fist translater / Dame Custance la gentil," 6430-31), but also that he could not have done it without her help: "Si sa dame ne li aidast, / ja a nul jor ne l'achevast," *Estoire des engleis,* 6439-40.

21. Giovanna Angeli suggested that these works, like the classical histories, were all done for the court of Henry and Eleanor, all connected in some way with the history that ultimately culminated in the Plantagenets; see Angeli, *L'Eneas e i primi romanzi volgari* (Milan: Riccardo Ricciardi, 1971).

22. "A Peitiers s'en ala, sun naturel manage; / N'i out plus prochain heir, qu'el fu de sun lignage, / . . ." 32ff., *Maistre Wace's Roman de Rou et des Ducs de Normandie,* ed. Hugo Andresen (Heilbronn: Gebr. Henninger, 1877), 208.

23. This is cited in the frontispiece of Wace, *Le Roman de Brut,* ed. Ivor Arnold, SATF 93.1.

24. See Yvonne Rokseth, *Polyphonies du XIIIe siècle: Le Manuscrit H 196 de la Faculté de Médecine de Montpellier,* (Paris: l'Oiseau-Lyre, 1935-39), vol. 4, 40; cited by Rebecca A. Baltzer, "Music in the Life and Times of Eleanor of Aquitaine," in *Eleanor of Aquitaine, Patron and Politician,* ed. William W. Kibler (Austin: University of Texas Press, 1976), 66. The story of Mordred's treachery, his adultery with the queen and his usurping of the crown, is told in much more detail than in Geoffrey, with emphasis on his shameful villainy and the queen's shame and sin. And when Arthur is carried off to Avalon, Wace adds that he is still there, that he might still be alive. Charlotte A. T. Wulf notes that in Wace, instead of leaving Guenever in Mordred's care, Arthur leaves the kingdom in the care of Mordred and Guenever; Wulf argues that Wace's Guenever is more active and motivated than Geoffrey's. See Wulf, "A Comparative Study of Wace's Guenevere in the Twelfth Century," in *Arthurian Romance and Gender,* ed. Friedrich Wolfzettel (Amsterdam: Rodopi, 1995).

25. Bezzola, *Les Origines et la formation de la littérature courtoise en occident (500-1200)* (Paris: Champion, 1944, 1960, 1963), vol. 3, 290, comments that even if Henry commissioned or sponsored such works, Eleanor was an important part of the audience, whose tastes contributed to the increasing importance of women and love in the plots.

26. Pallas's mother was right in terms of her son. The love story that is added at the end of the poem suggests that Lavinia's mother will be wrong about Eneas, but the story does not take us that far. And we are told that even Eneas recognizes he was wrong not to have gone to Lavinia after the combat; in other words, there may be some question about the strength of his love. For the French text, see *Eneas,* ed. J.-J. Salverda de Grave, 2 vols. (Paris: Honoré Champion, 1964, 1968), CFMA 44, 62; for an English translation, see John A. Yunck, *Eneas: A Twelfth-Century Romance* (New York: Columbia University Press, 1974), Records of Civilization, 93. For a study of Virgil in the *Eneas,* see Christopher Baswell, *Virgil in Medieval England: Figuring the Aeneid from the Twelfth Century to Chaucer* (Cambridge: Cambridge University Press, 1995), chapter 5. Baswell gives a lot of attention to the treatment of women in the French version; he sees them as finally contained within the imperial design. Marilynn Desmond suggests that Dido in the *Eneas* reflects Eleanor, "known for her resistance to the dominant gender ideologies," who was rumored to have led armies and committed adultery while

on crusade; see Desmond, *Reading Dido: Gender, Textuality, and the Medieval Aeneid* (Minneapolis: University of Minnesota Press, 1994), 118.

27. "Mieus vaut lor ris et lor baisiers / que ne fait Londres ne Peitiers," *Le Roman de Thèbes,* ed. Léopold Constans, SATF 30.1 (Paris: Didot, 1890). Constans's edition is a reconstruction based on all the available manuscripts. Raynaud de Lage (see next note), who follows one MS., does not cite these lines. It is, of course, impossible to tell when they got into or were left out of the text, but they do, as Bezzola says, seem to be directed at Eleanor.

28. The text is from *Le Roman de Thèbes,* ed. Guy Raynaud de Lage (Paris: Champion, 1968, 1969), 2 vols., CFMA 94, 96, which I have followed for most of my discussion. Martine Thiry-Stassin, "Interpellations féminines dans le *Roman de Thèbes,*" *Marche Romane* 27 (1977), 41–53, discusses female figures in the poem. She notes that about a third of the direct discourse involves women, that most of the women are royal, that women dominate situations "par le jugement ou par le sens," and that Jocasta is a woman of decision, "certaine de son pouvoir de mère et de suzeraine." It should be mentioned that Jocasta is said to be easily led as a woman to do what a man wants when she forgives Oedipus (440–42), which seems unfair since she is already committed to treating him well as the rescuer of the land, and nothing in the rest of the poem suggests such flightiness. I am, of course, assuming a date for the poem after 1152, since so much in it suggests that it was written after the marriage of Henry and Eleanor. Raynaud de Lage puts the poem between 1150 and 1160.

29. The riddle of the four/three/two-footed creature is told twice, emphasizing its message, that man begins and ends like an animal and only rises to a human state for the central period of his life. It is hard to avoid the sense that this is a comment on the behavior of most of the men in the story, who are given opportunities to act in a more civilized way but continually regress to selfish violence.

30. A minor example of the role of queen as peacemaker is given in the story of Lycurges's son, killed by a serpent when his nurse leaves him to help the drought-beset Greek army find water; instead of demanding the death of the girl, she asks for the head of the serpent, promising and giving a fief to the man who kills him (2589ff.).

31. Thebes is dominated through most of the poem by its king Ethiocles, who usurped his brother's rights, and at the end by Creon, who refused to let the dead be buried.

32. Adrastus tells Polinices and Thideus that his daughters are his heirs to whom he will give his realm (*annor*), but if the men marry the daughters, he will give it to them now, since he is old and tired: "ce sont mi oir / . . . / A mes filles m'annor dorré / . . . et, s'il vos plest, jes vous dorrai; / a vous deus m'annor partirai," 1021–26.

33. Benoît develops the love stories of Medea and Jason, Polyx and Achilles, and Briseida and Troilus in far greater detail than his sources (in some cases apparently making them up) and often with more sympathy for the woman. Briseida, the only nonroyal woman, is the most problematic.

34. *Le Roman de Troie par Benoît de Sainte-Maure,* ed. L. Constans (Paris: Firmin Didot, 1904–12), 6 vols., SATF, 52, 55, 57, 62, 66, 67. Douglas Kelly accepts Eleanor's patronage of Benoît and her inspiration for some of the women characters, particularly Helen, Medea, and Briseida, whose inconstancy is to be contrasted with the queen; see Kelly, "Le Patron et l'Auteur dans l'Invention Romanesque," in *Théories et pratiques de l'écriture au Moyen Age,* ed. Emmanuèle Baumgartner and Christiane Marchello-Nizia (Paris: Paris X-Nanterre, 1988), 25–39. Roberta L. Krueger raises questions about whether Benoît in his allusions to the "riche dame," is undermining female authority as much as acknowledging a powerful patron; see Krueger, *Women Readers,* 4. Krueger and I discuss some of the same works, but since her perspective is the reader's possible reaction to misogyny in romance and mine is to the patron's possible influence, we are looking for different things, so we sometimes read the same passages

in somewhat different ways, but I do not think our readings are finally incompatible. We both suggest that women were alert to and may have read the presentation of women in romance differently from men, she from the way they might have responded to misogyny, I from the sense they may have had of women in the real world as opposed to women in men's theory.

35. The Greeks are kind to her at first, but later the poet says she is hated in the camp. And even the Trojans have mixed feelings; when her father asks for her, Priam is so angry he says he would have her burned and torn apart, if she were not so noble, wise, and beautiful.

36. The eight children had been born by 1166, a probable date for the completion of the poem. On Benoît's privileging royal women, particularly Hecuba, see Martine Thiry-Stassin, "Interpellations feminines dans le *Roman de Troie* de Benoît de Sainte-Maure," in *Mélanges de langue et littérature françaises du moyen âge offerts à Pierre Jonin* (Paris: Champion, 1979), 645-60. It is likely that Thomas composed his *Tristan* for the court of Eleanor and Henry, where there is yet another notable queen, Ysolt, who is educated, composes *lais,* and has the medical skills to cure the hero, if she could reach him.

37. Helen's part in starting the war is played down, and men's violence played up. Even in Dares, Benoît's main source, Helen does little to cause the war: Alexander (Paris) is sent to get his aunt back, at which he fails, but he is attracted to Helen and takes her instead.

38. It has been argued that another woman with magic arts in the *Roman de Troie* who is usually presented negatively, Circe, is redeemed in Benoît's version; see Emmanuel S. Hatzantonis, "Circe, redenta d'amore, nel *Roman de Troie,*" *Romania* 94 (1973), 91-102.

39. On the probable relations between Marie and her mother, as they can be posited from the material we have, see June Hall McCash, "Marie de Champagne and Eleanor of Aquitaine: A Relationship Reexamined," *Speculum* 54 (1979), 698-711.

40. The text is from *Le Chevalier de la Charrete,* ed. Mario Roques (Paris: Champion, 1958), CFMA 86.

41. Madeleine Blaess mentions the "growing body of opinion" that Chrétien had links with the court of Henry II and knew England firsthand, though she believes that Marie, not Eleanor, was Chrétien's patron even in the early works; see Blaess, "The Public and Private Face of King Arthur's Court in the Works of Chrétien de Troyes," in *Chrétien de Troyes and the Troubadours: Essays in Memory of the Late Leslie Topsfield,* ed. Peter S. Noble and Linda M. Paterson (Cambridge: St. Catherine's College, 1984).

42. Krueger, *Woman Readers,* discusses Chrétien's narrative displacement of women (the queen in *Yvain,* Marie in *Lancelot,* where Marie's influence is displaced by the "male narrative bond between Chrétien and 'Godefroy,'" 37), as the beginning of "women's subsequent objectification in French fictions."

43. Perhaps Gawain represents someone like Evrat, writing on more serious matters for Marie but caught up in her views and therefore in danger of drowning. On Evrat and Marie, see June Hall McCash, "Marie de Champagne's 'Cuer d'ome et cors de fame': Aspects of Feminism and Misogyny in the Twelfth Century," in *The Spirit of the Court,* ed. Glyn S. Burgess and Robert A. Taylor (Cambridge: D. S. Brewer, 1985), 234-45. Marie expected men who wrote for her to espouse her views, and Chrétien makes it clear that he would prefer not to.

44. E. Jane Burns, in *Bodytalk: When Women Speak in Old French Literature* (Philadelphia: University of Pennsylvania Press, 1993), 161-62, 169-70, speaking of Chrétien as a poet who prefers not to write for women, notes that he transforms the masculine "conte d'avanture," "men's stories," into a feminine "*conjointure,*" "women's stories," and suggests that instead of replacing male combat with love, he is

(temporarily) substituting male coupling in combat with heterosexual union, turning the pleasure of the heroine's body into the pleasure of the romancer's text.

45. Laudine does read psalms, and there is a girl who reads a romance to her parents in the *Chevalier au lion (Yvain)*, but it seems to be nothing more than escape literature, since they are oblivious to the hundreds of girls being exploited in a sweat-shop in the same castle. Thessala has magic gifts, but she uses them to distort reality and deceive. Lunete rescues Yvain, at first, and temporarily manipulates him and her mistress but in order to accomplish what Yvain wants, and she is indebted to him for rescuing her in the past, as her life will be saved by him in the future. Only Lancelot is thoroughly manipulated by a woman, and has to be rescued from his (phallic?) tower prison by a woman, an event that does not occur in the part Chrétien admits to writing.

46. Male bonding is positive in *Erec,* because it brings the hero back into his world, but it never separates him from his wife; whereas in *Yvain,* it keeps him from the duties he has assumed. In *Lancelot,* where Lancelot keeps trying to find Gawain, it may be meant as a counter to the tyranny of love, and in *Perceval,* the company of the grail replaces any courtly society, of ladies or of knights.

47. The text of *Meraugis von Portlesguez* was edited by Mathias Friedwanger (Geneva: Slatkine Reprints, 1975, first pub. 1897).

48. The rescue of Gawain is particularly interesting, since the basic situation is not uncommon in romance—Erec rescues a knight from such a predicament, the Bel Inconnu rescues the lady from the knight who is "protecting" her, both by defeating the imprisoned knight—but in *Meraugis* the knight must be gotten out of the clutches of the woman by another (false) woman—the hero in disguise who plays dead and then dresses as a woman, saying "Vostre dame est venue" (*Meraugis,* 3366) when he reveals himself and his sword.

49. Krueger says *Ipomedon* "makes explicit the link between chivalry and misogyny"; see *Women Readers,* 82; see also her "Misogyny, Manipulation, and the Female Reader in Hue de Rotelande's *Ipomedon,*" in *Courtly Literature: Culture and Context,* ed. Keith Busby and Erik Cooper (Amsterdam: Benjamins, 1990), 395–409. For the text, see *Ipomedon: Poème de Hue de Rotelande,* ed. A. J. Holden (Paris: Klincksieck, 1979), Bibliothèque Française et Romane, 17. Holden notes how unfavorably women are presented and the author's cruel response to their suffering in his introduction. He dates the *Ipomedon* after 1174, which would put it in the same decade as *Lancelot,* and it makes most sense as a counterromance.

50. For the text, see Hue de Rotelande, *Protheselaus: Ein altfranzösischer Abenteuerroman,* ed. Franz Kluckow (Göttingen: Gesellschaft für Romanische Literatur, 1924).

51. That men are uncomfortable with women running lands is underscored by an episode in which the king of Denmark offers the hero the widowed Ismeine and her (husband's) land, Burgundy, as his vassal, but refuses to leave her to run it alone (5507ff.). Protheselaus defends her rights and then goes off on his own adventures.

52. Since leprosy was considered a venereal disease and was connected with adultery, the implications of the dangers of sex are obvious. See Saul N. Brody, *The Disease of the Soul: Leprosy in Medieval Literature* (Ithaca: Cornell University Press, 1974).

53. *Eracle,* ed. Guy Raynaud de Lage (Paris: H. Champion, 1976), CFMA, 102.

54. The edition I used is *Ille et Galeron,* ed. Yves Lefèvre (Paris: Honoré Champion, 1988), CFMA 109. Lefèvre dates the poem between 1167 and 1178. Gautier himself says that *Ille* was begun after *Eracle* (6592–602a), though it may have been finished earlier; see Frederick A. G. Cowper, "The New Manuscript of *Ille et Galeron,*" *Modern Philology* 18 (1921), 601–8. Cowper points out differences in the two manuscripts and suggests that Gautier may have offered somewhat different versions to Beatrice and to Thibaut, abbreviating his praise of the empress and omitting lovers' monologues and much of their courtship. Cowper based his edition (Paris: A & J Picard, 1956) on the

Wollaton MS. (W) but cites the longer praise of Beatrice from the Paris MS. (P) in the notes. Lefèvre bases his edition on P with insertions in italics from W to fill lacunae. Anthime Fourrier, in *Le Courant réaliste dans le roman courtois en France au moyen age* (Paris: Nizet, 1960), 207, suggests that Gautier edited his praise of Beatrice because he had been criticized for its excesses, perhaps even indirectly by Chrétien in his prologue to *Lancelot*, whose "Dirai-je tant com une jame / vaut . . ." may echo Gautier's "mout ama Dix honor de feme / quant nestre fist si bele geme" (cited from Lefèvre, 79-80).

55. Galeron retires from the marriage after three children to become a nun, choosing the unmarried life later rather than earlier.

56. Charles W. Dunn dates *Guillaume de Palerne* between 1194 and 1197 in *The Foundling and the Werwolf: A Literary-Historical Study of "Guillaume de Palerne"* (Toronto: University of Toronto Press, 1960), 141. Anthime Fourrier notes that Yolande had a translation done from Latin to French of the Pseudo-Turpin, which her brother Baudouin had left to her and suggests that that may have led the author of *Guillaume* to say she asked him to translate his story from Latin; see Fourrier, "La 'Contesse Yolent' de *Guillaume de Palerne*," *Etudes de langue et de littérature du Moyen Age offertes à Félix Lecoy* (Paris: Honoré Champion, 1973), 116-17. The text was edited by H. Michelant (Paris: SATF, 1876).

57. It is a small but intriguing detail that when the emperor of Greece receives a letter, he breaks the seal but has the letter read by a *clerc* (8450); when a letter arrives in the Spanish court, the queen breaks the seal and reads it herself. Presumably this underscores the public versus the private aspects of their actions, perhaps even the honorable versus the treacherous, but it also emphasizes the queen's literacy. Cf. the evil queen in the *Roman de Silence* who forges a letter in the king's name.

58. Krueger (*Women Readers,* 182) suggests that when "the lady and the poet in the frame are linked to the lady and the knight in the romance, the act of reading becomes a complex erotic interchange," which presents "a danger for the woman reader, who risks being subsumed within the discourse of desire." Krueger, 184, treats these women as fictional projections of the poet's fears and fantasies like the *domna* in Provençal lyric.

59. The generic name may be used to allow more easily for audience identification, or to make a comment on the two Isots, the one Tristan married being Isot-as-blancesmains, the one he loved Isot-la-blonde, which Renaut reverses: the Pucele is the hero's love, the Blonde Esmeree the woman he has to marry, one of many inversions of romance motifs in the poem. The text was edited by G. Perrie Williams (Paris: Honoré Champion, 1967) and more recently by Karen Fresco with a translation by Colleen P. Donagher (New York: Garland, 1992).

60. One of the adventures she puts him through involves rescuing her from an unwanted lover. She promised herself to anyone who could defeat all comers for seven years, and she finds herself with someone she does not want who has already lasted five years. Although this is a situation she has gotten herself into, it also turns a traditional motif of romance adventure on its head, and may well be a comment on women's vulnerability in marriages made for wealth or power, a problem that is alluded to in some of these romances.

61. Peter Haidu has suggested, rightly I think, that the heroine might be a surrogate for the poet, controlling the actions of the hero and the events of the story, though some of them get away from her, creating illusions like the hero's nightmares, but finally becoming a victim of the narrative machine. See Haidu, "Realism, Convention, Fictionality and the Theory of Genres in *Le Bel Inconnu*," *L'Esprit Créateur* 12 (1972), 37-60.

62. In *Florimont*, the hero's first love has magic powers, while the heroine is simply highly educated. In the other two, the heroine is highly educated and has magic powers

as well. All of them use their powers to help the hero, though they seem to lose some of the power when they allow themselves to fall in love.

63. The father had been told "qu'il n'avroit nul autre oir de moi," 4585. It is never explained whether the sister, Uraque, is illegitimate or a half-sister by her mother, or whether the prophecy meant that her father would not have sons or was simply wrong. Perhaps the topos of the educated heroine as an only child is so strong it overcomes even the facts of the plot. Perhaps the sister entered the story because the romance was written for the court of Blois, "very likely at the request of Alix," according to Hans-Erich Keller ("Literary Patronage in the Time of Philip Augustus," *The Spirit of the Court,* 197), daughter of Eleanor and Louis VII, younger sister of Marie de Champagne and half-sister of Philip Augustus. No patron is, however, named in the romance, which was edited by Joseph Gildea (Villanova: Villanova University Press, 1967-70), 2 vols.

64. In the course of the tourney, a knight declares his love to another woman, Persenis, who is in love with Partonopeu. She is very cautious about accepting the knight, saying she is the daughter of a count, not a king, and must have the emperor's permission. Melior and Partonopeu support the marriage, Partonopeu giving two counties to the knight to make him suitable for Persenis, who is the only heir to one of her own. This story is given in an appendix which would come around line 8970.

65. The story was, in fact, continued but whether by the same poet is not known. Krueger points out that the last words of the continuation, like the epilogue to the main romance, offer to write more, portraying the lady "primarily as a catalyst for future poetic activity," *Women Readers,* 190.

66. The need to keep love secret in order to preserve it is a motif that recurs, often as a practical matter in connection with adultery, as in *lais* of Marie de France and the Tristan stories, but it seems to me there is also a sense that once the knowledge is shared with others, the love is not the same.

67. The king's men wanted him to marry since he had no heir, male or female ("quant tu fil ne fille n'as," 951), recognizing the possibility of a woman inheriting though they hope for a man (900); her governess later reminds the heroine that if she died the land would be without an heir. The text is Aimon von Varennes, *Florimont,* ed. Alfons Hilka (Göttingen: Gesellschaft für Romanische Literatur, 1932). Though this romance is not much read now, apparently it was known to Christine de Pizan, along with other romances written for women, *Escanor* and *Cléomadès,* which suggests that women continued to read them for two centuries; see H. Michelant, introduction, in Gerard von Amiens, *Roman von Escanor,* ed. Michelant (Tübingen: Bibliothek Litterarischen Vereins in Stuttgart, 1886), and Krueger, *Women Readers,* 250.

68. The later romances also give greater roles to women, but in different ways. In the *Roman de Violette,* by Gerbert de Montreuil, composed for Marie, countess of Ponthieu, in the mid-thirteenth century, a wounded hero needs repeated healing by women; his faith in his lady is strong enough for him to stake his land on her constancy, but he is prey to deception and to a love-potion, while she remains absolutely loyal in the face of all kinds of vicissitudes. *Melusine,* by Jehan d'Arras, was composed in the late fourteenth century for the Duc de Berry and his sister, Marie, duchesse de Bar, about a fairy love, who gives wealth, governs well, builds a city, teaches the hero how to deal with all his problems, but is finally betrayed by his lack of faith.

69. Adenès emphasizes the role of the two women in his composition at the beginning and at the end of the work, so they are certainly among his patrons, although he sends the poem to a man, Robert count of Artois, and was apparently in the service of another man, Guy of Flanders (Dampierre) at the time. Adenès had begun in the service of Marie's father, Henry III of Brabant, who had him trained, and two of her brothers were also good to him. All of this is written into the end of the poem. But it is the two women who provided him with the story and commanded him to tell it. *Li Roumans*

de Cléomadès par Adenès li Rois, ed. André van Hasselt (Bruxelles: Victor Devaux, 1865), 2 vols.

70. Gerard also says "En escrit truis ci en ceste oevre, / si con li contes le descuevre" (61–2), which I take to mean "I composed it [le conte] in writing in this work, as the tale reveals it," not "I found it in writing in this work," which makes no sense.

71. "Mais et vouz et Kez, ce me samble / seriez trop bien conjoint ensamble / car il est I poi mesdisanz / et vouz r'estes trop despisanz / et de parler mal enseingnie: / si sera bone compaingnie," 11997–12002. But for all her sharp tongue, she hesitates to speak to Kay of love, because it would be ugly for a girl to do so.

72. Almost all the characters who matter in the story are given a suitable spouse; not only the hero's three sisters and the heroine's three companions but also her rejected suitor and his sister are appropriately matched, and even the widowed mother of the groom and father of the bride are married to each other. It is reminiscent of the marriages that occur at the end of *Kudrun,* a thirteenth-century German romance with a woman as the central character. She suffers from the wars brought on by male pride but, instead of taking revenge on her enemies, makes peace by arranging marriages. Neither the author nor the patron of *Kudrun* is known, but it is tempting to wonder if one of them at least was a woman.

73. The fictions include false names: Sare to the villain—is this meant to suggest she is Jewish and therefore not an appropriate wife to a king? He is from Africa, and nothing is said of his religion, but since the story is apparently Spanish, he might well be Muslim. Her other names are Trouvée, to suggest that she is a foundling and therefore again inappropriate for a king, and Perdue, presumably to suggest her state after the death of her supposed husband. But these names also mean something in her love story; she was "found" and then "lost" by Cléomadès, a double entendre only he would understand, like the conversation they have when he finds her again, which suggests madness to the others, but tells the hero what he needs to know.

74. *Les Enfances Ogier* is a rare example, as far as I know, of a chanson de geste presented to a woman, though it was commissioned by Guy of Flanders. The story includes two interesting women and several significant details. One woman is Charlemagne's aunt, Constance of Hungary, who governs her land for her son; she sends for help in defending it at the beginning of the poem, and sends thanks at the end, where she and her son have a double wedding with her rescuer and his daughter. The other woman, Gloriande, saves and then helps and guides the young hero, negotiates for him and for her own fiancé with Charlemagne and with her father, a pagan king whose land she inherits. Her people do homage to her, though her barons encourage her to marry. The poem was edited by August Scheler (Bruxelles: Closson, 1874).

75. *La Vie Seint Edmund le Rei, an Anglo-Norman poem of the Twelfth Century by Denis Piramus,* ed. Florence L. Ravenel (Philadelphia: J. C. Winston, 1906): "E Dame Marie altresi, / Ki en rime fist e basti, / E compensa les vers de lais, / ke ne sunt pas de tut verais; / Si en est ele mult loee, / E la rime par tut amee. / Kar mult laiment, si lunt mult cher, / Cunte, barun e chivaler. / E si en aiment mult lescrit, / E lire le funt, si unt delit, / E si les funt sovent retreire. / Les lais suelent as dames pleire. / De joie les oient e de gre, / Quil sunt sulum lur volente. / Li rei, li prince e li curtur, / Cunte, barun e vavasur, / Aiment cuntes, chanceuns e fables / . . . Kar il hostent e gettent penser, / Doil, enui e travail de quer, / E si funt ires ublier, / E del quer hostent le penser," 35–56.

5. WOMEN'S VISIONS OF WOMEN

1. The magistra was the presiding nun in a combined monastery of men and women under the rule of an abbot, as Schönau was. Elisabeth became magistra of Schönau in 1157, her brother abbot of Schönau in 1167.

2. For a comprehensive study of Elisabeth's life and works, the different versions in which they appeared, and sound arguments defending her literacy and analyzing the role her brother played in her work, see Anne Clark, *Elisabeth of Schönau, a Twelfth-Century Visionary* (Philadelphia: University of Pennsylvania Press, 1992). Clark, 24, citing Raoul Manselli, notes that the attacks Hildegard and Elisabeth made on Cathars and on the failure of the clergy to confront them led Elisabeth's brother Ekbert to compile a treatise of scriptural authority for use in examining Cathars. I am very grateful to Professor Clark for sharing material with me, for teaching me a great deal about Elisabeth, and for introducing me to her in the first place.

3. Although both went into religious life as children, Hildegard very young, the class system obtained even in the life of a recluse; Jutta, the noble recluse Hildegard joined, lived an austere life, but with a servant, a relative of lower birth. Neither Elisabeth nor Hildegard came from the highest nobility, but both could claim bishops among their relatives.

4. *Annales Palidenses, auctore Theodoro Monacho,* MGH, SS, 16.90, in an entry for 1158: "His etiam diebus in sexu fragili signa potentiae sue Deus ostendit, in duabus ancillis suis, Hildegarde videlicet in monte Roperti iuxta Pinguiam, et Elisabeth in Schonaugia, quas spiritu prophetie replevit, et multa eis genera visionum que scripte habentur per evangelium revelavit." The annals are from the monastery at Pöhlde, where Ruotger, a brother of Elisabeth and Ekbert, was provost from 1156 to 1163 (Clark, 5). While it is difficult to justify selecting only two of the many important women mystics from the twelfth and thirteenth centuries, Hildegard and Elisabeth seem appropriate choices. They were the first of major importance in the period who held respected positions within an established monastic order, whose revelations were widely sought by a varied and international audience, and they knew and supported each other's work.

5. Clark notes, 130, that the nature of her publications changed in the decade he was her secretary until her death in that the number of visions recorded decreased, but three major works were produced; at the same time, it was the angel's insistence that Elisabeth make the visions public that led to her need for Ekbert, not Ekbert's presence that made her publish them. All Elisabeth's works were edited by F. W. E. Roth, *Die Visionen der heiligen Elisabeth und die Schriften der Aebte Ekbert und Emecho von Schönau* (Brünn: Studien aus dem Benedictiner- und Cistercienser Orden, 1884).

6. Elisabeth's statements on the bodily assumption were cited in her lifetime and after, though they were never officially approved by Rome; see Clark, 27, 40–41. Peter Abelard, writing for the nuns of the Paraclete, also spoke for the bodily assumption.

7. Ruth J. Dean mentions a note in one manuscript in a Cistercian abbey in a thirteenth-century hand saying "this is read at meals"; see Dean, "Elizabeth, Abbess of Schönau, and Roger of Ford," *Modern Philology* 41 (1944), 209–220, particularly 217–18. Dean also cites a fourteenth-century historian, Nicholas Trevet, who mentioned Elisabeth in two of his works as a writer of some importance, giving details about her in the *Anglo-Norman Chronicle*—which he incidentally did for a woman, Mary of Woodstock, a nun and sister of Edward II. Dean also notes that Elisabeth's works are found among the writings of famous Benedictines and Cistercians, and Roth lists manuscripts, editions, and translations through the seventeenth century. For an up-to-date discussion of the transmission of Elisabeth's works, see Clark, appendix.

8. Not only did Hildegard accept Elisabeth's explanation of male members of the expedition, but the story of the pope's resignation became part of the official debate over a pope's ability to resign (Clark, 39); and Alberic des Trois Fontaines cited Elisabeth's as the true version in 1342 (Clark, 40).

9. In Clark's words (4), Elisabeth's "awareness of her femaleness and its implications for her place in the world and her attempt to articulate her specifically female religious identity are crucial aspects of her spirituality."

10. Elisabeth later sees those who killed themselves in a great abyss, suffering pain beyond estimation, unable to be freed (*Visionen,* 2.16), which suggests that her temptation had been a strong one. Clark notes (14) that *tristicia,* which had been a serious vice in monastic life, became "a medium of reflexive self-confrontation" in the piety of this period, but I think the state Elisabeth describes, like Abelard's in the *Historia calamitatum,* with the real possibility of suicide, is presented as morally dangerous.

11. Mary appears with Benedict, the founder of Elisabeth's order, again in 1.42 and 64, as if to give a feminine aspect to the order, which Benedict had conceived for men.

12. Caroline W. Bynum notes that Mary wears priestly vestments in a few late medieval paintings, but that such images have nothing to do with claiming sacerdotal functions for ordinary women: "Mary is priest because it is she who offers to ordinary mortals the saving flesh of God, just as the celebrant does in the mass"; see Bynum, *Fragmentation and Redemption: Essays on Gender and the Human Body in Medieval Religion* (New York: Zone Books, 1992), 212. The same may be true of Elisabeth's image, but I sense a psychological complication in her case, perhaps unconscious.

13. In one case, Elisabeth receives a sacrament in her vision, without benefit of human priest: she has a fever and sends for the abbot to give her the last rites, and with her magistra sitting beside her, she has a vision of a man who comes and talks with her and gives her the full rites, although he assures her she will not yet die, 1.65. Once she asked the brothers to celebrate the office of psalms in a field where the sisters could see it, but the field was flooded so they moved it; the lord, however, "recognized the desire of his handmaid, and I saw everything with the eyes of my mind" (1.44). She cannot control the brothers' actions, but she can supersede them with a higher authority.

14. All the women saints Elisabeth sees appear also in the third book of Christine de Pizan's *City of Ladies,* not surprisingly. They include some I have not mentioned, Afra, a prostitute who converted, gave everything to the poor, and was burned by pagans, and the eleven thousand virgins of Ursula's army, who became an important factor in Elisabeth's public life (1.30).

15. Communion plays a key role in Elisabeth's story. Not only does she go into ecstasy during the consecration (e.g., 1.76), though she often feels unworthy to receive the sacrament, but that small bread is able to weigh down her faults in the angel's scales. It is Mary who, accompanied by the apostles, turns the scales in her favor (1.77). Taking the body of Christ into oneself can be an imitation of Mary. For a study of later women and their relation to the host, see Caroline W. Bynum, "Women Mystics and Eucharistic Devotion in the Thirteenth Century," *Women's Studies* 11 (1984), 179-214, reprinted in *Fragmentation and Redemption.*

16. Cf. 2.23: Elisabeth asks the angel why she had such vexation of body, and again the angel says it is because she did not intend to take communion; when Elisabeth excuses herself, saying she feared she was not worthy enough, the angel asks how she can be worthy except through grace.

17. As her role begins to sound like Hildegard's, so do her words, "O homo surge," "rise, o man / human being" (1.67); "O homo cogita quid sis, quia pulvis et cinis es et vile figmentum," "O man, think what you are, for you are dust and ashes, and a vile figment" (1.68).

18. Elisabeth was certainly literate—she refers to her own reading of the psalms several times—but like Hildegard she was probably not schooled in Latin composition. In any case, it was in her (and her brother's) best interests to assert that the visions were composed by God, not by Elisabeth.

19. Clark (92) connects the "fili hominis" passage with Elisabeth's "self-consciousness about doing something (preaching the word of God) that is traditionally the exclusive vocation of men" and suggests (93) that the new image of herself as preacher and prophet "could not but collide with Elisabeth's sense of herself as a woman whose sole technique of affecting the world was prayer within her cloistered community."

20. The nun scribes who had been taking it all down certainly knew about her visions. Elisabeth says they showed the abbot "a part of the present book which you, brother, left with me, which I firmly proposed, as we discussed, to keep hidden to the end of my life." She does not make clear whether Ekbert gathered the notes the sisters made on their tablets or whether he took his own notes from what Elisabeth told him, in which case presumably she used their notes to refresh her memory. The sisters continued to take things down even after Ekbert was installed at Schönau, 3.8; see also Clark, 51–52.

21. This book has been translated by Thalia A. Pandiri in *Medieval Women's Visionary Literature,* ed. Elizabeth A. Petroff (New York: Oxford University Press, 1986), 159–70.

22. The priest spills some of the blood on the corporal, which Elisabeth, already in ecstasy, sees; the brother who did it cannot be consoled, and Elisabeth asks Mary what to do. Mary says the corporal should be put with the relics, where the Lord will protect it. After a year and many supplications for the negligence, Elisabeth sees a communion cloth suspended over the altar, with a small red spot which gets smaller day by day until it is gone, showing, the angel explains, that the negligence has been purged. (2.26).

23. Clark also makes a point of this episode, seeing the tension between Elisabeth's charismatic, visionary power and the abbot's liturgical power, 114–15. It might be mentioned that in the course of the twelfth century, as monastic males said more masses for the dead, there was a danger that people would ask monastic females less frequently for prayers for the dead, with economic repercussions for women's houses (Jo Ann McNamara mentioned this in a talk at Columbia University, April 10, 1993; cf. Johnson, *Equal in Monastic Profession,* 225–26). Elisabeth's interest in the prayers may reflect such a concern. Since Elisabeth is sure she is going to die (the angel implies it will be in three years, 2.17), her visions of purgatory and of heaven are all the more immediate. She sees various uncles in purgatorial situations (2.19), one of whom asks for masses, saying other prayers are like other food when one does not have bread and wine (2.20). On Elisabeth and purgatory, see Clark, 111ff., who points out that Elisabeth's references to it are not mentioned by Jacques LeGoff in his study (*La Naissance du Purgatoire* [Paris: Gallimard, 1981]), and indeed antedate the starting point he gives for it.

24. In the sermon on the way of martyrs, there is an injunction to mankind in darkness to raise the eyes of the intellect and look into the future and see the "blessed reformation of your body which will come from the saviour when he removes from your flesh the thorn of Adam" (4.12, p. 98).

25. The vision of Peter occurs in 2.29, which Roth puts after 2.27, since it is next in chronological order, noting that it follows that order in MS. A, see footnote, p.vi. In any case, the two episodes are not more than a few lines apart.

26. This piece had been very popular as a separate work. Ekbert fit it into the collected works roughly where it belonged chronologically in the autobiographical series.

27. Peter Damian's letter in response to his sister's questions about the beginning and end of the world gives a model for exchanges on theological subjects between religious siblings. It is conceivable that Elisabeth had such interests but was hesitant to speak of them until her brother gave her the occasion.

28. She asks him if, when souls are already in peace, prayers help. He answers that they give more joy to those who do not need them because they are benefitting those who do.

29. Ekbert insists he is no "doctor," no "dispenser of the mysteries of God," but a man of small sense, who answers out of love for his sister, asking her to pray that God will fill his mouth (as he does hers). Indeed, he says he uses the principle of interpretation he learned from her ("habito principio interpretationis ex te latius edisseram"),

and implies that she already knows some of the answers ("rightly I think you feel that," "according to what I have learned from you, adding little from my sense," and "why I chose this mode, you, my sister know, who were the cause of my digression," 3.31).

30. Clark suggests (95, 97) that this vision presents Elisabeth as a participant in the larger scheme of divine revelations, and that she recognized her special role in the divine order of history. The LVD was, in fact, a more popular work than the *Scivias,* judging from the number of known early manuscripts, twenty-nine to eight (Clark, 36), perhaps because its thrust is moral guidance rather than theology and complex allegory. Its popularity went beyond Germany: an English Cistercian, Roger, sent a copy of it to his abbot at Ford, which he had procured in France, telling him how eagerly it was read by abbots and bishops and asking him to have a copy made for Roger's mother's convent (Clark, 25); it continued to be read in various countries through the seventeenth century at least (Dean, 218).

31. This sermon includes attacks on venal women and vain men who put off virile seriousness and take on the softness of women, which may be connected with Hildegard's description of the corrupt world as womanish. It also tells women to obey their husbands and to bear even bad ones, making up for their iniquities with alms and prayer, and ends with an attack on Cathars, who reject the married way altogether.

32. Women were of course interested in this issue, since loss of virginity carried such heavy shame for the female sex. Hrotsvit also makes a point of the soul's ability to remain pure, whatever others might do to the body.

33. A cemetery had been excavated in 1106, but further excavations in 1156 turned up male bones, which cast doubt on the earlier identification of it as the burial place of Ursula's army. Bones from the cemetery were sent to various local monasteries, which were anxious to verify their authenticity. Elisabeth's visions about Ursula and her companions are the most popular of her works, judging from the seventy manuscripts in which they appear, far more, as Clark points out (37), than those of two later twelfth-century versions of the revised story. The book was translated by Marcelle Thiébaux, *The Writings of Medieval Women* (New York: Garland, 1987), as "The Book of Revelations of the Sacred Band of Virgins of Cologne," 146-62. Thiébaux also includes the first letter from Elisabeth to Hildegard, 138-43.

34. The importance of this explanation cannot be overstated. Clark notes (37-39) that medieval painters and chroniclers usually included the scene of the pope's resignation in Rome, which indeed was cited in debates over Celestine V's resignation.

35. This means, of course, that there were nonvirgin women accompanying the army, presumably over and above the eleven thousand virgins, but Elisabeth does not discuss that. One of the most surprising male presences, to Elisabeth, is that of Ursula's abandoned spouse, Etherius, a king, who was there with his mother, his sister, and a maternal cousin (5.11-12). He also had a vision, that he should exhort his mother to become a Christian and should join Ursula in her martyrdom. This does not completely satisfy Elisabeth, who still wants to know why he is said in the inscription to have lived a faithful life for twenty-five years, when he had to be instructed in Christianity for his betrothal to Ursula; she is told that the inscription referred to his modest and innocent life.

36. The last chapter of the book is a report from Ekbert to the abbot of Steinveld, answering questions he had asked Ekbert to put to Elisabeth about a saint buried in their church. The answer, a long one not included in the Thiébaux translation, includes two interesting details: that the angel is offended by what he considers a trick question put by the brothers, and that though Elisabeth takes questions from others, she puts them when she is ready (or when she remembers to).

37. The letter, addressed to Guda, Hadewig, and Regelind of Andernach, is in Roth, *Visionen,* 263-78.

38. Popes and emperors ask for her word on current events and her reputation as a prophet continued for many centuries. Marjorie Reeves cites Petrus de Aliaco in 1490

coupling her prophecy of Antichrist with Joachim's, and James Maxwell in 1615 putting her at the head of a list of Roman Catholic witnesses to the reformation of the church of Rome (*Joachim of Fiore and the Prophetic Future* [London: SPCK, 1976], 81, 157). In *Joachim of Fiore and the Myth of the Eternal Evangel in the Nineteenth Century* (Oxford: Clarendon, 1987), Reeves cites a list of false prophets by Gabriel Naudé in 1623 which includes Hildegard and Savonarola (13–14), the influence of Hildegard on neo-Johannites in the eighteenth century (194, n. 44), and circulation of her prophecies in connection with Pierre-Michel Vintras in the nineteenth century (197).

39. Barbara Newman and Peter Dronke have done a great deal to focus attention on Hildegard and to enhance our knowledge and understanding of her and her work. For more intense studies than I offer here, see particularly Newman, *Sister of Wisdom: St. Hildegard's Theology of the Feminine* (Berkeley: University of California Press, 1987); *Symphonia: A Critical Edition of the* Symphonia armonie celestium revelationum (Ithaca: Cornell University Press, 1988); and the introduction to *Scivias*, trans. Hart and Bishop (New York: Paulist Press, 1990). See also Dronke, *Poetic Individuality,* chapter 5; "Problemata Hildegardiana," *MlatJb* 16 (1981), 97–131; and *Women Writers of the Middle Ages* (Cambridge; Cambridge University Press, 1984), chapter 6. I owe a great deal to their studies as well as to their editions of texts.

40. Both incidents are recounted in the third book of her life by Godfrey of Disibodenberg and Theodoric of Echternach, which was heavily based on information Hildegard gave them and on autobiographical passages in her writings. Monica Klaes has edited the *Vita Sanctae Hildegardis,* CCCM 126 (Turnholt: Brepols, 1993). It is also in PL197, c.91–130 and has been translated by Anna Silvas in "Saint Hildegard of Bingen and the Vita Sanctae Hildegardis," *Tjurunga* 29 (1985), 4–25; 30 (1986), 63–73; 31 (1986), 32–41; and 32 (1987), 46–59. Godfrey, who was briefly her secretary, wrote the first book, Theodoric the other two. There is also a fragmentary life by Guibert of Gembloux (ed. Pitra and more recently among the letters of Guibert by Derolez Gb 38), and a long letter from Hildegard to Guibert about the nature of her visions, which Dronke edited in *Women Writers,* 250–64.

41. Newman points out that if only the humble could be exalted, women had a paradoxical advantage, in theory (*Sister of Wisdom,* 3, 35), that human weakness could be a sign of divine empowerment.

42. Guibert, her other biographer and last secretary, said that when he wanted to polish her style, Hildegard did not scorn his help but reminded him that Moses, though uncircumcised and ineloquent, spoke with God as a friend, and that Jeremiah demurred that he did not know how to speak (Gb38. 410–16). Hildegard seems also to have identified with Disibod, the patron saint of her old convent, whose abbot asked her for revelations about him. In the life she wrote, she describes him as a figure of humility and good works, who had to strike out on his own to be free (he from parents, she from her parent-monastery); he fought heresies virilely, attracted followers, and cured the ill and demonically possessed, and lived a long life (PL197. c.1095ff.).

43. She did celebrate historic women in her poems, though few by name. And in the life she wrote of Rupert, the saint whose church she chose for her new convent, she emphasized the saint's mother, Bertha, who suffered in her marriage to a pagan tyrant, vowed herself to God if she were freed, and when her husband died, built a church and removed herself and her son to it. She brought him up a good Christian and together they built a hospice and a city, resisted the attempt of nobles to draw him back to his secular heritage, and ministered to the needy. After his death, she continued her holy life for twenty-five years (PL197. c.1083ff.).

44. Newman calls Hildegard "the first Christian thinker to deal seriously and positively with the feminine as such," and also points out that as an abbess, spiritual

counselor, and physician, she was able to observe women and their particular gifts and problems (*Sister of Wisdom*, xvii-xviii). Bernhard Scholz speaks of Hildegard as "the first medieval woman to reflect and write at length on women"; see Scholz, "Hildegard von Bingen on the Nature of Woman," *American Benedictine Review* 31:4 (1980), 361. He sees in her writings "a profound disillusionment with a social order which gave women few rights and no power" (371), despite her acceptance of so many traditional views on the role of the sexes.

45. Guibert in his life of Hildegard, devotes the second chapter to Jutta, identifying her as a daughter of the count of Spanheim, beautiful, wealthy, young but mature of mind, who spurned all suitors, like St. Agnes, embraced celibacy virilely, and spent her life in meditation on divine law. He compares her to Judith, that most powerful virago, because she amputated the intellectual head of Holofernes, that is, lust, with the sword of the word of God. She attracted many followers and when she died at twenty-four, Hildegard was considered the most worthy to succeed her (Gb38).

46. Godfrey relates in book one that the pope, Eugenius III, had her writings investigated, read them himself to the council of Trier, and, with the support of Bernard of Clairvaux, gave his official confirmation and protection and encouraged her to continue to set down in writing any message from the Holy Spirit. In 2.1, Theodoric cites Hildegard's relation of these events. She does not mention Bernard, though we know he encouraged her from the exchange of letters between them; what she does say is that Eugene had them read publicly and read them privately himself, and ordered her to put in writing whatever she saw or heard in a vision. It is impossible to know which details are more accurate, but it is interesting that Hildegard's version has the pope giving her carte blanche, while Godfrey's limits the visions to those from the Holy Spirit.

47. Dronke, *Women Writers*, 160-62, offers an interpretation of this vision as referring to Hildegard's writings, the three visionary works, and perhaps the scientific treatises; the last and most ambitious book of visions (the *Liber divinorum operum*, still to come), would be represented in the vision by a fourth tower she could not see, but which was to be stronger and more excellent than the others.

48. Dronke, *Women Writers*, 164, suggests that the exorcism ritual was an "ingenious attempt at shock-therapy," and the later treatment cured the woman by allowing her to give vent openly to all her religious fixations. The lies the spirit uttered through the woman were catharist teachings, which attracted the attention of Elisabeth of Schönau's brother Ekbert, who followed up the information in them about certain Cathars, interrogated them, and, according to his biographer, turned them away from their heresy (Clark, *Elisabeth of Schönau*, 24).

49. Apparently God's voice also spoke in unpolished Latin, from which I assume Hildegard is making a distinction between oral and literary style. But Dronke argues for her command of Latin style, describing it as "forceful and colourful, and at times as subtle and brilliant, as any in the twelfth century" (*Women Writers*, 200, cf. 194). Dronke also notes à propos of her learning that people are still trying to track down her sources (ibid., 200); in "Problemata," he suggests Donatus and various Stoic sources for the *Scivias*, as well as Lucan and possibly Seneca and Cicero, 108ff.

50. The *Scivias* was edited by Adelgundis Führkötter, with Angela Carlevaris, CCCM 43-43a, 2v (Turnholt: Brepols, 1978); it was translated by Columba Hart and Jane Bishop (New York: Paulist Press, 1990).

51. The text has now been edited by Angela Carlevaris, *Hildegardis Liber vite meritorum*, CCCM 90 (Turnholt: Brepols, 1995). A translation based on the Pitra edition was done by Bruce W. Hozeski, *The Book of the Rewards of Life* (New York: Garland, 1994).

52. Since Richardis left her in 1151, long before the composition of the last two books of visions, Hildegard is either recalling the experience of the first book as the

crucial moment for her writing or alluding to other supportive companions. This seems less likely, even though she certainly had them, because her description of the pair, "the man I secretly sought and found" and the young girl is virtually formulaic. They are mentioned at the beginning of the LDO as well, "that man whom as I said in earlier visions I had secretly sought and found, and that girl I mentioned in previous visions."

53. In the first vision, Hildegard sees a fiery multitude looking at the precepts and arcane learning of God being written by the power of God (*virtus Dei*), sounding them like a very powerful trumpet (*fortissima tuba*) in every kind of music ("omni genere musicorum") but with one sound (*uno sono*). Hildegard also speaks of herself as a trumpet, which only sounds when God blows through it (in the letter to Elisabeth of Schönau). Given her musical interests and talent, it is not surprising that Hildegard thinks of herself as participating in the divine harmony.

54. See also Newman on Hildegard's "eccentric commentary" on Christ's reproach to his mother at the wedding at Cana, "Quid mihi et tibi est, mulier" (John 2:4), which she takes as a question about what God and the woman share.

55. Cf. Abelard's discussion of circumcision, n. 59 in chapter 2.

56. At the same time, she does say that women should not assume male clothes or male roles, and therefore should not approach the office of the altar, 2.6.77. Hildegard's God forbids cross-dressing except to save the life of a man or the chastity of a woman, though he apparently approves it in the symbolic figures who appear to Hildegard in the visions, where women (virtues) wear helmets and even bishop's mitres. To connect cross-dressing with the priesthood seems either to trivialize the prohibition or to emphasize that it is not essential. Newman (*Sister of Wisdom*, 214) says woman lacks the beard, which is required of a priest; Hildegard says "virilem personem nec in capillis nec in vestitu suo demonstrabit" ("she will not show a virile person in her hair or dress," ibid.), which may refer to facial hair but is not specific.

57. Newman notes that virginity and maternity were not mutually exclusive for Hildegard but "aspects of the unique feminine birthright that Eve unfortunately spoiled" (*Sister of Wisdom*, 188). Mary was both virgin and mother; Eve could have been.

58. Newman makes the eloquent point that Hildegard in seeing the church as a woman was "testifying that humankind in its totality . . . had a feminine face"; knowing that "her womanhood signified the divine humanity . . . she could . . . endure the misogyny of her culture with a serenity that is barely credible in our demythologized world" (*Sister of Wisdom*, 249).

59. The male/female psychological characteristics described here are not very different from what Carol Gilligan and Deborah Tannen have recently observed, another indication that Hildegard's study of the human condition included psychological as well as moral and physical traits.

60. That only a woman can represent the humility necessary to perfection is a point implicitly made by Dante in his allusion to St. Clare, the only human being in the Comedy whose life is described as "perfetta," Par. 3.97.

61. There is a brief allusion to Delilah, to the effect that when Samson's wife left him, he was deprived of his eyesight, as the synagogue forsook Christ, rejecting his doctrine (1.5.8). This is confusing, in that if Delilah represents the synagogue, she should be blind; if Samson is Christ, why is he blind?

62. Cf. his words to Christ: "you were born miraculously of a virgin, not conceived by the seed of a man," 3.6.15. In the LDO, Christ says, "I was sent from the father, I took on flesh in the maternal viscera without virile humidity [seed?]," 5.44.

63. Newman points out that statistically Hildegard puts much more emphasis on Christ's incarnation through the virgin than on his passion or crucifixion (*Sister of Wisdom*, 159 and n.5).

64. Both God and Christ continue to acknowledge Mary's importance in the incarna-

tion and the redemption in the second book of visions: "I [the living light] came, flaming, and rested in the womb of the virgin, incarnate from her flesh" (6.32); cf. 6.45, already cited, and 5.37, from the root of Jesse, a girl (*puella*) arose who divided lust in the belly of the serpent when she gave birth without the taste of lust in girlish innocence. In LDO 4.105, God speaks of "my son from the Virgin Mary," born without sin, of the word that took flesh in the womb of the Virgin, through the burning of the Holy Spirit.

65. In contrast, a suicide cannot be saved because he/she cannot do penance, 1.116. Hildegard, like Elisabeth of Schönau, is interested in the concept of purgatorial punishments which give more room for salvation. She includes a passage about purgatory in *Causae et Curae*, speaking of the fires as a kind of natural healing. She says the fires descend into places in the earth and gather where there are also rivers, so that certain souls can be examined in the fires and the waters; some of those rivers come up through the earth, as hot springs because of those inextinguishable fires which can be healing for people to bathe in (5.233).

66. The LDO describes ten visions, in three parts. The numbers I give in the text refer to the visions and their subdivisions, not to the three parts.

67. Physical adornment is, of course, an issue on which Hildegard had been criticized, by abbess Tengswind (VA52). She defended her nuns' elaborate dress on certain occasions with the example of the virgins in Revelations, adorning themselves for their husband, the lamb of God. Whether Hildegard was sympathetic to women, secular or religious, enjoying adornment is not clear, but not impossible.

68. In the moral allegory of the LDO, the female represents the body, the male the soul, because she "through the subtle knowledge of his work covers the man," 4.66; she was formed of flesh and blood, man of mud, so in his nudity he looked to her to be covered by her. Man (*vir*) who "according to God is strong and powerful" completes all his works with woman, who first gave the fall and through whom all ills were afterward repaired to better.

69. *Causae et Curae* was edited by Paul Kaiser for the *Bibliotheca Scriptorum Graecorum et Romanorm Teubneriana* (Leipzig: Teubner, 1903). I will refer to it as CC hereafter, giving book and page number. For a very useful study of Hildegard's medical writings on women, see Joan Cadden, "It Takes All Kinds: Sexuality and Gender Differences in Hildegard of Bingen's *Book of Compound Medicine*," *Traditio* 40 (1983), 149-74. See also her *Meanings of Sex Difference in the Middle Ages: Medicine, Science, and Culture* (Cambridge: Cambridge University Press, 1993). I am grateful to Professor Cadden for sharing her work on Hildegard's scientific writings with me over the years. Cadden pointed out that Hildegard wrote both medical works in her own voice, not in God's, without having recourse to either the female humility topos of frailty or the male learned topos of naming authorities. She seems to be her own authority in these works, drawing on her experience and observation, occasionally even giving German names for plants and animals used in treatment.

70. For a detailed analysis of the differences according to temperament, choleric, melancholy, phlegmatic, and sanguine, see Cadden, "It Takes All Kinds." Cadden calls Hildegard's independence and breadth of treatment on this subject "unusual, perhaps unique in the twelfth century" (165-66).

71. The infidelity of either parent can be harmful to the child, though a woman's adultery during early pregnancy is especially contaminating (2.68-69). "The children who are born from these just and unjust husbands or from just and unjust wives [if the child is conceived in wedlock, but one or the other parent has committed adultery], will be unhappy, since they have taken the origin of their conception from different customs and different blood, namely of men and of women" ("scilicet tam virorum quam mulierum," 2.68).

72. Speaking about woman's and man's pleasure, Hildegard says woman's is like the sun, spreading its heat over the earth so it brings forth fruit, man's like a storm or

fire (2.76). When the wind of pleasure comes from the woman's marrow to the matrix which adheres to the umbilical, it falls and moves the woman's blood to delight, and since the matrix is full and open around the umbilical, the wind dilates in her belly and therefore burns more gently . . . and also either from fear or from modesty she can restrain herself more easily from pleasure, so that the spume of seed is ejected more rarely by her than by a man, and is like a crumb to his loaf. The force of the winds of passion is dissipated in the broad space of a woman's womb, while in a man they enter a smaller area and so are more concentrated and harder to control (2.76).

73. This analysis is tantalizingly close to modern feminist interpretations of Genesis. See particularly Carol Meyers, *Discovering Eve: Ancient Israelite Women in Context* (New York: Oxford University Press, 1988), chapter 5.

74. The text of the *Symphonia armonie celestium revelationum* (Symphony of the harmony of celestial revelations) was edited and translated by Barbara Newman (Ithaca: Cornell University Press, 1988). Newman gives both poetic and literal translations; I cite from the literal, though I admire the power of the poetic, and occasionally I use my own words. I have taken the poems after the other works although they were probably composed earlier, because they were written and revised over a long period and cannot be dated with certainty (see Newman's introduction, 6–12).

75. See Newman, *Sister of Wisdom*, chapter 6, on Ecclesia in Hildegard's works.

76. In the cycle on the Holy Spirit that follows the poems to the Virgin, the third person of the trinity is described not only as a masculine spirit but also in the feminine as a "life-giving life" ("vivificans vita," 24), as charity (25), and the whole trinity is the creatrix of all things ("creatrix omnium," 26).

77. Newman connects the building metaphors that Hildegard uses for the Virgin Mary with the real buildings Hildegard had built for her new convent. Bruce Holsinger notes her emphasis on the boundless fertility and potential of the female body rather than its static utilitarianism in her descriptions of the Virgin ("The Flesh of the Voice: Embodiment and the Homoerotics of Devotion in the Music of Hildegard of Bingen (1098–1179)," *Signs* 19.1 [1993], 115); the Virgin's body experiences the touch of the holy spirit as grass experiences dew, not by penetration but by coating and immersion in moisture (109). He suggests that in "O viridissima virga" (*Symph* 19), *virgo* replaces *virga*, the phallic stem, acknowledging the unique powers, pleasures, and fruits of the female body, and radical irrelevance of the phallus (111).

78. Newman, in her introduction to the *Symphonia,* calls Hildegard "a maverick," who "exceeded the Carolingian composers in irregularity; her forms are so free that it is often hard to tell a sequence from a hymn" (16). On Hildegard's music, see Marianne Richert Pfau, "Music and Text in Hildegard's Antiphons," in *Symphonia*, 74–94 and her dissertation, "Hildegard von Bingen's *Symphonia armonie celestium revelationum:* An Analysis of Musical Process, Modality, and Text-Music Relations" (SUNY Stony Brook, 1990). See Holsinger on the nature and effect of Hildegard's music in relation to her view of women; he argues that various compositional strategies "express her profound awareness of the sonorous richness of the female body . . . and the constant refusal to repeat melodies and render them static throws the relationship Hildegard constructs into continuous flux" (115).

79. Cf. Caroline Walker Bynum on religious virgins: "the virgin (like Christ's mother, the perpetual virgin) was also a bride, destined for a higher consummation. She scintillated with fertility and power. Into her body, as into the eucharistic bread on the altar, poured the inspiration of the spirit and the fullness of the humanity of Christ." See Bynum, *Holy Feast and Holy Fast* (Berkeley: University of California Press, 1987), 20.

80. The translation is from Dronke, *Women Writers,* who discusses the letter and gives a partial translation, with text (196–98).

81. Cf. LDO, 5.23: man born in the fragile nature of Adam ("in fragili natura

Adae"); the fragility which arose from Adam ("de fragilitate quae sibi de Adam orta est").

82. Among her responses to the questions of the monks of Villers, Hildegard says that God spoke with angelic words which Adam understood, indeed Adam had knowledge of all languages through the wisdom he received from God and through the spirit of prophecy (solution to question 4). This links Hildegard's own source of knowledge, prophecy, to prelapsarian understanding. In CC, Hildegard says God sent many things to Adam in true prophecy, since he was not yet in a state of sin; so the soul of a sleeping man might see many truths if not weighed down with sin (2.82); cf. *Scivias*, 2.1.8: weighed down by sin, Adam could not rise to a true knowledge of God.

83. Hildegard occasionally connects women with fruit and flowers, in a spiritual sense (VA162), but not with agricultural labor.

84. The text says: "Adam enim uxorem suam culpare posset quod ei consilio suo mortem intulit, sed tamen eam non dimisit . . . quoniam illam sibi per divinam potentiam datam esse cognovit," 1.2.11, lines 271-74. The Hart-Bishop translation gives "Adam could have blamed his wife," but I think the force of *posset* is that he did blame her, but he did not give her up.

85. Ursula and her virgins were ministered to by religious and wise men, "For God / foreshadowed in the first woman / that woman should be nurtured / by the care [*custodia*] of man" (*Symphonia*, 63). In an exposition on the gospel about the birth of Christ (Pitra, 245ff.), Hildegard comments that God wished Mary to marry Joseph so that he would care for her, and she would be subject to him, because every woman who has a child should have a man caring for her (*procurantem*).

86. In a traditional image, Christ's wound in his side, from which sprang the church, wipes out the sin of Eve and Adam, after Eve was made from Adam's side, 3.2.21.

87. Although it does not occur in every vision, it averages to more than once per vision. I noticed allusions to Adam's transgression or sin ("divinum praeceptum transgressus est," "crimen transgressionis Adae," "casus Adae," "veterem culpam Adae," "praevaricationem Adae," "Adae peccatum," "vetus crimen Adae") in 1.4.4, 5, 30; 1.5.6; 2.1.8, 13; 2.3.18, 19, 24, 26, 34; 2.4.7; 2.5.12, 38, 60; 2.6.3, 18, 33, 62, 82, 83, 99; 3.1.5; 3.2.6, 7, 10, 21; 3.9.22; and 3.10.32. Christ's reparation of Adam's sin is mentioned in 2.1.13; 2.3.24, 34; 2.5.12; 2.6.18, 82; 3.2.15; 3.6.35.

88. But cf. 3.16: lust, the swallowings of the serpent's belly, grew in Adam and Eve through the hearing of their ears, when obedience vanished in them.

89. Passages in which I noticed an allusion to the sin or fall of Adam: 3.40, 3.80, 4.8, 4.53, 6.14, 6.16, 6.32, 6.33; to Adam and Eve together, 3.16, 5.27.

90. Hildegard alludes frequently in the LDO to Adam's transgression, fall, and exile: 4.69, 73, 92, 98; 5.18, 34; 7.17, 9.7, 10.5, 6. But she also connects Adam with Christ in 7.11 (angels wondered that you took your vestment from the mortal Adam, which you did so the transgressor would be revived), 7.14 (contrasting the wisdom of Christ with the ignorance of Adam), and 9.12 (the son of God descended into the Virgin's belly because Adam's transgression of God's precepts made him mortal).

91. Other examples: Adam lost the light of paradise at the fall and walked in the suggestion of the devil with all his sons/children (VA86 to an abbot); Adam perished for he did not complete the course of his circle (VA158r, to a deacon); Adam broke the law which led to death and exile (Schrader Führkötter, 130, to an emperor).

92. Though Hildegard tells an abbot (named Adam) that Samson and Solomon lost their power and glory through the foolishness of women, it is to keep him from doing the same, giving up his burden out of weariness (VA85r); that is, she is using the woman as a figure for the weaker side of man's nature, rather than as a historical source of trouble. She also mentions Adam's fall in this letter, saying God knew Adam would

be redeemed by charity (female), charity that had existed in the beginning and created Adam and Eve from the pure nature of earth.

93. A letter addressed to an abbess (VA110r) speaks of the serpent breathing on the woman through eloquence which she received, inclined herself to the serpent, and passed it on to her husband and it remained in man, since man (*vir*) carries through all things fully. That is, eloquence comes to man from the serpent via woman, as does knowledge: the first woman was formerly called night and she showed knowledge to the night, her husband (Christ is day). The letter also mentions God's choice of the virgin to carry his Word to humanity. In a letter to Hillin, archbishop of Trier (VA26r), the voice of Wisdom speaks of the first woman making a nod to the first man in deception, but then goes on to say that man has many strengths which woman can complete and that woman is the font of wisdom and full joy which man can complete.

94. The comment, "Let her look to God and not to man (*virum*), *whom first she did not want to have*," comes in the midst of a long letter which preaches the benefits of rejecting carnal husbands for the bedchamber of the supernal king. When she puts the face of her spirit in God, a woman may look like the eagle into the sun and like a dove through her windows, a forceful conjunction of male and female images. The passage seems to me one of the most significant remarks Hildegard makes about herself.

95. In a poem, Hildegard has holy widows who have now chosen marriage with Christ identify, in their previous marriage to a human husband, with Eve: "O father . . . who set (*constituisti*) us in the rib of the first mother, / who built for us a great fall into affliction— / we followed her / in our own right into exile, / joining ourselves to her pain" (*Symphonia*, 58).

96. "While the unhappy ones were blushing / at their offspring / walking in the exile of the fall, / then you cry out with a clear voice, / in this way lifting humanity / from this wicked / fall" (14). In a poem in which Ursula and her virgins are figures of Mary (65), Hildegard conflates the two, "the person whom He had formed from clay [Adam] / to live without mingling of man [Eve]," as the root in which God planted the burning bush. In the fourteenth century, Na Prous Boneta, a woman condemned for her apocalyptic visions, saw herself as the bearer or bestower (*donatrix*) of the Holy Spirit, as Mary was of the son. In her scheme, Eve is not responsible for the fall—she is a scapegoat blamed by Adam for what he did—while Adam's sin is replayed by the pope, John XXII. See Claudia Ratazzi Papka, "Fictions of Judgment: The Apocalyptic 'I' in the Fourteenth Century" (Ph.D. diss., Columbia University, 1996), 172–73.

97. The Eve/Mary contrast runs through Hildegard's poems. Besides the ones I have mentioned, it occurs in 10: against the prime matter of the world which Eve threw into confusion, God fashioned the word through which he had created it as man for Mary, "Hoc Verbum effabricavit tibi"; in 19: all that Mary is, blossoming, flower, aromas, dew on grass, wheat, food, joy, all these Eve scorned; and in 23: the spirit of God breathed on Mary and "sucked out what Eve bore away in the breach of purity."

6. WOMEN REPRESENTING WOMEN

1. I have nothing to add to the question of the identity of the author or authors of the life of Edward and the life of Catherine. The latter is certainly a more sophisticated work, but whether it is a later effort by the same author or the work of a different nun altogether is not clear. William MacBain, the editor of Clemence, seemed to accept her authorship of the earlier life in "The Literary Apprenticeship of Clemence of Barking," *Journal of the Australasian Universities Language and Literature Association* 9 (1958), 3–22, though he has apparently raised questions about it more recently, according to Elkins, *Holy Women of Twelfth-Century England*, 212, n. 17. My interest

is in the fact that both lives were written by a nun of Barking in a courtly style and form, with a courtly audience of "Seignurs" in mind.

2. "Muse eloquent entre les IX, Christine / nompareille que je saiche aujord'hui, / En sens acquis et en toute dotrine, / Tu as de Dieu science et non d'autruy; / Tes epistres et livres, que je luy . . . de grant philosophie . . . me font certain de la grant habondance / De ton sçavoir," *Oeuvres Complètes de Eustache Deschamps,* SATF 9, vol. 6, ed. le Marquis de Queux de Saint-Hilaire (Paris: Firmin Didot, 1889), balade 1242.

3. *Le Débat sur le Roman de la Rose,* ed. Eric Hicks (Paris: Champion, 1977), "Responsio de Gersonno ad scripta cuiusdam," 104-8.

4. "Loer assez je ne la puis / . . . Aux estrangiers pouons la feste / Faire de la vaillant Cristine, / Dont la vertu est manifeste / En lettre et en langue latine / . . . Froissart savoit bien le pratique / De bien dicter . . . / La mort Machaut, grant rethorique, / Les facteurs amoureux lamentent. / Les aultres d'Alain se dementent / Car il a le mieulx baladé. / . . . Mais elle fut Tulle et Cathon! / Tulle: car en toute eloquence / Elle eut la rose et le bouton; / Cathon aussy en sapience." The work is cited by Gaston Paris, "Un Poème inédit de Martin Le Franc," *Romania* 16 (1887), 415-16, from Raimond Thomassy, *Essai sur les écrits politiques de Christine de Pisan, suivi d'une notice littéraire et de pièces inédites* (Paris: Debécourt, 1838).

5. Charity Cannon Willard, *Christine de Pizan: Her Life and Works* (New York: Persea, 1984), 186, mentions the versions of the *Livre des Fais d'Armes et de Chevalerie* in which the sex of the author is suppressed.

6. On this manuscript and on Christine as a publisher of her own works, see J. C. Laidlaw, "Christine de Pizan—A Publisher's Progress," *Modern Language Review* 82 (1987), 35-75. For the letter to the queen, see Thomassy.

7. I discussed the epics in chapter 3. I will not attempt to deal with the scholarship on Hrotsvit here, except to mention again the important work done by Katarina Wilson and Peter Dronke (*Women Writers*), both of whom take her deservedly seriously as a writer. The text I use is *Hrotsvithae Opera,* ed. Helen Homeyer. Translations have been done by M. H. Wiegand, *The Legends of Hrotsvitha: Text, Translation, and Commentary,* (Ph.D. diss., St. Louis University, 1936); K. M. Wilson, *The Dramas of Hrotsvit of Gandersheim* (Saskatoon: Peregrina, 1985), also L. Bonfante and A. Bonfante-Warren, *The Plays of Hrotswitha of Gandersheim* (New York: New York University Press, 1979); and the epics by Mary B. Bergman, *Hrosvithae Liber Tertius,* text and translation (Covington, Ky.: Sisters of Saint Benedict, 1943).

8. Dronke suggests that Hrotsvit's diminutives are "self-assured, even self-assertive, by being self-deprecating" (*Women Writers,* 82); he takes her insistence on her frailty and her incompetence as an ironic approach to the double standards of the male-dominated world.

9. In the invocation to Mary which precedes the first poem, she claims that one who made the foolish ass speak and the virgin conceive can loose her tongue, comparing herself in humility to the ass, but at the same time as an instrument of God's will to the virgin who bore the ruler of all in her womb, *Historia nativitatis,* 29-38. She will sing gratefully, rather than be condemned for ungrateful laziness (40-41), that is, she has something to be grateful for.

10. She does not mention that she is also correcting Terence's misogyny, but that is another effect of the women she presents. One might add that besides the brothel scenes, some of the torture descriptions which like so many martyrdoms of virgins have aspects of violent pornography might also be titillating to a court audience.

11. Note that Hrotsvit's sources are not always traditional: they are oral as well as written, pagan as well as Christian, apocryphal as well as orthodox. That not only extends her scope, it also gives her more freedom to play with the material.

12. Hrotsvit mentions Adam by name but not Eve, blaming him or both the first

parents for the fall: *Ascension*, [Christ] "qui solus culpae fuerat sine sordibus Adae," 18; *Gongulf*, "culpis / quas protoplastes obtinuere patres," 35–36 (though Gongulf's wife is seduced by a serpent, an implicit connection with Eve); *The Fall and Conversion of Maria*, "quis te seduxit?" "qui protoplastos prostravit," 7.3. Eve is referred to separately only in connection with the counterbalancing Mary: "Carnis veram sumpsit de virgine formam / virginis ut gustum primae deleret amarum," *Theophilus*, 450–51.

13. Hrotsvit emphasizes songs of praise in her nativity story, with a certain self-reference: Anna's to God sound like Hrotsvit (see 316, 322), and Mary studies the songs of David, her ancestor and a model for Hrotsvit.

14. There is one thoroughly unregenerate woman in Hrotsvit's poems, the wife of the martyr Gongulf, who is seduced by the serpent, has an affair with her husband's secretary, plots her husband's murder, rejects any possibility of repentance, and denies miracles. But Gongulf is a saint at least in part because he "drew in faith with milk from his mother's breast," so the holy woman has a greater effect on him than the evil one.

15. See Dronke, *Women Writers*, 59, on the importance of Roman models for the Ottonians, in connection with Hrotsvit.

16. William MacBain calls it "by far the most original treatment of the St. Catherine legend in medieval French," in his edition of another life, *De Sainte Katerine: An Anonymous Picard Version of the Life of St. Catherine of Alexandria* (Fairfax, Va.: George Mason University, 1987), x. MacBain also edited *The Life of St. Catherine by Clemence of Barking* (Oxford: Blackwell, 1964), ANTS 18. For the life of Edward, see *La Vie d'Edouard le Confesseur, poème anglo-normand du XIIe siècle*, ed. Östen Södergard (Uppsala: Almquist and Wiksells, 1948). The life of Edward is based on the life written by Aelred of Rievaulx, the life of Catherine on an eleventh-century Latin life, itself a version of a tenth-century Greek life, and on an earlier Anglo-Norman poem which Clemence says was out of fashion. Neither of the Barking lives is a slavish translation, though both follow the storyline. I assume therefore that what they include and emphasize is what they consider important.

17. Södergard notes that Thomas Becket was murdered in 1170 and his sister became abbess of Barking in 1173, making it unlikely that Henry would be mentioned so benevolently by a nun of that convent, 25–26; Legge agrees, *Anglo-Norman Literature*, 60–61. MacBain points out that in 1175 Maud/Matilda, a natural daughter of Henry II, became abbess and might easily encourage praise of the king (*Life of St. Catherine*, xxv, n.2), but this does not answer the other arguments against the later date. The life of Catherine is thought to be later, somewhere in the last quarter of the century, though probably impossible to date more closely (MacBain, xxiv–v). I would suggest, however tentatively, that Clemence's treatment of the pagan emperor as susceptible to female beauty but an obstinate enemy of the faith and frustrated as he becomes more isolated, and her very sympathetic treatment of the empress, might reflect Eleanor's imprisonment, and be dated between 1174 and 1189.

18. I wonder if there is a punning allusion to Edith in an earlier passage describing Edward's goodness which is known through all lands and increased by his good fame, "bone fame," 812 and 814. To those hearing the poem, this might suggest his good wife.

19. The nun also shows sympathy for the plight of a secular woman in the telling of one of Edward's miracles: a woman with a double grief, she cannot have a child and she has an ugly tumor on her face which makes her husband avoid her and want her to die. Even her relatives hate her; as happens to people with great trouble, their friends want to be rid of them rather than help (3085ff.).

20. The Vulgate text, which MacBain gives as the main Latin source for Clemence, is given in Appendix B of his *De Sainte Katerine*, from an edition by Hermann Knust. The main differences I noticed between the Latin and Clemence's French are an emphasis in the Latin on the unexpected strength and constancy of the weaker

sex as compared to bearded men and the remark that Catherine conquered her sex (177–78). Additions in the French include the creation of reasoning men and women ("humes e femmes raisnables fist," 701); a description of the fall, "the enemy deceived the woman with the apple, which she ate. She and her lord ate, that he ate was madness. From this disobedience sorrowful pain grew in the world," 703–8); and a sermon about Christ's goodness. There are small but telling additions, like the name of Constantine's mother, Helena, which is there only, I assume, to remind the audience of another holy woman.

21. Cf. Marie in the Prologue to the Lais: "Ki Deus ad duné escïence / E de parler bon eloquence / Ne s'en deit taisir ne celer, / Ainz se deit volunters mustrer. / Quant uns granz biens est mult oïz, / Dunc a primes est il fluriz," 1–6. The edition is Marie de France, *Lais,* ed. A. Ewert (Oxford: Blackwell, 1969).

22. In this naming of herself, Clemence again sounds like Marie: "Marie ai num, si sui de France" at the end of the *Fables,* ed. and trans. Harriet Spiegel (Toronto: University of Toronto Press, 1987).

23. "Clerjastre" (486) has its equivalent in the Latin, "unum ex clientulis nostris" (187), but "plaideresse" (479) does not. The specific insult to the woman who argues is the woman's addition.

24. The emperor also argues that he has to punish the empress or she will set a bad example for women who will lead or deceive their husbands into error which will be disruptive to the state, the man worrying about the government, the women about religion (2219–30).

25. For the texts of both poems and discussion, see Katharina Städtler, "The *Sirventes* by Gormonda de Monpeslier," in *The Voice of the Trobairitz: Perspectives on the Women Troubadours,* ed. William D. Paden (Philadelphia: University of Pennsylvania Press, 1989), 129–55.

26. This occurs in the last dialogue; see *Andreas Capellanus on Love,* ed. P. G. Walsh (London: Duckworth, 1982), 158–59. In the debates Andreas stages, he has women undercut male arguments and show up the hypocrisy of their rhetoric, just as they do in Provençal pastorelas and Italian lyric debates; see my "Male Fantasy and Female Reality in Courtly Literature."

27. See Angelica Rieger, *Trobairitz,* which includes twenty-six dialogues, three women with women, the others between women and men as well as twenty other poems by women. I use her text and her numbering. It is interesting that the word "trobairitz" does not occur in contemporary poetry, treatises, or *vidas,* but is found in a Provençal romance, *Flamenca,* describing a woman (the heroine's maid) who makes clever verbal responses to a man, see Paden, Introduction, *Voice,* 13. So in its first literary use, the word is connected with an exchange of words. But for the debate poems we have, it is virtually impossible to determine if they are male- or female-authored fictions, or if they are actual exchanges between two individuals.

28. Boutière and Schutz, *Biographies des Troubadours,* 23. Maria is identified by the editors as the daughter of Raimon II of Turenne, and wife of Eble V, vicount of Ventadorn, who died c. 1222. One other text, a razo of Na Lombarda, presents a poem as an exchange, in this case between her and her lover: describing her as noble, beautiful, charming, educated, and author of lovely amorous poems, it says he sent her a poem before he went away, and she answered in astonishment that he had left, 60. Among the one-hundred-one texts in Boutière-Schutz, only seven are about women poets; the others are Castelloza, Azalais de Porcairagues, the Countess of Dia, Tibors, and Almucs and Iseut together. But that is a higher percentage than the number of poems (not including dialogues or debates) that have come down to us in manuscripts; not more than one percent of the known (some 2500) Provençal poems, are attributed to women (see Geneviève Brunel-Lobrichon, "Images of Women and Imagined Trobairitz in the Béziers Chansonnier," Paden, *Voice,* 211).

29. Kathryn Gravdal, in "Metaphor, Metonymy, and the Medieval Trobairitz," *Romanic Review* 83 (1992), 411-26, suggests that Maria is underscoring the literary nature of male powerlessness, in contrast to the situation in life.

30. Marianne Shapiro says of the trobairitz' work: "As a whole the poems affirm only by negation, whose pervasiveness eclipses even that of repetition." See Shapiro, "The Provençal *Trobairitz* and the Limits of Courtly Love," *Signs* 3 (1978), 565.

31. I did a preliminary study of these questions in "Notes toward the Study of a Female Rhetoric in the Trobairitz," Paden, *Voice*, 63-72. For an extreme example of the use of negatives, see the one incomplete stanza we have by Tibors (39), in which there are eleven negatives in just over eight lines, although the stanza is a positive statement of love: "Lovely, sweet friend, I can tell you truly (or 'in verse') / that I have never been without desire / since I knew you or (*ni*) took you for a true lover / nor have I even been without the wish, lovely, sweet, friend, to see you often / . . . never, if you went away angry, / have I had joy until you returned, nor . . ." Tibors is, incidentally, one of the few women for whom we have a *vida*; we are told that she was a lady from a castle in Provence, that she was courtly, educated, charming, and a "master" ("fort maïstra," BS, 79), and knew how to compose poetry ("saup trobar"), that she was in love and loved by the good men of the country and feared and obeyed by all the worthy women. This suggests that there was a good deal more to her corpus than the eight lines we have.

32. Gravdal, "Metaphor," argues very interestingly that what some critics see as masochism in female description of suffering for love is an attempt to correct the fictions of male love poetry. That is, women suffer for love in life, men suffer in literature. And some men, like Bernart de Ventadorn, take pride in their suffering.

33. Sarah Kay says, "The women poets give no impression of confidence either in their inherent worth or in their ability to bargain for it," speaking of the absence of feudal and financial imagery from their poems; see Kay, *Subjectivity in Troubadour Poetry* (Cambridge: Cambridge University Press, 1990), 127. Looking at the trobairitz within a larger study of Provençal poetry, Kay shows how uncomfortable they are with the role of *domna*, how difficult it is for them to express their subjectivity within the established gender system, 101-11. Looking at them from the perspective of women's letters and women-sponsored literature, I am inclined to see more positive assertiveness in what they say.

34. In an envoi that appears in only one manuscript, she says her distress comes from Aurenga (49-52). Raimbaut was a fellow poet, perhaps a model, perhaps a patron or friend, see Rieger, notes to lines 41 ff. Kay notes similarities between her canso and two of Raimbaut's, 104-5. In the *vida*, N'Azalais de Porcairagues is said to have come from Montpellier, to have been a noble and educated (*enseingnada*) woman, who fell in love with Gui Guerrejat, brother of Guillaume de Montpellier; she knew how to compose poems, and made many good songs (*cansos*) about him (BS, 52). Gui was the brother of Guillaume VII of Montpellier, and died in 1177, but whether he was Azalais's lover is not known.

35. Elizabeth W. Poe, in a detailed discussion of the poem, its history, and its possible connections with Clara's *canso*, which it seems to answer, and a *canso* which Uc de Saint Circ sent to Azalais, telling her about his problems with his love, his reformation, and his second chance, argues ingeniously that the poem attributed to Azalais may have been written by Uc himself, whose *razo* (Boutière and Schutz 33B, which mentions his love for Clara), says he wrote letters for ladies. Though the argument is intriguing and the manuscript provenance suggestive, Poe admits that it is not conclusive. See Poe, "Another *salut d'amor?* Another *trobairitz?* In Defense of *Tanz salutz et tantas amors,*" ZrP 106 (1990), 314-37.

36. It is a tribute to the power of Castelloza's poetry that she has inspired so many differing but valid readings: "The Poems of the *Trobairitz* Na Castelloza," ed. William

D. Paden, Jr., *Romance Philology* 35 (1981), 158-82; Peter Dronke, "The Provençal *Trobairitz*: Castelloza," in *Medieval Women Writers,* ed. Katharina M. Wilson (Athens: University of Georgia Press, 1984); Amelia E. Van Vleck, "'Tost me trobaretz fenida': Reciprocating Composition in the Songs of Castelloza," Paden, *Voice,* 95-111; H. Jay Siskin and Julie A. Storme, "Suffering Love: The Reversed Order in the Poetry of Na Castelloza," *ibid.,* 113-27; Matilda T. Bruckner, "Fictions of the Female Voice: The Women Troubadours," *Speculum,* 67 (1992), 865-91, which includes a section on the Countess of Dia. Paden and Dronke include English translations of Castelloza's four songs. Her *vida* says only that she was from Auvergne, noble, married to Turc de Mairona (a lord of Meyronne), gay, educated, and beautiful, and that she had a lover, N'Arman de Breon, about whom she composed many poems (BS 49).

37. *Preiar* can be translated "ask," "beg," "court," "pray," "woo." I prefer "ask" only because it does not seem to carry as many connotations as the others, leaving the reader to supply whatever the context suggests. I also use "lady" for "dompna" rather than "woman" when it is juxtaposed to "knight" ("cavalliers") since "dompna" denotes status and perhaps power. For a study of *midons,* the masculine form applied to women in Provençal poetry, which questions some of the accepted views, see W. M. Hackett, "Le problème de 'midons,'" in *Mélanges de philologie romane dédiés à la mémoire de Jean Boutière,* ed. Irénée Cluzel and François Pirot (Liège: Soledi, 1971), vol. 1, 285-94.

38. Cf. 29.32: "de sol lo dich n'ai eu lo cor gauzen," "from the word alone my heart rejoices," referring to what he told her (not to worry), but it could also mean, "from the telling alone," that is, even if he did not mean it, it gives her pleasure to record what he said. Paden et al. note that she threatens suicide or madness in all her poems and that forms of *morir* occur very frequently, "The Poems of . . . Castelloza," 166-67.

39. Amelia E. Van Vleck suggests that Castelloza is seeking a poetic exchange with the man, on the basis of possible double entendres: "tost mi trobaretz fenida," 31.38, which might mean "you will soon compose a tornada or farewell couplet for me," as well as "you will soon find me dead"; and when she asks him to come as soon as he has heard her song, promising "sai trobetz bella semblanssa," she may mean not only "here you will find a fair appearance," but also "compose a beautiful semblance," a likeness to her song, the response she has waited for ("Reciprocating Composition in the Songs of Castelloza," Paden, *Voice,* 103-4).

40. The Countess's emphasis on rank and prestige suggests that she is a countess in her own right. The *vida* says only that she was the wife of William of Poitiers, a good and beautiful woman, who fell in love with Raimbaut d'Aurenga and made many good songs about him (BS 69). Much has been suggested but nothing is known about her or who her husband or her lover(s) were.

41. Bruckner (*Speculum,* 1992) connects the idea of mutality in love with the play on masculine and feminine rhymes through the poem, "Ab ioi et ab ioven m'apais" (34), 877ff.

42. For the text of the *lais,* I used Marie de France, *Lais,* ed. A. Ewert, and the translation *The Lais of Marie de France* by Robert Hanning and Joan Ferrante (Grand Rapids, MI: Baker Books, 1995, first published 1978). I number the lines within each *lai* following Ewert. For the fables, Marie de France, *Fables,* ed. and trans. Harriet Spiegel (Toronto: University of Toronto Press, 1987), I give the number of the fable with the line numbers. The literature on Marie is vast, and I mention only a few studies that are particularly relevant to my perspective here, with apologies to the many scholars who have written so well about her.

43. For more on this, see Karen K. Jambeck, "Truth and Deception in the *Fables* of Marie de France," in *Literary Aspects of Courtly Culture,* ed. Donald Maddox and Sara Sturm-Maddox (Cambridge: Brewer, 1994), 221-29.

44. Rupert Pickens suggests that Marie is concerned with female-generated textuality in the *lais,* a way of appropriating male poetics; see Pickens, "The Poetics of Androgyny in the *Lais* of Marie de France: *Yonec, Milun,* and the General *Prologue,*" in *Literary Aspects of Courtly Culture,* 211-19.

45. If there is any feminine humility in Marie's approach to her art, it is in her choice of short narrative forms, the lai and the fable, even for a story like Eliduc which lends itself to much longer development, as in *Ille et Galeron.* Hrotsvit also started with shorter forms, and moved to historic epics in her last works. If Marie translated the *Espurgatoire Seint Patriz,* which has been questioned, she too moved to a longer form.

46. On Marie's sources, see Mary Lou Martin in her translation, *The Fables of Marie de France* (Birmingham, Ala.: Summa, 1984), 20-24.

47. I do this with full awareness of the attendant risks, but hoping that the material I have presented in earlier chapters of this book helps me to avoid the worst blunders. Heather Arden has recently read Marie's lais in the light of Carol Gilligan's work with female community and attachment and male hierarchy and separation; see Arden, "The *Lais* of Marie de France and Carol Gilligan's Theory of the Psychology of Women," in *In Quest of Marie de France, a Twelfth-Century Poet,* ed. Chantal A. Maréchal (Lewiston: Edwin Mellen, 1992), 212-24.

48. For Marie's pursuit of *pris* through writing, see Prologue, 31, *Guigemar,* 1-11; for men pursuing it with violence, *Guigemar,* 51, 69, *Milun,* 124, 311, 333, 335, 338, *Eliduc,* 199. Robert Hanning suggested many years ago that "the androgynous stag [in *Guigemar*] serves as an emblem of complete humanity, in which 'male' aggressive elements intertwine and coexist with a 'female' impulse toward passion and affection," in "Courtly Contexts for Urban *Cultus:* Responses to Ovid in Chrétien's *Cligès* and Marie's *Guigemar,*" *Symposium* 35 (1981), 47.

49. Nonetheless, Michelle Freeman has made a very good case for the mother in "The Power of Sisterhood: Marie de France's 'Le Fresne,'" *French Forum* 12 (1987), 5-26. She notes that the young woman who prevents the baby's murder has been kept and raised by the mother, and greatly loved and cherished by her, so the mother is not "an unregenerate stock villainess," 16. Freeman also suggests that the mother's original action, the slander, was caused by her fear that the report of the neighbor's double success would show up her own failure to produce a male heir, which certainly makes it a less gratuitously cruel act, 10-11. The problem of sterility and fertility is projected onto the names of the two daughters, 11.

50. I had written and taught this reading of *Bisclavret* for some time before I came across the same suggestion made by one of her students and reported by Laurie Finke in a review of Krueger, *Women Readers,* MFN 19 (1995), 33. I was delighted with this modern corroboration.

51. Robert Hanning suggested to me that there is a play on the Annunciation in the woman's prayer to God that it be done according to *her,* not his, will: "Il en face ma volenté," 104.

52. Because the woman wills the lover to come to her and when he comes he assumes her form to take the Eucharist, and because the world to which she follows him seems to be a dream world, I see him as a very powerful figment of her imagination, powerful enough to give her the strength to cope with the husband and make her fertile, but finally existing only in her mind. Michelle Freeman discusses the fantasy/fiction aspect of *Yonec* in "The Changing Figure of the Male: the Revenge of the Female Storyteller," *In Quest of Marie,* 243-61.

53. It is intriguing that in the work of the male poet, Thomas, it is the heroine, Iseut, who composes a lai about the sad love of Guirun, whereas in the work of a female poet, Marie, it is the hero, Tristan, who composes a lai about the joy he had with his love. What Marie says is "for the joy he had from his love whom he saw, and

because of what he had written as the queen had told him, to remember the words" ("Pur la joie qu'il ot eüe / de s'amie qu'il ot veüe / e pur ceo k'il aveit escrit, / si cum la reïne l'ot dit, / pur les paroles remembrer," 107-11). This is normally taken to refer to the message he carved in wood, as she had directed, but he only carved his name on that (54), though it conveyed much more. What are the words the queen told him? Could they refer to a lai she composed?

54. Men do seem gullible in the fables, ready to believe even that they are pregnant (42, 43), perhaps Marie's way of commenting on "male fantasy" and "female reality."

55. For a discussion of women's concerns and female activity as Marie presents them through animals in the fables, see Harriet Spiegel, "The Woman's Voice in the *Fables* of Marie de France," *In Quest of Marie*, 45-58. Spiegel notes that Marie's "interest in the females of her fables . . . suggests a writer who saw herself as a woman, addressing an audience that may well have included women" (57).

56. On Christine's responses to misogyny, see Susan Schibanoff, "Taking the Gold out of Egypt: The Art of Reading as a Woman," in *Gender and Reading: Essays on Readers, Texts and Contexts*, ed. Elizabeth A. Flynn and Patrocinio P. Schweickart (Baltimore: Johns Hopkins University Press, 1986), 83-106; Renate Blumenfeld-Kosinski, "Christine de Pizan and the Misogynistic Tradition," *Romanic Review* 81 (1990), 279-92; and Krueger, *Women Readers*, 217-46.

57. For the text, see *Le Livre de la Mutacion de Fortune*, ed. Suzanne Solente, 4 vols. (Paris: Picard, 1959-66). Editions of the other texts cited are *Le Livre des Fais et Bonnes Meurs du Sage Roy Charles V*, ed. Suzanne Solente, 2 vols. (Paris: Champion, 1936-40); "The Livre de la Cité des Dames of Christine de Pisan: A Critical Edition," ed. Maureen Curnow, Ph.D. diss., Vanderbilt University, 1975 (Ann Arbor: UMI, 1975); trans. Earl Jeffrey Richards, *The Book of the City of Ladies* (New York: Persea, 1982); *L'Avision-Christine*, ed. Mary Louis Towner (Washington: Catholic University, 1932)—I follow her numbering from the manuscript; trans. Glenda K. McLeod, *Christine's Vision* (New York: Garland, 1993); Angus J. Kennedy and Kenneth Varty, "Christine de Pisan's 'Ditié de Jehanne d'Arc,'" *Nottingham Medieval Studies* 18 (1974), 29-55, 19 (1975), 53-76; *The Treasure of the City of Ladies or The Book of the Three Virtues*, trans. Sarah Lawson (Penguin, 1985).

58. Christine begins the first book of *L'Avision* with an echo of Dante ("Ja passe avoye la moitie du chemin de mon pelerinage, comme un iour sus lavesprir me trouvasse pour la longue voye lassee et desireuse de heberge"). Dante is also a model for her in the *Chemin de Longue Estude*, so she does not, in fact, shrink from such comparisons.

59. France had earlier used the negative side of the birth image, saying that like a woman who wants to see the fruit of her womb but worries about the pain, she looks forward to the good that God promised would come, but not the evil she has to pass through to get there. For an analysis of birth and nursing images in Christine, see Suzanne C. Akbari, "'Laict' et 'Lettres': Maternity and Authorship in the Writings of Christine de Pizan," *Exemplaria*, forthcoming.

60. Reason explains that God formed woman from the side of man, signifying that she should stand at his side as a companion, not (from his feet) that she should lie at his feet like a slave; but she leaves out the third part of the lesson, not from his head, to dominate (cf. Hugh of St. Victor, *De sacramentis christianae fidei*, 1.6.35), that is, Reason does not exclude the possibility of woman's domination of man.

61. Karen Sullivan comments on Christine's feminism: "I would argue, however, that it is precisely owing to the instability of her location as a woman that Christine is most profoundly feminist and that it is precisely in her difference from feminist truisms that feminists have most to learn from her." See Sullivan, "At the Limit of Feminist Theory: An Architectonics of the Querelle de la Rose," *Exemplaria* 3.2 (1991), 466.

Bibliography

PRIMARY SOURCES

Abelard, Peter, *Hymnarius Paraclitensis,* ed. Joseph Szövérffy, 2 vols. (Albany: Classical Folia, 1975).

Abelard, Peter, *Opera Petri Abaelardi,* ed. V. Cousin, 2 vols. (Paris: A. Durand, 1849, 1859).

"Abelard's Letter of Consolation to a Friend, *Historia Calamitatum," Medieval Studies* 12 (1950), 163-213; "The Personal Letters between Abelard and Heloise," ed. J. T. Muckle, MS 15 (1953), 47-94; "The Letter of Heloise on Religious Life and Abelard's First Reply," ed. J. T. Muckle, MS 17 (1955), 240-81; "Abelard's Rule for Religious Women," ed. T. P. McLaughlin, MS 18 (1956), 241-92.

Adam de Perseigne, *Lettres,* ed. Jean Bouvet (Paris: Editions du Cerf, 1960).

AEthelward, *Chronicon AEthelweardi, The Chronicle of AEthelweard,* ed. and trans. A. Campbell (London: Thomas Nelson, 1962).

Aimon von Varennes, *Florimont,* ed. Alfons Hilka (Göttingen: Gesellschaft für Romanische Literatur, 1932).

Alcuini Epistolae, ed. Ernestus Dümmler (Berlin: Weidmann, 1895), MGH, EpKar 2.

Andreas Capellanus on Love, ed. P. G. Walsh (London: Duckworth, 1982).

Anglo-Latin Satirical Poets and Epigrammatists of the Twelfth Century, ed. Thomas Wright, 2 vols. (London: Longman, 1872).

Annales Palidenses, auctore Theodoro Monacho, MGH, SS, 16.90.

Anselm, *Sancti Anselmi Cantuarensis Archiepiscopi Opera Omnia,* ed. F. S. Schmitt (Edinburgh: Thomas Nelson, 1946).

Augustine, *Sancti Aureli Augustini Hipponiensis Episcopi Epistulae,* ed. A. Goldbacher, 4 vols. CSEL (Vienna: Tempsky, 1911).

Baudri of Bourgueil, *Le Epistole metriche di Baldericus Burguliensis,* ed. M. Teresa Razzoli (Milan: SAEDA, 1936).

Baudri of Bourgueil, *Les Oeuvres poétiques de Baudri de Bourgueil,* ed. Phyllis Abraham (Paris: Slatkine, 1974, first pub. 1926).

Bernart de Ventadorn, *The Songs of Bernart de Ventadorn,* ed. and trans. Stephen G. Nichols, John A. Galm, and A. Bartlett Giamatti (Chapel Hill: University of North Carolina Press, 1965).

Bertran de Born, *The Poems of the Troubadour Bertran de Born,* ed. and trans. William D. Paden, Tilde Sankovitch, and Patricia Stablein (Berkeley: University of California Press, 1986).

Biographies des Troubadours, ed. J. Boutière and A.-H. Schutz (Paris: Nizet, 1964).

Castelloza, "The Poems of the *Trobairitz* Na Castelloza," ed. William D. Paden, Jr., *Romance Philology* 35 (1981), 158-82.

Chrétien de Troyes, *Le Chevalier de la Charrete,* ed. Mario Roques, CFMA 86 (Paris: Champion, 1958).

Christine de Pisan, *L'Avision-Christine,* ed. Mary Louis Towner (Washington, D.C.: Catholic University, 1932).

Christine de Pisan, *Le Débat sur le Roman de la Rose,* ed. Eric Hicks (Paris: Champion, 1977).

Christine de Pisan, *The Livre de la Cité des Dames of Christine de Pisan: A Critical Edition,* ed. Maureen Curnow (Ph.D. diss., Vanderbilt University, 1975).

Christine de Pisan, *Le Livre de la Mutacion de Fortune,* ed. Suzanne Solente, 4 vols. (Paris: Picard, 1959-66).

Christine de Pisan, *Le Livre des Fais et Bonnes Meurs du Sage Roy Charles V,* ed. Suzanne Solente, 2 vols. (Paris: Champion, 1936-40).

"Christine de Pisan's 'Ditié de Jehanne d'Arc,'" ed. Angus J. Kennedy, and Kenneth Varty, *Nottingham Medieval Studies* 18 (1974), 29-55; 19 (1975), 53-76.

Dante's Lyric Poetry, ed. K. Foster and P. Boyde, 2 vols. (Oxford: Clarendon Press, 1967).

De Sainte Katerine, an Anonymous Picard Version of the Life of St. Catherine of Alexandria, ed. William MacBain (Fairfax, Va.: George Mason University Press, 1987).

Deschamps, Eustache, *Oeuvres Complètes de Eustache Deschamps,* ed. le Marquis de Queux de Saint-Hilaire, SATF 9 (Paris: Firmin Didot, 1889), vol. 6.

Donizo, *Vita Mathildis Carmine Scripta a Donizone Presbytero,* ed. Luigi Simeoni (Bologna: Zanichelli, 1930-34).

Elisabeth of Schönau, *Die Visionen der heiligen Elisabeth und die Schriften der Aebte Ekbert und Emecho von Schönau,* ed. F. W. E. Roth (Brno: Studien aus dem Benedictiner- und Cistercienser Orden, 1884).

Elisabeth of Schönau, letters, in P. Schmitz, "'Visions' inédites de Sainte Élisabeth de Schoenau," *Revue Bénédictine* 47 (1935), 181-83, and Van Acker, L., "Der Briefwechsel zwischen Elisabeth von Schönau und Hildegard von Bingen," *Instrumenta Patristica* 23 (1991), 409-17.

Encomium Emmae Reginae, ed. and trans. Alistair Campbell (London: Royal Historical Society, 1949), Camden Third Series, vol. 72.

Eneas, ed. J.-J. Salverda de Grave, CFMA 44, 62 (Paris: Champion, 1964, 1968).

Enfances Ogier, ed. August Scheler (Brussels: Closson, 1874).

Ennodius, *Magni Felicis Ennodi Opera Omnia,* ed. William Hartel, Corpus Scriptorum Ecclesiasticorum, 6 (Vienna: Geroldus, 1882).

Epistulae duorum amantium, ed. Ewald Könsgen (Leiden: Brill, 1974).

Eracle, ed. Guy Raynaud de Lage (Paris: Champion, 1976), CFMA, 102.

Ermoldus Nigellus, *In Honorem Hludowici Ermoldi Nigelli Exulis Elegiacum Carmen,* in *Poème sur Louis le Pieux et épitres au roi Pépin,* ed. and trans. Edmond Faral (Paris: Champion, 1932).

Fortunatus, *Venanti Fortunati Opera Poetica,* ed. Fridericus Leo (Berlin: Weidmann, 1881).

Gaimar, Geffrei, *L'Estoire des Engleis,* ed. Alexander Bell, ANTS 14-16 (Oxford: Blackwell, 1960).

Gerard von Amiens, *Roman von Escanor,* ed. H. Michelant (Tübingen: Bibliothek Litterarischen Vereins in Stuttgart, 1886).

Gilbert of Foliot, *The Letters and Charters of Gilbert of Foliot,* ed. Z. N. Brooke, Dom Adrian Morey, and C. N. L. Brooke (Cambridge: Cambridge University Press, 1976).

Gormonda de Monpeslier, Städtler, "The *Sirventes* by Gormonda de Monpeslier," in Paden, *Voice.*

Gregory VII, *Das Register Gregors VII,* ed. Erich Caspar, MGH Epistolae Selectae (1920–23).

Guiberti Gemblacensis, Epistolae, ed. Albert Derolez, CCCM 66 and 66a (Turnholt: Brepols, 1989), cited as Gb.

Guillaume de Palerne, ed. H. Michelant (Paris: SATF, 1876).

Hilarii Versus et Ludi, ed. John B. Fuller (New York: Holt, 1929).

Hildeberti Cenomannensis episcopi, *Carmina Minora,* ed. A. Brian Scott (Leipzig: Teubner, 1969).

Hildegard of Bingen, *Analecta Sancte Hildegardis opera,* ed. J. B. Pitra, *Analecta sacra,* vol. 8 (Typis Sacri Montis Cassinensis, 1882), cited as Pi.

Hildegard of Bingen, *Causae et Curae,* ed. Paul Kaiser, *Bibliotheca Scriptorum Graecorum et Romanorm Teubneriana* (Leipzig: Teubner, 1903), cited as CC.

Hildegard of Bingen, *Scivias,* ed. Adelgundis Führkötter, with Angela Carlevaris, CCCM 43–43a (Turnhout: Brepols, 1978).

Hildegard of Bingen, *Symphonia, A Critical Edition of the Symphonia armonie celestium revelationum,* ed. and trans. Barbara Newman (Ithaca: Cornell University Press, 1988).

Hildegardis Bingensis Epistolarium, ed. Lieven Van Acker, CCCM 91 and 91A (Turnholt: Brepols, 1991, 1993), through ep.250r, cited as VA.

Hildegardis Liber Vite Meritorum, ed. Angela Carlevaris, CCCM 90 (Turnholt: Brepols, 1995).

Hrosvithae Liber Tertius, ed. and trans. M. B. Bergman (Covington, Ky.: Sisters of St. Benedict, 1943).

Hrotsvitha, *The Legends of Hrotsvitha: Text, Translation, and Commentary,* ed. and trans. M. H. Wiegand (Ph.D. diss., St. Louis University, 1936).

Hrotsvithae Opera, ed. H. Homeyer (Paderborn: Schöningh, 1970).

Hue de Rotelande, *Ipomedon, poème de Hue de Rotelande,* ed. A. J. Holden, BFR 17 (Paris: Klincksieck, 1979).

Hue de Rotelande, *Protheselaus, ein altfranzösischer Abenteuerroman,* ed. Franz Kluckow (Göttingen: GfRL, 1924).

Hugh of Fleury, *Hugonis Liber qui Modernorum Regum Francorum Continet Actus,* MGH, SS 9.376–77.

Ille et Galeron, ed. Yves Lefèvre, CFMA 209 (Paris: Honoré Champion, 1988).

Jerome, Saint, *Sancti Eusebii Hieronymi Epistulae,* ed. Isidorus Hilberg, 3 vols. (New York: Johnson, 1970, repr. of 1910).

Jerome, Saint, *Opera exegetica,* CCSL 76, 76a (Turnhout: Brepols, 1969, 1970).

John of Fécamp, *Un Maitre de la vie spirituelle au XIe siècle, Jean de Fécamp,* ed. Jean Leclercq and Jean-Paul Bonnes (Paris: Vrin, 1946).

Könsgen, Ewald, "Zwei unbekannte Briefe zu den Gesta Regum Anglorum des Wilhelm von Malmesbury," *Deutsches Archiv für Erforschung des Mittelalters,* 31 (1975), 204–14.

The Life of Christina of Markyate, ed. C. H. Talbot (Oxford: Oxford University Press, 1959).

The Life of St. Catherine by Clemence of Barking, ed. William MacBain, ANTS 18 (Oxford: Blackwell, 1964).

Marbod of Rennes, ed. Walther Bulst, "Liebesbriefgedichte Marbods," *Liber Floridus, Mittellateinische Studien Paul Lehmann Gewidmet,* ed. Bernhard Bischoff and Suso

Brechter (St. Ottilien: Eos, 1950), 287–301.

Marie de France, *Fables*, ed. and trans. Harriet Spiegel (Toronto: University of Toronto Press, 1987).

Marie de France, *Lais*, ed. A. Ewert (Oxford: Blackwell, 1969, first published 1944).

Martin le Franc, ed. Gaston Paris, "Un Poème inédit de Martin Le Franc," *Romania* 16 (1887), 415–16.

Meraugis von Portlesguez, ed. Mathias Friedwanger (Geneva: Slatkine Reprints, 1975, first pub. 1897).

Metel, Hugh, letters, in *Sacrae antiquitatis monumenta*, ed. C. L. Hugo (Saint-Die: J. Charlot, 1731), vol. 2, 348–49, epp.16, 17.

Origenes Werke, 9. Die Homilien zu Lukas in der Übersetzung des Hieronymus und Die Griechischen Reste der Homilien und des Lukas-Kommentars, ed. Max Rauer (Berlin: Akademie Verlage, 1959).

Osbert of Clare, *The Letters of Osbert of Clare*, ed. E. W. Williamson (London: Oxford University Press, 1929).

Partonopeu de Blois, ed. Joseph Gildea, 2 vols. (Villanova: Villanova University Press, 1967–70).

Paul the Deacon, *Die Gedichte des Paulus Diaconus*, ed. Karl Neff, Quellen und Untersuchungen zur lateinischen Philologie des Mittelalters, 3 (Munich: C. H. Beck, 1908).

Pauli Diaconi Historia Romana, ed. Amedeo Crivellucci (Rome: Tipografia del Senato, 1914).

Peter Damian, *Die Briefe des Petrus Damiani*, ed. Kurt Reindel (Munich: MGH, 1983), BDKz.

Peter the Venerable, *The Letters of Peter the Venerable*, ed. Giles Constable, 2 vols. (Cambridge: Harvard University Press, 1967).

Quellen zur Geschichte der Sächsischen Kaiserzeit, ed. and trans. Albert Bauer and Reinhold Rau (Darmstadt: Wissenschaftliche Buchgesellschaft, 1971).

Raimbaut d'Orange, *The Life and Works of the Troubadour Raimbaut d'Orange*, ed. W. Pattison (Minneapolis: University of Minnesota Press, 1952).

Renaut de Bâgé, *Le Bel Inconnu*, ed. Karen Fresco, trans. Colleen P. Donagher (New York: Garland, 1992).

Renaut de Beaujeu, *Le Bel Inconnu*, ed. G. Perrie Williams (Paris: Champion, 1967).

Le Roman de Thèbes, ed. Guy Raynaud de Lage, CFMA 94, 96 (Paris: Champion, 1968, 1969).

Le Roman de Thèbes, ed. Léopold Constans, SATF 30.1 (Paris: Didot, 1890).

Le Roman de Troie par Benoît de Sainte-Maure, ed. L. Constans, SATF, 52, 55, 57, 62, 66, 67 (Paris: Didot, 1904–12).

Li Roumans de Cléomadès par Adenès li Rois, ed. André van Hasselt, 2 vols. (Brussels: Victor Devaux, 1865).

Sordello, *The Poetry of Sordello*, ed. and trans. J. J. Wilhelm (New York: Garland, 1987).

Trobairitz, Der Beitrag der Frau in der altokzitanischen höfischen Lyrik, ed. Angelica Rieger (Tübingen: Niemeyer, 1991).

La Vie d'Edouard le Confesseur, poème anglo-normand du XIIe siècle, ed. Östen Södergard (Uppsala: Almquist and Wiksells, 1948).

La Vie Seint Edmund le Rei, An Anglo-Norman Poem of the Twelfth Century by Denis Piramus, ed. Florence L. Ravenel (Philadelphia: J. C. Winston, 1906).

Vita AEduuardi Regis qui apud Westmonasterium Requiescit, in *Lives of Edward the Confessor*, ed. Henry R. Luard, RBMAS 3 (London: Longman, 1858).

Vita Mathildis reginae antiquior, ed. Rudolf Köpke, MGH, SS 10 (1849), 573-82, cited as VMRA.

Vita Mathildis reginae [posterior], ed. Georg H. Pertz, MGH, SS 4 (1841), 282-302, cited as VMRP.

Vita Sanctae Hildegardis, ed. Monica Klaes, CCCM 126 (Turnhout: Brepols, 1993).

Vita S. Margaretae Scotorum Reginae, in *Symeonis Dunelmensis Opera et Collectanea* I, ed. Hodgson Hinde (Durham: Andrews, 1868), Publications of the Surtees Society, 51, 234-54.

Wace, *Maistre Wace's Roman de Rou et des Ducs de Normandie,* ed. Hugo Andresen (Heilbronn: Gebr. Henninger, 1877).

Willelmi Malmesbiriensis Monachi, De gestis regum Anglorum, ed. William Stubbs, RBMAS 90 (London: Eyre and Spottiswoode, 1887).

SECONDARY SOURCES

Abelard, *The Hymns of Abelard in English Verse,* trans. Jane Patricia (Lanham, Md.: University Press of America, 1986).

Abelard, *The Letters of Abelard and Heloise,* trans. Betty Radice (Harmondsworth: Penguin, 1974), cited as R.

Akbari, Suzanne C., "'Laict' et 'Lettres': Maternity and Authorship in the Writings of Christine de Pizan," *Exemplaria,* forthcoming.

Althoff, Gerd, "Causa Scribendi und Darstellungsabsicht: Die Lebensbeschreibungen der Königin Mathilde und andere Beispiele," in *Litterae Medii Aevi, Festschrift für Johanne Autenrieth,* ed. Michael Borgolt and Herrad Spilling (Sigmaringen: Jan Thorbecke, 1988).

Angeli, Giovanna, *L'Eneas e i primi romanzi volgari* (Milan: Riccardo Ricciardi, 1971).

Anna Comnena, *The Alexiad of Anna Comnena,* trans. E. R. A. Sewter (Harmondsworth: Penguin, 1969).

Arden, Heather, "The *Lais* of Marie de France and Carol Gilligan's Theory of the Psychology of Women," in Maréchal, *In Quest of Marie.*

Augustine, *Saint Augustine Letters,* trans. Wilfrid Parsons, 5 vols. (New York: Fathers of the Church, 1951-56).

Baltzer, Rebecca A., "Music in the Life and Times of Eleanor of Aquitaine," in *Eleanor of Aquitaine, Patron and Politician,* ed. William W. Kibler (Austin: University of Texas Press, 1976).

Bandel, Betty, "The English Chroniclers' Attitude toward Women," *Journal of the History of Ideas,* 16 (1955), 113-18.

Barlow, Frank, *Edward the Confessor* (Berkeley: University of California Press, 1970).

Bartlett, Anne C., "Commentary, Polemic, and Prophecy in Hildegard of Bingen's *Solutiones Triginta Octo Quaestionum,*" *Viator* 23 (1992), 153-65.

Baswell, Christopher, *Virgil in Medieval England: Figuring the Aeneid from the Twelfth Century to Chaucer* (Cambridge: Cambridge University Press, 1995).

Berschin, Walter, *Bonizo von Sutri, Leben und Werke* (Berlin: de Gruyter, 1972).

Bezzola R. R., *Les Origines et la formation de la littérature courtoise en occident, 500-1200,* 3 vols. (Paris: Champion, 1944, 1960, 1963).

Blaess, Madeleine, "The Public and Private Face of King Arthur's Court in the Works of Chrétien de Troyes," in *Chrétien de Troyes and the Troubadours, Essays in*

Memory of the Late Leslie Topsfield, ed. Peter S. Noble and Linda M. Paterson (Cambridge: St. Catherine's College, 1984).

Bloch, R. Howard, *Medieval Misogyny and the Invention of Western Romantic Love* (Chicago: University of Chicago Press, 1991).

Blumenfeld-Kosinski, Renate, "Christine de Pizan and the Misogynistic Tradition," *Romanic Review* 81 (1990), 279-92.

Bond, Gerald A., *The Loving Subject: Desire, Eloquence, and Power in Romanesque France* (Philadelphia: University of Pennsylvania Press, 1995).

Brody, Saul N., *The Disease of the Soul, Leprosy in Medieval Literature* (Ithaca: Cornell University Press, 1974).

Brown, Peter, *Augustine of Hippo, A Biography* (Berkeley: University of California Press, 1967).

Brown, Peter, *The Body and Society: Men, Women, and Sexual Renunciation in Early Christianity* (New York: Columbia University Press, 1988).

Bruckner, Matilda T., "Fictions of the Female Voice: The Women Troubadours," *Speculum* 67 (1992), 865-91.

Brunel-Lobrichon, Geneviève, "Images of Women and Imagined Trobairitz in the Béziers Chansonnier," Paden, *Voice*.

Bumke, Joachim, *Mäzene im Mittelalter, Die Gönner und Auftraggeber der Höfischen Literatur in Deutschland, 1150-1300* (Munich: C. H. Beck, 1979).

Burns, E. Jane, *Bodytalk, When Women Speak in Old French Literature* (Philadelphia: University of Pennsylvania Press, 1993).

Burns, E. Jane, "The Man behind the Lady in Troubadour Lyric," *Romance Notes* 25 (1985), 254-70.

Burns, E. Jane, and Roberta Krueger, eds., *Courtly Ideology and Woman's Place in Medieval French Literature, Romance Notes* 25 (1985).

Bynum, Caroline Walker, *Fragmentation and Redemption, Essays on Gender and the Human Body in Medieval Religion* (New York: Zone Books, 1992).

Bynum, Caroline Walker, *Holy Feast and Holy Fast* (Berkeley: University of California Press, 1987).

Bynum, Caroline Walker, *Jesus as Mother: Studies in the Spirituality of the High Middle Ages* (Berkeley: University of California Press, 1982).

Bynum, Caroline Walker, *The Resurrection of the Body in Western Christianity, 200-1336* (New York: Columbia University Press, 1995).

Cadden, Joan, "It Takes All Kinds: Sexuality and Gender Differences in Hildegard of Bingen's *Book of Compound Medicine*," *Traditio* 40 (1983), 149-74.

Cadden, Joan, *Meanings of Sex Difference in the Middle Ages: Medicine, Science, and Culture* (Cambridge: Cambridge University Press, 1993).

Campbell, Miles, "The *Encomium Emmae Reginae*: Personal Panegyric or Political Propaganda?" *Annuale Mediaevale* 19 (1979), 27-45.

Cherewatuk, Karen, and Ulrike Wiethaus, eds., *Dear Sister, Medieval Women and the Epistolary Genre* (Philadelphia: University of Pennsylvania Press, 1993).

Chibnall, Marjorie, *The Empress Matilda, Queen Consort, Queen Mother and Lady of the English* (Oxford: Blackwell, 1991).

Christine de Pisan, *The Treasure of the City of Ladies or The Book of the Three Virtues*, trans. Sarah Lawson (Penguin, 1985).

Christine de Pizan, *The Book of the City of Ladies*, trans. Earl Jeffrey Richards (New York: Persea, 1982).

Christine de Pizan, *Christine's Vision,* trans. Glenda K. McLeod (New York: Garland, 1993).

Cipollone, M., "In margine al *Problemata Heloissae,*" *Aevum* 64 (1990), 227-44.

Clark, Anne L., *Elisabeth of Schönau, A Twelfth-Century Visionary* (Philadelphia: University of Pennsylvania Press, 1992).

Clark, Elizabeth A., *Jerome, Chrysostom and Friends: Essays and Translations,* Studies in Women and Religion, 1 (New York: Edwin Mellen, 1979).

Clark, Elizabeth A., *The Origenist Controversy: The Cultural Construction of an Early Christian Debate* (Princeton: Princeton University Press, 1992).

Coakley, John, "Gender and Authority of Friars: The Significance of Holy Women for Thirteenth Century Franciscans and Dominicans," *Church History* 60 (1991), 445-60.

Constable, Giles, *Letters and Letter-Collections* (Turnhout: Brepols, 1976).

Corbet, Patrick, *Les saints ottoniens, Sainteté dynastique, sainteté royale et sainteté féminine autour de l'an Mil* (Sigmaringen: Jan Thorbecke, 1986).

Cowper, Frederick A. G., "The New Manuscript of *Ille et Galeron,*" *Modern Philology* 18 (1921), 601-8.

Cutler, Kenneth E., "Edith, Queen of England, 1045-1066," *Medieval Studies* 35 (1973), 222-31.

Dean, Ruth J., "Elizabeth, Abbess of Schönau, and Roger of Ford," *Modern Philology* 41 (1944), 209-20.

de Plinval, George, *Pélage, sa vie, ses écrits et sa réforme* (Lausanne: Payot, 1943).

Desmond, Marilynn, *Reading Dido: Gender, Textuality, and the Medieval Aeneid* (Minneapolis: University of Minnesota Press, 1994).

Dewart, Joanne E. McWilliam, *Death and Resurrection* (Wilmington: Michael Glazier, 1986).

Dickinson, J. C., *The Origins of the Austin Canons and Their Introduction into England* (London: SPCK, 1950).

Dronke, Peter, *Medieval Latin and the Rise of European Love-Lyric,* 2. vols. (Oxford: Clarendon Press, 1968, 1st ed. 1965).

Dronke, Peter, *Poetic Individuality in the Middle Ages, New Departures in Poetry* (Oxford: Clarendon Press, 1970).

Dronke, Peter, "Problemata Hildegardiana," *Mittellateinisches Jahrbuch* 16 (1981), 97-131.

Dronke, Peter, "The Provençal *Trobairitz:* Castelloza," in *Medieval Women Writers,* ed. Katharina M. Wilson (Athens: University of Georgia Press, 1984).

Dronke, Peter, *Women Writers of the Middle Ages, A Critical Study of Texts from Perpetua to Marguerite Porete* (Cambridge: Cambridge University Press, 1984).

Dunbabin, Jean, "What's in a Name? Philip, King of France," *Speculum* 68 (1993), 949-68.

Dunn, Charles W., *The Foundling and the Werwolf, A Literary-Historical Study of "Guillaume de Palerne"* (Toronto: University of Toronto Press, 1960).

Elkins, Sharon K., *Holy Women of Twelfth Century England* (Chapel Hill: University of North Carolina Press, 1988).

Eneas, A Twelfth-Century Romance, trans. John A. Yunck, Records of Civilization 93 (New York: Columbia University Press, 1974).

Ennen, Edith, *Frauen im Mittelalter* (Munich: C. H. Beck, 1984), trans. Edmund Jephcott as *The Medieval Women* (Oxford: Blackwell, 1989).

Farmer, Sharon, "Persuasive Voices: Clerical Images of Medieval Wives," *Speculum* 61 (1986), 517-43.

Ferrante, Joan M., "Male Fantasy and Female Reality in Courtly Literature," *Women's Studies* 11 (1984), 67-97.

Ferrante, Joan M., "Notes toward the Study of a Female Rhetoric in the Trobairitz," in Paden, *Voice*.

Ferrante, Joan M., *Woman as Image in Medieval Literature from the Twelfth Century to Dante* (Durham, N.C.: Labyrinth, 1985, first pub. 1975).

Flanagan, Sabina, "Spiritualis Amicitia in a Twelfth-Century Convent? Hildegard of Bingen and Richardis of Stade," *Parergon* 29 (1981), 15-21.

Fourrier, Anthime, "La 'Contesse Yolent' de *Guillaume de Palerne*," *Etudes de langue et de littérature du Moyen Age offertes à Félix Lecoy* (Paris: Champion, 1973).

Fourrier, Anthime, *Le Courant réaliste dans le roman courtois en France au moyen age* (Paris: Nizet, 1960).

Freeman, Michelle, "The Changing Figure of the Male: The Revenge of the Female Storyteller," in Maréchal, *In Quest of Marie*, 243-61.

Freeman, Michelle, "The Power of Sisterhood: Marie de France's 'Le Fresne,'" *French Forum* 12 (1987), 5-26.

Gaunt, Simon, "Poetry of Exclusion: A Feminist Reading of Some Troubadour Lyrics," *Modern Language Review* 85 (1990), 310-29.

Georgianna, Linda, "Any Corner of Heaven: Heloise's Critique of Monasticism," MS 49 (1987), 221-53.

Goffart, Walter, *The Narrators of Barbarian History, A.D. 550-800* (Princeton: Princeton University Press, 1988).

Goldin, Frederick, "The Array of Perspectives in the Early Courtly Love Lyric," in *In Pursuit of Perfection, Courtly Love in Medieval Literature*, ed. J. M. Ferrante and G. D. Economou (Port Washington: Kennikat, 1975), 51-100.

Gravdal, Kathryn, "Metaphor, Metonymy, and the Medieval Trobairitz," *Romanic Review* 83 (1992), 411-26.

Gregory, Tullio, *Anima Mundi, La filosofia di Guglielmo di Conches e la scuola di Chartres* (Florence: Sansoni, 1955).

Guenée, Bernard, *Histoire et culture historique dans l'occident médiévale* (Paris: Aubier Montaigne, 1980).

Hackett, W. M., "Le problème de 'midons,'" in *Mélanges de philologie romane dédiés à la mémoire de Jean Boutière*, ed. Irénée Cluzel and François Pirot (Liège: Soledi, 1971), vol. 1, 285-94.

Haidu, Peter, "Realism, Convention, Fictionality and the Theory of Genres in *Le Bel Inconnu*," *L'Esprit Créateur* 12 (1972), 37-60.

Hanning, Robert W., "Courtly Contexts for Urban *Cultus*: Responses to Ovid in Chrétien's *Cligès* and Marie's *Guigemar*," *Symposium* 35 (1981), 34-56.

Hatzantonis, Emmanuel S., "Circe, redenta d'amore, nel *Roman de Troie*," *Romania* 94 (1973), 91-102.

Hildegard von Bingen, *Briefwechsel*, trans. A. Führkötter (Salzburg: Müller, 1965).

Hildegard of Bingen, *The Letters of Hildegard of Bingen*, trans. Joseph L. Baird and Radd K. Ehrman (New York: Oxford University Press, 1994), vol. 1 of Van Acker edition.

Hildegard of Bingen, *Scivias*, trans. Columba Hart and Jane Bishop (New York: Paulist Press, 1990).

Holsinger, Bruce, "The Flesh of the Voice: Embodiment and the Homoerotics of Devotion in the Music of Hildegard of Bingen (1098-1179)," *Signs* 19.1 (1993), 92-125.

Holum, Kenneth G., *Theodosian Empresses* (Berkeley: University of California Press, 1982).

Holzknecht, Karl J., *Literary Patronage in the Middle Ages* (New York: Octagon, 1966, first pub. 1923).

Hozeski, Bruce W., *The Book of the Rewards of Life* (New York: Garland, 1994), trans. of Hildegard *Liber vitae meritorum*.

Hrotsvit, *The Dramas of Hrotsvit of Gandersheim,* trans. Katharina Wilson (Saskatoon: Peregrina, 1985).

Hrotswitha, *The Plays of Hrotswitha of Gandersheim,* trans. L. Bonfante and A. Bonfante-Warren (New Work: New York University Press, 1979).

Huneycutt, Lois L., "The Idea of the Perfect Princess: The *Life of St. Margaret* in the Reign of Matilda II (1100-1118)," *Anglo-Norman Studies* 12 (1989), ed. Marjorie Chibnall, 81-97.

Jambeck, Karen K., "Truth and Deception in the *Fables* of Marie de France," in Maddox, *Literary Aspects.*

Jerome, *Selected Letters of St. Jerome,* trans. F. A. Wright (London: Heinemann, 1933).

John, Eric, "The Encomium Emma Reginae: A Riddle and a Solution," *Bulletin of the John Rylands Library* 63 (1980), 58-94.

Johnson, Penelope, *Equal in Monastic Profession, Religious Women in Medieval France* (Chicago: University of Chicago Press, 1991).

Karph, Ernst, *Herrscherlegitimation und Reichsbegriff in der Ottonischen Geschichtsschreibung des zehnten Jarhhunderts* (Stuttgart: Franz Steiner, 1985).

Kay, Sarah, *Subjectivity in Troubadour Poetry* (Cambridge: Cambridge University Press, 1990).

Kearney, Eileen, "Heloise: Inquiry and the *Sacra Pagina,*" in *Ambiguous Realities, Women in the Middle Ages and Renaissance,* ed. Carole Levin and Jeanie Watson (Detroit: Wayne State University Press, 1987).

Kearney, Eileen, "Peter Abelard as Biblical Commentator: A Study of the Expositio in Hexaemeron," *Trierer Theologische Studien* (1980), 199-210.

Kelly, Douglas, "Le Patron et l'Auteur dans l'Invention Romanesque," in *Théories et pratiques de l'écriture au Moyen Age,* ed. Emmanuèle Baumgartner and Christiane Marchello-Nizia (Paris: Paris X-Nanterre, 1988).

Kelly, J. N. D., *Jerome, His Life, Writings, and Controversies* (New York: Harper and Row, 1975).

Krueger, Roberta, "Misogyny, Manipulation, and the Female Reader in Hue de Rotelande's *Ipomedon,*" in *Courtly Literature, Culture and Context,* ed. Keith Busby and Erik Cooper (Amsterdam: Benjamins, 1990), 395-409.

Krueger, Roberta L., *Women Readers and the Ideology of Gender in Old French Verse Romance* (Cambridge: Cambridge University Press, 1993).

Laidlaw, J. C., "Christine de Pizan—A Publisher's Progress," *Modern Language Review* 82 (1987), 35-75.

Lawless, George, *Augustine of Hippo and His Monastic Rule* (Oxford: Clarendon Press, 1987).

Legge, M. Dominica, *Anglo-Norman in the Cloisters* (Edinburgh: Edinburgh University Press, 1950).

Legge, M. Dominica, *Anglo-Norman Literature and Its Background* (Oxford: Clarendon, 1963).

Legge, M. Dominica, "La précocité de la littérature anglo-normande," *Cahiers de Civilisation Médiévales* 8 (1965), 327-49.

Legge, M. Dominica, "Les Origines de l'anglo-normand littéraire," *Revue de linguistique romane* 31 (1967), 44-54.

LeGoff, Jacques, *La Naissance du Purgatoire* (Paris: Gallimard, 1981).

Leyser, K. J., *Rule and Conflict in an Early Medieval Society, Ottonian Saxony* (London: Edward Arnold, 1979).

Lifshitz, Felice, "The *Encomium Emmae Reginae:* A 'Political Pamphlet' of the Eleventh Century?" *Studies in Medieval History, Journal of the Haskins Society* 1 (1989), 39-50.

LoPrete, Kimberly, "The Anglo-Norman Card of Adela of Blois," *Albion* 22 (1990), 569-89.

Lot, Ferdinand, *Les Derniers Carolingiens, Lothaire, Louis V, Charles de Lorraine* (Paris: Bouillon, 1891).

Luecke, Janemarie, "The Unique Experience of Anglo-Saxon Nuns," in *Medieval Religious Women*, vol. 2, *Peaceweavers*, ed. Lillian T. Shank and John A. Nichols (Kalamazoo: Cistercian Publications, 1987).

MacBain, William, "The Literary Apprenticeship of Clemence of Barking," *Journal of the Australasian Universities Language and Literature Association* 9 (1958), 3-22.

Maddox, Donald, and Sara Sturm-Maddox, eds. *Literary Aspects of Courtly Culture* (Cambridge: D. S. Brewer, 1994).

Maréchal, Chantal A., ed., *In Quest of Marie de France, a Twelfth-Century Poet* (Lewiston: Edwin Mellen, 1992), 20-24.

Marie de France, *The Fables of Marie de France*, trans. Mary Lou Martin (Birmingham, Ala.: Summa, 1984).

Marie de France, *The Lais of Marie de France*, trans. Robert Hanning and Joan Ferrante (Grand Rapids, MI: Baker Books, 1995, first pub. 1978).

McCash, June Hall, ed., *The Cultural Patronage of Medieval Women* (Athens: University of Georgia Press, 1996).

McCash, June Hall, "Marie de Champagne and Eleanor of Aquitaine: A Relationship Reexamined," *Speculum* 54 (1979), 698-711.

McCash June Hall, "Marie de Champagne's 'Cuer d'ome et cors de fame': Aspects of Feminism and Misogyny in the Twelfth Century," in *The Spirit of the Court*, ed. Glyn S. Burgess and Robert A. Taylor (Cambridge: D. S. Brewer, 1985), 234-45.

McDonald, William C., with Ulrich Goebel, *German Medieval Literary Patronage from Charlemagne to Maximilian I* (Amsterdam: Rodopi, 1973).

McKitterick, Rosamund, "Frauen und Schriftlichkeit im Frühenmittelalter," *Weiblicher Lebensgestaltung im Frühenmittelalter*, ed. H. W. Goetz (Cologne: Böhlau, 1991).

McKitterick, Rosamund, "Women in the Ottonian Church: An Iconographic Perspective," in *Women in the Church*.

McLaughlin, Mary, "Peter Abelard and the Dignity of Women: Twelfth Century 'Feminism' in Theory and Practice," *Pierre Abélard—Pierre le Vénérable: Les Courants philosophiques, littéraires et artistiques en Occident au milieu du XIIe siècle* (Paris: Editions du Centre National de la Recherche Scientifiques, 1975), 287-333.

McNamara, Jo Ann, "Cornelia's Daughters: Paula and Eustochium," *Women's Studies* 11 (1984), 9-27.

McNamara, Jo Ann, *Sainted Women of the Dark Ages,* ed. and trans. McNamara and John E. Halborg, with E. Gordon Whatley (Durham, N.C.: Duke University Press, 1992).

McNamara, Jo Ann, *Sisters in Arms: Catholic Nuns through Two Millenia* (Cambridge, Mass.: Harvard University Press, 1996).

Medieval Feminist Newsletter (numbers 7 and 8, 1989 and 1990).

Meyers, Carol, *Discovering Eve, Ancient Israelite Women in Context* (New York: Oxford University Press, 1988).

Murphy, James J., "Anonymous of Bologna: The Principles of Letter-Writing (1135 A.D.)," in *Three Medieval Rhetorical Arts,* ed. James J. Murphy (Berkeley: University of California Press, 1971).

Murphy, James J., *Rhetoric in the Middle Ages* (Berkeley: University of California Press, 1974).

Nelson, Janet L., "Perceptions du pouvoir chez les historiens du haut moyen âge," in *La femme au moyen-âge,* ed. Michel Rouche and Jean Heuclin (Mauberge: Maulde et Renou-Sambre, 1990).

Newman, Barbara, "Authority, Authenticity, and the Repression of Heloise," JMRS 22 (1992), 121-57.

Newman, Barbara, *From Virile Woman to Woman Christ: Studies in Medieval Religion and Literature* (Philadelphia: University of Pennsylvania Press, 1995).

Newman, Barbara, *Sister of Wisdom, St. Hildegard's Theology of the Feminine* (Berkeley: University of California Press, 1987).

Nichols, Stephen, "An Intellectual Anthropology of Marriage in the Middle Ages," in *The New Materialism,* ed. M. S. Brownlee, K. Brownlee, and S. G. Nichols (Baltimore: Johns Hopkins University Press, 1991).

Origen, *On First Principles,* trans. G. W. Butterworth (New York: Harper and Row, 1966).

Paden, William D., ed., *The Voice of the Trobairitz, Perspectives on the Women Troubadours* (Philadelphia: University of Pennsylvania Press, 1989), 129-55.

Papka, Claudia Ratazzi, "Fictions of Judgment: The Apocalyptic 'I' in the Fourteenth Century" (Ph.D. diss., Columbia University, 1996).

Partner, Nancy, ed. *Studying Medieval Women: Sex, Gender, Feminism, Speculum* 68.2 (1993).

Paterson, Linda, *Troubadours and Eloquence* (Oxford: Clarendon, 1975).

Petroff, Elizabeth A., ed. *Medieval Women's Visionary Literature* (New York: Oxford University Press, 1986).

Pfau, Marianne Richert, "Hildegard von Bingen's *Symphonia armonie celestium revelationum:* An Analysis of Musical Process, Modality, and Text-Music Relations" (Ph.D. diss., SUNY Stony Brook, 1990).

Pfau, Marianne Richert, "Music and Text in Hildegard's Antiphons," in Hildegard, *Symphonia,* ed. Newman.

Pickens, Rupert, "The Poetics of Androgyny in the *Lais* of Marie de France: *Yonec, Milun,* and the General *Prologue,*" in *Literary Aspects of Courtly Culture.*

Platelle, Henri, "Les Relations entre l'abbaye Saint'Amand de Rouen et l'abbaye Saint'Amand d'Elnone," *La Normandie bénédictine au temps de Guillaume le Conquerant, XIe siècle* (Lille: Facultés Catholiques, 1967), 83-106.

Poe, Elizabeth W., "Another *salut d'amor?* Another *trobairitz?* In Defense of *Tanz salutz et tantas amors,*" ZrP 106 (1990), 314-37.

Previté-Orton, C. W., *The Shorter Cambridge Medieval History,* 2 vols. (Cambridge: Cambridge University Press, 1953).

Reeve, Michael D., "Freculf of Lisieux and Florus," *Revue d'Histoire des Textes* 19 (1989), 381-90.

Reeves, Marjorie, *Joachim of Fiore and the Myth of the Eternal Evangel in the Nineteenth Century* (Oxford: Clarendon, 1987).

Reeves, Marjorie, *Joachim of Fiore and the Prophetic Future* (London: SPCK, 1976).

Rokseth, Yvonne, *Polyphonies du XIIIe siècle: Le Manuscrit H 196 de la Faculté de Médecine de Montpellier,* 4 vols. (Paris: l'Oiseau-Lyre, 1935-39).

Saint Augustine Letters, trans. Sister Wilfrid Parsons, 5 vols. (New York: Fathers of the Church, 1951-56).

Schibanoff, Susan, "Taking the Gold out of Egypt: The Art of Reading as a Woman," in *Gender and Reading, Essays on Readers, Texts and Contexts,* ed. Elizabeth A. Flynn and Patrocinio P. Schweickart (Baltimore: Johns Hopkins University Press, 1986).

Scholz, Bernhard, "Hildegard von Bingen on the Nature of Woman," *American Benedictine Review* 31:4 (1980), 361-83.

Schrader, Marianna, and Adelgundis Führkötter, *Die Echtheit des Schrifttums der heiligen Hildegard von Bingen* (Cologne: Böhlau, 1956).

Schulenberg, Jane, "Saints' Lives as a Source for the History of Women, 500-1100," in *Medieval Women and the Sources of Medieval History,* ed. Joel T. Rosenthal (Athens: University of Georgia Press, 1990).

Searle, Eleanor, "Emma the Conqueror," in *Studies in Medieval History Presented to R. Allen Brown,* ed. C. Harper-Bell, C. J. Holdsworth, and J. L. Nelson (Woodbridge: Boydell, 1989).

Sestan, Ernesto, "Qualche aspetto della personalità di Paolo Diacono nella sua 'Historia Romana,'" *Italia Medievale* (Naples: ESI, 1966).

Shadis, Miriam, "Motherhood, Lineage, and Royal Power in Medieval Spain and France: Berenguela de Leon and Blanche de Castile" (Ph.D. diss., Duke University, 1994).

Shapiro, Marianne, "The Provençal *Trobairitz* and the Limits of Courtly Love," *Signs* 3 (1978), 560-71.

Sheils, W. J., and Diana Wood, eds., *Women in the Church* (Oxford: Blackwell, 1990).

Shields, Hugh, "Philippe de Thaon, Auteur du Livre de Sibylle?" *Romania* 85 (1964), 455-77.

Silvas, Anna, "Saint Hildegard of Bingen and the Vita Sanctae Hildegardis," *Tjurunga* 29 (1985), 4-25; 30 (1986), 63-73; 31 (1986), 32-41; and 32 (1987), 46-59.

Simon, Gertrud, "Untersuchungen zur Topik der Widmungsbriefe mittelalterlicher Geschichtsschreiber bis zum Ende des 12 Jarhhunderts," *Archiv für Diplomatik Schriftgeschichte Siegel- und Wappenkunde* 4 (1958), 52-119; 5/6 (1959-60), 73-153.

Siskin, H. Jay, and Julie A. Storme, "Suffering Love: The Reversed Order in the Poetry of Na Castelloza," in Paden, *Voice.*

Spiegel, Harriet, "The Woman's Voice in the *Fables* of Marie de France," in Maréchal, *In Quest of Marie.*

Stafford, Pauline, *Queens, Concubines and Dowagers, The King's Wife in the Early Middle Ages* (London: Batsford, 1983).

Stanger, Mary D. "Literary Patronage at the Medieval Court of Flanders," *French Studies* 11 (1957), 214-29.

Sullivan, Karen, "At the Limit of Feminist Theory: An Architectonics of the Querelle de la Rose," *Exemplaria* 3.2 (1991), 435–66.

Thiebaux, Marcelle, *The Writings of Medieval Women* (New York: Garland, 1987).

Thiry-Stassin, Martine, "Interpellations féminines dans le *Roman de Thèbes*," *Marche Romane* 27 (1977), 41–53.

Thiry-Stassin, Martine, "Interpellations féminines dans le *Roman de Troie* de Benoît de Sainte-Maure," *Mélanges de langue et littérature françaises du moyen âge offerts à Pierre Jonin* (Paris: Champion, 1979), 645–60.

Thomassy, Raimond, *Essai sur les écrits politiques de Christine de Pisan, suivi d'une notice littéraire et de pièces inédites* (Paris: Debécourt, 1838).

Tyson, Diana B., "Patronage of French Vernacular History Writers in the Twelfth and Thirteenth Centuries," *Romania* 100 (1979), 180–222.

van Houts, Elisabeth, "Women and the Writing of History in the Early Middle Ages: The Case of Abbess Matilda of Essen and Aethelweard," *Early Medieval Europe* (1992), 1.53–68.

Van Vleck, Amelia E., "'Tost me trobaretz fenida': Reciprocating Composition in the Songs of Castelloza," in Paden, *Voice*.

Ward, Elizabeth, "Agobard of Lyons and Paschasius Radbertus as Critics of the Empress Judith," in *Women in the Church*.

Ward, Elizabeth, "Caesar's Wife, The Career of the Empress Judith, 819–29," in *Charlemagne's Heir, New Perspectives on the Reign of Louis the Pious (814–40)*, ed. Peter Godman and Roger Collins (Oxford: Clarendon Press, 1990).

Wattenbach, W., "Lateinische Gedichte aus Frankreich im elften Jahrhundert," *Sitzungsberichte der Akademie der Wissenschaften*, Berlin (1891), 97–120.

Weiss, Judith, "The Power and the Weakness of Women in Anglo-Norman Romance," in *Women and Literature in Britain, 1100–1500*, ed. Carol M. Meale (Cambridge: Cambridge University Press, 1993).

Wemple, Suzanne F., *Women in Frankish Society: Marriage and the Cloister, 500–900* (Philadelphia: University of Pennsylvania Press, 1981).

Wessley, Stephen, "The Thirteenth Century Guglielmites: Salvation through Women," in *Medieval Women*, ed. Derek Baker (Oxford: Blackwell, 1978).

Wiethaus, Ulrike, "In Search of Medieval Women's Friendships: Hildegard of Bingen's Letters to Her Female Contemporaries," in *Maps of Flesh and Light: The Religious Experience of Medieval Women Mystics*, ed. U. Wiethaus (Syracuse: Syracuse University Press, 1993).

Willard, Charity Cannon, *Christine de Pizan, Her Life and Works* (New York: Persea, 1984).

William of Malmesbury's *Chronicle of the Kings of England*, trans. J. A. Giles (London: Bohn, 1847).

Wilmart, André, "Eve et Goscelin," *Revue Bénédictine* 46 (1934), 414–38, and 50 (1938), 42–83.

Wilson, Katharina, *Hrotsvit of Gandersheim, The Ethics of Authorial Stance* (Leiden: Brill, 1988).

Wolf, Gunther, "Theophanu und Adalheid," in *Kaiserin Theophanu, Prinzessin aus der Fremde—des Westreichs Grosse Kaiserin*, ed. Gunther Wolf (Cologne: Böhlau, 1991).

Wulf, Charlotte A. T., "A Comparative Study of Wace's Guenevere in the Twelfth Century," in *Arthurian Romance and Gender*, ed. Friedrich Wolfzettel (Amsterdam: Rodopi, 1995).

INDEX